MARK WAUGH

THE BIOGRAPHY

MARK WAUGH

THE BIOGRAPHY

JAMES KNIGHT

Collins Willow

An Imprint of HarperCollins*Publishers*

First published in Australia in 2002
byHarperSports
An imprint of HarperCollins*Publishers*, Australia

First published in UK in 2002 by
CollinsWillow
An imprint of HarperCollins*Publishers*, London

A CIP catalogue record for this book
is available from the British Library

ISBN 0 00 714521 7

Printed and bound in Great Britain
by Clays Ltd, St Ives plc

The HarperCollins website address is
www.**fire**and**water**.com

To Mr Reading.

Thank you for looking after the Gunnedah South School nets.

And to Gran.

For keeping the orange juice cold.

CONTENTS

ACKNOWLEDGMENTS / IX
A NOTE FROM MARK WAUGH / XIII
FOREWORD BY ALLAN BORDER / XV

CHAPTER ONE / 1
THE ARRIVAL

CHAPTER TWO / 4
TWINS

CHAPTER THREE / 28
THE ROAD TO SUCCESS

CHAPTER FOUR / 42
THE AWAKENING

CHAPTER FIVE / 53
PARTNERS

CHAPTER SIX / 64
ONE OF THE LADS

CHAPTER SEVEN / 73
AUSTRALIA CALLING

CHAPTER EIGHT / 89
MISTAKEN IDENTITY

CHAPTER NINE / 100
WORTH THE WAIT

CHAPTER TEN / 113
VIOLENCE IN PARADISE

CHAPTER ELEVEN / 126
DROPPED

CHAPTER TWELVE / 136
SRI LANKAN DUCKS

CHAPTER THIRTEEN / 152
EVERYTHING OLD IS NEW AGAIN

CHAPTER FOURTEEN / 170
HONG KONG

CHAPTER FIFTEEN / 182
JOHN AND SALIM

CHAPTER SIXTEEN / 191
GRANDSTAND DRIVER

CHAPTER SEVENTEEN / 198
REVERSE SWEEPS AND POINTED FINGERS

CHAPTER EIGHTEEN / 206
WELCOME BACK, FRANK

CHAPTER NINETEEN / 219
JUSTICE AND BOMB BLASTS

CHAPTER TWENTY / 228
BEATEN BUT NOT BROKEN

CHAPTER TWENTY-ONE / 238
STAYING ON TOP

CHAPTER TWENTY-TWO / 250
A BAD GUT FEELING

CHAPTER TWENTY-THREE / 259
UNDER PRESSURE

CHAPTER TWENTY-FOUR / 272
TOUGH TIMES

CHAPTER TWENTY-FIVE / 288
COURAGE UNDER FIRE

CHAPTER TWENTY-SIX / 298
NEW MILLENNIUM

CHAPTER TWENTY-SEVEN / 307
THE RIGHT TO DECLINE

CHAPTER TWENTY-EIGHT / 321
A REMARKABLE SERIES

CHAPTER TWENTY-NINE / 330
GOODBYE?

CHAPTER THIRTY / 342
THE FINAL WORD

STATISTICS / 347
SOURCES / 363
INDEX / 365

ACKNOWLEDGMENTS

Thank you to Mark for his endless enthusiasm and support during many long interviews. My thanks also to Sue Porter for her hospitality and support, Bev Waugh for digging through numerous boxes of old newspaper articles and photos, and Allan Border for writing the foreword. I'm also extremely grateful to the following people for giving up precious time to talk to me.

NEIL FOSTER	GEOFF MARSH	HARRY SOLOMONS
BRIAN FREEDMAN	RODNEY MARTIN	MICK STEPHENSON
GLENN FROST	GREG MATTHEWS	MARK TAYLOR
IRIS GREENHALGH	NSW CA LIBRARY	DAVID THOMPSON
PETER GREENHALGH	REBECCA OVERTON	ANNE TURNBULL
ADAM GILCHRIST	MARK PATTERSON	PETER V'LANDYS
BOB HAGAN	RON PERRETT	DANNY WAUGH
IAN HEALY	RAFF PISANO	DEAN WAUGH
RONNIE IRANI	RICKY PONTING	RODGER WAUGH
LEO KARIS	JONTY RHODES	STEVE WAUGH
GEOFF LAWSON	BOB SIMPSON	MIKE WHITNEY

Thank you to everyone at HarperCollins: Shona Martyn, Alison Urquhart, Mel Cain, Karen-Maree Griffiths, Vanessa Radnidge, Graeme Jones, Luke Causby, Helen Beard, Ali Orman, Rodney Stuart, Tegan Murray. Also thanks to Amanda O'Connell, Ross Dundas, Michael Wyatt and Frances Paterson.

Finally, a big hug to Mum, Pete, Ando, Tombsy, Grego, Carissa and Ange for their never-ending encouragement.

'It is not the critic who counts, not the man who points out how the strong man stumbled, or where the doer of deeds could have done better. The credit belongs to the man who is actually in the arena; whose face is marred by the dust and sweat and blood; who strives valiantly; who errs and comes short again and again; who knows the great enthusiasms, the great devotions and spends himself in a worthy cause; who at the best, knows in the end the triumph of high achievement, and who, at worst, if he fails, at least fails while daring greatly; so that his place shall never be with those cold and timid souls who know neither victory nor defeat.'

President Theodore Roosevelt
Sorbonne, 1910

A NOTE FROM MARK WAUGH

To Allan Cowie. One of Australia's most promising jockeys who had his career tragically ended when his mount fell in a race on Magic Millions Day. In a split second, he became a paraplegic.

To Glenn McEnallay. A courageous and law-abiding citizen and policeman who lost his life to a cowardly act of crime.

Both of the above are absolute tragedies. And let's not forget all the lives that were lost, and have been changed forever as a result of what happened on 11 September 2001.

When you look at some of the cards people can get dealt, I am very thankful and grateful for what I have. So far, I have been able to live a healthy and fulfilling life. Writing a book on me is almost embarrassing when I think of all the people in Australia and the world who have made much more important, and life-saving, contributions to society. Having said that, to represent your country in sport, or anything else, is a great honour. It's something I will always cherish.

Like anyone, I have had my ups and downs, and made my mistakes, but hopefully people will remember me as someone who had tremendous pride in wearing the green and gold. There are so many people to thank for making my cricket career what it is, and I hope I haven't forgotten too many along the way.

Putting this book together must have been a never-ending road for James Knight, piecing together statistics, tours, events, milestones and so on. To James, thank you very much for your patience, commitment, passion, and for just being a damn good bloke. Without you, and of course HarperCollins, this book would not have been possible.

To my team-mates and coaches in all the teams I have played in, your friendship, support and attitudes are major reasons for my success, and I thank you all for that.

To the cricket fans and supporters out there, thank you for your loyalty and enthusiasm through the good and bad times. Without you I'm sure the Aussie team wouldn't be as successful, and have as much fun as it does.

To my sponsors, starting with Harry Solomons at the Kingsgrove Sports Centre, right through to my friends at Slazenger and Bolle, who have been with me all the way, may the partnerships continue. Thank you to all the other sponsors who have been with me over the years.

To Raff Pisano and Michael Shatin, the legal team that had the belief and confidence in me to get me through one of the toughest periods of my life, a special thank you.

I also thank all the people James has acknowledged in giving up your time and help for the book. I am extremely grateful. Many of you are very close friends.

Apart from my family, there is one person who has been with me all my career as a professional cricketer. Leo Karis has been my manager, enabling me to perform at my best on the field, while he has been doing all the dirty work off the field. Juggling my needs, keeping happy all the sponsors, media, and anybody else who has wanted to get involved in my life. Leo is not just my manager, but a close friend, and someone I can trust. Thank you.

To my family. To Mum and Dad. If it wasn't for all the sacrifices you made, I wouldn't be where I am now. Bringing up four boys who played every sport under the sun was a huge job. Showing us how to conduct ourselves on and off the sports field is a credit to you and your parents. To my brothers, Dean, Danny and Stephen, thanks for putting up with me as a brother, and for really being there when I've needed you.

To Nanny, Gran, and the rest of my family, thank you for being a very important part of my life, especially Dorothy Bourne and Ella Waugh and your late husbands whom I remember very fondly when we were youngsters being looked after.

And finally, they say behind every man there is a great woman, and Susan Porter, my fiancée, certainly is worthy of the tag. Without your loyalty, advice, friendship and love, I wouldn't be the person I am today. To you and your family, thank you for your great support.

I am lucky to be surrounded by such people.

FOREWORD

It's a great pleasure to be asked to write about one of my all-time favourite cricketers. I have a very soft spot for 'Junior' Waugh because of what he has brought to the game. Unlike me, with my often intense style, Mark is very laid-back, easygoing, and has never become too frustrated, yet he is as competitive as anyone, and has that rare streak of genius that makes him a very special player.

I've got no doubt that he can be considered one of the game's greats, not only because of his gifted batting, but also for his exceptional all-round ability. First, look at some of the catches he has taken. Some have defied description, and although they mightn't have looked fantastic, we knew as cricketers that they were freakish. One moment stands out during the second Test against Pakistan in Hobart in 1999–2000, when Mark turned the match with a catch to dismiss Inzamam-ul-Haq. Justin Langer and Adam Gilchrist quite rightly got the credit for winning the Test after their magnificent centuries, but Australia was only allowed to get to that stage because of what had happened before. Before Mark took that catch off Shane Warne's bowling, the Test was slipping away from Australia, then all of a sudden his brilliance allowed his team to get back into it. There weren't too many players of any era who could have taken that catch. Even though he didn't score many runs in that game, Junior kept us in it by turning the momentum. That ability alone makes him a priceless player.

Then we have his bowling. In his younger years he bowled quickish medium pace. He was very aggressive, loved bouncing batsmen, and often made vital breakthroughs. His off-spinners were just as valuable because he claimed some very big wickets with them, and once again he had the knack of getting them when Australia really needed them.

And what can you say about his batting? I have been at the other end when he has been in full flight and I've just had to shake my head and think, 'Gee this bloke is something out of the ordinary.' Those sorts of players don't come along too often. Mark has never been a statistical person or a ruthless run accumulator. He's an entertainer who probably gets bored with himself at times. That has cost him percentage points in statistics, but his value goes so far beyond that. Although he normally scores his runs at a good clip, he has also shown throughout his career that he can play tough when he has needed to. He has been both a matchwinner and match-saver — you can't say that about too many players. When he has played well, Australia has won.

I said during the interview for this book that it is no coincidence that Australia's success in the last 10 years has coincided with the rise of Mark Waugh. How many other countries can boast one of the best one-day batsmen of all time, one of the best stroke-players of all time, a world record-breaking fieldsman who can turn a match in a split second and can be outstanding anywhere from the slips to the deep, a wicket-taking fast bowler, a wicket-taking slow bowler, a very competitive and aggressive player, someone who is rarely injured, and a player with a very knowledgeable cricket brain. You would have to look a long way to find a collection of cricketers with those abilities, but Mark Waugh has them all rolled into one.

One of my fondest memories of Mark is when he came to replace me at Essex in 1988. I was asked by officials if I knew of a young Australian who might be worth a go. I thought of Mark straight away because he could do everything. He came out in his first game and scored a sensational hundred and took two wickets. The Essex officials were beating the door down to sign him up, and I was left looking like a genius for picking him! He went on to become one of Essex's favourite overseas players, and his time in England helped his development as a cricketer, and obviously helped the future of Australian cricket too.

I have seen the development of Mark from his earliest days as a first-class cricketer. Back then, he gave the impression that he just expected things to happen with his game. But it didn't take him long to realise he had to work hard if he was going to go further. And he has. People who believe it has come too easy for him just don't realise the hours he has put in, his determination and his competitive spirit.

Off the field, I liked the bloke from the first time I met him. At the time he came onto the scene for New South Wales, it was quite extraordinary to see a young bloke who didn't drink a hell of a lot. He didn't like being out of control or having hangovers. He was his own man. And he always has been. As the years went on, we all got to know him as being very image conscious, and at some time or another all his team-mates have given him a ribbing about his hair and his looks. He loves a punt, has a very dry sense of humour, always says what he thinks, and is very loyal to his friends, family and team-mates. He's just a good bloke to be around.

Being a twin, it's obvious he is going to be compared with his brother Stephen, but they both deserve to stand alone as cricketers and as people.

As far as Mark goes, I consider myself very lucky to have played with and against him. Every team he has played for has been lucky, whether it be Bankstown, New South Wales, Essex or Australia. And everyone who has seen him play has been lucky because Mark is simply not the type of player who comes along very often in any sport. Once again I have no hesitation in calling him one of the greats of cricket.

Thanks Junior.

Allan Border
April 2002

CHAPTER ONE

THE ARRIVAL

Elegant. Brilliant. Poetic. Freakish. Imperious. Lazy. Soft. Carefree. Sleepy. Frustrating. Enigmatic ... All words that have been used to describe Mark Edward Waugh during his cricket career. Among others, there is also 'intriguing'. Certainly it is one of many ways to characterise an incredibly gifted sportsman about whom there has always been just one certainty — sooner or later he would reach the very highest level of his sport.

Yet in the mid to late 1980s, Mark was in the shadow of his twin brother, Stephen, on the cricket field. Steve had made his Test debut in 1985–86 against India. Although Mark had secured a berth in Australia's one-day squad from 1988–89, by the end of the decade he was still to make an appearance in the Test arena despite a glowing first-class record.

His conspicuous absence became the topic for much discussion. From Australia to England. From press box to pub. From dressing room to living room. In a sport in which players, fans and the media have endless hours to fiddle with their thoughts, it was no surprise that Mark's campaign eventually became the target of cricket wit.

In December 1979, long before Mark had even dreamed of playing for Australia, Afghanistan had been invaded by troops from the Soviet Union whose aim was to ensure the return to power of a Soviet-backed communist government in the Muslim country. The Soviets remained until 1989, and although their presence prompted the United States to boycott the 1980 Moscow Olympics, the longer the fighting dragged on, the less attention it attracted across the globe. The conflict became a forgotten war.

And so came the tag 'Afghanistan' — the Forgotten Waugh.

The moment Mark could shake off his unfortunate nickname came in somewhat bizarre circumstances on the evening of Monday, 21 January 1991, four days before the fourth Test against England, at the Adelaide Oval. Mark was visiting his parents' home at Revesby, in Sydney's western suburbs, when Steve walked in and told his brother, 'Congratulations, you're in the Test team.'

For a flickering moment it appeared that history was dusting off a new page to record the selection of the first set of twins to play Test cricket together, but before celebrating, Mark asked the obvious question: 'Who's been dropped?'

'Me,' replied Steve in his matter-of-fact style.

The twins would have to wait another three months before they created history, but in the meantime Mark headed to Adelaide for a long-awaited and overdue appointment. He recalls:

I wasn't really nervous. I already had twenty-five first-class tons, so I was pretty experienced. It was pretty low-key. I remember going to the manager's room to pick up my gear in a box. There was no ceremonial presentation of caps as there is now. I was pretty quiet, just minded my own business in the dressing room and at training. Obviously the press had made a big deal out of me replacing Stephen, but it was just one of those things. I knew he'd be back, and in the meantime I'd been given my chance.

Back then players still had to share rooms. I had Merv Hughes, which was probably a good thing because it helped me relax. There's no-one quite like him. It's pretty hard to get too tense when you've got a bloke ordering midnight pizzas, and waking you up in the morning by jumping on you.

The Test itself became just another game. I had a close call first ball when I nearly got caught off the glove down leg side off Phil DeFreitas. But after that everything fell into place. It was a lot easier than I thought. I went out there,

played my natural game and peeled off a hundred. It was too good to be true,
really. I just remember thinking that Test cricket wasn't that hard. I had no
inhibitions, I didn't have the worry of a form cloud hanging over my head, or
the pressure of the media. I just went out there, backed my instincts and batted.
Looking back, I suppose it was a pretty good start to my career.

Mark is a master of the understatement, his innings being much more than a 'pretty good start'. The very first signs that Australian cricket was welcoming the arrival of a unique player happened the moment the slim 25-year-old walked out to bat on the first day with his side in trouble at 4–104. Wearing a sleeveless jumper, long hair hiding a partially upturned collar, he set his own style. Team-mate Greg Matthews, who combined with the debutant for a 171-run sixth-wicket stand, considered his partner a 'pretty boy'.

'It was an enormous compliment I was paying him,' says Matthews. 'It was just about the way he played. He just looked so damn pretty. Never a hair out of place, always wore a jumper, never had grass stains, just one of those guys who'd always walk out neat and tidy.'

In an innings that stretched into the second day, he scored 138 in just a breath under four hours. He reached his hundred with a regal square-drive in the final minutes of the opening day, the performance prompting Fairfax journalist Phil Wilkins to suggest in the *Sydney Morning Herald* (26 January 1991):

'Such a maiden Test century could hardly have been surpassed for commanding presence.'

Nowadays, a photo capturing the celebrations after he reached his ton hangs low on a wall, almost out of sight behind a bar that is crowded with memorabilia in his Sydney home. It reveals something very rare: Mark acknowledging his achievement by taking off his helmet, a sight that has rarely been seen since. It was a brief glimpse behind the mask of a private man, who in the years to come would sometimes struggle under the heat of the spotlight.

But on 25 January 1991, there were no booing fans, acid ink in the press or anti-corruption investigators to trouble him. On that day, Mark Waugh was comfortable showing his face. And on that day, it seemed the face and the name could no longer be forgotten.

CHAPTER TWO

TWINS

Four minutes. Time enough for New South Wales horse Archer to win the first Melbourne Cup in 1861, and a British medical student named Roger Bannister to run a mile in 1954. It was also more than enough time for exuberant American boxer Muhammad Ali to land his 'phantom punch' against Sonny Liston to retain the world heavyweight crown in 1965. And in the same year, it was time enough for a promising teenage tennis player from Sydney to deliver the second of two would-be aces to the world.

The pregnant Beverly Waugh was just nineteen when she was taken by her twenty-year-old husband, Rodger, to Canterbury Hospital in Sydney's western suburbs on 2 June 1965. It ended a fortnight of false alarms, during which Bev was continually woken by labour pains in the early hours of the morning.

When the real moment finally arrived, Bev caught medical staff by surprise, and was alone except for a young nurse who had never delivered a baby. Despite their inexperience, Bev and the nurse rose to the occasion, and opened their account with two healthy boys. The first, a thin baby, wide awake with flowing black hair, arrived at 8.14 p.m.; the second, four pounds [nearly 2 kilos] heavier than his brother, sleepy and nearly bald, arrived at 8.18.

Beverly and Rodger could smile. They had twins. Stephen and Mark.

'As soon as Mark was born, two of his major characteristics were pretty evident to me,' recalls Bev. 'He was sound asleep. Dead to the world. He's been a good sleeper ever since. When he wasn't sleeping, he was eating. When the nurses brought him in for feeding, his mouth would be sucking all the way up their arms. They used to make a joke of him: "Here comes this hungry baby." Sleeping and eating have always been two of Mark's favourite pastimes.'

The births continued a frenetic pace for Bev and Rodger who'd married only the year before. It was in the most literal sense a true courtship, the two having met while playing tennis in the Bankstown district. At the time of the births, the young couple were living at Bev's parents' home in Panania, and although every effort had been made to ensure the twins enjoyed a smooth transition from hospital to house, there was an unexpected complication when Rodger contracted a severe case of measles. His early days of fatherhood were spent in isolation in one bedroom, while Bev and the babies stayed in another. Despite her youth, Bev was a natural mother, feeling 'privileged and very special' to have twins. However, her time with them was curtailed because she had to return to work as a teacher with the New South Wales Department of Education when the boys were just six weeks old. Rodger was already spending long hours away from his family, leaving home each weekday morning at seven o'clock to catch a train from Revesby into the city, where he worked in management at the National Bank on George Street. When he wasn't playing tennis on weekends, he was invariably coaching to supplement the household income so that the new family could move into a home of their own.

While Mum and Dad were working, Steve and Mark were split between their grandparents.

'Every morning was hectic,' recalls Bev. 'I'd breastfeed them, then deliver a baby with milk to one mum, then it was off to the other home before heading to work. I could never have left them with anyone but our parents.'

Mark was usually cared for by Bev's mother, Dorothy Bourne, as Steve, the smaller baby, was easier to handle for Ella Waugh, who'd suffered from polio when she was in her late teens. She and husband Edward lived in Earlwood, about twenty minutes drive from the Bournes'.

After twelve months of living between Earlwood and Panania, Rodger and Bev finally upheld the great Australian dream by buying a one-storey house that was within a short drive of the grandparents' homes, but far enough away for the founding of a new family life. Fifty-six Picnic Point Road, Panania was in the Bankstown shire, a mixture of fibro, weatherboard and brick dwellings that signified a typical blue-collar area. But unlike some of its neighbouring suburbs that were scarred by too much concrete and too little space, Panania was flanked by bushland that scampered down to the picturesque Georges River. The young Waugh family had discovered a slice of suburbia with a peaceful sprinkling of country charm.

'It's a good down-to-earth place,' says Mark, who continues to live in the area. 'It hasn't changed a lot actually. There are a few more restaurants and shops, a lot more town houses and units have gone up, and the area along the river has now become fairly sought after, but back when we were growing up, it was an out-of-the way sort of place.'

Although being twins ensured Mark and Steve would attract additional attention and ceaseless comparisons that continue to this day, there was nothing extraordinary about their early development. Mark gained a head start on his brother after he took his first tentative steps when he was little more than nine months old. Steve followed about six weeks later. Both began talking at about eighteen months, Steve more loudly, but neither spoke excessively — a Waugh trait had seemingly taken hold already. Bev remembers:

> They didn't talk a lot but had this funny sort of language between them at the start. They muttered words like 'moonie' and 'goolie'. I remember writing them down in the diary while thinking, 'What have I reared here?' It was just their own little way of communicating. But there was no talking a lot of the time. They spoke through simple actions, not many words. They seemed to understand each other even though they were so different. I can't ever remember them being aggressive, or trying to hurt each other.
>
> Mark had to be the first one bathed all the time because he was always the hungriest baby. There were even a few episodes when he gulped his food down so quickly that he got severe colic. He was also very, very clumsy at first. He'd fall over his own shadow very easily.

They played a lot together, and were always watching each other. They had one favourite toy that they got for Christmas once. It was a little train of plastic pieces that they pushed around by hand. Other than that, they'd play on old cane chairs out the back, or jump into cardboard boxes and improvise.

As the boys grew, their personalities became more obvious. Steve was the louder and more reckless of the two. Mark primarily sought security. He was quite often unsettled when he and Steve were separated between their grandparents, and was so attached to his dummy that he almost took it to school with him. He had long matured from the sucking stage, but felt comfortable with the dummy in his pocket. To the outsider, identical clothing was the easiest way of determining the boys were twins. Garish short-sleeved shirts tucked into shorts that were looped with white vinyl belts showed the Waughs were unfortunate victims of the forgettable fashions of the late 1960s and 1970s. Many of the clothes were painstakingly made by Bev.

'It wasn't a good look. The red and black cowboy outfits were head-turners too,' laughs Steve, who remembers he not only shared clothes with his brother, but almost everything else as well. 'We tended to get things at the same time. We got our first cricket bats at Christmas together, we got our first bikes together. That meant we could experiment with them together as well. We appreciated all the material possessions that we got. We didn't have a lot, but Mum and Dad always provided for us, so we made sure we took pretty good care of everything.'

Mark and Steve were easily amused — an obvious advantage of being twins was that neither boy had to look beyond the other side of the back yard, the living room, or the bedroom for a companion. Steve was the organiser of most activities, including fancy-dress games using Bev's old clothes, hats, handbags and a wig. Mark was a somewhat reluctant follower on such occasions, but there was never any hesitation when it came to picking up a bat or a ball of any description.

The bloodlines suggested sport was destined to have a bearing on the twins' upbringing. Grandfather Edward, a greyhound trainer in his early years, was a passionate race follower and small-time gambler who didn't mind a two-bob each-way flutter. Growing up in the far North Coast town of Bangalow, near Lismore, he'd been a very good swimmer and was fullback for the New South Wales Country rugby league team. He was set to join the Eastern Suburbs club in the Sydney premiership, but his career ended prematurely when he helped nurse Ella through polio. In his later years, he excelled in lawn bowls for Earlwood's number one pennants team.

Rodger, an only child, was an excellent tennis player who'd been ranked number 8 in Australia as a junior during the founding years of a golden era. He'd won the New South Wales Under–14 grass-court final, and a few years later joined John Cottrill to claim a National Under–19 doubles title. Ray Ruffles, Alan Stone, Tony Roche and future Wimbledon champion John Newcombe were other players of the day.

On the opposite branch of the family tree, Bev also spent much of her youth with a racquet in her hand. One of four children, she travelled to tournaments throughout southern and western New South Wales where her father taught in one-teacher schools. Keith Bourne was widely respected throughout the region as a good tennis player and cricketer. Bev recalls learning her early skills playing with her dad on a court overrun with grass in the tiny town of Brungle, near Gundagai. She would later win the South Australian Under–14 Singles Championship, and team with Ray Ruffles to claim the New South Wales Under–19 mixed doubles title. Significantly, Bev's eldest brother, Dion, was a talented opening batsman who went on to play first grade for Bankstown. He remains the club's all-time leading run-getter in the Sydney Cricket Association competition. Sadly, Keith saw few of his son's innings. He died when he was just fifty-two, suffering a heart attack while playing tennis with his other daughter, Coral. At the time Steve and Mark were only three years old.

Mark's earliest sporting memories are of watching his parents play tennis at weekend tournaments throughout Sydney. While Rodger and Bev were on court, the twins often amused themselves by throwing, catching and kicking whatever balls they could find. They had the regular boyhood toys of trucks and cars, but more often than not reverted to games involving hand, eye and foot co-ordination. In between matches, Rodger and Bev became extra playmates, hitting catches to the boys off their racquets. Bev remembers the boys enjoyed any sort of ball game, and although a little uncertain she thinks they were catching from when they were about twelve months old. In a sporting family that had considerable interest in horse racing, was it an omen that the Bart Cummings trained Light Fingers won the Melbourne Cup the year Mark and Steve were born?

Because of Rodger's long work hours — he sometimes didn't arrive home until the boys were in bed at night — Bev played a bigger role in the formative years of her children. Three and a half years after her eventful debut at Canterbury Hospital, she returned to the maternity ward to give birth to her third son, Dean. The house grew with the family, an extension out the back completed soon after the birth.

The Waughs were a normal suburban family. Mark remembers that he and his brothers weren't spoilt, but had a 'loving upbringing'. They enjoyed simple pleasures such as trips in the family's Ford Falcon station wagon to Edward and Ella's home where lollies and drinks were always waiting. Excursions to the Bournes weren't as exciting because they lived just around the corner. Undoubtedly the biggest adventures were on the long weekends when the Falcon was packed to the roof top with pillows, bags and tennis equipment for journeys to satellite tournaments at Gloucester and Taree, or inland, over the Blue Mountains, at Bathurst.

'They were really good fun,' says Mark. 'Even the car trips used to be exciting. We'd load all the gear, and away we'd go. I clearly remember all the pillows, sleeping in the back and stopping off along the way. There was another time when we went to Bomaderry down near Nowra on the South Coast. I cut my foot on an oyster shell; I thought a shark had bitten me. It was a big cut, blood everywhere. I think I've always been a bit scared of the water since then, actually.'

A scar near Mark's left ankle is a permanent reminder of the occasion. These days, the right fetlock also sports a memento: the numbers 349 and 105 are etched in green, signifying Mark's position in Australian cricket's roll call for Test and one-day selection. They're surrounded by five gold stars with green borders — the Southern Cross. Three decades apart, an oyster shell and a Somerset tattooist both left their mark on the boy, then the man, from Bankstown.

Recollections of Mark's journey from childhood to adulthood are embedded as deeply in Bev's mind as the stars on her younger twin's skin. She remembers a well-organised boy who never wanted to find trouble.

Mark was never a daring boy. Stephen was the one who'd organise anything that was a little bit sinister or mischievous, but Mark was often afraid to follow.

He was scared of horses and dogs, and I remember one June long weekend when
I took them to Australia's Wonderland [a Sydney theme park]. Dean was just a
baby, so the twins must have been four or five.

Stephen ran over to this high slippery dip because he couldn't wait to get to
the top, but Mark stood at the bottom. I knew he was scared. Stephen kept
saying, 'Come on Mark, come on.' So Mark cautiously got up to the top, but then
he looked across at me, and I could see that he was too frightened to go down. He
was calling out for me, so I tore up the slippery dip telling him to wait until I
could help him. Just as I got to the top, he let go and down he went. I went flying
down after him, but in the kerfuffle the long plastic coat I had on got caught at
the top and by the time I reached the bottom it was ripped off to about waist
length. I ripped a thumbnail off as well. That was the end of our trip!

It just amazes me to think he was so scared of so many things, and yet now
he goes out and faces the fastest bowlers in the world.

Similar stories from Mark's childhood are abundant. In hospital for a minor operation when he was just three, he was too afraid to tell the nurses he didn't like the peaches that had been poured all over his cornflakes. Fearing he'd be in trouble if he didn't eat all his breakfast, he quietly tipped the fruit behind his bed onto the floor. Not surprisingly his action caused more commotion than a more public abstinence would have.

There was also the occasion when he raided the supply of his father's favourite biscuits. He thought he would have less chance of being discovered if he took a whole packet, instead of just a small handful. That night when Bev tucked the twins into their beds in the same room they would share for the first seventeen years of their lives, she was surprised to find a hefty supply of orange slice biscuits stashed everywhere from Mark's pyjama pockets to underneath his pillow.

And then there was the time in kindergarten when Mark was caught with his pants down. Too frightened to explain himself to the shocked teacher, he later told Bev that he was simply inspecting the damage after he'd been pricked in the bottom by a girl with a pin.

However, Mark rarely stumbled into the teacher's bad books. At Panania Primary School, just five hundred metres from the Waugh home, he was considered a polite and conscientious student who wanted to please. Unlike

Steve, he hated being late, always finished his homework on time, and his books were frequently used by teachers to set a good example for other children.

His mid-year fifth class report was a typical reflection of his character: 'Mark's ratings in academic and other spheres indicate the high standard of his school involvement. He approaches his work in a thoughtful, tradesmanlike manner and is, at all times, well behaved and dependable.'

By this stage, sport was already playing a very big role in the Waugh twins' lives. They were just six when they had their first taste of organised competition in the East Hills T-Ball League. Mark's most vivid memory is of the maroon and white uniform he wore, but Bev has a more telling recollection.

'It was so competitive for them. Every time they batted, they put their heads down and really tried hard for home runs. It was just in them. They had each other as models, but were always trying to outdo each other. It spurred them on.'

Registration for the Revesby-Milperra Lions soccer club followed at the same age, and the next year, amidst occasional tennis matches, the boys began playing cricket for Panania East Hills RSL Under–10s in the Bankstown District Association competition. In the immediate years to come, their ability to find the back of the net, or hit over it, was as noticeable as their progress with bat and ball. However, their opening game of cricket did nothing to parade their talents: playing three years above their age, they both scored ducks — Mark's a golden one, while Steve lasted just two balls. Although in their first two seasons they didn't dominate the scorebooks to the same extent as they would in their teenage years, their natural talents were nevertheless recognised as something out of the ordinary.

Bankstown club stalwart Brian Freedman, who at the time was coaching a rival team that included his son, the future New South Wales spinner, David, says it was obvious to everyone that they were very special.

They were only eight when I first saw them in the Under–10s. My first impression was that they could catch like no-one else. And their running between the wickets was so much better than any of the others, especially when they ran together. They never spoke, they just looked at each other and away they went. You'd never run them out when they were together, but you always thought you had a good chance when they were running with someone else because the other kids were never as good as them. They were just so natural.

Freedman also recalls that the twins were quite reserved, but much more competitive than their team-mates. While other boys were prone to letting their minds wander — it's not uncommon on any junior sporting field to see a boy waving at his parents or paying more attention to catching butterflies than balls — Freedman says Mark and Steve were focused only on doing as well as each other, and winning.

They made their first representative team, the Bankstown District Foster Shield Under–10s, when only eight years of age. Bev remembers her boys being 'very, very excited', but they struck unexpected trouble before either had a chance to make an impact.

'For the occasion my mum knitted them these little vests which had the blue and white colours of Bankstown on their sleeves. The boys thought it was big time with the vests and long trousers. But they were both sent off the field because of the colours; everyone else was in plain white. I can still see these little boys walking off Padstow Park really embarrassed.'

Only fate could have forecast that in years to come Mark and Steve would be welcomed onto fields all over the world wearing the green and gold of their country. However, some people stared into the crystal ball with incredible foresight. As he watched the progression of the Waugh boys through the junior ranks, Freedman used to say: 'Those kids will play for Australia.' At first it was the sort of throwaway statement that countless adults have uttered more in jest than serious conviction, but as time and the twins matured Freedman's faith in his prediction continued to grow.

Throughout those early years, rival teams hoped to draw Panania East Hills RSL in the first round of competition each season because the Waughs would generally be away on holidays at that time. 'If you got them while they were away, at least you had a chance,' remembers Freedman.

The boys' initial coaches were Alan Dougherty, a veteran park cricketer, and his son Neil, who both ensured the boys had a cricket education beyond Bankstown Shire. On Sunday mornings their ute was often a tangle of at least half a dozen excited youngsters heading to watch a Test or Sheffield Shield match at the Sydney Cricket Ground.

'I remember watching both New Zealand and the West Indies play,' says Mark. 'But my best memory is of the ute stopping at a pub in St Peters for the coaches' benefit.'

By the time Mark and Steve were 10, the Waugh family alone could have filled the Dougherty's ute after Bev gave birth to yet another boy, Danny, prompting the addition of a second storey to the house. The three older brothers took great pride in looking after the new arrival, although on one occasion their treatment of Danny's sanitary requirements was akin to abattoir workers handling a sheep's carcass. With no desire to come too close to their soiled kid brother and his nappy, Mark and Dean held Danny's legs, while Steve the supervisor washed the affected area with a hose.

Most other incidents of physical mishandling occurred during the almost ceaseless sporting contests that took place in the front and back yards. The brothers threw themselves into soccer, golf, tennis, scooter races, Australia–England cricket tests and rugby league games between Cronulla Sutherland, in the person of Mark, and Steve's 'team', Western Suburbs. (Their respective loyalties were the result of jumpers their parents had given them. Both would later change their allegiances to the local club, Canterbury-Bankstown). While his brothers continued to 'look after me', Danny recalls there was no sympathy given during the games. 'I was normally the fielder, and because I was the smallest I was the one who had to go under the house all the time to get the balls.' As expected in a family of boys, there were animated calls of cheating that led to arguments, a few half-hearted punches, the tossing away of a bat, a ball thrown in anger.

'There were never any proper fights,' says Mark. 'Maybe a few low blows in the kidneys, but nothing like punching anyone in the face. We were a close, tightknit bunch.'

Among Steve's memories is one particular scooter race down the front yard's steep driveway, which also doubled as a cricket pitch. The most dangerous part of the circuit was a sweeping left-hand turn that had to be negotiated to avoid crashing into the garage. The race between the twins was neck and neck until Steve, with the inside running into the bend, pushed out his right leg, knocking Mark off balance and sending him spearing into the garage door.

'We had some colossal races,' says Steve with a laugh. 'Mark would have got me back later on. It was never a case of one of us having too much on the other one. It was give and take, and always very even. Everything we did was a contest, but we must have got on pretty well because we played for hours in the front yard, the back yard, by the side of the house. While there was the occasional blue, we enjoyed each other's company. When Dean was old enough, he joined in too.'

Dean recalls, 'I used to trail behind a bit because I was younger, but Stephen and Mark always wanted to involve me. We were no different from any other family.'

At school, there were the regular playground activities of 'tag' and throwing tennis balls against walls, and much importance was placed on the winter craze at the time — football card collecting. To have a full set of teams sweetly scented by sticks of bubble gum was a highly sought after honour.

Panania Primary was a strong supporter of sport, although Mark and Steve needed no encouragement to play most games. In 1976, the eleven-year-olds became the youngest ever members of the New South Wales Primary Schools soccer team. Bev's heavyweight collection of memorabilia includes yellowing letters of congratulations to Mark and Steve from the Panania Primary Ladies Auxilliary. The final sentence in each letter is an indication of the boys' first experience of professional sport: 'Enclosed is a cheque for the value of $10.00 which we would like you to accept and use for spending money whilst you are away.'

Playing as strikers, the twins also swept their school to victory in the Umbro International Shield, a statewide knockout. In the final, Panania played Cardiff South Primary from the city of Newcastle, about 140 kilometres north of Sydney. At the full-time whistle, the winners' scoresheet read: Steve Waugh 2 goals, Mark Waugh 1. Panania won 3–1.

Mark has patchy memories of the games played, but he clearly recalls 'Mr Barnard', the devoted English soccer coach who ran very disciplined training sessions. Any boy caught misbehaving was usually banished with words uttered in a strong West Country accent: 'Go home boy, you're no use to me.' Mark never suffered that punishment, but on one occasion he did fall from grace after he smashed his coach's glasses, the result of a wayward delivery in a playground cricket match.

There was little doubt that sport was fast becoming the headline act in Mark's life. In their final two years at primary school, he and Steve played dominant all-round roles in Panania's successive triumphs in the state cricket knockout, and in their last year, 1977, they were also members of their school's tennis team that finished runner-up across New South Wales. Rugby league was the only absentee on their championship list. Although Mark enjoyed watching league games, he laced up the boots only once, admitting the physical contact was 'probably a bit rough for me, but it never stopped me in soccer'.

Even if he had the inclination for league, it's doubtful he would have had any time to pursue it. That year, 1977, was the most hectic of all Mark's primary years because he captained both the New South Wales cricket and tennis teams to victory in the national schools championships. Not the least surprisingly, Steve was at the helm of the soccer side, and had also earned cricket selection.

The cricket squad boasted phenomenal talent, including future Australian off-spinner Gavin Robertson and the multi-gifted Mark Patterson, who would graduate to senior New South Wales honours in both cricket and rugby union.

'Mark and Steve were the guns back then,' recalls Patterson. 'Being from the country I'd never seen anyone like them. They were outstanding. They were batting 4 and 5, and if you were behind them, you wouldn't pad up because you didn't think you'd get a hit.'

Patterson's claim certainly rang true in the game against South Australia when the twins were involved in a 150-run partnership. However, their exceptional abilities inevitably led to conflicts between sports, and none was more significant than their de-registration from the Bankstown Junior Soccer Association after they withdrew from an Under–12 representative game. The boys had legitimate excuses: Mark was playing tennis for New South Wales and Steve was in the soccer team at the national primary schools championships in Adelaide. Bankstown officials took the hard line, prompting the principal of Panania Primary, Bernie Gregory, to write to the *Daily Telegraph* newspaper in protest. At twelve years of age, Mark and Steve had caused their first controversy. It was a hint that they would have to make serious decisions about their career paths in the not too distant future. But at that stage, the dispute was a minor disruption because the twins soon registered with the nearby Auburn Association, which was already grooming another young prodigy, future Australian player Robbie Slater.

Mark identifies this period as the time when he and Steve began to rise above their peers. He says they were 'equally keen' on soccer and cricket, and although he had just as much potential on the tennis court, he disliked the individual element of 'sitting around all day by yourself waiting to play'. He enjoyed team environments where he could blend in with the pack and try not to be noticed, a difficult task considering his talents. Even at this age, he admits he felt uncomfortable about his brief appearances in the spotlight. 'I was pretty shy. When I got trophies I used to get embarrassed going up to get them. I'm still a bit the same way now, actually.'

Bev, too, acknowledges the reserved nature of the twins. When, as six-year-olds, they received their very first awards for sports participation, they walked with their heads bowed to the presentation stage at the local YMCA. 'It was impossible to get a good photo,' says Bev.

It was a role the boys had to become accustomed to. No matter what the sport, trophies and representative selection flowed as easily as runs, goals and forehand winners. Before stepping into secondary education, they won an Under–12 double wicket competition in the neighbouring suburb of Padstow, were presented with Slazenger bats as joint winners of the weekly New South Wales Cricket Association–*Sunday Telegraph* Encouragement award and were also regular recipients of the Sports Star of the Week award that was staged by the local paper, the *Bankstown Torch*. In his most impressive performance to that time, Mark had also topped the district's Under–12 representative batting aggregate with 244 runs at the Bradmanesque average of 122.

Bev and Rodger had every reason to be proud, and although they were always full of encouragement, they were never the annoying sideline parents who pushed their boys beyond the limits, or campaigned for them at the expense of others.

'I knew sport was always going to be their game right from the word go,' says Rodger. 'But no matter how well they were playing, enjoyment was always the main thing. Bev was particularly strong about that, and also playing hard but fair. Take your losses well, and show sportsmanship. A lot of credit goes to her for that.'

Bev's influence is still strongly evident today. As the teacher in charge of the special swimming scheme for handicapped children in Sydney's south-west, she has an important message for any new student: 'Look after yourself. Be proud of yourself. Do the best that you can do.'

'Some of the children may only end up swimming one metre at the end,' says Bev. 'It may disappoint their parents, yet that little kid has put in 150 per cent. Always be appreciative of other people's talents and efforts. When you lose, sometimes it's your fault, other times you have to accept that your opponent was better than you. I've tried to instil that in the boys as well.'

However, such was their dominance, the twins were rarely on losing teams, and consequently they were frequent but reluctant recipients of more praise than their peers. Coaches, parents, team-mates, officials, senior players and the local media believed that Mark and Stephen Waugh were heading towards greater triumphs. Despite the attention they were receiving in the Bankstown district — this wasn't due only to their individual sporting achievements but also to society's curious fascination with twins — the Waughs weren't known to everyone. On their first day at East Hills Boys Technology High School their surname was pronounced by some teachers as 'Woff' and by others as 'Wow'. It wouldn't be the last time that tongues were troubled — to this day in India, Mark and Steve are affectionately known as the 'Wog brothers'.

East Hills Boys was a little further from the Waugh home than Panania Primary, but was still within a twenty-minute walk, a five-minute push-bike ride or, frequently, a hasty trip in the Falcon when the boys slept in.

Sport was again an important part of the curriculum. The school had already helped nurture former Australian rugby union fullback Laurie Monaghan and Olympic swimmer Graeme Windeatt, while in the future it would educate its biggest international star of all — swimming phenomenon Ian Thorpe, whose father, Ken, had played first-grade cricket for Bankstown.

'The school has a reputation of producing good sporting teams and individuals,' says former sports-master and current careers adviser Ron Perrett, who watched with interest as the twins passed through their teenage years. 'I don't know if we can necessarily take much of the credit for it. All the top kids who have gone through would have been successful anyway, but the state school system gave them the opportunity to represent. That's very important, especially for the kids of Steve and Mark's era when school sport was highly regarded. In some people's eyes it was more important than weekend sport, but it's gone the other way now.'

To the Waugh twins, sport was sport, no matter where it was played. Their school and weekend commitments worked together, one helping the other to further the boys' development and reputations. An early sign of the partnership came during the 1978–79 summer when Mark and Steve were completing their first year at East Hills Boys. On the invitation of their uncle, Dion Bourne, the first-grade captain of Bankstown, the twins were invited to trial for the club's Green Shield Under–16 team. They were only thirteen, but Bourne had no doubt his nephews were ready to take the next step into a competition that was the traditional feeder of talented youngsters into the grade ranks. Both were selected. Mark had few opportunities, scoring 31 runs at an average of 15.5 from three innings, while Steve tallied 73 at 18.25. It was an inauspicious start, but their potential caught the attention of club officials who earmarked the 'aggressive' batsmen as already having the ability to graduate to the seniors.

The following season they entered the grade ranks as gawky fourteen-year-olds. Mark's first game came just before Christmas, the notorious period for teams to suffer from player shortages. He was called into the Fourths, making his debut against Randwick at Kensington Oval.

'It was a bit daunting,' Mark recalls. 'Even just going into the dressing rooms was intimidating. I was really shy, and it actually scared me a bit. It opened my eyes seeing blokes drinking and smoking after the game. It was so different from school. I got about 20 batting number 7 or 8, and bowled a bit of medium pace. I didn't realise how big a deal playing grade cricket at such a young age was, but looking back it was an important part of my development. It took me out of my comfort zone. I was testing my skill against better and much stronger players, so that accelerated my learning curve.'

Mark completed the season in Fourths, his top score was 41 not out, and there was no doubt much bigger innings were tapping him on the shoulder. So too were the opportunities at school. In the same season as their grade debuts, the twins were selected in the East Hills Boys First XI. It was 1980, the beginning of Year 9. In one of his early matches in the statewide Alan Davidson Shield knockout, Mark scored an unbeaten 63 and took 2–29 against Busby High — a small sign of what was to come.

Each Wednesday afternoon East Hills would play schools in the local Edmonson zone, a pool of rich talent that boasted future first-class cricketer Brad McNamara and New South Wales Under–19 representative Mark England. The same zone would later groom Dean before he became the third Waugh to play Sheffield Shield cricket. Other products of the area included Scott Hookey, Wayne Holdsworth and Corey Richards, all of whom would reach the first-class level, while in soccer there was no better player than Mark Bosnich, the upcoming Australian and English Premier League goalkeeper.

Ron Perrett remembers the impact the twins had.

When they'd arrived in Year 7, they came with the fanfare of being outstanding sports kids. By the time they got to the first-grade teams in Year 9, they'd be there every Wednesday afternoon playing soccer in winter, cricket in summer.

Back then I must admit at the back of my mind I didn't think they'd go on to play Test cricket, but certainly by the time they got to Year 11 there was a big chance they'd go all the way. Looking back now, I really think they could have gone on to be successful at the top level in any number of sports — soccer, tennis, golf. They just had that gift.

They were well respected, very well liked and had lots of friends. That's the case with a lot of kids who are very good at sport. It's like bees around the honey pot, they tend to attract other kids who like sport.

Both boys were also considered above average in the classroom. Just as he had been at primary level, Mark says he was a quiet high school student who achieved 'reasonable' results, but there was never any thought the scholar would stand above the sportsman.

I wouldn't say I looked forward to school, but I did look forward to all the sport. We had some really good and supportive teachers. Our PE master was Olympic decathlete Peter Hadfield. For me, it was just sport and more sport.

Girls were never a distraction because we just didn't get to see them much. East Hills Girls High was across the street, and all I can remember is throwing fruit at them every now and again. We never had much interaction at all.

Mark's only serious high school love was sport. Not only did he play cricket, soccer and tennis, he also found time to excel at squash, and once took Rodney Martin to five sets in an Under–14 final at nearby Engadine. Martin would later become a five-time national senior champion who peaked at number 2 in the world rankings.

Mark could excel at nearly any sport he tried. He was a natural. He also showed promise as a track and field athlete. His still skinny frame was well suited to 800-metre running, but he defied the stereotypes when he succeeded in the burly domain of shot-putting. He enjoyed competing at school carnivals, but curiously he believes athletics toyed with his nerves more than any other sport he had tried. 'I don't know why, but the 800 used to make me really tense. Maybe it was sizing up all the other runners before the start. It was really unusual for me because in most sports I was pretty casual.'

Casual but serious. Although he was still playing tennis — he made the semi-finals of an Under–14 metropolitan event at the prestigious White City — the individual nature of the sport had little appeal compared to Mark's team commitments. Soccer and cricket headed his priorities. During the 1980 winter, he and Steve played for Auburn in the state soccer league. It was usual for the twins to play two games in a row: the first in their proper age group, then they'd take on boys at least a year older. The back-to-back commitments continued until Mark was forced to cut back when troubled by Osgood-Schlatter Disease, a repetitive stress injury that affects the knee, most commonly suffered by teenage boys. He visited a Sydney specialist who suggested Mark, just hovering above five feet [1.52 metres] and shorter than Steve at the time, wouldn't grow any more. Bev remembers Mark looking 'absolutely devastated'. It wasn't until he was sixteen and grew nearly a foot in a year that there was cause for relief.

Because of sport, the twins led somewhat sheltered lives. Whether at school or outside, their routines were dictated by travel, training sessions and matches. There was little time for anything else in their early adolescence, but there were no complaints. Mark's view was simple: 'How good is this?' It's an outlook that remains with him today. Sport is his life.

By the time he was fifteen, cricket was beginning to take centre stage. Brother Danny remembers Mark 'worked really hard. He was always in the garage hitting a stocking with a ball in it practising his shots.' During the 1980–81 season Mark and Steve would play junior matches in the morning, then hurry off to their second season of grade cricket in the afternoon. After scoring 124 against Manly in Fourths, Mark was elevated to Thirds where he again turned heads, one innings in particular — 103 not out against Penrith — confirming he was on a fast track to the top grade. He shared a match-winning and club record-breaking 201-run fifth-wicket partnership with his captain, Mick Stephenson, who recalls the day clearly.

We played out at Cook Park, appropriately named because it was about forty degrees. Stinking hot. We were in a bit of trouble. Steve was already out for a duck in the middle of a hat-trick, but Mark made up for it. Third grade is usually the grade that sorts the kids out. They come from scoring hundreds against lollypop attacks in the juniors, then they start to come up against a few of the hard heads, but Mark handled it easily. I most noticed the time he had to play his shots. Just so much time. He was working the ball either side of the pitch, and was extremely strong on the pull shot. He was obviously just a natural. And above all else, he played the entire innings with his helmet on. In forty-degree heat! Over the years I don't think he's changed his game at all, technique wise.

Mark also impressed in the Green Shield team, captained by Steve, to the extent that he was selected in Bankstown's Poidevin-Gray Under–21 side for the final two matches of the season.

Mark barely had time to stand still — unless he was taking guard. That 1980–81 season he scored his first century for his school — 104 not out against Bankstown Boys High — and also destroyed his opponents with the ball, taking match figures of 8–32. Steve returned 8–53 in the same encounter. Two games earlier, Mark had scored an unbeaten 63 and snared 6–59 against Birrong Boys, while Steve, not wanting to be outdone, had a collective haul of 5–73 and chipped in with a first innings 87.

They kept stride with each other — Mark as an opening batsman and first-change bowler, Steve as an opening bowler and first-drop batsman. Quite often, a two-man team. However, it was the opportunities cricket offered that Mark cherished as much as his performances.

The reason we played cricket was for the companionship and the trips. We'd travel to some places by train, which was great fun. I can remember going all the way to Albury [on the New South Wales–Victoria border] once for a Davidson Shield game. Then we'd get billeted out. That used to be a nerve-wracking time. You'd get to the school and line up in front of all these strange people waiting to be told who they'd be looking after. A teacher would read your name out, then you'd look across at the people ready to take you home, and you'd suss them out. I was as nervous getting billeted as I was playing. Most of the time Stephen and I were billeted together, which was an advantage. We actually used to get put with a lot of girls. I think we got on okay most of the time, but I can remember we made one girl cry. I don't know what happened there!

The trip to Albury wasn't a memorable one for on-field performances. East Hills Boys were basically beaten by one player, an upcoming opening batsman named Geoff Milliken who scored a half-century, and would later play alongside the Waughs in the New South Wales Sheffield Shield side.

A small but significant step was taken towards that side in December 1980 when the twins were named in the New South Wales Under–16s for the national carnival in Launceston, Tasmania. Mark was vice-captain, deputy to young all-round sportsman Glen Tobin from the Illawarra region, south of Sydney. Both twins were enjoying their share of leadership roles. Neither was considered to have more tactical knowledge than the other.

As the cricket commitments increased, Bev was a most devoted team extra, rarely missing a match, and sometimes being called upon for scoring duties. She also clocked countless kilometres as a shuttle driver for various teams. Danny was still at an age needing considerable attention and Bev found little time for herself, but she relished the chance to share in her sons' achievements. However, with a touch of Chevvy Chase taking the Griswald family on vacation, there were times when the transport didn't run smoothly. Bev recalls a few breakdowns and running out of petrol with half a team in the back, while on one occasion her bearings took her in the opposite direction from a representative match in which Mark was already running late to open the batting. The familiar white station wagon arrived just in time for Mark to hurry out to bat.

Bev admits she was overprotective, but she preferred to do everything herself instead of leaving the boys in someone else's hands. She says she was never relaxed until she saw them all at home again. However, time at 56 Picnic Point Road was becoming less plentiful for the twins, and also Dean, who was beginning to rise through age representative teams in the Bankstown district.

Any thoughts the Waugh family had of a quiet recovery period after the 1980–81 season were bumped quickly out of the way by another winter of soccer. The twins continued playing for Auburn and were also part of a very strong school side that made the final eight of the Tasman Cup, a similar competition to the Davidson Shield. Mark scored a goal in the quarter-final against Woonona High School. He admits he was intimidated by a very parochial crowd and by the size of his opponents, who were 'all much bigger' than he was. Woonona eventually won in a penalty shoot-out after extra time couldn't separate the sides. Afterwards, the East Hills goalkeeper told his team-mates that he'd been pelted with stones thrown by people standing behind the net during the sudden-death decider. Woonona went on to win the championship.

Although sport was seemingly running their lives, the twins were entering an important stage of their education. The two final years of their studies were looming, meaning electives had to be chosen. For students considering tertiary education, electives were prerequisites for acceptance into many courses. Rightly or wrongly, this was the time careers had to be contemplated. The whole process was aided by the standard Year 10 practice of work experience, during which students were hosted by local businesses to gain a taste of the life they would lead once the school gate had shut for the final time. When careers adviser Ron Perrett put up a list of work opportunities outside his office, Mark was in no hurry to make a choice. By the time he had to make a decision, nearly all the jobs had been taken. Not through any desire, he ended up wearing old clothing and hard shoes and working as a laboratory assistant at British Paints. The 8.30 a.m. to 4.30 p.m. hours contributed to the longest week of his school life. 'I was certainly never going to be a lab assistant after that,' he laughs.

But what was he going to do? Perrett remembers clearly. 'He and Stephen both told me they wanted to play for Australia. They wanted to be professional cricketers.'

Both, however, would first make the play-for-pay ranks in soccer. While still at school they moved from the junior ranks at Auburn to join the Sydney Croatia reserve-grade team in the senior state league. Mark was a defender, Steve a forward. They were paid minimal amounts for each game, but motivation quickly deserted Mark. The more talented Steve stayed for longer, but he too lost interest when the demands started creeping in on his cricket.

The 1981–82 season further added to their hunger for the summer game when they were both chosen in Bankstown's Second-grade side, Mark as a middle-order batsman and medium pacer. He finished the season with 307 runs at an average of 19.19, and he took seven wickets. In the club yearbook, captain John Dunn suggested the youngest player in the team continually showed promise but often fell victim to playing across the ball.

Mark's cricketing education was also starting to encompass the social scene. One of his early girlfriends was scorer for the Second-grade side, but he quickly discovered time spent with the 'boys' was just as important. On Saturday nights after matches, his team-mates frequently took him to inner city pubs, the Orient Hotel at The Rocks being the most popular venue. It was the first time that Mark had experienced adult nightlife. He only had the occasional beer, but the whole experience opened his eyes to not only Bankstown's but Australia's sporting culture — play hard, play to win, then have a good time once the game is over.

The inevitable promotion to the top grade came in 1982–83 when Mark and Steve made their debuts as seventeen-year-olds against Western Suburbs at Bankstown Oval. Mark's first trip to the crease as an opener was unforgettable — he showed he could handle the rise in standard by scoring a patient 97 in four hours against an attack that included Greg Matthews. Steve was dropped back to Seconds after four games, but Mark played out the season He recalls:

First grade was a real introduction to tough cricket. I'd been lucky to have some pretty good grounding at training. From the moment we joined Bankstown no-one ever took it easy on me or Stephen. Lennie Pascoe [Test fast bowler] would be steaming in bowling bouncers, and everyone just accepted if we were there we were good enough to handle whatever was thrown up. But that didn't mean I thought I was ready for First grade. It wasn't only the climb in standard, but Firsts was a lot harder mentally. I remember playing Petersham who had some really tough competitors like Graeme Hughes [New South Wales Sheffield Shield batsman and First Grade rugby league player for Canterbury Bankstown], Dave Chardon, Brian Riley and Greg Hartshorn.

They didn't mind having a chat, and were always at me. It was my first experience of sledging. It was nothing serious, but they just chirped away with things like, 'Go back to Green Shield where you belong!'

We made the final that year against Penrith. Steve Smith opened the batting for us. He was the first player I'd actually seen bat in grade cricket a few years earlier when I was about twelve or thirteen. Back then, Stephen and I used to work the scoreboard at Bankstown Oval. I also remember watching Steve [Smith] score a double hundred against Victoria when the ABC used to cover Sheffield Shield matches on TV. I thought he was a great player, but in the final against Penrith he was trapped early on by Graeme Pitty, who was pretty sharp. I was watching from the boundary thinking, 'Geez, these blokes are too good for me. If Steve Smith can get cleaned up, how am I meant to do well?'

Mark replaced Smith at the wicket, and after showing glimpses of promise he was dismissed for 21, a disappointing yet considerable tally in a team total of just 140, 44 runs behind Penrith in a low-scoring match. However, the season had been a profitable one for the younger Waugh twin who finished second in the aggregates and averages with 427 runs at 30.5. His medium pace also proved successful: 14 wickets at 10.71.

Team-mate David Thompson, four years older than Mark, offers an intriguing insight into his close friend.

> I can remember when he first started bowling in First grade. He'd never even mark out his run-up. He'd just walk to a spot, turn around, run up and bowl. It was just so natural, like he was still playing in the back yard. He and Stephen were very competitive. There was one game where they were bowling together at Sydney University. Stephen happened to get a couple of wickets, and Mark turned to me and said, 'That shits me. I soften them up and Stephen gets the wickets!'
>
> He was great to bat with. We put on several big opening partnerships over a few seasons, and I was just in awe of the bloke. Just the shots he could play, even at that age. He had the ability to make me feel comfortable when I was batting with him. It just seemed to take the pressure off. It rubbed off on me, and made me play better at the other end. He was just so relaxed. I was a fairly hard hitter, and sometimes after I hit a four, he'd come up to me in between overs and say, 'Thommo, the ball only has to reach the fence, not go through it.' He may have been shy, introverted and guarded when necessary, but he was also very funny.
>
> In those early days we used to rib him about a few things, especially his shower habits. He always kept his towel on until he went into the shower behind a brick wall out of our sight. Then we'd see the towel come over the top. He was pretty bashful. Sometimes he wouldn't have a shower after a day's play. That was a big thing in those days in the dressing room. You had to have a tub, it was part of the culture.

Amidst the good-natured humour from his team-mates there were perceptive observations from officials — Mark thinks this is where he earned his long-standing nick-name of 'Junior', in relation to being Steve's younger brother. After Mark capped his successful 1982–83 club season with a batting average of 45.33 in the Poidevin-Gray competition, manager John Mackinnon wrote of

'Junior' in the Bankstown yearbook: 'Proved to be an accomplished opening bat, and apart from the occasional lazy shot in no-man's-land has the ability and temperament to go to the top. A very good right-hand medium-pace bowler and one of the safest pairs of hands in the club.'

High praise and representative selection were common for Mark. In the same season, he and Steve were members of both the New South Wales Combined High Schools team and the state Under–19s. However, one honour eluded them — they hadn't been able to help East Hills Boys win the Davidson Shield. Ron Perrett recalls:

> To be Shield champions, you were basically looking at winning eight
> consecutive matches. I took over coaching the team when the twins were in their
> final year. We made it pretty easily to the quarter-finals, then we played
> Normanhurst Boys at Pennant Hills Oval. Mark opened and scored 20 or 30.
> Stephen went in at first drop, slashed at his first ball outside off-stump and was
> caught behind. Well, the coach of Normanhurst almost went through the roof of
> the old grandstand, while I just sat there with my head and shoulders slumped.
> We weren't chasing that many to win, but the effect the two dismissals had on
> the other kids in the side was incredible. You could see their body language
> suggesting, 'Oh no, what are we going to do now?' The impact of Stephen and
> Mark on the entire team was that great. We didn't get the runs, and
> Normanhurst went on and won the final.

East Hills eventually won the final in 1984, the year after the twins left school, but the Waugh influence was still strong. That season marked the First XI debut for Dean, a hard-hitting middle-order batsman. The school took out the competition again in 1991 when all-rounder Danny continued the family tradition of cricketing excellence. Although the two younger brothers weren't to reach the same spectacular heights as the twins, they both enjoyed considerable representative success in the age ranks. Dean graduated to the first-class arena, representing both New South Wales and South Australia, while Danny remains an important member of the Sydney University First-grade side in the Sydney Cricket Association competition.

Throughout their younger years, both shared in the success of their elder brothers. In 1983–84, there were frequent reasons for quiet family celebrations, the greatest of which was the selection of the twins in the Australian Under–19s for a Test and one-day series at home against Sri Lanka. Mark's progression into the team was highlighted by his Player of the Series performances at the Caltex New South Wales Schoolboys Championships in Sydney in December 1983, a month after finishing the New South Wales Higher School Certificate and leaving school. As opening batsman and first-change bowler for the Combined High Schools First XI, his returns included 105 not out and 4–32 against Combined Catholic Colleges, and 132 not out against Combined Associated Schools.

It was obvious that Mark and Steve's careers were lengthening stride towards the first-class arena. Among their enthusiastic team-mates was a likeable left-handed opening batsman from the southern New South Wales country town of Wagga Wagga. Former Australian captain Mark Taylor says:

I always joke that Mark and Stephen didn't have to bat or bowl at trials. All they'd have to do was turn up and they'd get picked. I actually don't think that was altogether untrue. I was about fifteen or sixteen when I first met them. Coming from the country, it was a couple of years before I started making selection trials for under-age cricket, but all the way along, everyone knew who the Waugh twins were.

Then I started to make a few sides with them, and I remember in particular going down to Young to play at the Combined High Schools carnival in November 1983. Steve was in the Metropolitan Firsts, and Mark and I were in the Seconds. We all ended up going quite well, and eventually made it to New South Wales CHS Firsts together. We also played state Under–19s in Melbourne, and from there were lucky enough to get picked in the Australian Under–19s. That's the first time we really started to play together on a regular basis.

A new era in Australian cricket was beginning to take shape.

CHAPTER THREE

THE ROAD TO SUCCESS

It's ironic that someone as naturally co-ordinated as Mark finds it difficult to drive a manual car. When learning, Steve was happy to test his feet on a clutch pedal, but Mark cautiously took the automatic route to his provisional licence. Bev remembers the difficulties she had teaching her younger twin.

Mark did practically what I told him to do to the point that we once nearly had an accident when I was trying to get him to do a U-turn. He was in the driver's seat in the old Falcon, which was a great big tank to handle. We were on a quiet stretch, but Mark was going too fast before turning. It wasn't very fast, but quick enough to have me worried. I kept telling him, 'Slow down, slow down. If you don't we'll hit that telegraph pole!' But he wasn't slowing. So I told him, 'If you don't slow down, get out of the car!' Next thing you know, he opened the door and got out of the car while it was still going. I had to jump across in a hurry and take the wheel. He said afterwards that he thought the car would stop because it was an automatic. He and Stephen both got their licences on their first go. How, I'll never know.

Although the old Falcon would continue to play an eventful role with the Waugh clan, the road to further teenage cricketing success was much smoother. After being selected in the Australian Under–19s in January 1984, Mark, Steve and Mark Taylor joined a list of future first-class and international players for three Tests and three one-dayers against Sri Lanka. The Australian team, captained by South Australian batsman Jamie McPhee, also included New South Wales left-arm spinner Mark England, Tasmanians Richard Soule and Danny Buckingham, and Victorian fast bowler Denis Hickey. The visitors were led by Aravinda de Silva, who together with team-mate Asanka Gurusinha launched into a battle against the Waughs and Taylor that wouldn't reach its climax until the controversial World Cup on the subcontinent twelve years later.

The Australians won the first four-day Test, in Canberra, by an innings and 11 runs. Opening the batting, and having the additional role of vice-captaincy, Mark scored 47, and took 1–19 in the second innings after being the fourth bowler introduced to the attack. The undoubted star of the match was a lean red-headed paceman from Queensland who hammered 81 and claimed four wickets in each innings. Only nine months later, the same player shot into the senior Test ranks for Australia's home series against the most destructive team of the 1980s, the West Indies. Craig McDermott was on his way to the top.

Although the second Test against Sri Lanka ended in a draw, the match offered Mark the chance to become acquainted with the Adelaide Oval, a ground on which he was to experience more highs and lows during his career than any other venue across the world. His introduction was memorable: he top scored with 123 and took a wicket in each innings, bowling first change. His efforts weren't wholly recognised in the newspaper reports that continually referred to 'New South Welshman, Michael Waugh'.

The final Test, in Melbourne, was also drawn. Mark compiled 32 before falling caught behind to de Silva. After scoring a half-century in the previous match, Steve demolished the Sri Lankan attack with a brilliant 187 off only 216 deliveries.

Australia completed a successful campaign by winning the one-day series 2–1. Mark remained consistent with scores of 37, 23 and 28. His best bowling return was 2–41 in the final match in Melbourne.

'I never knew whether a cricket career was going to come off, but by the Under–19s I was hoping things would go my way, that's for sure,' says Mark.

The Under–19 team wasn't the first Australian honour for Mark. In 1983 he'd won selection in the national indoor cricket side. The modified game, run as much as a business as a sport, boomed in the 1980s. Some centres were built specifically for the indoor sport, others were converted storage facilities and warehouses in suburban industrial areas, an inglorious contrast to the grand outdoor arenas the twins would become accustomed to in the years to follow.

Mark and Steve had been introduced to indoor cricket by one of their junior coaches, Glen Russell, and were soon playing with Bankstown first-grade captain Bob Vidler and Steve Smith. Mark remembers:

Everyone was into it back then. It might have been very different from real cricket, but it helped me develop some important skills with my fielding. That's where Stephen and I learnt a lot of our backhand flicks. I used to keep as well, with only one glove on and the other hand free for throwing. At the top level the game was really quick, and it helped my reactions and anticipation in the real game. But batting and bowling weren't good for us at all. It was all about playing across the line and working the ball into side nets. I used to play proper shots, play straight, and go for fours and sixes off the back net.

We had a lot of fun though. New South Wales won the national titles twice while we were playing, and the trips away were always a chance for the guys to cut loose a little. One trip to Melbourne for the national titles was the first time I'd ever been sick from alcohol . . . and the last. We had a big night out at the end of the series, the next morning at the presentation I spent most of the time in the toilets!

But the game started to wear thin after a while. It was really aggressive, and players used to Mankad batsmen, and give high fives every time a wicket fell or a four was hit. It was a bit over the top, I lost interest, but had enjoyed it at the start.

The twins were also umpires, earning about thirty dollars each a night for three games. Sitting on their high chairs at the back of the courts, they were a safe enough distance away from heated disputes that occasionally led to push-and-shove contests between players. It wasn't uncommon to see a batsman shoulder-charge a fieldsman out of the way, or suddenly be ducking a ball thrown angrily in his direction. Mark recounts with a smile the times when players would try to unsettle him by climbing the net nearest the umpire's chair and hurling insults. Mark would sometimes issue 5-run penalties for bad conduct, knowing the offenders would 'shut up for a while'. When games were running late he occasionally cut some bowlers a few balls short every over to make up for lost time.

Mark was still playing indoor cricket during his second season of First grade for Bankstown in 1983–84. While the year's highlight was unquestionably his performances for the Australian Under–19s, he added another innings to his collection of memories when he scored his initial first-grade century, 108, against Mosman. His Poidevin-Gray returns further enhanced his reputation: 283 runs at 70.75 and 14 wickets at 12.07. However, statistics meant little to him. Even at this stage he was just as concerned with how he made his runs as how many runs he made. His distinct leg-side play was becoming a feature of his game, and at just eighteen years of age he was recognised throughout the club ranks as an elegant batsman who not only made batting look easy, but had the rare and enviable quality that sifted a class player from a good player — he always seemed to have time to play his shots.

Time was something he also had much of away from the cricket field. After receiving his HSC results — he can't remember his exact mark, but believes it was just above 250 out of 500 — he was still to decide what he would do in what he hoped would be merely a transition period between part-time player to full-time professional. Reflecting a feature of his character that is still very much apparent today, Mark preferred not to think too far ahead. He hadn't considered a career outside cricket, and had no desire to go to university, acknowledging that he wasn't a natural learner.

'Stephen and I had both been hopeless at Maths. I was quite good at Economics and Geography, and did well in English without reading a book! But it was great when school had finished — no more study.'

Mark was fortunate to have a strong support base which included Harry Solomons, an inspiring example of an immigrant who'd come to Australia with little money, but with a wealth of ambition and an unwavering desire to succeed. Originally from Sri Lanka, Solomons arrived in Sydney in the 1970s and worked his first job as a prison officer at Long Bay Gaol in the city's eastern suburbs. Willing to take risks and work hard, he ventured into business and established the Kingsgrove Sports Centre, which is now recognised as the heartbeat of the world's largest chain of specialist cricket stores. Solomons first met the twins when they were fifteen. He was seeking up-and-coming youngsters to sponsor with his new range of Symonds equipment that was readily identified by its logo of a charging rhinoceros. At the time he was looking after the needs of Bankstown players David Thompson and Gary Crowfoot, and Western Suburbs all-rounder Brad McNamara, whose journey through the junior representative ranks was keeping pace with the Waughs'. The three all suggested Solomons consider adding Mark and Steve to the Symonds stable. Solomons recalls:

I was on a pretty tight budget, and could only afford to support one of the twins. Steve was the first to come and see me, he was the hungry one, whereas Mark was quiet and didn't push himself forward. So obviously Steve got the deal, and I recommended Mark to a friend of mine, Peter Sutton, the sales manager at Stuart Surridge. About three to four weeks later I ran into Mark and discovered that he was still waiting for a sponsorship. I felt really sorry for him, and gave him gear as well. At that stage both boys were beginning to make names for themselves in Sydney's metropolitan squads. They were very, very highly thought of.

I started employing them part-time when they got picked in the New South Wales Under–17 side the following year. When they left school, I found a place for Steve because he had the slightly higher profile, but I couldn't find a place for Mark, so I arranged a job for him with another cricket distributor, ML Sporting Goods at Alexandria. This was just after he'd made the Australian Under–19s. He was a horrible worker, he was the sort of guy who needed a few kicks up the butt to get him moving. I don't think Mark was interested in work, he was a bit of a lazy bugger. One day his bosses went looking for him in the warehouse, but couldn't find him until they discovered him asleep in a box! That was Mark. He was very casual and probably only got tolerated because of his cricket ability.

But at first I don't think he was hungry enough with his cricket either. When they came back from the Under–19s series I remember one day going to their home. While we were having dinner I asked Steve in front of the whole family, 'Do you think you'll play for Australia?' His prompt answer was, 'Yes.'

I turned and asked Mark the same question, but he was busy concentrating on his food. He could eat like a horse. He was getting stuck into the pasta, and answered in between licking his fingers. 'Yeah, maybe, yeah, we'll see.' To me it was obvious that Steve would play first. He had a little more hunger.

Solomons' strong support of Mark was evident right from the beginning. Only the day after receiving his first kit of equipment, Mark had all his gear stolen out of his car at Revesby Swimming Pool. Solomons replaced everything the following day.

Solomons became a close friend of Mark. Not only did he arrange job and sponsorship opportunities, but he was soon to find himself offering advice to Mark about an office relationship that was certain to raise eyebrows and cause considerable heartache and conflict. However, at the end of the 1983–84 season, Mark was still to discover his love for Harry's first employee, Susan Porter.

Another step up the representative ranks was taken in 1984–85 when Mark and Steve were included in the New South Wales train-on squad. Mark admits being 'overawed and a little intimidated' by his inclusion. With a very slender physique, poor dress sense (according to other squad members) and a notable hairstyle that was characterised by an almost shoulder-length flow at the back — nowadays coined comically a 'mullet' — nineteen-year-old Mark was every inch a boy among men in a squad that had a plentiful collection of strong and diverse personalities including Greg Matthews, Geoff Lawson, Mike Whitney, Murray Bennett and Steve Rixon. Lawson remembers the first time he saw the 'Junior' Waugh bat in the nets.

He looked to be pretty loose, but very talented. He hit the ball well, but didn't care where it went. He just played a lot of shots. I could understand how he'd made a lot of runs in grade cricket, but I thought it was going to be a lot tougher for him when he got to first-class cricket. He'd have to hone up his act, sharpen it up. He used to play a lot of shots to good length balls that everyone else was leaving. He'd try to whack them past point, sometimes doing it well, but not on other occasions.

His bowling was quite sharp, and he was always willing to bowl. You never had to ask him.

He was also pretty quiet and kept to himself. I think he's still quite shy now.

If, as Lawson suggested, Mark needed technical improvement in his game, his elevation into the New South Wales squad came at an opportune time because it coincided with the appointment of Bob Simpson as coach. Simpson played 62 Tests for Australia, scoring 4869 runs and taking 71 wickets. He is recognised as one of cricket's all-time great slips fieldsmen, once holding the national record with 103 catches. He is also a noted technician able to pick up even the most minute faults in a player's game.

He first witnessed the twins' abilities when the New South Wales squad gathered for winter training at Cranbrook College in Sydney's eastern suburbs. Mark and Steve were just eighteen. Simpson recalls:

I honestly hadn't heard of either of them because I'd been out of cricket for a while. I saw these two contrasting players. People had to tell me they were twins because I never would have picked it. The talent was obvious, there was a naturalness in both of them. Stephen was more natural than he is today. Mark is basically the same player today, with a little more safety valve than he had when I first saw him. Back then I was delighted to think there were these two young boys who were at the right age to hopefully be shown a few things.

There is the old story that too much talent can be a hindrance as well as a great thing to have. Too much talent can take you to a certain level, probably when you're about seventeen, and then you get to the real world. I think that's the area Mark and Stephen were in when I first saw them.

Mark was very shy and introverted. He sometimes put up a defensive wall, and was perhaps less sure than Stephen about his destiny. But I found him easy to work with. He was a good listener.

And a good watcher. Mark remembers absorbing the atmosphere at training sessions, and more often than not he tried to develop his own game by observing others. He was not one to ask many questions. He recognises Simpson had a strong influence, particularly in fielding where the great slipper of yesteryear helped mould his brilliant successor. Simpson's philosophy is that a slips fielder's hands have to feel as though they are loose enough to drop off. He stresses that catchers behind the wicket have to let the ball come to them, not go after the ball. From very early on, Mark epitomised that.

Mark can't remember Simpson trying to change his batting in any significant way. There were the obvious discussions about building innings and shot selection, but Simpson was mindful not to inhibit the Waugh flair. It was a few years later when Mark was on the edge of Australian selection that Simpson, by then the national coach, had reason to discuss the need for added discipline, especially when it came to leg-side play.

The most significant change for Mark during the 1984–85 season was the loss of his lifelong playing partner. After a golden run of form in grade, Steve was selected in the Sheffield Shield team, taking a sizeable step ahead of his brother. From this point on, the twins, who were so used to being side by side during their junior and school years, would experience very different journeys to stardom. Journeys that Beverly Waugh would travel in spirit with her sons.

I was watching Dean play a game at Taren Point when I heard on the radio that Stephen was selected for the Shield. Well I got all tingly and thought, 'Who can I tell?' I just wanted to tell everyone because that was the realisation of a dream — playing for New South Wales. Then at the back of my mind I thought, 'If Stephen can do it, Mark can too.' It felt as if they'd both been chosen. That was the most exciting moment I've had in their cricket careers because it was the first indication I got that they might represent Australia.

In my heart I knew that if all things went according to plan, they'd both get there one day. That was the only time I sat back and realised they were a chance of going all the way.

While Steve became accustomed to first-class cricket, beginning with his debut against Queensland in Brisbane in early December, Mark was forced to bide his time in the New South Wales Colts and Second XI teams. His best returns came for Bankstown where he topped the first-grade batting aggregates with 717 runs. In Steve's absence Mark assumed captaincy of the Poidevin-Gray side, a notable moment coming when he took a hat-trick — all bowled — against Sydney.

Away from cricket, the Waugh twins had developed a reputation for their driving. The big white Falcon station wagon was a familiar sight on the streets of Panania and beyond. Being frugal when it came to purchasing petrol, the boys rarely filled up beyond what was immediately needed. Three dollars here, four dollars there, but never a full tank. Running out of fuel was a common occurrence. Perhaps it was a genetic disposition because Bev had been known to run on empty, and on one particular occasion when she asked a service station attendant for the use of a jerry can to carry to her thirsty car, she was told, 'I'm sorry, but two young blokes borrowed it the other day, and they haven't brought it back yet.' No points for guessing who the two offenders were!

Mark experienced a number of embarrassing moments behind the wheel, none greater than his bout of forgetfulness at a Revesby service station. He was in such a hurry to make it to state training that he drove away without paying for his petrol. He was completely unaware of his lapse until he arrived home that night to be told by Bev that police were looking for the accidental thief. Mark quickly drove back to Revesby and paid his dues.

On another occasion, the car broke down on the eternally hectic Parramatta Road when Mark was driving Mark Taylor to state training. The Falcon was eventually put to pasture when it would only travel in reverse!

Mark's cricket continued to head in the opposite direction. Towards the end of the 84–85 summer, the twins signed a deal to spend the Australian winter playing for the Egerton club in northern England's Bolton league. Under the competition's rules, each club was allowed one professional of any nationality, and an overseas player. Steve had been appointed the club pro, but would split his income with Mark.

In Egerton, about half an hour's drive from Manchester, the twins' impending arrival was publicised in Bolton's *Evening News*. Locals Peter and Iris Greenhalgh, who had no strong connections with cricket, or passion for the game, read the article with interest. Iris, speaking with a delightful mix of cockney and northern accents, remembers:

It said that the Egerton Cricket Club was looking for accommodation for the season for these nineteen-year-old twins who'd never been out of Australia. Peter said to me, 'Will we have them here?' And I asked how long it would be. He told me, 'Only a couple of weeks.'

It wasn't a massive house or anything. We had four small bedrooms, two of them were spare. So, after a bit of a think we decided to give it a go and contacted the cricket club. Two lads came down, had a look around and thought everything was fine. So that's how it started.

Stephen and Mark slept for twenty-four hours when they arrived. Then they came down the following morning in shorts and T-shirts. It was something like the beginning of April, and it was absolutely freezing. They settled in and it was only then that Peter told me they were going to stay for five months! I thought, 'Oh my God! But well, they're here now.'

We just wanted to carry on as normal. They just had to live with us the way we were. They were no trouble whatsoever, they were brilliant lads, lovely lads.

We bought loads of Foster's beer because we thought being Australians they'd want loads of beer, but they never drank in the house. We'd had no experience with Australians before that. We thought these were nice lads but they were totally different; I thought they'd be very much alike in personality. They didn't seem to talk to one another much, but there was a real understanding between them. Stephen rang home a lot, Mark didn't. I even had to remind Mark to write or ring. After having two girls in the family it was quite a novelty having two boys.

When they first came we took them out to see one or two sights. I can remember them running out of a restaurant in Southport to take photos when it started to snow. They had never seen snow before. It was just so brilliant having them. Absolutely brilliant.

However, a complex and at times controversial chain of events significantly altered the twins' winter. Towards the end of the Australian summer, rumours had simmered about plans for a rebel team to tour the apartheid-scarred South Africa, a cricket outcast since 1970. Players from England, Sri Lanka and the West Indies had already made tours, but Australia had remained staunchly opposed. The opportunity to tour South Africa prompted former, current and potential Test players to jeopardise their careers. The list of Australian rebels was headed by the recently-deposed Test skipper Kim Hughes, but the most significant names to affect the Waughs were those of John McGuire and Carl Rackemann. The Queensland pacemen had been named in Australia's Ashes squad to tour England from late April, but when they refused to sign statutory declarations stipulating they wouldn't go to South Africa, they were replaced by Jeff Thomson and young New South Wales fast bowler Dave Gilbert. As a result, Gilbert was forced to forfeit his Esso scholarship, a prestigious award allowing four young Australians to play Second XI cricket on the English county circuit. Steve, with little more than half a season of first-class cricket to his credit, was named as Gilbert's replacement. He headed south to Essex, leaving Mark as Egerton's new professional after just one game. It was the first time in the twins' lives that they'd been separated for any significant length of time. Mark recalls he actually enjoyed it.

'I had a room to myself, wasn't being compared to someone all the time and could be my own person. I was probably a bit lonely for a couple of days, but after that I settled in well. I obviously made a lot of friends at the cricket club, and Pete and Iris were really good to me.'

Fellow countryman Mark McPhee would later join Mark as the overseas player. Sadly, the widely respected West Australian would die in a car accident in his home state more than a decade later. Mark remembers, 'He was a top bloke and a very good friend. It was very sad.'

While the Lancashire and Central Lancashire leagues were considered the two main cricket championships in the area, Bolton boasted a small but very competitive league that included two other Australian professionals — Greg Shipperd (Heaton) and Rod Tucker (Farnworth) — and Indian Test players Dilip Vengsarkar (Westhoughton), Mohinder Armanath (Kearsley) and Chetan Sharma (Tonge). Mark comments:

It was a good little competition. It was very different from playing in Sydney — the furthest you had to travel for a game was about fifteen minutes. The whole experience was obviously different for me because it was my first time away from home. The fact that I was the number one player in the team put a bit of pressure on me. The local members of the club are pretty tough people, and if the pro doesn't do any good, they'll let you know. The first three or four weeks I didn't do much at all, and the officials were starting to say, 'Oh this lad's no good. He's roobish!'

The first game we played was in snow, not exactly ideal cricket weather. It's a bit hard to perform at your best in weather like that.

But when I got used to everything, I started to do quite well, and actually ended up playing one game for the Lancashire Second XI against Nottinghamshire. I batted about number 9, made about 20 not out and took 4–20 bowling seamers. It was a good introduction to English cricket.

Mark also clearly remembers dismissing Vengsarkar caught and bowled from a leading edge when Egerton played Westhoughton. It was his first international wicket. By this stage, as Bolton's *Evening News* reported on 6 August, Mark was 'rapidly becoming the talk of the league'. After watching their pro peel off six centuries by the end of the season, club officials replaced 'roobish' with 'brilliant'. Despite losing Steve, they had made a wise choice in keeping Mark, whose success prompted not only small financial bonuses, but an unusual fringe benefit. About seven years earlier Mark had two teeth knocked out during a picnic cricket match near the Waugh home. Although he'd had them repaired, he'd never had them crowned, an expensive procedure that was too much for the family pocket. However, not long after his arrival at Egerton he was given an incentive: if he scored at least 800 runs and took 50 wickets, he would have his teeth fully repaired by local dentist Peter Moss who just happened to be captain of the Egerton side. By little more than halfway through the season Mark had a much brighter smile!

He eventually finished his stint with 1460 runs, strolling past the club record by more than 200 runs and falling just 75 short of the league's all-time mark set the previous year by Bankstown team-mate Rod Bower. He also claimed 70 wickets with his medium pace, but was hampered in the latter stages by back pain that would cause greater problems a few years later.

While Mark left a significant impression on the Egerton club, there was little doubt his biggest impact was on the Greenhalghs. Iris recalls:

He was great, he was just one of the family. I used to wait on him like I did the girls. He was a very pleasant lad. Always nice, always happy. And very, very clean. He must have showered a couple of times a day.

I think he pulled our legs a little bit sometimes. He used to say, 'Can you make me a pavlova, please? My mum makes a great pavlova.' Well I just wasn't good at that sort of thing. He used to pull my leg about my cooking. He was just such an easy, nice lad. When we took him to the airport there were tears all round.

We still follow what the boys do. Even now, when they're playing our lads, I don't want England to win, I want Australia to. If Peter sees them on television he'll always say, 'Come on, your boys are on.'

Mark remains in contact with the Greenhalghs. Christmas cards are swapped, and whenever the twins have played in Manchester, the Greenhalghs have been spectators and dinner companions. The Egerton experience offered Mark a teaser of life on the road as a paid cricketer. He wasn't an adventurous tourist, admitting he was too shy to go out by himself. 'If someone wanted to take me somewhere I'd go, but I wouldn't go out on my own around the countryside looking at things like some people do. I just played my cricket and that was about it really.'

After his first successful campaign abroad Mark returned to Sydney full of confidence for the 1985–6 season, his early form prompted speculation in the media that he would soon join Steve in the New South Wales Shield team. He launched into grade with the same aggression that underlined his performances at Egerton. The highlight was a score of 177, including twenty-three fours and two sixes against Petersham at Petersham Oval. The innings, lasting five hours, ensured Mark's position as an opening batsman in the state's Second XI. Continued good form would surely enhance his first-class prospects.

For the second time in six months Mark's claims were helped by the rebel cricket controversy. The fourteen players who'd signed to tour South Africa from late October had been banned by the Australian Cricket Board from playing Tests for three years, and state cricket for two. This meant that New South Wales selectors were searching for two new openers to replace Steve Smith and John Dyson, who'd both agreed to the rebel trip.

Mark's main rivals were Mark Taylor and former Bankstown batsman Steve Small, who was profiting from a stint at the Penrith Club. Taylor and Mark had the inside running after opening in the season's early Second XI matches, but on the day the New South Wales team was chosen for its first Shield game of the year against Tasmania, the two youngsters endured mixed fortunes against Victoria's second stringers at Manly Oval, in Sydney's north. In front of the chairman of selectors, Dick Guy, Taylor crafted a watchful 102 in nearly five hours, while Mark spent much of the innings in the grandstand after being dismissed for a duck. However, selectors had already identified his talent, and that night a phone call from journalist Greg Growden was cause for celebration. Mark was in the team, but his immediate response to Growden, as reported in the *Sydney Morning Herald* (22 October 1985), was disbelief: 'What? You're kidding. I really can't believe it, you beaut. I was feeling pretty down in the dumps earlier in the day after getting out second ball, but you can bet I am a lot better now.'

Mark Waugh, the slender, gifted twenty-year-old from Panania, was four days away from making his Sheffield Shield debut. It appeared destiny was in his hands.

CHAPTER FOUR

THE AWAKENING

Young. It was the most fitting way to describe Mark before his first Sheffield Shield match. A photo of the twins published in the *Sydney Morning Herald* on the opening day of the match against Tasmania showed Mark to be lithe, narrow-shouldered and with a fresh face still to be hardened by the cricketers' lotion of sun and experience. His hair, a few centimetres shorter than Steve's collar-teasing flow, was cut in an unflattering square fringe at the front and sides, and his clothes were more suitable for the dance-floor than the dressing room, especially the light-coloured body shirt that folded open to reveal a thick necklace. A boy entering a man's domain.

Tasmanian captain David Boon won the toss, and sent New South Wales in on a very hard pitch at Hobart's Tasmania Cricket Association ground. The decision returned early rewards — Mark, fellow debutant Taylor and captain Dirk Wellham were all dismissed cheaply, leaving New South Wales struggling at 3–60. However, Greg Matthews (184), Steve (107), and Peter Clifford (98) repaired the damage in a total of 561. Mark had scored just 13 before falling to West Indian paceman Winston Davis. He remembers 'battling away, but feeling reasonably comfortable'. In the second innings he was dismissed for 28 by another new cap, fast bowler Michael Hill. When stumps were pulled in the drawn match, Taylor was 56 not out, a belated present for his twenty-first birthday the day before.

There was, however, a much more infamous moment concerning Taylor's coming of age. On the eve of his birthday — the second night of the match — the team went out to celebrate. Mark left early, returning to the hotel for a good night's sleep, and assuming his room-mate Taylor would arrange the morning wake-up call. Hours and more than a handful of beers later, Taylor came back and put himself to bed, expecting Mark to have organised the call. The following morning the phone did ring, but when Taylor answered, there wasn't the pleasant voice of a hotel employee at the other end of the line. The conversation was brief.

Taylor: Who is it?

Voice: Bob Simpson.

Taylor: No bullshit, who is it?

Voice: It's Bob Simpson. The team is down at the ground and you're late!

Needless to say the slumbering rookies were penalised when they reached the ground, still wiping sleep from their eyes. Simpson hammered them with fielding drills. 'We must have taken about 300 catches each that morning,' recalls Mark, who took his opening first-class catch later that day when he held a skied shot to deep mid-wicket from Roger Woolley off the bowling of veteran leg-spinner Bob Holland. Although the sleep-in was an unfortunate way to launch a first-class career, perhaps the Simpson grilling helped lay the foundation for two of the greatest slips fieldsmen of recent years.

New South Wales played Victoria four days later in the steel city of Newcastle. It was here that Mark really noticed the step up in class after being dismissed twice by fast bowler Merv Hughes — for 0 and 4 — in the Blue-bags' 90-run win. Mark says:

It was the toughest game I'd encountered. To that stage I'd never played Merv's aggressive type of fast bowling. Or not to that standard anyway. The closest I'd come was in the grade final against Graeme Pitty a couple of years earlier. But Merv was a different story. He was a Test bowler, and a bloody scary one at that. I got caught behind in the first innings and bowled in the second. I wasn't in long enough for him to say anything to me. I just remember it being the best fast bowling I'd ever faced. I thought I was out of my depth, just not quite ready for it. Certainly not as an opener anyway. I'd opened in the Under–19s, but I'd never really considered that was my best position. At grade level I'd started off in the middle order, and although I was moved to the top of the order, opening for your club is a very different thing to the Sheffield Shield.

I was also a bit naive and still felt very young. I didn't know my game that well, or what should be my approach to first-class cricket. I was just happy to be there, and took the view that whatever happened, happened. I didn't think too much about it.

It was a challenging introduction to the first-class arena. So familiar with being successful, Mark was in the unusual position of having to prove himself to his team-mates. He was no longer a brilliant kid with potential, but a young man who had to uphold that potential and the accompanying faith so many people had shown in him since his junior years. If only it was as easy as picking a Melbourne Cup winner, which Mark managed to do when the John Meagher trained What A Nuisance pipped Koiro Corrie May by a short head to win Australia's legendary two-mile event.

What A Nuisance could have easily been used the following week by Australia's players as an appropriate description of masterful New Zealand bowler Richard Hadlee, who demolished the home side with 15 wickets, including 9–52, in the Kiwis' innings and 41-run win in the first Test, at Brisbane.

After the victory, New Zealand travelled south to play New South Wales at the Sydney Cricket Ground. Mark knew his position was under scrutiny, and although Hadlee was rested, the younger Waugh twin was still certain to be tested by the competent new-ball attack of Ewen Chatfield and Lance Cairns. He saw off the shine only to depart for 17, victim of left-arm orthodox spinner Steven Boock. It wouldn't be the last time Mark would surrender to that type of bowler in the running battle he has waged against slow men since his earliest days at the top level.

Mark wasn't as fortunate in the second innings after a mid-wicket mix-up with Taylor pushed him back through the players' gates for his second duck in four innings. So far, his first-class career had returned 62 runs at an average of 10.3. He wasn't surprised, or upset, when he was dropped for the following match, against Western Australia in Sydney. 'I knew I was young enough and good enough to come back, but probably not as an opening batsman.'

However, only the most fearless of fortune-tellers would have predicted Mark's selection for the final four matches of the season as a new-ball and first-change bowler who batted in the middle order. After being overlooked for five games, Mark returned to play Queensland at Brisbane's Woolloongabba Cricket Ground in late January. By this stage Steve had been selected for Australia's Test and one-day teams, and was on the brink of being chosen for his first senior tour — a three-Test campaign in New Zealand. The obvious and at times seemingly never-ending questions were being asked. Now that Steve had made a sizeable statement in his career, would Mark's actions speak just as loudly? Mark comments:

> *The comparisons had happened right through our teenage years, then into First grade. We learnt to live with it and the media hype. We were playing our own games. People thought that because we were twins we'd always be getting picked in the same teams at the same time. It was inevitable that someone was going to go ahead a bit sooner or later. Even now, when we go through good and bad times, people always like to compare us.*

Bowling first change behind Mike Whitney and Phil Blizzard, Mark took 4–130 off 33 overs in Queensland's first innings of 389. He claimed the first three wickets to fall: Andrew Courtice, Robbie Kerr and captain Kepler Wessels. On a good batting pitch that had surprisingly seen Wellham send the home side in after winning the toss, Mark gained considerable bounce, and showed a willingness to attack the batsmen. Simpson remembers: 'He was genuinely quick and loved bouncers. His bowling was my stand-out recollection of him in his early days of Shield cricket.'

Batting at number 6, Mark scored 12 in the New South Wales reply of 487, the innings dominated by hard-hitting middle-order batsman Mark O'Neill, who scored 147. Again coming on at first change, Mark finished wicket-less in Queensland's second innings as the match crept to a draw.

He not only kept his spot for the next match, against Tasmania in Sydney, but he was promoted to taking the new ball with Whitney. It was difficult to believe that in the space of five first-class matches, his role had swung so dramatically.

'We had a lot of injuries that year which meant the team was chopping and changing a fair bit,' says Mark. 'By that stage I'd worked out I wasn't an opening batsman, but to come back in as a fast bowler was a bit of a shock. I didn't even open the bowling in club cricket, then all of a sudden I was doing it for New South Wales. I suppose it was good because it showed I had a few strings to the bow.'

While he continued to struggle with his batting — he was dismissed by Tasmanian captain and future cricket writer Mark Ray for 1 in the only New South Wales innings — Mark further impressed with the ball, taking 2–31 off 15 overs on the opening day of the match. He bowled seven wicket-less overs in the second innings before surrendering the ball to Bob Holland who cut through the Tasmanians with 5–25, sweeping his side to an innings victory.

Holland and Mark represented two very different faces of New South Wales cricket. At one end there was a thirty-eight-year-old with a kitbag full of experience and a gentlemanly manner dusted with the grey hairs of distinction that ensured respect in the dressing room. At the other, a twenty-year-old who was not only coming to terms with his rise to first-class cricket, but also sported a head-turning rock-and-roll hairstyle that was the subject of much good-natured ribbing from team-mates.

'Yeah, the mudflap [mullet] and the peroxide hair wasn't a great look I suppose,' laughs Mark. 'But everyone had a mudflap in those days. For some reason before the Tasmanian game I wanted a bit of colour in my hair. It was meant to turn out blond, but Mum did it, and it ended up near orange.'

Mike Whitney was among the smirking team-mates.

How could you forget it? The peroxide mullet and the tight body shirt with long sleeves. But boy, what about his bowling! I remember the first day he opened he was two yards quicker than me. He was really slapping them into the gloves and I was down at fine leg thinking, 'Geez, he's getting them through quite handy.' Bang! Bang! Play and miss! Bang! When I'm running in at the other end the slips cordon starts yelling out, 'Come on old fella, what about upping the tempo? We're getting a bit of pace from the other end, how about you?' He bowled really well, and really quickly. Real quick. But he was only ever regarded as a seamer. When he wanted to turn it on he bowled

genuine pace. It was right up there, just off this shortish sort of run. He was a
good thinking bowler too. And he just loved using the bouncer. A typical
batsman! They get a rock in their hand and they want to pay everybody back
for the short ball. He ended up getting a lot of people out bouncing them. I
loved watching him bowl quick. I was a very big fan.

Mark and Whitney again opened the attack for the final preliminary match of the season, against Queensland on a dusty turner at the SCG. While Holland and left-arm orthodox spinner Murray Bennett assumed much of the workload, Mark collected four wickets in the drawn match, including 3–49 in the first innings. He scored 27 in his only chance with the bat.

The game proved a dress rehearsal for the five-day final a fortnight later in Sydney. New South Wales needed only a draw to win the Sheffield Shield for the second successive season, and for the thirty-ninth time overall. Their chances weren't helped by the absence of Steve, Greg Matthews and Dave Gilbert, who were touring New Zealand with the Australian team. Queensland, still striving for its first triumph since entering the competition in 1927, was missing Allan Border, Craig McDermott and Greg Ritchie.

The visitors dictated play from the moment Kepler Wessels won the toss and batted, declaring at 9–436 in their first innings. Wessels (166) and Glenn Trimble (112) were the mainstays. Being the only two front-line pacemen playing for New South Wales, Mark and Whitney assumed heavy workloads, bowling 27 and 34 overs respectively. Mark's return of 1–71 — bowling Trimble was his only success — was completely overshadowed by his partner's return of 6–65. New South Wales used seven bowlers in an innings that spanned 165 overs and almost two days.

By stumps on the third day, New South Wales were 6–246, a much healthier position than when wicket-keeper Greg Dyer had joined Mark at the wicket in the final session. The pair shared a critical unbroken stand of 97 that took their side past the follow-on mark of 236 that had hovered threateningly in the thoughts of the New South Welshmen earlier in the day. Batting at number 7, Mark displayed immense composure in an unbeaten 39 that inspired the outspoken Bill O'Reilly, legendary Test leg-spinner of the 1930s and 40s, who was already a noted Steve Waugh fan, to write in the *Sydney Morning Herald* (17 March 1986):

Until yesterday I had no idea that Mark Waugh had such outstanding capacity with the bat.

So good is he at using his nimble feet in getting safely well down to the pitch of the ball that it made me feel that I had some very important advice to offer the famous Waugh twins.

First, I caution Steve in New Zealand to keep a weather eye wide open for his brother back here at home. He threatens to bulldoze his way into next year's New South Wales team as a batsman — even over the head of his kinsman if need be.

As for Mark, I believe the quicker he can walk away from his new-ball bowling brief the better.

I see no future in that department for him, but I see no limit to his prospects bat in hand.

O'Reilly's hopes of settling into the press box to admire another exhibition of Waugh talent on day four lasted just a matter of minutes before Mark edged Jeff Thomson to wicket-keeper Ray Phillips after adding only two runs to his overnight score. Dyer held the innings together with an unbeaten 88 in a disappointing total of 294.

With a lead of 142, Queensland sought quick runs in a bid to set up a declaration before the end of the day. Mark bowled just five overs, claiming 0–25, an insignificant return that would have further consolidated O'Reilly's assessment of the younger twin.

Wessels called the innings closed at 7–133, setting New South Wales a target of 276 in little more than a day. The home side began solidly, with Wellham and Steve Small both scoring half-centuries, but the middle order crumbled, wrecking any chance of victory. Mark had looked at ease again in an all too brief innings of 24. It seemed making starts at this level was no longer a problem; the next step was how to convert them into long stays at the crease.

In a thrilling finish to the match, New South Wales, eight wickets down and 22 runs short of the target, nervously relied on tailenders Bennett and Holland to bat out the final overs and force a draw. Whitney, the next man in, had been in the dressing room calling the match ball by ball down the phone line to Steve, Gilbert and Matthews, who were anxiously awaiting the result across the Tasman. Mark remembers:

It was really tense at the end. But we got there. It was a great feeling to be part of a winning team in my first year. Looking back, I was reasonably happy with my performances. I'd actually batted quite well in the final few matches, but just didn't know how to get a big score. I wasn't quite comfortable at that level. I'd get to 20 or 30 then get out a bit softly.

There is an education period when you get into first-class cricket. It's pretty rare for players to come and just start blazing centuries, especially when you're fairly young. It does take a while to acclimatise, get into the system and believe in yourself.

We were a very successful team, a good side. When you have a winning culture you learn how to play the right way, and develop a never-give-up attitude. New South Wales had a lot of ability too; you can naturally improve when you're with higher class players because you try to lift yourself.

It helped when the players were so helpful. Whit [Mike Whitney] was a good fella, one bloke who'd make anyone feel welcome in his company. He was a bit intimidating to start with, but it was good to get to know him. Murray Bennett and Bob Holland were also really helpful. They were the ultimate gentlemen. They probably wouldn't fit in as well these days because the game is much more cut-throat.

Overall, it wasn't what I really expected. Cricket has changed a lot over the years. It was certainly a lot more social back then. When we played, we meant business, but once a game was finished, everyone knew how to have a good time. There were certainly no recovery sessions, going to the pool or drinking Gatorade.

Mark's initial season of seven first-class cricket matches yielded: 167 runs at an average of 15.18; 11 wickets at 32; and 6 catches. Much of his fielding time had been spent in the covers and gully, although occasional stints in the slips suggested a more permanent arrangement was beckoning.

Three weeks before the Shield decider, Mark had made his limited-overs debut at the SCG when Victoria beat New South Wales by four wickets in a McDonald's Cup semi-final. Coming in fourth wicket down, he was caught behind for 13 off the bowling of left-arm spinner Paul Jackson, and he took 1–28 off nine overs with the new ball.

The season was capped off by the announcement that Mark had won an Esso scholarship to spend the 1986 winter as a member of the MCC Young

Cricketers squad at Lord's. The other three recipients were Queensland all-rounder Glenn Trimble, who was to join Sussex, Tasmanian batsman Keith Bradshaw and Victorian fast bowler Denis Hickey, who were both bound for Glamorgan. Although the scholarships were highly sought after, Mark was disappointed with the outcome.

> I thought I got the raw deal. It was okay, but I didn't end up experiencing any quality cricket. We played a few Second XI counties, but most of our opponents were teams from the army or navy. The standard wasn't great.
>
> When I wasn't playing or training, I had to go and bowl in the nets to the MCC members. Every day I had to go into Lord's. I helped with the covers during an England–New Zealand Test, but one day it was raining so hard I stayed in the sheds and thought, 'Bugger this, I'm not here to do this.' I also worked the scoreboard in a Middlesex county game, and kept thinking, 'I've come over to improve my cricket and here I am working on the MCC ground staff.' I wasn't overly impressed.

His fondest memories are of the Wembley flat he shared with four other young MCC cricketers. It was Mark's first experience of fending for himself, and the results nearly put him in hospital with food poisoning towards the end of his stay. The living conditions were so unhygienic that the flat not only housed five naive youngsters, but also a despicable array of maggots!

Practical jokes were common, and Mark, admitting he has a gullible nature, proved an easy target. On one occasion he was told by his colleagues that because he was an overseas player, he had been invited to meet Queen Elizabeth II at Lord's during the England–New Zealand Test. In preparation, he had his MCC jacket dry-cleaned, his trousers pressed, his shoes polished. On the eagerly awaited day, a nervous but resplendent young Australian cricketer waited for his call-up, only to be told the truth by his chuckling team-mates an hour before the Queen's arrival. The off-field camaraderie was unmistakably the feature of an otherwise frustrating trip.

Nevertheless, Mark returned to Sydney with high expectations for the 1986–87 season. After glimpses of form teased him the previous year, he was keen to consolidate his position in the New South Wales team as both a bowler and batsman. However, a niggle he had first felt in his lower back while bowling in the Bolton league shattered his hopes. Before the Sheffield Shield season was underway, Mark was diagnosed with stress fractures, the curse of so many fast bowlers. He recalls:

All the bowling I'd been doing hit me all of a sudden. I was pretty thin up top, not overly strong, and I suppose an injury was waiting to happen. There were times when I couldn't walk, and could barely move because I was in so much pain. The fact that I played so much sport growing up might have had something to do with it too. Whatever the reason, it was a season to forget.

Years later, New South Wales team physiotherapist Pat Farhart discovered that Mark, Steve and Bev all had similar weaknesses on the lower left sides of their spines.

Mark made just one Shield appearance that season as an all-rounder in a drawn match against Western Australia at the SCG. He failed to score in the first innings, trapped lbw by medium pacer Ken Macleay, and surrendered to English spinner Vic Marks for 26 in the second. His bowling was restricted to eleven overs, time enough to dismiss opener Mark McPhee on the final day. He also played two McDonald's Cup matches, failing with 4 runs against the West Australians, but impressing with 46 against Victoria, his highest score for New South Wales at that time. Most of his season was spent playing solely as a batsman for Bankstown, finishing on top of the run tally with 582.

It was a difficult period for Mark. He'd felt his game developing every year since he'd begun playing grade, but suddenly he was treading water, uncertain of what lay ahead. In between his limited cricket commitments, and his stints on the physiotherapy table, he was helped by Harry Solomons, who readily offered work at Kingsgrove Sports Centre. Solomons recalls:

Mark was starting to get a bit of a profile. He and Steve both had jobs at the shop, but I was happy to give them time off when they needed it. Mark was not the best of salesmen. I remember him once yawning while selling a bat to a customer who obviously couldn't play. I had to pull him aside and tell him to show some enthusiasm.

Mark was somewhat protected from Solomons' watchful eye by Sue Porter, who worked in the mail-order section.

'I covered his butt a fair bit, but I didn't mind,' says Sue. 'It was just second nature to me, just my protective nature I suppose. Harry would come down and ask me what Mark had done, and I'd tell him, "He's been really good, he's done everything that needs to be done."'

Sue, married with three children, had reason to be protective because she and Mark had quietly begun seeing each other outside work. Neither of them knew at this stage whether their close friendship would develop into something more serious, nor what the personal and emotional costs might be. While Mark was forced to put his cricket career on hold, he was about to enter the most important partnership of his life.

CHAPTER FIVE

PARTNERS

M ark's memories of his early associations with the opposite sex are few and far between. He kissed a teacher when still at infants school — 'We had very friendly teachers' — and in primary he enjoyed his first serious peck on the lips with his first girlfriend, Kim. Throughout his adolescence, 'dates' were nothing more than days in the calendar marking the next game he'd play. He'd had a couple of girlfriends, but admits he wasn't 'Mr Smooth in the female department'. His commitment to sport ensured he led a sheltered life in which the only considerable brush with femininity came via his mother.

However, when he began working part-time at Kingsgrove Sports Centre, he met Sue Porter, a cheerful woman, who despite being thirteen years older than Mark had a very young and enthusiastic outlook on life. At this stage Mark was still at school, a teenager recognised in the shop as one of the talented cricketing twins who Harry Solomons was always ready to help. No-one could have foreseen just how much that help would be needed in the not too distant future.

Initially Sue knew Steve the better of the twins, but by the time the older brother was chosen for Australia, the younger was building a strong friendship with her. At first, that is all it was — a friendship.

'Even though there was an age difference between me and Sue we got on really well,' Mark remembers. 'It wasn't love at first sight. Sue was married, and I was just a young fella who was a bit naive when it came to girls.'

When Mark returned to Sydney following his Esso scholarship, the friendship discreetly moved into a more serious stage. Sue was having problems with her marriage, and found Mark very supportive. It was soon obvious that deeper feelings were developing.

'It came as a shock really that an older woman would be interested in me,' says Mark. 'We just seemed to hit it off; we didn't see the age difference as a hindrance at any stage. Obviously we'd spend a lot of time together at work, then on Thursday nights we'd [Kingsgrove Sports Centre's employees] often all go out, and Sue and I started to get closer. It all snowballed from there.'

Sue acknowledges they tried to fight the relationship in the early stages, but both were overtaken by their emotions. The older woman and the younger man. Thirty-four and twenty-one. That alone would turn heads, but when Sue's marital status was added, there was little doubt the situation would arouse mixed feelings among the people who recognised what was happening. Harry Solomons, a friend of both families, quietly warned Sue and Mark to be careful. He admits he was worried, finding it hard at first to understand the relationship, but as time passed he realised that 'Mark was definitely in love with Susan'. Mark's Bankstown team-mate and close friend, David Thompson, was also a confidant and adviser during this period, acknowledging it 'was a very difficult time'.

The relationship continued quietly through, then past, Mark's injury-affected 1986–87 season. In September 1987, having recovered from his stress fractures, he was selected in a New South Wales touring team to play eight matches against Zimbabwe. While away, he rang Sue nearly every day, and when home again, delivered an ultimatum. Sue recalls:

He came home and said, 'Something has to give here.' He told me he couldn't carry on the way things were. Neither of us could, so the crunch time came. It was something that snuck up on us really. I kept thinking, 'What am I doing with a young boy? God help me!' It had really helped being good friends first — I just knew him as a cricketer and a work colleague. He was a very caring person towards me, he'd helped me through some very difficult times in my marriage. I didn't see what he was like with other people because I had tunnel

*vision — once love takes over that's all you see. It was tough. It's not easy to
have a marriage, a normal life, a family, then start thinking, 'Oh God, do I give
all this up?' But that's what I decided to do.*

*It was difficult, but we managed. Our families didn't own us for a little
while, but they didn't realise the extent of our relationship. There were people
against us, but we just had to see it through.*

The change shocked Mark. He was suddenly confronted with the reality that he
was moving out of home to live with a woman for the first time. The initial step
was 'to look for somewhere to live quick smart'. Solomons provided immediate
support, offering the couple a room in his home until they found a flat to rent
in the suburb of Punchbowl about a fortnight later. Susan recalls Solomons
remained a close and sympathetic ally throughout the whole ordeal.

*We actually had our first Christmas with Harry. We were sitting in our little
flat all by ourselves thinking, 'What are we going to do?' Mark's parents had
gone away, and I'd seen my kids in the morning. Then Harry rang and asked us
what we were up to. I welled up in tears over the phone, everything had just
been so hard, but Harry said, 'For heaven's sake, just get over here.' So off we
went with nothing in our hands to spend Christmas night with Harry. He has
been a really good friend to us all the way through.*

*I was obviously worried about the kids when all this started to happen. Chad
was about to go into high school, Tim was a year younger, and Lauren was only
five. They all remained with their father. The boys were really good about it,
they accepted what was going on right from the start. Lauren was a little bit
different. It is really hard for a mother to leave her daughter, but we survived.
Mark really became her stepfather but he never imposed that on her. She lives
with us now, and she and Mark are really good friends. You see them mucking
around the house. Lauren worked her magic on Mark right from the start. He
was a sucker for her.*

*In those days we only had the kids once a fortnight — never in between. I'd
speak to them every day, and I'd also see them because they went to school near
where I worked. We'd cross paths every afternoon. I wasn't the kind of mother
who needed them under my feet every five minutes — as long as they were
happy and healthy, that's all that mattered.*

Amidst the drama, Mark and Sue discovered their time in Punchbowl proved a surprisingly welcome distraction from the dramatic changes to their lives. Their closest neighbours in a bland block of flats were a diverse assortment of characters whose appearances and habits could have been taken directly from a television soap. A single mother with a young girl lived next door to Mark and Sue, while Ronald Hubbard, the much adored star of the 'show', lived across the hallway. An older man with few teeth, Ronald had a Scottish flat-mate, who when drunk was inspired to play the bagpipes. Underneath, a young woman, Debbie Rae Williams, lived quietly on her own. She remains a good friend of Mark and Sue to this day, and has been a regular spectator at Australia's limited-overs games in Brisbane. Sue recalls:

> They were all fantastic to us. We had a lot of hysterical times. Ronald was a keen fisherman. He'd go out and return with these whopping fish that were so big they wouldn't even fit in the oven. He was a mad, mad man, but he and the others helped keep us going through that time. We went away once to the Hunter Valley for a weekend. We all shared the one room, so being the only couple, Mark and I got the bed, but we ended up with everyone in it. No-one got any sleep, we were all a bit drunk, but it was a great escape from what had happened around us.

Throughout the upheaval, Mark managed to concentrate on his cricket. At the start of the 1987–88 season, Ronnie and company didn't really know who their neighbour was, but by the end of the summer, the name Mark Waugh was known far beyond the bricks and mortar of Punchbowl.

The standard was set during the pre-season tour of Zimbabwe where Mark was the most successful New South Wales batsman. His top score, 93 not out, came off only 67 balls in a one-day match at the Harare Sports Club. The explosive innings included eight sixes, five of which were blasted in a row against off-spinner Babu Meman. Mark remembers:

> The fifth six won us the game. We all began walking off, then it was decided we'd finish the over to see if I could get six sixes. The last ball was bowled flat, fast and wide, and I could only hit it for four.

Zimbabwe had a pretty good side back then. They had Dave Houghton, who was a world-class batsman, Eddo Brandes, who was pretty quick, and Graeme Hick before he moved to England.

It was a good tour. I did play really well.

Mark returned home full of confidence, but knowing competition for positions in the Sheffield Shield team would be intense following the return of rebel players Steve Smith, John Dyson and Steve Rixon. He boosted his claims in Sydney the week before the team was selected when he slammed 150 in 219 minutes for the state's Second XI against their Victorian counterparts. That innings, and some impressive early form for Bankstown, was more than enough for Mark to secure a batting spot in a line-up that included his brother, Mark Taylor, Steve Small, Mark O'Neill and Greg Matthews. In a display of loyalty to existing players, the selectors did not choose any of the rebels.

A week after Allan Border led Australia to World Cup glory on the subcontinent, New South Wales opened their Sheffield Shield season with a six-wicket win over South Australia at the SCG on a pitch that visiting captain David Hookes condemned as underprepared, and not fit for first-class cricket. Mark scored 28 and 25.

There were no 'starts' in the next game, against Queensland at the Newcastle Sports Ground. After being trapped lbw for a duck by Craig McDermott, Mark was dismissed by left-arm paceman Dirk Tazelaar for 9 in New South Wales' disastrous second innings of just 83. The team was all out in 21 overs, after little more than an hour and a half. McDermott was the destroyer, taking 7–54, and 10 wickets for the match in his side's 333-run win.

Once again Mark was in the uncomfortable position of looking over his shoulder after scoring 62 runs in four innings, but he held his spot for the encounter with Tasmania at Devonport in early December. Batting first after winning the toss, the home side struggled to 134 against an attack inspired by opening bowlers Geoff Lawson (3–22) and Mike Whitney (2–31). By stumps on the second day, New South Wales were in complete command at 4–393. Steve Smith, returning for his first game since completing his two-year ban, scored 84, and Mark Taylor, 72. However, the unbeaten batsmen drew much of the attention. Mark O'Neill walked to the crease the following day with 111 next to his name, and at his shoulder was Mark Waugh with 50. The pair thumped the attack for an hour, taking their side to 467 before New South Wales declared 333 runs ahead. Captain Murray Bennett had hung on long enough to allow Mark to record his opening first-class century, 101 not out from just 125 balls in an unbroken fifth-wicket stand of 187 with O'Neill (130 not out). If there had been any doubt about the young Waugh's position, the fears had been swept away in just two and a half hours. Mark recalls:

> Devonport had an old bike track around the ground, and cars were parked on the hill. It wasn't the most prestigious ground in the world to make my first hundred. I really didn't think much of it. I simply thought, 'Well, I've scored runs, got a hundred. That's great, let's keep enjoying it.' I don't think I was hyped up about it, or thinking it was a big relief. I certainly can't remember any big celebrations in Devonport.

New South Wales cruised to victory by an innings and 38 runs, but the team's fortunes suffered an abrupt slap in the face when Western Australia inflicted an innings defeat a week later at the West Australian Cricket Association Ground in Perth. Mark also thudded back to the pack with scores of 5 and 6. It was the first time for the season he'd batted in the same spot — number 6 — for both innings of a match. Until then, he'd been juggled up and down the order, spending time in every position in the top six, with the exception of opener, a slight irony considering he'd begun his career against the new ball. However, after constant experimenting, it was considered by selectors and captain Greg Dyer that Mark's free-flowing approach was best suited to the middle order. Their decision was justified in the following match when their youngest player scored an unbeaten 114 in the first innings against a Victorian attack depleted by a hamstring injury to Merv Hughes, who bowled only 10 overs. Nevertheless Mark still had to overcome Australian swing bowler Simon Davis, and soon-to-be Test all-rounder Tony Dodemaide. Mark was at the crease for a little under three hours, and his second fifty came in just 45 devastating minutes. It was a notable outing for the Waughs — Steve had earlier made 170 in the innings of 9 declared for 438. Rain played the most significant hand, ensuring a draw.

While Mark hadn't yet performed well enough to attract considerable attention from national selectors, his progress had certainly interested one Australian leader, the prime minister, Bob Hawke, who chose the in-form batsman to play for the Prime Minister's XI against New Zealand two days before Christmas. Batting without a helmet against Richard Hadlee, he top-scored with 35, but it wasn't enough to stop the Kiwis from securing a 37 run win.

Australia's bicentennial year, 1988, began with its share of confrontation between the colonials and the mother country when Queensland hosted New South Wales from 1 January at the Gabba. On the final day of the match, Mark and boisterous English all-rounder and Maroon recruit, Ian Botham, engaged in a captivating duel at twenty-two paces after the visitors had been set 353 to win. Mark had taken the earlier rounds, his bowling haul of five wickets for the match including Botham's scalp in each innings. However, he'd failed in his first chance with the bat, falling caught behind to Dirk Tazelaar for 4. When he walked to the crease the second time, an eager Botham was waiting. In the now extinct *Sun* newspaper (6 January 1988), Phil Wilkins wrote:

It was the best battle of wits and willpower seen at the Gabba in ages.

In the maroon corner was the tough old champ and world record-holder Ian Botham. In the blue corner was the young batsman extraordinaire and would-be international, Mark Waugh.

Botham bounced Waugh and was hit to the fence. Botham moved a man to square leg and bounced Waugh again, and watched the ball crack into the boundary hoarding again. Botham moved fielders, kept bouncing the New South Wales right-hander, and Waugh kept hooking the ball, threading it finer or squarer of the three men between fine leg and mid-wicket.

Botham saw Waugh top-edge another bouncer on to the greyhound track for six and retired, bruised but unbowed, his five overs having cost 27 runs.

However, Botham could afford the final chuckle when he caught Mark in the slips off Tazelaar for 88, the top score in the innings of 300. Despite being on the losing side, Mark stole more than his share of column space in the following day's papers. His three-hour innings had shown he wouldn't buckle under pressure or reputations; the media predicted he was moving closer to joining Steve in the Australian team.

He scored 72 in his only chance at the crease during the next outing, against South Australia at the Adelaide Oval. The home side won by 63 runs, but Mark again found significant room in the press. He was undoubtedly a preferred subject of the scribes. A young, elegant batsman from Sydney's working-class suburbs campaigning to join his twin brother in the national Test and limited-overs teams made a good yarn. Perhaps the only sporting story to be creating as much interest at the time was a battling Queensland trainer who used to tow his one prized galloper in a two-horse float to meetings up and down Australia's east coast. Vic Rail and his untidy, unlikely champion Vo Rogue were favourites of the nation. The day after the Shield match finished in Adelaide, the mighty Vo won the $200 000 William Reid Stakes at Melbourne's Moonee Valley track.

The sporting stablemates continued to share headline space for the rest of the summer and into autumn. In the same week the galloper won the Orr and Blamey Stakes, the cricketer scored an unbeaten 100 in the second innings of the drawn Shield match against Victoria at the MCG. Mark then briefly and successfully converted his campaign from staying to sprinting when New South Wales opened its McDonald's Cup season against Queensland at the Gabba. In a pleasing all-round performance, he slammed 27 off 28 balls in a sizeable total of 7–287, then took 3–23 as the Maroons crumbled for 134. Ian Botham was again a Waugh victim, but this time it was Steve who claimed the honours. His brother, however, had taken the catch.

Just like Vo Rogue, Mark had become a frontrunner. The leading New South Wales run-getter for the season added to his already impressive tally, scoring 95 in the first innings of the hosts' 131-run Shield win over Western Australia at the SCG in late February. It could have easily been his fourth century of the summer if three sweetly struck straight drives in his innings hadn't rattled the stumps at the bowler's end. *Sydney Morning Herald* journalist Greg Growden praised Mark's performance (25 February 1988):

Nothing was strained. He was always perfectly balanced and everything was natural as he lovingly caressed the ball.

Unlike most players who appear hurried and cramped when facing pacemen, Waugh batted as if he was impatiently waiting for the ball to arrive in his danger zone — so sweet and effortless was his timing.

While New South Wales had long slipped from Shield calculations, the players finished the season impressively, beating Tasmania by eight wickets at the SCG. Yet again Mark dominated the headlines after scoring 116 in the first innings. Untroubled by any bowler during his four-hour stay, he eventually fell the only way he looked likely to be dismissed — run out after a mix-up with Peter Taylor.

It was his final Shield innings for the year, taking his tally to 833 runs at an average of 64.08. A one-man show. Mark Taylor's return of 459 at 25.50 was the next best. Mark recalls:

> *Everything just seemed to click that year. I was finally working out my own game at the first-class level. I felt on top of it for the first time. Once I'd got that century in Devonport, I was right. I got my confidence and knew what I could do. Until that happens, it can be a hard time for any new player. That's what I reckon has happened with New South Wales over the past four or five years. There's been quite a few young blokes who've done what I did by getting a few 20s and 30s. But as soon as you can work beyond that stage, you're on your way. You just have to hope that selectors aren't too short-sighted by not sticking with you and giving you a go. It took me about 10 games over three seasons to find my feet.*

In a season of few opportunities with the ball — he bowled only 46 overs — Mark took six wickets at 26.33. His fielding had brought greater rewards — 18 catches. Geoff Lawson recalls:

> *Junior could field everywhere. Infield, outfield, he just had these great hands and incredible reactions up close to the bat. He didn't spend a lot of time in the slips in the early days. Most of his time was spent around cover and mid-wicket. But I remember one game where we needed an extra slip, and Steve suggested Junior. He ended up taking an extraordinary catch travelling low to his left. It was something only he could have taken.*
>
> *He wasn't too keen for bat-pad — he wouldn't put himself forward at first — but once he caught a few that no-one else would have got a hand on, he got the job.*

After finishing third on the Shield ladder, New South Wales sought to make amends in the McDonald's Cup. They beat Tasmania by four wickets in a rain-affected match at the SCG — Mark scored 32 and claimed 1–17 off five overs — then strolled past Victoria by five wickets in the semi-final played in Sydney. Mark maintained his consistent run, taking 1–22 off seven overs, and again making 32. The following day Vo Rogue finished second behind 125–1 long shot Dandy Andy in the Australian Cup. Was it an omen for the final between New South Wales and South Australia to be played a fortnight later at the SCG? Thankfully for Mark and his team-mates, it wasn't.

After winning the toss, New South Wales captain Greg Dyer decided to bat on a typically slow-paced Sydney pitch. Apart from opener Scott Hookey, the top seven all reached double figures. Middle-order batsman Trevor Bayliss top scored with 44, Graeme Smith made 42, and Mark, 38. Although 7–219 wasn't a daunting total to chase, the South Australians were plagued by ill-timed wickets whenever they looked to be in promising positions. They ended their fifty-over chase at 6–196 — Steve claimed 2–37, but Mark wasn't required to bowl — allowing New South Wales to be crowned limited overs champions for the second time.

It ended a solid four-match campaign for Mark: 129 runs at 32.25, five wickets at 12.4, and two catches. Following his brilliant first-class season, it was inevitable he would be named New South Wales Cricketer of the Year in early April. It was the first time in the award's twelve-year history that the judges had been unanimous in their decision, a fitting indication of Mark's dominance throughout the season. However, the announcement was tinged with disappointment as only days earlier selectors could only find room for Mark as a reserve for Australia's tour of Pakistan in September. His omission was criticised by the media, but the player at the centre of it all knew his time would eventually come. So, too, his partner who had endured the most trying time of her life, yet was still able to offer remarkable support and guidance amidst the turmoil of a marriage breakdown. Mark confesses:

Sue has always been the rock. Because she's a bit older, she's obviously very level-headed. People say she's changed me for the good, even my dress sense! She knows what's going on, and right from the start she kept me in line. If I ever got carried away she was always the first person to bring me down to a normal level.

It was tough when we started because of her marriage. It would have been a big decision for her to leave home. I was single, so it wasn't as hard for me. She made a big commitment, so it was up to me to support her and make it work. Cricket was the way for me to do it.

I think even now people are interested in our relationship because of the age difference. It's old news, but people seem to make a big deal of it. To us, it's just a normal relationship. We have similar interests, get on well and are good friends — that's the most important thing in any relationship. Sometimes people make fun of the fact that she's a lot older than me, you see the banners in the crowd or you might hear something, but it doesn't worry me too much. You take notice, but each to themselves. It's none of their business really. I don't care what people think. If we cared what people think, we wouldn't be here now together.

After negotiating the volatile and unpredictable journey through 1987–88, Mark and Sue discovered there was one final surprise waiting for them. Just days before the New South Wales presentation night, they were involved in a frightening car accident while driving in heavy rain at Terrigal on the Central Coast of New South Wales. An oncoming vehicle turned right in front of them, forcing Mark to swerve suddenly, but not successfully. He clipped the back of the offending car, and went hurtling across the road straight into a stormwater drain. His brown Sigma flipped onto its side, and was on the verge of tipping upside down. Water began coming into the car while Mark and Sue, both very disorientated, struggled to undo their seat belts and crawl free of the wreckage. They were grateful that some locals who'd seen the accident rushed over and were able to pull them out. A fire brigade arrived soon afterwards, one fireman making the most of the situation by asking the still dazed Mark for an autograph!

'I was shaking so much I couldn't sign it,' he recalls. 'Everything had happened in slow motion. It was the only accident I'd really had. The Sigma was a write-off, Sue and I were okay, but we were still pretty shaky for a while afterwards. It was the closest I've ever come to thinking I was going to die.'

It was a symbolic ending to one of the most dramatic periods in Mark and Sue's relationship. No matter what problems they faced, they survived. The season of break-ups and breakthroughs, 1987–88, was just the beginning. Whatever challenges lay ahead, he and Sue were ready to take guard together.

CHAPTER SIX

ONE OF THE LADS

F riday night, July 1988, the middle of winter. Mark had gone to the Harold Park trots at Glebe in inner Sydney, and Sue was by herself in the Punchbowl flat. The phone rang, and after hearing the voice at the other end of the line, Sue thought it was close friend David Thompson playing a practical joke.

'It's Allan Border here,' said the distant voice.

Sue replied with little respect, 'For God's sake Thommo, give it a rest. It's late.'

She hung up. After all, why would the Australian captain be ringing Mark in the middle of the off-season?

The phone rang again.

'It's Allan Border here,' repeated the voice.

'Are you serious?' asked Sue.

'Yes.'

The captain had indeed spoken!

After a few hasty apologies, Sue took a brief message, promising Mark would return the call as soon as he could. Border was in England, about to complete his stint as overseas professional with Essex, one of the strongest clubs in the county championship. His stay had been shortened because of Australia's upcoming tour of Pakistan in September. He recalls it left officials seeking his help.

They asked me if I knew of any Australians who might fit in and fill the role at Essex, because they liked Aussies, they had a history of choosing them there.

I told them there was a young bloke whose name they'd know — Waugh. But it was Mark, not the Stephen they were familiar with. I said he was a quality batsman who also bowled sharpish medium pace and fielded like they wouldn't believe. They thought I must have been wrapping this kid up too much, but they were keen to get someone and took my word.

Mark was 'really surprised' when Border told him about the offer, but he had no hesitation in accepting. It was a gamble. A young player with just one full season in the first-class arena was replacing one of cricket's most respected and recognised batsmen who, by the time of his replacement's arrival, had scored six centuries during the English summer. Essex was brimful of international experience with Test players Graham Gooch, Derek Pringle and Neil Foster forming the nucleus of the side.

It was only a six-week stint, but time enough to leave lasting impressions in a competition in which overseas players could secure lucrative contracts. Essex was undoubtedly taking a chance, but officials could afford to take a risk. They already had a good side, and even if Mark failed they would still be a good side. The time was right to offer an audition to a young player when the pressure wouldn't be great.

The debut of the twenty-three-year-old Australian came on 14 August against Nottinghamshire on one of Essex's outer home grounds, Colchester. It was a Royal Assurance limited-overs match, Mark's first game of cricket for four and a half months. To use an analogy from his much loved world of horse racing, it was impossible to read his form because he was resuming after a lengthy spell. Despite having a few net sessions after his arrival, he was unquestionably short of a gallop.

Essex batted first; Mark was in the middle order. He recalls going to the crease and barely being able to hit a ball properly for the first twenty minutes. It was a less than inspiring start, but after striking a few boundaries he began to find his touch against an attack headed by West Indian Franklin Stevenson. Any doubt officials had about Border's replacement was soon knocked away by a series of trademark flicks through mid-wicket and majestic off-drives. Mark dominated the bowlers, racing to 103 off only 94 balls, his second fifty coming off just 28 deliveries. In a modest but dry-witted summary of his innings that included one six and fifteen fours, Mark says he 'fluked a few and ended up getting a ton'. He then followed up by claiming 2–16, including the wicket of England's Test batsman Derek Randall. Essex won by 77 runs, and their new recruit had shown he would be worth following during the rest of his campaign. On the same day Steve, already having passed 1000 county runs for Somerset, scored a handsome 38 in his side's 2-run win over Yorkshire at Scarborough. The twins' performances were early warning signs that English cricket would face a double-barrelled family assault in years to come.

Mark's opening performance in the county championship against Surrey at The Oval wasn't as eye-catching: 29 runs in his only innings and 0–75 off just 12 overs. However, in his next match, against Leicestershire on the main Essex ground at Chelmsford, he enjoyed back-slaps in the dressing rooms after scoring 86. He scored 35 and 28 in his final county game against Northamptonshire at Chelmsford. His three first-class outings had yielded 178 runs at an average of 44.5, while his haul from five limited-overs games was: 158 runs at 31.6, and three wickets at 42.

Essex team-mates and officials were impressed. Pace bowler Neil Foster recalls:

It was a huge thing coming across to find your feet on your own. He turns up, gets a hundred on his Sunday League debut, so we were pretty well sold straight away. To come in and do that as a twenty-three-year-old was a huge achievement really.

He was a pretty quiet fella, a real homebody who wasn't interested in the drinking or the nightlife. Certainly when he came to Essex he didn't really seem interested in drinking, and the English game had perhaps more of a drinking culture than Australian cricket. So he seemed pretty straight on the way he was going to run his career.

He was very unassuming, but put him on a cricket field and you'd see the other side of him — he was very, very competitive. He really fitted in with us ever so well.

Foster, who would later confront Mark in the international arena, became a close friend. He was aware of the loneliness that overseas players could suffer away from home, and involved Mark in as many activities outside cricket as possible. Mark was a regular visitor to the Foster residence, and to this day has not forgotten the hospitality and thoughtfulness displayed by his team-mate and his wife. Likewise, Foster has indelible memories of an Aussie who was very much his own man. Among his stories is that of the day Essex player Alan Lilley proudly displayed his infant daughter to the team. The newborn baby had a very obvious birthmark on her forehead, and while most of the side politely ignored it, Mark had no qualms about asking, 'What's that on her melon, mate?'

Foster also remembers Mark's habit of smothering nearly all his food in tomato sauce: 'He is a little more refined now, I am pleased to say.'

Mark may not have been a gourmet, but his batting was undoubtedly flavoured with the rich delights of elegance that separated him from the bangers-and-mash batsmen who had to work hard for their runs on the county circuit. He had shown more than enough during his brief stay to whet the appetites of Essex officials who invited him to return for the 1989 season. His availability would depend on whether he was selected in Australia's Ashes squad. Either way, he was set to return to England in another seven months time.

Mark's campaign for Ashes selection was a popular topic in the media in the lead-up to the 1988–89 season. While Allan Border was leading the Test team on an unsuccessful tour of Pakistan — the host nation won the three-Test series 1–0 — Mark was the subject of numerous articles. Could he continue the golden run he'd enjoyed the previous Sheffield Shield season? If he reproduced last season's form, did he believe he deserved a Test position? Was he eyeing off a spot in the Ashes squad? Or was he hoping for a call-up into Australian colours sooner? In his typical understated way, Mark's response was to take the 'one game at a time' approach. This is regarded as a sporting cliché, but it is another example of Mark's philosophy of life — never think too far ahead. It wasn't until later in the season that he expanded on his goals in an interview with *Australian Cricket* magazine (January 1989), he told writer Jim Hope:

I wasn't really disappointed at missing out on going to Pakistan, as I had only had one good year in Shield cricket and I knew there were a couple of players ahead of me. But I've set my sights on making the England tour, which is probably the best tour to go on with the atmosphere and tradition.

Mark had held these hopes since the beginning of the season, but hadn't voiced them, preferring his performances to make his statements. However, in the opening Sheffield Shield match against Queensland in Brisbane, his bat didn't lift above a whisper. In the first innings Mark was dismissed by Dirk Tazelaar for a duck, edging a ball to wicket-keeper Ian Healy, who'd just returned from playing his debut Test series in Pakistan. In all, four New South Wales batsmen failed to score in an innings of 291 that was saved from disaster by centuries from Steve (118), and Greg Matthews (108). Only one other batsman, Peter Taylor (34) reached double figures. The home side replied with a meagre 212. Mark was given little time to make an impression at the bowling crease, delivering just three overs for the costly return of 0–21.

Mark Taylor (85) held the New South Wales second innings together, while his former opening partner cruised to 18 before being lured out of his crease by off-spinner Peter Cantrell. Healy did the rest.

In what proved a remarkable run-chase, Queensland reached 8–329, the highest total of the match, to win by two wickets. Greg Ritchie led the way with 92, and was well supported in a scorecard that showed just one batsman making single figures. Mark completed his disappointing season opener bowling three wicket-less overs.

New South Wales engaged in another thrilling finish against Victoria the following week at the SCG. Set 334 to win on the last day, the Blue-bags finished at 7–312. After falling caught behind off Simon O'Donnell for another first innings duck, Mark, elevated to first drop, showed scintillating form in a breezy second innings of 46. His strokeplay flowed from the moment he worked the first ball he faced, a Merv Hughes delivery, to the square-leg boundary. Further leg-side artistry followed, but just when it appeared he was settling in for an important stay, he misjudged a single to Warren Ayres at mid-off who threw the stumps down from twenty metres. At the time it appeared the only way Mark was likely to surrender, such was his command over the bowlers. The all-too-brief but threatening contribution was an example of the type of innings that would later draw criticism from some sections of the media. At different stages throughout his Test career Mark would be labelled a player who could make batting look easy yet fall to a 'soft dismissal' when seemingly set for a big score. His New South Wales team-mates quickly learnt to accept the lapses. Mike Whitney says:

I can remember a game not long after he got into the side when he was caught hooking after we'd lost a couple of early wickets in the first hour. I just bagged him in the dressing room, then Stephen had a go at me, saying I was quick to applaud Mark when he got runs off similar shots, so I shouldn't be so quick to criticise him when he failed. He snapped at me and said, 'It's just the way he plays.' Stephen and I spoke about it later and apologised to each other. He was just being a protective brother.

The bottom line is that you have to acknowledge and even appreciate that it's part of Mark. I asked him one day about it and he said, 'Do you think I mean to do it? Do you think I mean to nick a wide one? Do you think I mean to hole out at fine leg or get run out when I'm set? It happens, it's just the way I play.'

With Mark Waugh, I learnt very early on that you had to be happy with what you saw. If he got 20, it was the best 20 you'd ever see. It would have three boundaries in it, two cover drives, and a nudge around the corner for a single. If you saw him get a hundred, then wow, you were lucky. Sure he made mistakes, but we all do. It's better to see him get a few runs, then get out, than not see a player like him bat at all.

Normal people can't do what he does. When I used to bowl to him in the nets, he was never in a hurry, and his bat always seemed so wide. It's really unfortunate that he has been labelled with this 'makes it look so easy' tag. But the truth is he does make it look so easy. You just watch him when the ball is in the slot and he plays that cover drive. Bang! By the time he's followed through the ball is into the boundary without it looking as though Mark has hit it hard. The next ball is nearly in the same spot. Bang! It goes through mid-wicket for four. Elegant is not a good enough word to describe him. They used to say that David Gower was elegant. Mate, you see Mark Waugh bat, and it can be just like watching honey dripping off his bat with a minimum of fuss. He might have got himself out a few times for New South Wales, but we were lucky to watch him, and the team was lucky to have him.

However, national selectors were yet to be convinced of that view. Mark had an important chance to parade his talents when New South Wales played the West Indies at the SCG four days after the draw against Victoria. After winning the toss the home side batted first on a very slow, almost laborious pitch that did little to suit the calypso pacemen Patrick Patterson, Winston Benjamin and Ian Bishop.

Mark had only this match left to press his claims before the first Test began a week later in Brisbane. There'd already been considerable speculation on both sides of the country that the younger Waugh twin and the in-form West Australian all-rounder Tom Moody, were close to being called-up.

After watching Mark Taylor and John Dyson combine for a 162-run opening partnership, Mark strode to the crease under the close scrutiny of national selector John Benaud. Nine runs later he returned to the dressing room the victim of a Bishop delivery edged to Richie Richardson in the slips. A golden opportunity had been missed. Taylor (82) and Dyson (79) were the leading scorers in a total of 8 declared for 401. In reply, the visitors were dismissed for 329, after their captain, Viv Richards (101), became the first West Indian to score 100 first-class centuries. It was Mark's first close look at a player he'd always admired. Mark admits:

I never really had idols, or put players up on a pedestal, but Viv was a bit of an exception. I loved the way he played the game, the way he'd always want to dominate the bowlers, take it to them, and show them that he was in control. He was a great player. He could demoralise an attack, and change the game in a couple of overs or half an hour at the crease. It was good to watch him bat, even if I was in the field.

The roles were reversed in the second innings when Richards became the spectator as Mark struck form, building on a slow start to craft a mostly free-flowing 103 not out. In the *Sydney Morning Herald* (15 November 1988), journalist Mike Coward observed:

He refused to grow impatient and watched closely as the pacemen tackled the thankless task that broke hearts and backs, and shrewdly assessed what impact the slow bowlers — this time including orthodox left-armer Keith Arthurton — could have on the last day.

When he was satisfied his readings were complete he demonstrated he is also a most able player on the back foot and played some delightful pulls and cuts in reaching his fifth first-class century — 103 with seven boundaries and a six from 163 deliveries.

Mark and Dyson, who completed a wonderful match with 100 not out to add to his first innings success, added 192 runs for the second wicket before New South Wales declared at 1–261, leaving the West Indians to batting practice as the match meandered to a draw.

Afterwards, Richards told the media that: 'Mark certainly looks a good player and did everything right today.' A simple statement that nevertheless summed up the performance. Mark had indeed done everything right. Or almost everything. For a player already renowned for his sweet striking of the ball, he was left rueing one vital ingredient — timing — because Australia's team for the first Test team had been announced a day before, and M.E. Waugh was not among the twelve names.

His absence didn't stop media talk of his impending breakthrough. He may have been overlooked for the Tests, but with the Benson & Hedges limited-overs series against the West Indies and Pakistan less than a month away, he was among a pool of fringe candidates that included Moody, lanky West Australian left-armer Bruce Reid and Greg Matthews.

He had two more matches to prove himself before a thirteen-man squad would be chosen. The first was against Tasmania in Devonport, scene of his opening first-class century the previous season. History repeated itself, but not as Mark would have wished — for the third consecutive Shield match he failed to score in the first innings, this time falling to all-rounder Peter Faulkner. Geoff Lawson clearly remembers the dismissal and Mark's reaction, which again illustrated his attitude to batting.

We got sent in on a pretty ordinary wicket. Mark Taylor was out quickly, then Junior comes in and gets out straight away playing a cut shot. David Boon took a great catch in the gully, but it was first or second ball! That put us in a bit of trouble. Later on when we were going for a walk around the ground I asked him about the shot and said, 'Shouldn't you have had a look at the bowling, you know, sussed it out a bit first?'

Mark just answered, 'Yeah, but it was a good catch.'

'Yeah, but you hit it in the air and put us in trouble.'

But Mark was adamant. He said, 'I don't care what the game situation is. I'd play the same shot every time.'

You couldn't tell him to be circumspect on some occasions. I reckon he worked it out about twelve years later!

Mark recovered some lost ground in the second innings, scoring 100 not out in another unbroken century partnership with Dyson (53 not out). The rain-interrupted match ended in a draw, ensuring New South Wales remained at the bottom of the Shield table with only two points.

Their fortunes finally changed in their next encounter when they beat Western Australia by 134 runs in Newcastle. Mark enjoyed some solid time in the middle with innings of 69 and 39 on a good batting pitch. But was it enough to earn Australian selection?

The answer came a few days later when Mark was relaxing with Sue in their newly-purchased town house in Revesby, just 10 minutes drive from Panania. The phone rang, but it wasn't a joking friend, or even Allan Border on the end of the line. This time it was Australia calling.

CHAPTER SEVEN

AUSTRALIA CALLING

Dion Bourne had heard the news of his nephew's selection on the radio. He immediately rang Mark, who couldn't hide his surprise: 'Get lost! How can that be?' he asked. Nearly an hour passed before official confirmation came from the Australian Cricket Board. Mark was in the squad to play the opening matches of the triangular series against the West Indies and Pakistan beginning in a week's time. After all the talk in the media, the moment had finally come — for the first time in history, twins would play cricket for Australia. Mark says:

I knew I was close to selection because there'd been some paper talk with so-called experts pushing my case. I'd had a few ups and downs in the Shield, but I'd been in pretty good form. It's a funny feeling while you're waiting, you're not human if you don't start thinking a bit about what it would be like to play for Australia. And then when you're selected, there's still a part of you that wonders if you really deserved to be picked. But I knew I was ready.

Having Stephen there was a bonus. Obviously we'd grown up together and played most of our cricket together, so it wasn't hard to think I was going into just another team with him. We knew that we were going to cause a lot of attention, but we'd already become used to a lot of press about the twins issue. It was nothing new to us. I know he was proud of me, and I was proud of him.

It was indeed a proud moment for the whole Waugh family, all of whom were accustomed to achieving sporting success at breakneck speed. Steve comments:

Mark had to wait a bit longer than me, but it still happened pretty quickly for both of us. Just a few years earlier we were at high school, and I don't think either of us knew how we were going to get to the next level. We were always watching cricket on TV and thinking, 'Yeah I wouldn't mind getting there, but how?' We knew we were as good as anyone else our age, but we weren't sure how to make the next step up to the big grade. But by the time we got into First grade we'd played that much competitive cricket over the years that we were pretty battle-hardened, and we could see the pathway to the next level. When we finally got into the same Australian team, it was hard to believe where we had come from. I was happiest for Mum and Dad because they were the ones who'd given us the grounding and support to make it all possible.

Mark and Steve were given the chance for a rehearsal when they were picked in the Prime Minister's XI to play the West Indies in Canberra just days before the Benson & Hedges World Series began. However, consistent rain forced the abandonment of the match without a ball being bowled.

Mark discovered he had little more to do when he made his much awaited international debut against Pakistan the following Sunday, 11 December, at the Adelaide Oval. After winning the toss, the visitors were dismissed for 177 in the forty-sixth over. Merv Hughes, Australia's other limited-overs debutant, returned a man-of-the-match haul of 3–30. Waiting to bat at number 5, Mark spent the innings watching Geoff Marsh (86 not out) and Dean Jones (55 not out) steer their side to a nine-wicket win. Victory aside, the encounter was a most insignificant way to begin a career. Of course there had been considerable pre-game hype, but once play was underway Mark slipped into the new surroundings as quietly as a latecomer to Sunday mass. In many ways it was a fitting introduction for a shy young man who'd already told the media he wasn't 'all that keen' on the level of attention he'd attracted after his selection was announced.

There was no chance of avoiding the spotlight two days later when he walked onto the SCG to join his brother in a tense run-chase under lights against the West Indies, who'd set Australia a target of 221 for victory. Earlier, Mark had taken his first catch at this level when he combined with off-spinner Peter Taylor to remove opener Gordon Greenidge for 52. However, the pressure was much greater when standing 22 metres away from the world's most intimidating bowlers: Malcolm Marshall, Curtly Ambrose and Courtney Walsh. Mark looked comfortable from the outset of his innings, working the ball into gaps on both sides of the wicket. He and his brother were building a promising stand when the sixth sense that twins allegedly have let them down — Steve was run out for 40. Mark fell soon afterwards, bowled by Winston Benjamin for 18 off 19 deliveries. In a nerve-tingling finish, Ian Healy held the tail together with an unbeaten 23, ensuring the result came down to the final ball. Australia needed two to win, but Craig McDermott hit the deciding delivery, a full toss from Ambrose, straight into Viv Richards' hands at mid-wicket. This was as thrilling as one-dayers could be, and a sample of what Mark would become accustomed to in years to come when Australia played some of the most memorable and incredible matches in limited-overs history.

In the furious non-stop swirl of the one-day tournament, the West Indies defeated their hosts again two days later at the floodlit MCG. Chasing 237, the Australians were dismissed for 202 after losing their last six wickets for 18 runs. Mark was seventh man out, bowled by Ambrose for 32 off 37 balls. His innings was overshadowed by the run-out of Steve for 54 — the second time in as many outings that the twins were separated by poor judgement.

After the match, they briefly went their separate ways. Steve returned to the Test fold for the fourth match of the series, against the West Indies in Melbourne, while Mark joined New South Wales for a three-day game against Pakistan at the SCG. Brilliant left-arm paceman Wasim Akram bowled him for a duck in the first innings — his fourth of the summer — but he showed his class in the second with an eye-catching 63 not out as the encounter headed for a draw.

Mark was overlooked for the next three limited-overs internationals, two of which Australia won, before he returned for the run into the final series in mid-January. He scored 12 off 13 balls against Pakistan at the MCG in a game dominated by Geoff Marsh's innings of 125. The Australians won the rain-interrupted encounter, then humbled the West Indies for the second game straight with a 61-run triumph in Sydney. Mark played an important part in the success, scoring 42 from 53 balls — his best performance of the series.

However, it wasn't enough to keep him in the side for the first final in the best-of-three encounter against the West Indies at the MCG. In front of 73 000 fans, Australia won another tight contest by two runs. Mark replaced Simon O'Donnell in the team for the remaining two matches in Sydney. In the first, he shone in the field, taking two catches in the inner circle, including one off Steve's bowling to dismiss Richie Richardson. He continued his consistent form with the bat, making 22 off 25 deliveries before hitting a return chance to Ian Bishop. Viv Richards' side cruised to a 92-run win, and won again in the anticlimactic decider that intermittent rain turned into a farce. After an unbeaten 93 from Dean Jones guided the hosts to 4–226 in their shortened innings of 38 overs — Mark was bowled by Carl Hooper for 5 — they watched helplessly as further rain interruptions presented the West Indies with a ludicrous revised target of just 108 from 18 overs. They reached it in only the fourteenth over with eight wickets to spare. Richards led the way with a brutal 60 not out from only 40 deliveries. The swaggering kings from the Caribbean had won their fifth Australian limited-overs title in 10 years.

For Mark, the tournament had offered a mixed introduction to top-level limited-overs cricket. In and out of the team, he'd played seven matches, totalling 131 runs at an average of 21.83. He recalls:

I was comfortable being a middle-order batsman who could bowl a bit if needed. In those days, batting at 5 or 6 meant you generally didn't get much of a hit because Swampy [Geoff Marsh] or Boonie [David Boon] would take up most of the early overs, then you had Dean Jones coming in. He was a great one-day player. Most of the time I had to come in and try to get a run a ball in the final overs. That's all I contributed really. I didn't have time to build an innings.

I enjoyed one-day cricket right from the start. Looking back now, it's mentally not as stressful as Test cricket. In a lot of ways it's an easier game; I don't find there's the same mental pressure. If you're opening the batting you know when you're going to bat, and if you're down the order you know there's a fair chance you'll be needed at some stage. Until last season [2001–02], you didn't have to worry about the bouncer, you generally knew the type of field placings — there wouldn't be people crowding around the bat, and the bowlers were limited to 10 overs, so you could see them off relatively quickly when compared with Test cricket — it could be a bit more relaxing, you could have a bit more fun, you didn't seem to have to worry as much.

Before the one-day series had begun, former Test captain and national selector Greg Chappell stated in the media that the shortened version of the game was the right place to introduce Mark to the international arena. The question now beckoned: was it time to open the door into the Test team for the Ashes tour? Chappell's brother, Ian, as tough and astute a cricketer as any to play for Australia, had made an interesting observation in the *Sun-Herald* (1 January 1989) during the Benson & Hedges tournament:

It will probably help Mark now that his brother Steve is a fully fledged Test player.

Steve has proved his temperament at the top level and the selectors must believe there's a fair chance his twin brother will be similarly equipped. He certainly has the skill.

One thing the selectors will need to watch closely with Mark Waugh is his tendency to be a little too casual at times. There's no sign of that trait in Steve's make-up and Mark would be well advised to try to subdue any urge to lairise.

The labels that had already been fixed to Mark in the Sheffield Shield were spreading. Was he too casual? Even lazy? Or did his elegance and ease at the crease forge a false impression? Was he a mixture of apparent ease and veiled effort? A wonderful player to watch, yet a source of frustration because he was perceived to have a wandering mind? Mark says:

No matter how I look, I'm always out there trying. It's bloody hard work, you know. Looking back there have been days I suppose when I did get out to soft dismissals, but so have renowned tough players. When I did get out like that we were normally in a really strong position already. I can be in trouble for erring on the side of aggression, but right from the start of my career, even before coming into first-class cricket, I always wanted to score runs as quickly as

*possible. I enjoyed it most that way, and I also knew we had a responsibility to
entertain.*

*I like being called effortless and elegant, and I suppose there've been times
when it's fair to call me casual, but most of all I want to be known as someone
who is always trying. No matter what it seems to look like, I never give up and
am always trying to put the team in a winning position.*

Views about Mark's approach were plentiful. Allan Border, Australian captain
at the time, was still acquainting himself with his new player's temperament
and style, but he'd already seen enough to recognise rare qualities.

*You could just tell he was going to be something special. Everyone thought of
Steve as the real hard-nosed, eye-of-the-tiger player because you could see that
in him. Everyone also thought Mark was the real casual one — there was a
certain amount of truth in that, but there was a lot of steel as well that you
could see behind the scenes.*

*He was always going to put up with the labels, it's the price he paid for the
way he played. He could almost be called elegant and lazy in the same
innings. While you're going hammer and tong, people rave about you, but as
soon as you play the shot that gets you out, people immediately say, 'How lazy
or casual was that?' Even when he first started in the Australian team he
could play twenty-five cover drives that scorched through the field, but the
twenty-sixth one that he got out to was the one that everyone would complain
about.*

*He was a victim of his own style. You look at someone like Justin Langer
who puts so much effort and intensity into even playing the forward defence,
whereas Junior always looks like he's doing it so easy. He always has. Right
from the start.*

Wicket-keeper Ian Healy, who was still finding his own feet in the Australian
team, remembers Mark 'did a lot naturally in the game at the start. He got
through and produced what he did on pure natural instincts and skill.'

Steve offers a similar appraisal by emphasising that his brother 'always had
natural talent, good instincts and the confidence to express his ability in a way
other people mightn't have wanted to do, or had the courage to do'.

Rodger and Bev Waugh at the christening of the twins. Mark is on the left.

A howling Mark makes it known to everyone within earshot that Stephen has stolen his dummy.

Later in his childhood Mark took a disliking to water after he cut his ankle on an oyster shell.

Mark jokes that this was the last time the twins had a cuddle!

Off to school at Panania Public. Mark was significantly taller than Stephen in the early years.

Dressing-up was a favourite pastime that Mark says the twins have thankfully outgrown.

Second class at Panania Public. Even in photos the twins couldn't be separated. Mark is in the third row, second from right.

The twins' first soccer team. The Revesby-Milperra Lions Under-6s. Mark is in the second row, first on right. Stephen is behind him.

Rodger, Dean Waugh and the two cowboys at Rodger's parents' home in Earlwood.

Stephen, Dean and Mark enjoying a summer pastime away from cricket. Mark's broad-brimmed hat would later be replaced by his trademark 'white-floppy'.

Dean and the twins on the driveway that saw many scooter races and accidents. The concrete was also a favourite cricket pitch.

Stephen and Mark in their early representative days. The stances have changed significantly!

Throughout their lives, the twins have always been in successful teams. Mark is second from right in the back row, Stephen is second from left.

The Under-12 Bankstown representative soccer team. Mark is third from left in the first row, Stephen is far right on the second row.

The twins with balls on a string. Both showed natural gifts in many sports.

Throughout his early years, Mark divided his time playing soccer, cricket, and tennis.

Rodger and the twins during a tennis trip to Taree.

Thirteen-year-old Mark in the Bankstown District Under-14 representative team in 1978–79.

Danny Waugh stands proudly between his brothers after they were chosen in the NSW Under-16 cricket team.

Bev with all her sons, Danny, Stephen, Mark, and Dean.

Mark walks off after an innings for Essex during his first stint with the English county.
(Photo by Jon Nicholson/Getty Images.)

The end of a long wait. Mark salutes the crowd after scoring a Test century on debut against England at the Adelaide Oval (1990–91).

All four Waugh boys played cricket for NSW at some level. Danny is the only left-hander. This photo was taken at Bankstown Oval.

However, Mark's courage and lack of inhibition on the field undoubtedly affected his progression towards Test selection. Bob Simpson, by then in his third year as Australian coach, suggests, 'The greatest disappointment in life as a coach is always the boys you can't get that little bit extra out of. More often than not it's the over-talented person who's never had to think too much about it, and I think to some extent that was Mark. He did it all too naturally.'

Rightly or wrongly, the labels of 'casual' and 'lazy' were sticking firmly to one of Australian cricket's newest and most exciting products. Mark had five Shield matches and no more than four domestic one-dayers remaining in the season to prove to selectors he would be an asset on the Ashes tour.

The renewed campaign began badly against Victoria at the MCG in late January. New South Wales lost by 200 runs, Mark contributing just 7 and 5. He had only one chance in his next encounter, scoring 29 in the first innings of a draw with South Australia in Sydney. By this stage, the West Indies had completed a 3–1 victory over Allan Border's Test troops, Mark Taylor making his international debut in the second last match. The series result was a disappointing build-up to the Australians' bid to win the Ashes for the first time since Greg Chappell led a side to a 2–1 triumph at home in 1982–83.

The rest of Mark's first-class summer was consistent without being outstanding. He scored 38 and 37 in the 67-run win by New South Wales over eventual champions Western Australia in Perth; 19 and 85 in a draw with Tasmania in Sydney; and 2 and 58 in another draw at the SCG against Queensland. In the nine Shield matches he played, he tallied 552 runs at an average of 34.5, well short of the state's leading run-scorer, Taylor, who guaranteed his Ashes ticket with 981 runs at 57.7. New South Wales finished fourth on the ladder behind Western Australia, South Australia and Queensland. In the newly named one-day series, the FAI Cup, in which New South Wales reached the semi-finals before losing to Victoria, Mark's top score was 51 off 72 balls against Western Australia. After bowling 22 wicket-less overs during the Shield season, he wasn't required for one solitary over in the one-dayers. His heavy commitments left him with few opportunities to play for Bankstown.

Despite a continued push by some journalists, Mark was overlooked for the Ashes. Apart from captain Allan Border, the batsmen chosen in the squad were Geoff Marsh, Mark Taylor, David Boon, Mike Veletta, Dean Jones and Steve.

Most significantly for Mark, twenty-four-year-old all-rounder Tom Moody had also won a berth. Although there was some initial disappointment, he accepted his inconsistent form hadn't warranted his inclusion. Nevertheless, he had shown enough glimpses when given the chance at the top level, albeit in the shortened version of the game, to suggest the Test incumbents needn't look too far over their shoulders to see a player marking time.

While not yet a favourite of national selectors, Mark had endeared himself to the cricketing public with his stroke play and aggression. Not surprisingly he'd also gathered a considerable female following, especially among teenage girls who adored his flowing hair and good looks. Such was his influence, he inspired young cricketers across the nation to grow their hair long. One of them had the opportunity to play with the Waugh twins when a handful of New South Wales players visited Lismore in the state's far north for a Tooheys Cup promotional game. The 'youngster' recalls:

> I was still at school. The Tooheys Cup matches were the highlight of the cricket calendar for us. Six New South Wales players would come out to towns across the state and join in with the local teams. I was finally old and experienced enough to get picked in the Lismore team, and Mark was on our side; Stephen was in the opposition. I thought it was going to be the highlight of my career, but the game was washed out. But I'll always remember the photo with Mark and the big, long hair — he had the mullet happening then. My girlfriend at the time, who now happens to be my wife, looked at the photo, saw the mullet and thought, 'Gee, that looks pretty cute!' She thought Mark was cute, so I thought I had to grow my hair into his style. I'm not too proud to say that I really tried to copy his hairstyle, which was an interesting result for me.

Thankfully the impressionable teenager has since grown up and out of the look. These days his short style can barely be seen under the baggy green cap, but he still frequently reminds Mark of his younger years. Wicket-keeper Adam Gilchrist has come a long way!

Although the mullet was to remain for some time, by the end of the 1988–89 season, team-mates had witnessed some notable changes in Mark's appearance. Mike Whitney recalls when the twins first arrived at state training, their dress sense was 'very, very, ordinary'.

Mo [Greg] Matthews, who was the exact opposite and was right on with
everything that was happening in the fashion world, used to shake his head
when Mark and Stephen came along. Mo would say to me, 'What about the
clothes that these guys wear!'

But we all saw the difference once Sue got hold of him. She not only turned
his dress sense around 180 degrees, but put him into a spin. He started turning
up in some really good gear.

Eighteen months after the turmoil of her marriage break-up and the decision to
settle into a relationship with Mark, Sue Porter was having a significant influence
on her partner. Throughout New South Wales cricketing circles, she was
recognised as giving Mark stability, security and a new sense of assuredness.

'She has always been a strong person who loves helping people,'
acknowledges Mark. 'Her guidance and support really helped me establish
myself. She has always been a very kind person to others, but doesn't do
enough for herself really.'

Sue laughs when asked about her influence.

Oh yes, he's come good. I've definitely given him a bit of finesse. It's nice to
think that I played a part in his development as a cricketer, but the credit goes to
him. You could never change him too much. What you see is what you get. For
better, for worse.

There were many times when we didn't talk much cricket. If he was to get a
hundred he wouldn't come home and make a fuss about it; if he got nothing he'd
come home, sometimes curse a bit, but never carried on with it. He has never
been moody about it at all with me.

Another stage in their relationship came when Mark returned to Essex for the
1989 winter. His brief six-week stint in England the previous year had been
tough for Sue. It was the longest time she'd been apart from her partner, but
she was already learning to accept that this was simply the way it was for a
cricket widow. She says:

It can be hard being alone for such long periods of time, but you just have to
make the best of it. You have to have a good network of friends around you.

Harry Solomons was always a good friend, Thommo [David Thompson, Mark's Bankstown team-mate] and his wife Karen were also very good to me. They all understood me totally and never excluded me from anything. I thought I was a bit luckier than most because I also had the children.

Despite the hardship, there was a positive aspect for Sue. The woman raised in Sydney's inner suburbs had never left Australia, but when she farewelled Mark at Sydney airport in April, she was excited by the knowledge that she would join her partner during a four-week holiday from Kingsgrove Sports Centre later in the season.

In the meantime, Mark was warmly welcomed back to Essex for what would be an eventful, and at times controversial, season. There was much greater pressure on him than the previous year when he had been an unknown commodity. He was engaged to play the complete season as the overseas professional and expectations were high. Allan Border and South African player Ken McKewen had set a high standard the previous years, and officials expected nothing less from Mark. Good results weren't desired, but demanded.

The county season began slowly for Mark, who registered just one fifty — 77 against Derbyshire — in his first six innings. However, after returning a promising double of 92 and 3–23 off 12 overs against Cambridge University, he ran into a consistent patch of form that returned three fifties in his next six times in the middle, including a highly entertaining 89 not out against Leicestershire. In the same match he took 2–9 off four overs in the second innings. His growing belief that he was on the brink of his first hundred was vindicated in the following match against Hampshire at Ilford in late June. After scoring 20 in the first innings, he left a lasting impression when he scored 109 in the second innings, mastering an attack led by West Indian Test great Malcolm Marshall. The majesty of his front-foot shots on both sides of the wicket soared above the strokeplay of his peers. It was a special performance. Mark remembers:

I was pretty proud of that hundred because Malcolm Marshall was one of the best bowlers in the world at the time, and I remember it being a pretty lively pitch. It's always nice to make runs against world-quality bowlers. It was good for me personally and also for my future as a player because people would recognise that I'd made a hundred against Marshall, and for that reason alone they'd think I must have played pretty well. That was the good thing about playing county cricket back then because we continually came across some of the best overseas players.

By that stage I was finding a bit of confidence. I don't remember ever sitting down and listening to someone saying you gotta do this, you gotta do that. I think my game just naturally evolved, and I was adjusting to the different level of play. I learnt my game myself just watching others and listening to them — I was working it out for myself.

There was still room for development, but there was little doubt he had graduated from a player with potential to a player beginning to uphold it. By the time Sue touched down in London, Essex were acknowledging a different arrival — the arrival of Mark Waugh as an international player of class.

The busy schedule of the county cricketer seemed likely to prevent Mark picking up Sue from Heathrow Airport. As a precaution, he gave club official Graham Saville a photo of his partner. Sue, excited but a little apprehensive about her first trip abroad, was preparing to put herself in the hands of a stranger, but at the last minute Mark was able to change plans and be waiting at the gate for his travel-weary mate.

The couple stayed with Saville's mother, Queenie, near Chelmsford, but much of their time together was spent at cricket grounds, in hotel rooms and on the road travelling the length and breadth of England between matches. It was another new experience for Sue who witnessed at close range the lives of the busiest professional first-class cricketers in the world. The county circuit offered little chance for a player to put his feet up and enjoy the spasmodic charm of a British summer.

After his century against Hampshire, Mark had every reason to feel confident about the second half of the season, but he discovered the constant grind of competition forced him to battle bouts of wavering concentration. His performances in late June and early July were a mixture of failures and frustrating starts with only one memorable finish, an unbeaten 112 against Glamorgan in a Royal Assurance one-dayer at Neath. His county championship returns were much less spectacular: 1 and 2 against Warwickshire; 0 and 8 against Sussex; 26 against Derbyshire; 21 against

Glamorgan; and 29 against Kent. The disappointing sequence continued when Mark was dismissed for 27 and 0 against Yorkshire in a match tainted with controversy. Essex won the contest but were stripped of 25 championship points after the English Cricket Board deemed the pitch at Southend to be of substandard quality under regulations introduced to prevent counties rigging pitches to suit their bowling attacks. Mark recalls:

Southend was one of Essex's outer grounds. Chelmsford was the main venue, then they had three outer grounds — Ilford, Colchester and Southend, where they held week-long carnivals each season. The Southend ground was owned by the local council, so the pitch was prepared more by council workers than professional groundsmen, although the curator at Chelmsford went down to overlook what was going on. It obviously didn't have the preparation that went into the main ground, but it wasn't as though the pitch was doctored — it was just the way the wicket was. It was very dry, and the ball started going through the top on the first day, but I don't think it got any worse. It was the same for both teams. At that stage there were a lot of poor pitches around the country, but there was no way we'd doctored the pitch.

But doctoring did go on. I remember playing one game at Nottingham, at Trent Bridge. On the morning of the game, Nottingham saw our team and actually changed pitches. They'd obviously prepared two of them, and when they saw that we had spinners they changed to a mainly grassy pitch. Obviously you prepare a pitch that's going to suit your bowlers — it's common sense isn't it? I suppose the ECB thought there was just too much of it going on, and the pitches were too results oriented.

They were a bit harsh taking the points off us. There were a lot worse wickets we played on around the country throughout the year. Because Essex were one of the contenders for the championship and were a really good county at that stage, I think they just wanted to make an example of us. There was real disappointment among the players because we had no control over the pitch, we didn't prepare it, and it wasn't that bad anyway.

While Essex officials protested to the ECB, Mark preferred to concentrate on the job he was paid to do, and was relieved to find form again with 110 in the following match against Middlesex at Uxbridge. A further and most satisfying century — 100 not out off 165 deliveries — came five games later when Essex played Border's Australians, who at that stage had already regained the Ashes with a 4–0 lead after five games of the six-match series. Mark remembers:

Nowadays the overseas professional rarely gets picked against touring teams, but I wanted to play against Australia and really wanted to perform well. Essex made a little badge up before the match with Stephen and me wearing our respective caps. The whole game turned into a bit of a reunion because Stephen, Merv Hughes and Allan Border had all spent time at Essex. It was a big game, and a really big crowd.

I had a bit of luck in my innings — I got dropped a couple of times by Tim Zoehrer [wicket-keeper], but it didn't stop me enjoying it. It was nice to make a hundred, but it was a bit of a different feeling to do it against blokes I normally played with. I got 57 in the second innings as well, so it turned out to be a pretty pleasing game for me.

It was a bit awkward playing against Stephen. I actually bowled to him, but it was still really competitive. I certainly didn't want him to hit me for four.

Steve, having already proved a batting sensation in the Tests with two centuries, wasn't to be outdone, and emulated his brother's feat with a hundred off just 101 balls.

Australia won the match by 150 runs, but there was little disappointment shown by Essex supporters, who were laying claim to contributing to the development of the Waugh twins.

After the match, Mark and Steve went their separate ways — Steve to London for the final Test, a draw at The Oval, and Mark back to the county grind. He made one more century for the season, 165 in the final outing against Leicestershire at Leicester. It completed a solid performance in the first-class arena: 24 matches with 1537 runs at an average of 43.91.

Essex finished second in the county championship, just six points behind Worcestershire who admittedly would have enjoyed a bigger winning margin if their last match hadn't been ruined by rain. However, it was obvious that the ECB's pitch-doctoring decision had affected the season's outcome. In a move that left no-one in any doubt as to who they thought should have claimed the title, Essex officials awarded their players championship-winning bonuses.

It wasn't the only sour note for the county. In the Royal Assurance League limited-overs competition, Essex players were furious when their penultimate away match of the season against the eventual winners, Lancashire, was abandoned. It was another controversial ruling that influenced the results table.

Chasing 136 for victory off a rain-shortened twenty-eight overs, Essex were 0–53 in the eleventh over when they were forced from the field because of further poor weather. By the time the skies had cleared and the covers were removed, the umpires decided there wasn't enough time remaining for Essex to receive twenty overs, the minimum needed to constitute a match. Mark remembers:

> The players thought an enormous amount of time had been taken to get the ground ready. We thought we could have been playing sooner. In those days there was a lot of north–south rivalry. The north thought they never got a fair go, especially in national team selections. They always thought Essex, Surrey and Middlesex got the bulk of the Test players, whereas Lancashire and Yorkshire rarely got a look in. I think this was a payback. They took an extraordinary amount of time to clear the covers. They were smart.

Essex finished third in the competition, but enjoyed better fortune in winning the Royal Assurance Cup. Apart from a first-round exit in the NatWest trophy, the county had a successful limited-overs season that culminated with an appearance in the final of the Benson & Hedges Cup against Nottinghamshire at Lord's. The match was a thriller.

Batting first, Essex reached 7–243 off 55 overs. Alan Lilley top scored with an unbeaten 95, Graham Gooch made 48 and Mark contributed 41 off 58 balls. His innings was described in the 1990 *Wisden Almanack*.

> Mark Waugh, capped on the eve of the game, was upright, authoritative and clean hitting, yet, like so much of the Essex innings, his knock was not totally satisfactory. He suggested so much more than he achieved, before hitting Evans limply to mid-wicket after he and Lilley had put on 82.

Nottinghamshire was always in sight of the target due to constructive innings from captain Tim Robinson (86), Paul Johnson (54) and Derek Randall (49). However, when Randall fell in the second last over, Essex's hopes lifted.

Veteran left-arm medium pacer John Lever, in his twenty-third and final first-class season, delivered the fifty-fifth over. Nine runs were needed, three wickets remained. Nottinghamshire were still four short of victory with one ball remaining. Tailender Eddie Hemmings, as unlikely a hero as there could be, backed away to the leg side and forced the ball through gully to the boundary. Nottinghamshire celebrated, Essex team-mates consoled Lever, and Mark was left with one of the most vivid recollections of his season.

It is a stand-out memory. There was a lot of tension, the crowd was on edge, everyone was pretty nervous during the last over. It's great being part of those games. It was a good experience for me at the time because I was still watching and learning as much as I could. Every game gave me the chance to further my own game in some way.

The whole season was part of a continued learning curve for me. I got the chance to play a lot of innings under different conditions against different attacks. Facing guys like Marshall on dodgy pitches was quality training. Playing nearly every day could wear you down, but it made me a better batsman. It really tested my concentration.

I learnt a lot socially, too. The biggest change for me was having to wear a coat and tie to the ground every day. When I first went over there, I didn't even take a tie with me. I eventually reformed and started putting one on, but I didn't feel comfortable. You couldn't even wear jeans after the game on an away trip. The rules were so old-fashioned that they really surprised me, I thought it was ridiculous. Why would you wear a coat and tie to a game? Why not a tracksuit? I thought it was very strange.

To interested onlookers, the season was an invaluable and timely part of Mark's cricketing education. Allan Border says:

I really think the experience helped his cricket a hell of a lot. When I'd first recommended him to Essex, I thought it would be good for Essex, good for Mark and good for Australia's future. The day in, day out style really toughened him up. He got a bit more direction about his game. He was obviously disappointed about missing the Ashes tour, but there are processes you have to go through before you make it to play for Australia. By the time he scored his hundred against us at Chelmsford you could just tell he was starting to make some inroads. Mind you, we helped him out with a few short ones outside off, and a few full ones on leg stump!

Essex paceman Neil Foster makes a similar assessment:

Without doubt coming to Essex was a real boost for him, it really helped him along. It gave him the opportunity to get lots of innings under his belt and develop a hunger. I actually think he found it quite hard at first, not having time to put his feet up.

He had this reputation, if you like, of being a bit of a softy; I think partly in comparison to Stephen. That was probably true, but he seemed to know what his game was and became more assured the further he went along. He was a very good player off his legs, a very fluent, elegant player. He often scored runs in situations when we really needed runs, and on poor wickets a lot of the time. Quite often he got us runs to win us a game — that is the mark of a good player.

He was also a top fella. We still have great affection for him.

One fascinating by-product of Mark's Essex stint was a change in batting style. He came home to begin his 1989–90 summer with a very upright stance, which he believes was the result of subconsciously copying Graham Gooch's technique. He quickly reverted to his old ways, but he was destined to stand taller than ever before in the season ahead.

CHAPTER EIGHT

MISTAKEN IDENTITY

The dining room at the Cricketers Club in central Sydney was packed with players, officials, sponsors and high expectations. Surrounded by trophies of eternal lustre and ageing photos of the greats — Bradman playing a pull shot, Trumper dancing down the pitch, O'Reilly rolling his arm over — everyone present at the 1989–90 season launch for the New South Wales team held optimistic hopes. Geoff Lawson was to captain a side widely regarded as the best in the Sheffield Shield competition, even before a ball had been delivered. A quick glance through the players' list supported the critics' predictions that New South Wales would sweep all before them during the season; Lawson, Mark Taylor, Steve Small, Mark O'Neill, Greg Matthews, Mike Whitney, Peter Taylor and Phil Emery were all part of the dynamic squad. And then there were the Waugh twins. It was impossible to forget them, but was it possible to mistake them?

Former brilliant Australian all-rounder Alan Davidson stood at the front of the gathering in his role as New South Wales Cricket Association President. He was beaming with Blue pride when he said, 'Geoff Lawson is here, Peter Taylor. I saw Steve Waugh earlier ... not sure if Mark's here.' It was an unfortunate gaffe because Mark was the only one of the twins present. Dressed in a perfectly pressed New South Wales blazer, he sat quietly, looking unperturbed at a nearby table. It wasn't the first time his and Stephen's identities had been confused, despite their appearances and personalities being significantly different.

Mark had become accustomed to being referred to as 'the other Waugh', but any doubts anyone still held that he would ever emerge from his brother's shadow were soon to be swept away.

The mistaken Waugh, who by this time was widely known as 'Junior', launched into the domestic season with a renewed appetite for success. Despite performing consistently during the previous home summer's Benson & Hedges series and being one of the leading limited-overs batsmen in England during his season with Essex, he wasn't chosen in Australia's squad for the six-nation Nehru Cup in India in late October. Pakistan won the tournament, but it was a disappointing time for Allan Border's men, who failed to reach the semi-finals after winning just two of their five preliminary matches. They returned home to prepare for Tests against New Zealand, Sri Lanka and Pakistan, with the last two countries to play also in the Benson & Hedges series.

Although Australia's Test line-up appeared settled after its commanding display against England, Mark was still hopeful of forcing his way into the team through sheer weight of runs. The batting incumbents from the final Ashes Test were Geoff Marsh, Mark Taylor, David Boon, Border, Dean Jones and Steve. Mark says:

At about that time I thought I was getting ripe for Test selection. I'd strung together a couple of pretty good seasons and felt comfortable with my game. I'd become used to all the talk in the papers about my chances, but tried not to read too much into it. It was hard to see any changes to the Australian team after they'd played so well in England, but that didn't mean I could lose interest. There were a few guys in the same boat, like Greg Matthews and Tom Moody. We all knew that we had to keep playing our best because you never knew when something could happen. I'd never wish it upon anyone, but if someone got injured or lost a bit of form, the guys on the edge had to be ready for a call-up. Waiting for a chance was hard, but looking back it didn't do me any harm. Nowadays there are blokes who have to wait for five or 10 seasons before they

get a go, so I didn't have to wait that long really. Guys like Darren Lehmann
and Matt Hayden have had to wait a lot longer.

Despite Mark's belief in his own game, there were significant reasons he hadn't progressed beyond fringe candidacy. Former Australian coach Bob Simpson recalls there was a feeling among selectors that the younger Waugh twin's batting lacked some discipline.

He was basically kept out of the Australian side for a little longer because we felt
he was getting out too easy the same way. Even though it had been discussed
with him, he was having a lot of trouble controlling the flick off his hip and he
was being caught at square leg too often. The thing that used to get him in
trouble was the fact that he was just too cocky on the on side. Natural talent
allowed him to get away with a lot of it. While he was getting a lot of runs in
England, we also took the decision at that time not to be overly impressed by
people who were getting big scores in county cricket because of the standard.

At the time, Australia's selection panel comprised Simpson, John Benaud, Jim Higgs and Lawrie Sawle. If their assessment was heeded, Mark faced the difficult challenge of tightening up his game without losing his aggressive flair and natural style, two of his most valuable, and at times priceless, assets. He needed to find a fine balance in his strokeplay.

After scoring 32 against Western Australia and 0 against Tasmania in the first two FAI cup matches in late October, Mark swung his attention to the Sheffield Shield opener against South Australia, at the Adelaide Oval. The pitch proved a run haven. Sent in by SA captain David Hookes, New South Wales amassed a total of 7 declared for 516. Mark Taylor maintained his brilliant Ashes form, scoring 199, while Mark, his former opening partner, batting at number 5, cut, drove and flicked his way to a masterful 172 from 301 deliveries, the highest score of his career. While his aggression caught the spectators' eyes, his defence captured the attention of the critics. Journalist Phil Wilkins wrote about a 'changed man' in the *Sun-Herald* (12 November 1989):

Last summer his defensive shot was an automatic mechanism which took
the ball out to square leg. Now he stands as straight as a grenadier guard.

His cover drives and cuts blazed as spectacularly as ever for his twenty boundaries, but the risk has gone.

It was as near perfect a start to the season as Mark could have hoped. He had made a telling statement: no matter what the views of selectors, he was maturing and had undoubtedly benefited from his time in England.

Incredibly, his performance and that of Taylor were overshadowed during the SA innings when beefy nineteen-year-old left-hander Darren Lehmann scored 228 to ensure the home side took first innings points in the drawn match.

Four days later, New South Wales hosted the Sri Lankans in a four-day match at Canberra's Manuka Oval. In his only chance with the bat, Mark strolled to 42 off 59 balls before edging a delivery from medium pacer Graeme Labrooy into the slips. He took three wickets for the game, including one in the second innings as opening bowler in the absence of injured captain Geoff Lawson. When stumps were drawn, the visitors were seven wickets down and still 119 runs short of victory.

As expected, Mark wasn't picked for Australia's one-off Test against New Zealand in Perth at the end of November. Selectors made only one change to the top six who had played the last Ashes Test: Geoff Marsh was replaced by West Australian team-mate Tom Moody who proceeded to score 61 on debut, increasing the edge he had over Mark in the battle for a long-term Test spot.

Mark's next opportunity came in the 32-run win by New South Wales over Queensland at the Newcastle International Sports Ground. In a low-scoring match he made 46 and 18, but his most significant contribution was at the bowling crease with returns of 1–31 and 2–34. His twenty-five overs for the match were more than he'd bowled in the entire 1988–89 Shield season.

While Moody, batting at number 3, continued to impress with a century in the two-Test series against Sri Lanka in December — Australia won 1–0 — Mark also boosted his reputation with 100 not out in the second innings of the drawn match against Victoria in the NSW country town of Albury. It wasn't enough to win selection in the Australian squad for the opening matches of the Benson & Hedges series. Moody also missed out, but would force his way in for the second half of the tournament.

Mark had to be content with state cricket for the time being. His first match for 1990 gave no indication of what lay ahead that year when he was bowled for 30 by Test and limited-overs medium pacer Terry Alderman in a rain-marred draw against Western Australia, at the SCG. His following two outings with the bat were forgettable: 0 in his only innings in Hobart, against Tasmania who claimed outright points after a generous New South Wales declaration, and 4 in the 81-run win by the Prime Minister's XI over Pakistan, in Canberra. However, he impressed with the ball against the visitors, taking 2–13 off five overs.

Despite the batting stumbles, there was media speculation Mark would be a late inclusion in the one-day squad, perhaps at the expense of Steve whose bowling had been limited by a stress fracture in his back. He improved his chances by scoring his second unbeaten hundred of the season against Victoria at the MCG in yet another draw. The stylish innings proved an entrée to Mark's spectacular performance against South Australia at the SCG. After losing the toss, New South Wales were sent in to bat by David Hookes, who hoped his bowlers could exploit a damp patch at one end of the pitch. By the end of the day, the visiting captain was regretting his decision after the home side reached 7–351. Mark's innings was the indisputable highlight — 137 off 185 balls, including a massive six over mid-wicket off former Test leg-spinner Peter Sleep. The ball went within centimetres of hitting the clock-tower on top of the Members Stand, prompting Geoff Lawson to describe it as the longest hit he'd ever seen. The contemptuous shot illustrated Mark's view that spinners were there for easy runs. Simple as that. Bankstown player David Thompson remembers an incident before a grade match that summed up his close mate's attitude.

> We were driving to Mosman for a game. Mark had been away for the week, but had made himself available for the club, which he always did whenever he could. When we were running through the team I told him about a spinner who was making his debut. Mark immediately said, 'You're joking! I could hit him for six every ball.' He was dead serious. He just didn't rate spinners at all.

In all, his fourteenth first-class century included two sixes in the space of three deliveries from Sleep, and thirteen fours. *Daily Telegraph* journalist John Taylor suggested Mark 'was like a younger version of Viv Richards', while in the *Sydney Morning Herald* (16 February 1990) Ian Cockerill wrote:

Wherever Hookes placed his fieldsmen Waugh would imperiously render them obsolete, going over, between and sometimes through them.

It would almost have been reckless if it hadn't been done so clinically. He did not give a chance until his demise, keeping the ball on the ground with flawless technique except for his occasional attacks on the clock-tower.

The innings came on the same day that a thirteen-man Australian squad was announced to play one Test and a limited-overs series in New Zealand in March. Mark wasn't included, but he enjoyed some consolation when he received an emergency call-up to replace the flu-ridden Craig McDermott for the final preliminary Benson & Hedges Cup match against Pakistan, in Sydney, five days later. It proved a frustrating case of so close yet so far when he was chosen to carry the drinks. However, he finally popped the cork on his international season when he was chosen in the eleven for the second final against the Pakistanis, at the SCG. He replaced his brother who was dropped from an Australian team for the first time since he'd made his Test debut four years earlier. The older twin, who was still struggling to bowl, had played 87 one-day matches for his country; the younger twin had just seven to his credit.

Australia won the match by 69 runs, completing a 2–0 victory in the finals. Batting at number 5, Mark made 14 off as many balls before being run out, and he wasn't needed to bowl. It was his only appearance in Australian colours all summer, a disappointing result considering his handful of matches the previous season.

A double failure awaited his return to the Sheffield Shield when he scored just 5 and 11 as New South Wales surrendered to Western Australia in Perth. He took 2–55 in the second innings, but perhaps his most telling contribution was in the field. Although his stints in the slips were still quite rare, because he was considered just as valuable elsewhere in the inner circle, he took three catches in the cordon for the match, further underlining a skill that left team-mates shaking their heads in disbelief. Mike Whitney, still in awe of Mark's ability, says:

He was just phenomenal. Just absolutely phenomenal! Even in those days before he became a full-time slipper, he was just unbelievable. I thought Ian Botham was extraordinary because he used to wait with his hands on his knees, and I used to wonder how he ever got them into position. But Mark was a step above. He just had the gift. I can look back now and say that he's the best I've ever seen. I know that's a really huge wrap, but he makes half-chances look easy catches. I've played with some great slip fielders — Rick McCosker, Allan Border, Mark Taylor, Greg Chappell, Shane Warne, and I thought Stephen was great in gully, but even some of those guys wouldn't have got a hand on some of the things Mark's taken. From the first time he went into the slips he was taking half-chances going down low to his right but not even falling over when momentum should have rolled him on his back or at least off his feet. How many times did I see him hit the deck? Very, very few. He was just so well balanced. Just watching him when he first went into slips, it wasn't hard to know that's where he'd end up spending a lot of time.

Whitney wasn't alone in his praise. Greg Matthews would later suggest Mark was 'the most well-balanced white man in the world'.

Mark was looming as a critical factor in New South Wales' Sheffield Shield hopes. After a slow start to the season, the Blue-bags needed to beat Tasmania in their last preliminary match to move into the final. The absence of Steve, Mark Taylor and Peter Taylor, all in New Zealand with the Australian team, placed Mark under pressure. It was a position he relished. In reply to the visitors' meagre first innings of 117, New South Wales were struggling at 3–33 when the scattering of fans at the SCG saw the familiar sight of a slim, loose-limbed batsman walking through the players' gate with helmet already on and a long sleeveless jumper stretching below his backside. Three hundred and ninety deliveries later, the figure walked off the field at stumps on the second day with 198 not out against his name.

Unfortunately, inclement weather prompted Lawson to declare overnight, preventing Mark from registering his first double century. The decision was a relief for Tasmania's bowlers who'd had no answer to a superb range of front and back-foot strokes that sprinted to all parts of the ground.

Mark's fifth first-class century for the summer had dominated the 224-run partnership with wicket-keeper Phil Emery (81) and resulted in a record sixth-wicket stand for New South Wales–Tasmania Shield matches.

By this stage, Mark had begun using a bat with a blade that was an inch and a half [3.8 cms] longer than average. At two pounds ten [1.35 kilos], it was quite heavy, but it wasn't wielded as though it were a blacksmith's hammer pounding on glowing metal. Instead, it worked together with the ball. Willow and leather were partners in subtlety and softness, but rarely brutality. He may have been from a blue-collar suburb, but Mark was fast becoming renowned for his aristocratic touch. Bob Simpson recalls:

> *From the very first time I saw him, he had the rare ability to hit the ball so hard*
> *and smoothly without any apparent anger. Even when he went down the wicket*
> *to hit it over the top he didn't need to throw everything at it — he'd just stroke*
> *it, yet he could hit the ball as far as anyone in the game. There was never any*
> *real anger, he just kept that balance.*

While Simpson missed the innings because of Australia's tour across the Tasman, he and his fellow selectors would surely have nodded their heads in approval at media reports that not only underlined Mark's elegance, but also his staunch discipline and discreet shot selection.

New South Wales won by an innings and 156 runs, and advanced to the final at home against Queensland. Both teams were boosted by the return of their Australian players, but predictions of a close encounter disappeared after Queensland crumbled for 103 in their first innings, a long way behind the New South Wales total of 360 in which Mark fell for 3, caught by Healy off Allan Border's left-arm orthodox spin. He made amends with an unbeaten 78 when New South Wales batted again and declared at 9–396. The visitors folded for 308, ending a one-sided affair. The biggest talking point throughout the match was the late appointment of Mark Taylor as captain after Lawson was forced out with a shoulder injury. The twenty-six-year-old stand-in skipper celebrated with a century in each innings.

New South Wales weren't as successful in the FAI Cup, losing their semi-final to South Australia the week before the Shield decider. Mark had impressed with a half-century off 78 balls, his highest score of the series.

However, all the telling statistical statements were made in the first-class arena. Mark finished the season as the Sheffield Shield's leading scorer with 967 runs at an average of 80.85. Together with Lawson and Darren Lehmann he was named in the 1990 *ABC Australian Cricket Almanac* as Player of the Year, an award he also received at state level. Mark acknowledges:

My own form was helped by being in a winning team. Winning certainly breeds
a more confident player, a player who believes in his own ability. If you're
playing in a losing team, you can tend to go into your shell a bit more and
worry about your own game. Everyone is just fighting for survival. But I had
no worries about that during the season. I was part of a good aggressive team
that played the way I liked to play. It was easy to do well.

What Mark doesn't mention is the two-way street that success travels in.
Winning teams can help breed greater confidence in their players, but winning
teams also need confident players to begin with. Such was the case during the
1989–90 season. Mark and New South Wales enjoyed a symbiotic relationship.

A report in the ABC *Almanac* confirmed that the younger Waugh twin
'seemed a more mature, more complete batsman. He still played with his
characteristic blend of dash and elegance, but his batting seemed to be
reinforced now by extra application and determination.' The report finished
with the prediction that 'if he can keep this up, the selectors will not easily
resist his claims for a place in the Test side'. Mark comments:

I really tried hard not to think about the talk. The Australian team was going
well. And I knew it was going to be very hard to replace any of the batsmen in
the team. I just hoped that my time would come if I kept scoring runs. I was
really disappointed not to have played more one-day matches — I thought I'd
really done nothing wrong the season before, but I just couldn't get a look in.

His only option was to keep making big scores, and in his 1990 season at Essex,
the runs came at a phenomenal rate.

After arriving back in England and settling into a flat in Cheltenham, Mark
quickly revived his love for the county game, scoring 166 not out in his fourth
match of the season, against Worcestershire at Worcester. He scored 125 in the
next game, against Hampshire, whose attack was still led by West Indian
speedster Malcolm Marshall, and after relative failures of 39 and 59 in the
following outing with Middlesex, he cracked the double-century barrier for the
first time, scoring 204 against Gloucestershire at Ilford. The visitors' attack
included Marshall's calypso team-mate Courtney Walsh, who struggled to
contain his rival on an easy-paced pitch. The 267-ball innings was over in a

stroke under five hours, and included 92 runs in boundaries. The run feast continued against Warwickshire where Mark scored 103, his fourth ton in seven innings. The golden run ended with a first innings duck against Somerset, but in the five games prior to that Mark had tallied 735 runs in seven innings at an average of 122.5.

For a player who generally acknowledged statistics with nothing more than a roll of the shoulders, Mark was pleased with his form. Reminders of his triumphs weren't only recorded in scorebooks but on a most unusual honour board — Mark's thigh pad. He says:

> To this day I'm not sure how it came about. I think Keith Fletcher [former coach and Essex player] started it during the 1989 Essex season. He must have been bored one day. The next thing you know I picked up my thigh pad in the dressing room, and it had all these little stickmen drawn on it.
>
> I just wondered what would I do with a thigh pad that had stickmen all over it. Then I thought, 'Why not use it? Why not put a stickman on it every time I scored a century?' So I decided to write down the score, and the team each hundred was scored against. If it was a double century, I'd put on a double-headed stickman. It was good because every time I put on my thigh pad I'd see the hundreds and that would reinforce the belief that I had in myself. It made me think about how well I'd done in the past, and that became an incentive for the future.

Nowadays, the thigh pad is in a cupboard in Mark's home. He stopped recording his achievements on it a few years ago, but he hopes one day to update it — because of his emotional attachment to it, he wore it until it was so thin it offered nothing more than psychological protection.

During the 1990 season, Mark's pen was nearly as busy as his bat as he continued his relentless and successful pursuit of big totals. After raising the bat at Edgbaston, he scored four more centuries during the county championship: 126 against Derbyshire at Colchester; 103 not out against Sussex at Hove; 169 against Kent at Chelmsford; and 207 not out against Yorkshire at Middlesborough. He finished with 2072 first-class runs at 76.74. Since January he'd amassed 2635 runs, just shy of the magical 3000, a phenomenal mark he'd pass by the end of the year.

'At the end of the day, 3000 runs in a calendar year is only a statistic,' Mark says. 'It's not the be all and end all, but it does confirm you must have been consistent with big scores over a pretty long period. To make so many runs puts you up there with some very good players. It's pleasing to see something for your efforts, but now, who really cares?'

His success at Essex was further underlined by a limited-overs century against Lancashire, and he claimed his best first-class bowling figures, 5–37 off 12 overs, against Nottinghamshire. It was a golden summer. Admittedly the dry weather had opened its arms to run-making, but as a report in the 1991 *Wisden Almanack* suggested, there was no more pleasing craftsman at the crease than Australia's Test hopeful.

Mark Waugh with an ease bordering on elegance displayed a rich talent, and even when confronted with the occasional pitch giving encouragement to the bowlers, he showed an ability to gather runs fluently.

Mark was named the Essex Player of the Year, the County Player of the Year, and one of Wisden's Cricketers of the Year, an honour he shared with Indian batsman Mohammad Azharuddin, West Indian opener Desmond Haynes, and local products Mike Atherton and Alan Butcher. Only the previous year Steve had been one of Wisden's best after scoring 506 runs at 126.5 during the Ashes campaign. Mark was described in *Wisden* as: 'the type who can have 30 on the board without the bowlers realising he has his pads strapped on'. Needless to say, the pads were firmly attached to his legs for much of the season.

His performances helped Essex finish runners-up in the county championship for the second successive year. Their limited-overs form wasn't as imposing — a quarter-final appearance in the Benson & Hedges Cup was their most rewarding return.

For Mark, the season put the final touches on his cricket apprenticeship. He left Essex not knowing if he'd ever return. He was just as uncertain about his immediate future in Australia. Was he closer to Test selection? Or would he remain on the outside looking in? He hadn't had a break from the game for twenty-six months, but surely the sheer weight of his performances meant his career was just about to begin.

CHAPTER NINE

WORTH THE WAIT

After proving almost unstoppable at the crease during England's 1990 summer, Mark finally discovered an opponent who could match him at the start of the following Australian season — himself! An infected finger forced him out of the opening round of grade cricket with Bankstown, but he recovered in time to score a blistering 87 retired in the New South Wales trial match between City and Country in Sydney. The innings included six fours and four sixes. He shared a 154-run partnership with all-rounder Brad McNamara who described Mark's performance as 'awesome'. New South Wales selector Neil Marks threw some spice into the pre-season mix when he said in the media Mark had to be selected in Australia's Test team for the upcoming defence of the Ashes. It seemed everything old was new again. Another season about to begin, and another set of headlines calling for Mark's promotion to a side that had a well-established top six. He again shared column space with Tom Moody, and the much publicised newcomer to the race, Darren Lehmann, who'd celebrated his twentieth birthday the previous summer when twelfth man for the third Test against Pakistan, in Sydney. There was no change in Mark's attitude — he just had to keep scoring runs.

New South Wales launched their summer with an FAI Cup fixture against Queensland in Brisbane. The limited-overs series would be completed before the end of the month, unlike previous seasons in which it was interwoven with the Sheffield Shield.

Mark returned a solid all-round performance, taking 2–26 and scoring a sedate 31 off 62 balls in his side's four-wicket victory. Two days later at the SCG, New South Wales beat Tasmania by 88 runs after Mark contributed a rollicking 59 from 65 deliveries. He maintained his form with 64 off 83 balls as New South Wales triumphed at home against Victoria.

The three straight successes booked the Blue-bags a spot in the final against Western Australia in Perth. Sent in by WA captain and Test opener Geoff Marsh, the visitors compiled 7–235 off 50 overs. The innings was propped up by an unbeaten 74 from the richly gifted twenty-year-old left-hander Michael Bevan. Mark made only 1 before he was bowled trying to work a ball through the leg side off gangly left-armer Bruce Reid. Western Australia reached the target in the forty-fifth over due to an unconquered 91 from Marsh, who was named man of the match.

Attention quickly swung to the Sheffield Shield competition in which New South Wales were at home for their first game of the season, against Tasmania. The Blue-bags won by an innings and 20 runs. Mark Taylor's 183 was the dominant notation in a scorecard that also read ME Waugh, caught Boon, bowled Pearce, 49.

Mark missed the next Shield match with good reason — he had been chosen in the Australian XI to play England in Hobart. He failed to make the most of the opportunity, falling for 15 and 12, but the lean return was quickly swept away by attractive innings of 74 and 65 when New South Wales hosted New Zealand's champion provincial side, Wellington. It seemed that Mark was beginning to warm to his task.

In the meantime, national selectors remained loyal to their Test batsmen for the opening Ashes Test in Brisbane. Taylor, Marsh, David Boon, Dean Jones, Allan Border, Steve Waugh — a list of names that not only presented England's bowlers with formidable obstacles, but faced Mark with the harsh reality that he could be watching from beyond the boundary for yet another season unless there was a dramatic change of form and fortune in the Australian team.

However, he was encouraged when picked in the Benson & Hedges squad for the campaign against England and New Zealand. He admits:

It was a relief to be back. If I'd missed the team again it would have been hard to take. I really felt I deserved my chance to have a full season of games and show what I could do. The one-day game was a lot different back then. It was more or less a case of just turning up and getting into it. There was no real planning, and some players still found it hard to accept it as real cricket. But I really enjoyed it. You had a good chance to be involved most of the time — as a batsman, a bowler, and you generally had a fair bit to do in the field. I didn't really think my performances could boost my Test chances, but it wouldn't do them any harm if I played well.

The Benson & Hedges series offered an important challenge fifteen months before the staging of the World Cup in Australia and New Zealand. If Mark was to play a part in his country's defence of the trophy that had been won in India in 1987, the time had come for him to show his true value. Although his batting was the key element of his game, his bowling could prove a valuable asset. All-rounders, such as Victoria's hard-hitting batsman and medium pacer Simon O'Donnell, were much sought after. Mark knew he had the opportunity to create a similar position for himself when the campaign began just four days after Australia had cruised to a 10-wicket triumph in the opening Ashes Test.

Critics of the limited-overs game suggested it could be difficult for players to adjust between 'traditional' and 'pyjama' cricket, but Allan Border's men showed few signs of Test lag when they beat New Zealand by 61 runs in a rain-affected match at the SCG. Batting at number 5, Mark made a welcome return with an entertaining 40 off 32 deliveries, including two fours and a six. He also bowled for the first time in his international career, a sign that Allan Border was keen to test his player's all-round talents. However, Mark was replaced after delivering three unconvincing overs that cost 21 runs.

He ensured the first impression wouldn't prove lasting when he took his first wicket, Martin Crowe, in the following contest with the Kiwis, at the Adelaide Oval. Although still expensive — he claimed 2–25 off five overs — he showed his worth as a bowler who could make breakthroughs at critical times. Crowe, who'd just reached 50, was steering his side to a threatening total when he offered Dean Jones a catch at mid-wicket. His departure started a minor collapse during which Mark claimed his second victim, left-hander Chris Harris, caught behind by Ian Healy. The visitors made 7–208, a target reached by Australia for the loss of just four wickets. Mark (7 n.o.) and Steve (4 n.o.) added the final touches to the victory.

Mark's performances with the ball outshone his batting in the early matches. By the time the series went into a two-week break from mid-December, Mark had totalled 75 runs from six innings, and taken five wickets, including 3–23 against New Zealand in Melbourne. His batting returns may not have been substantial, but the chances to build an innings were rare because he frequently came to the crease amidst the fury of the final overs. It was impossible to tell if he was battling poor form because he wasn't in long enough to find out. It was hit out or get out.

Nevertheless he was hungry for a long innings when he, Steve, Mark Taylor and Peter Taylor returned from Australian duties to bolster the New South Wales team for the Shield match against Western Australia in Perth.

As he had done two months earlier in the FAI Cup final, Geoff Marsh decided to give his bowlers first use of the WACA's notoriously bouncy pitch after winning the toss. In charge of a formidable attack that included Terry Alderman, Bruce Reid, Chris Matthews and Ken Macleay, Marsh was confident the batsmen could suffer early problems. Although they didn't celebrate a rush of wickets, the West Australians were pleased enough when their rivals were teetering at 4–137 midway through the afternoon session. Another wicket or two, and the home side would be into the tail. A satisfying start indeed. But who would have been bold enough to suggest what would follow?

By stumps, New South Wales were in control at 4–375 following a blistering 238-run stand in just 206 minutes. The Waugh twins had struck! Their partnership, a New South Wales record for the fifth wicket, was simply breathtaking. Mark (128 n.o.) and Steve (112 n.o.) not only took the initiative away from the home side, but crushed it, tearing it into little pieces that drifted away in the afternoon's Fremantle doctor. It was a display that at times crossed the fine border between confidence and arrogance. After describing the bowling attack as 'being reduced to a gibbering rabble', journalist Greg Growden wrote in the Sydney Morning Herald (21 December 1990):

In the end, the partnership became a playful game, with the twins trying to establish who could play the most extravagant strokes, who could get a century first and who could push the fielding cordon back further.

Growden also stated that Mark and Steve 'even determined what bowlers they'd face'.

Mark reached his century off 141 balls. The innings was a delightful mixture of leg-side flicks, cover drives and cuts that continually split the heavily populated off side field. Mark says:

There's nothing better than crunching a cut. The leg-side flick has become my signature shot, but it actually isn't my favourite. I think I hit off the back foot through point nearly as well. Taking a one-handed catch, crunching a cut shot or hitting a six, whether it be off a slow bowler or a fast one, is the best feeling in the game. It's like hitting a great drive in golf or hitting a hole in one. I really felt that most of the time through my innings. Along the way I was just in the zone, almost in a trance, aware of nothing else except batting. I wasn't thinking of anything. I don't know why it happens, it just happens. You're almost on autopilot. It just happens so easily that it makes you think: 'Why can't I do this every time?' Everything just clicked.

When the century-makers returned to the dressing room that evening, Greg Matthews, the next batsman in, made a light-hearted bet with the twins. Undeniably the team's most eccentric player, he'd spent all afternoon with his pads on, watching and waiting. He joked to Mark and Steve that if they remained unbeaten the following day, he'd wear his pads out on the town that night.

Every shot on the second day pushed Matthews a step closer to setting the new fashion trend. As the off-spinner contemplated which jeans would match his leg-wear, Mark and Steve showed no signs of relenting in the middle. Mark enjoyed a double celebration after reaching his 150 — he'd passed 3000 runs for the calendar year.

Within sight of the tea interval, Geoff Lawson decided enough was enough, and declared at 4–601. Mark (229 n.o.) and Steve (216 n.o.) had shared a 464-run partnership in 408 minutes, or little more than a day at the crease together. They'd set a new world record for a fifth-wicket partnership, erasing two legendary names — Don Bradman and Sid Barnes — who'd compiled 405 against England in 1946–47. It was also an Australian record for any wicket, eclipsing the 462 carved by South Australia's David Hookes and Wayne Phillips, against Tasmania in 1986–87.

Mark's century included thirty-five boundaries and one enormous six off Macleay. Geoff Lawson recalls:

> It was some of the most phenomenal batting I've ever seen. Ken Macleay started bowling about two feet outside off stump, and in the dressing room Mike Whitney said, 'Oh, Mark won't put up with that.' A couple of balls later Junior comes down the wicket and hits the ball straight back thirty rows over the sightscreen. Macleay had no idea where to bowl after that.

For the few spectators at the ground, the partnership was a once-in-a-lifetime memory worthy of a gilt-edged frame. Batting of such irresistible quality had rarely been seen throughout cricket's history. In typically humble fashion, Mark says:

> Looking back, it's my individual highlight in Shield cricket. I'd always struggled in Perth. No New South Wales player normally did very well over there, so it came out of the blue. I certainly remember it very clearly. When you're out there playing, you are still just taking each ball as it comes. You don't know what's going to happen next ball, so you never look too far ahead. But once I got to 100, I started looking at the scoreboard a bit and thought, 'A hundred, yeah that's not bad. A hundred and fifty, yeah that's pretty good.' Then when I got to 200 and still saw Steve at the other end I knew we were achieving something pretty special. The fact that we did it together obviously meant it had added significance. It will always stand out in our careers. At the time it was the best innings I'd ever played, and is still right up there with my best first-class hundreds.
>
> The funny thing is we could have gone on and got more. Stephen was very disappointed when Geoff Lawson declared.

'Disappointed' is an understatement. Mike Whitney still laughs at the scenes in the dressing room afterwards.

They come off, and Mark walks in first. The room is full of back-slaps and
pumped-up guys. Mark takes his helmet off, walks over to the mirror and wants
to make sure his hair is still looking good. He doesn't have a blemish, not even a
bead of sweat running down his forehead. It looks like he's just gone out at one
minute past eleven. Then Stephen comes in, he has sweat pouring out of him,
and he's pissed off. He says to Henry [Geoff Lawson], 'Fuck, why did you
declare? We could have got 600!' Who knows, they could have got a thousand!

I just sat back in the dressing room looking at Stephen and Mark in front of
me and thinking, 'Twins who are worlds apart.'

They scored more runs that day than I scored in my whole career.

The final lines in the partnership were written that night when a new fashion statement was made by Matthews. After walking through Perth's streets, quite happily acknowledging the occasional cry of 'Idiot!', he and his team-mates ended up at a night-club where he boasts his protective attire 'was a bit of a bonus because I could crash my way through the crowd'.

It was obvious the partnership would have the media's fingers cracking in anticipation of writing about Mark's Test selection. But the wait continued. After watching Australia take a 2–0 lead in the Ashes with an eight-wicket victory in the Boxing Day Test at the MCG, Mark moved back into the national line-up for a Benson & Hedges match on New Year's Day in Sydney. He may not have been the type of person to make resolutions, but his best performance of the limited-overs series was the first indication that 1991 was going to be the year for new beginnings. He made 62 off 69 balls, the innings described by Terry Brindle of the *Australian* as 'played with the timing of a Swiss watch-maker'. At one stage the home side was in strife at 5–93, but Mark and Simon O'Donnell (71) repaired the damage with a 112-run partnership off 140 balls. Australia ended up winning by 68 runs.

For Mark, it was an all too brief appearance at the top level. While the Test players regathered for the third Ashes fixture three days later at the SCG, Mark flew to Brisbane to play Queensland. He scored 97 in the first innings, and a duck in the second as New South Wales surrendered by 110 runs. In the meantime, the third Test was heading for a draw.

Once again the players jumped from the Test to the limited-overs merry-go-round for the remaining matches in the Benson & Hedges series. The

Australians, having lost only one match of the preliminary games, did not need to win their last outing against England in Melbourne to qualify for the final. However, it was a vital game for their opponents who needed a victory to advance. In a tight finish, Graham Gooch's team fell four runs short after Mark wrecked their hopes by taking 4–37 off 10 overs. Earlier, he'd struck 36 off 46 balls before being run out — Steve was again the batsman at the other end.

After their convincing display throughout the competition, Australia were expected to take just two matches to claim the trophy in the best of three finals against New Zealand. And so it proved. A six-wicket win in Sydney — Mark took 3–29 and was dismissed for a duck, lbw to fast bowler Danny Morrison — was followed by a seven-wicket triumph in Melbourne. In what was an anti-climactic finish for Mark, he failed to take a wicket and was 3 not out when the championship-winning runs were scored.

However, it had been an impressive series for the lesser known twin, who was quickly emerging from his brother's long shadow. In 10 matches, he tallied 176 runs at 22.00 — not shattering figures, but highly acceptable for a middle-order player used to coming in at the death of an innings. His bowling statistics were exceptional no matter how they were viewed. Mark led the averages with 12 wickets at 15.92, and further capped a successful season by taking six catches, the most by an Australian.

His immediate future in the shortened version of the game seemed assured; it was now only the Test scene that tormented him. When he rejoined his New South Wales team-mates to tackle South Australia in Sydney four days later, he was unaware just how close he was to feeling the torment lift because the fourth Test team was to be chosen and announced before the end of the match. At the close of the second day New South Wales were 3–167, chasing their opponent's first innings total of 293. The home side's sound position was strengthened by the knowledge that Mark and Steve would resume batting the following morning. They'd already looked comfortable in a 55-run partnership, prompting considerable chat in the stands. Was it possible to see a repeat of Perth?

The answer was no, but the third day, Monday 21 January, proved to be just as eventful as the epic at the WACA. The twins added a further 91 runs, taking their stand to 146 before Steve fell, caught behind off Colin Miller, who at that time in his career was a medium pacer.

Mark continued his resistance in a three-hour stay that swept him to 112, taking his first-class tally to 7501 runs in 100 matches — a formidable record for a player still to wear the baggy green cap of his country. In contrast to previous moments in his career, his timing was perfect because selectors were choosing the Test team the same day.

That night, he went with Sue to his parents' home. Beverly Waugh always enjoyed the visits of her sons. Their presence sometimes triggered her favourite cricket memories of when her boys were little. She says:

> There was friendship between the [other] parents in the team. Back then, we'd talk about matches the week before, how we were going to go; we'd be organising the lunch, who'd take the champagne, who'd take this and that. It was a real family picnic atmosphere when the boys were little. I think every mother's fondest memories of their children are when they are safe and secure in your little nest.

When Steve visited the nest later in the evening, Beverly discovered one of the hardships of parenting: how to feel happy for one child, yet console another in the same breath. Steve delivered the news that the Test team had been chosen — he was out, Mark was in. Bev says:

> It's just lucky we're not an emotional family. I think we were more excited for Mark than disappointed for Stephen because knowing Stephen's nature, we knew that it wasn't going to be permanent.
>
> One of the good points about having four boys was that it was rare for all of them to come home ecstatic from a game. There was always going to be at least a couple who'd be disappointed, so we learnt not to get too carried away with success.

The following morning the reality of selection struck when a blur of cameras, interviews, handshakes and phone calls greeted Mark at the SCG. It was a difficult situation for the twins and their team-mates who still had a day to play in the Shield match. At lunch, a newspaper photographer asked the brothers to pose together. Although obliging, Steve, when asked to smile, queried what he had to smile about.

'It was very tough on Stephen,' says Mark. 'Seeing him dropped took some of the gloss off my selection. It was uncomfortable for both of us, but he handled it very well. I knew he'd be back.'

Steve maintained his self-belief, acknowledging 'at the time I knew it was the right time to be dropped. Mark had done well in first-class cricket. He was ready to be picked, and I knew he'd do well. It was up to me to accept the challenge to get back in the team with him.'

Not surprisingly, they struggled to concentrate for the remainder of the match. Mark was dismissed for a duck, and Steve managed only a single before joining his brother as one of Miller's six second-innings victims. Chasing 113 for victory off 17 overs, New South Wales finished at 7–83. It was Mark's last Shield appearance for the season, and if everything went according to plan he'd have few opportunities to play for his state for a few years to come.

The night before he headed to Adelaide to launch his Test career, he and Sue enjoyed a quiet celebration with his parents over a bottle of champagne. It wasn't only a new beginning for Mark, but his partner too had to come to terms with what lay ahead. Sue remembers:

> I was so excited for him — that had always been his ultimate goal. There was nothing better in the world for him. It was like winning the lottery. Then I thought, 'Oh my God, what does that mean for me?' I knew Lynette [Steve's fiancée at the time, and now his wife] didn't see Stephen all that often. I can always remember her saying how different it was when Stephen began playing for Australia. She said he was away a lot. I wondered how I was going to cope because I didn't have the children living with me. I'd be on my own. I didn't voice my opinions to Mark, but I did a lot of thinking. Then all of a sudden he was gone. I knew our lives would change. I always remember thinking, 'I can't get there. I should be there.' But I had to work.

Mark, too, had to work. Ten years after telling his high school careers adviser he wanted to play cricket for Australia, he was finally upholding the bold statement. This was the job he'd wanted since he was a teenager — to be a professional Test cricketer.

His new team-mates recall Mark was quiet in the days leading up to the match. He was the centre of media attention, but handled it considerably well

— aside from slight touches of embarrassment that suggested he'd rather be preparing for the biggest moment of his career in a dark alley than on a main drag. At this stage, he had no resentment towards the media. In his simple and innocent way he believed journalists were there to 'write good things about the team'. Who was to know that seven years later press columns would be full of sinister sentences when Mark was preparing for another game against England at the Adelaide Oval.

However, on 25 January 1991 'good things' were all that could be written in describing a performance of rare quality and grace. What had taken his brother 43 innings to climb, Mark had scaled in one — he had reached the heights reserved for century-makers, becoming the fifteenth Australian to record three figures on debut. The adjectives flowed in the media: 'glorious', 'majestic', 'elegant', 'pure' — but for Mark, the word was 'satisfied'. His wait on the outer had been worth it. He had proven beyond doubt that he was not only ready for Test cricket, but would succeed in Test cricket.

The day was full of moments that became priceless anecdotes. In her office at the Kingsgrove Sports Centre, Sue had been 'batting every ball' with her partner while watching Channel Nine's television broadcast. To her horror, as Mark was approaching his century the commentators bade farewell to New South Wales viewers because of news commitments. It was six o'clock Sydney time, half an hour ahead of Adelaide. It was likely Mark would reach his century in a matter of minutes, but how would Sue know? She looked frantically for a radio, but on finding one her fumbling fingers couldn't tune it correctly. Left with no other option, she waited until the sports segment of Channel Nine's news began at about twenty past six. She cheered and breathed a sigh of relief. Mark had made it. She says when he rang later that night 'he was still very, very excited'. Mark recalls:

Before the match, I wasn't really sure what to expect. I was probably unaware of all the pressures that went along with Test cricket, so I didn't have anything to worry about. It was a case of just turning up and playing really. I was more like a kid in his first couple of games just enjoying it and taking it in. I hadn't really got involved in team discussions or any of the important lead-up talks. I just minded my own business. In those days we had a lot of experienced players, so I was just in the background. The innings went very quickly. It actually helped knowing most of the English guys as well from county matches. That sort of puts you at ease when you are playing someone you know pretty well. Makes you more comfortable. Most of the time they were very quiet, didn't say much at all, and when they did say something none of it was negative. I can remember Robin Smith at bat-pad saying to me, 'You can let the handbrake off now. You can give it some.' It didn't seem like a Test match at all, not that I knew what to expect.

Mark finished his first day of Test cricket 116 not out after sharing an unbeaten 145-run partnership with Greg Matthews (29 n.o.). When he returned to the dressing room, Allan Border was one of the first to congratulate him. Border recalls:

It was a fantastic debut. We were in a bit of strife when he was called on to bat, and he just peeled off one of those magnificent Waugh hundreds that he'd become known for. He was ready for Test cricket. I remember making a comment along the lines of, 'Well done, first up hundred, great work.' He just replied with, 'You should have picked me years ago!' He always had confidence in his ability.

Mark says the comment was made in jest. Perhaps he should have been picked earlier — certainly some journalists believed so — but now that his wait was over it was time to look forward. Australia resumed the following morning at 5–269, a much healthier position than when Matthews had joined his novice partner the afternoon before. Their partnership had dug the home side out of trouble, and although they added only a further 29 runs together, they'd ensured England would be chasing at least a reasonable total.

Mark was the first dismissed, bowled by paceman Devon Malcolm for 138. The innings, off just 188 deliveries, included eighteen boundaries, many of which were through the square leg to mid-wicket region or the covers. Bob Simpson remembers:

My initial thought was, 'What a brilliant innings.' Then when I started to analyse it I wondered if the Poms would be as kind to him in the future because they bowled a lot towards middle and leg, which was absolutely fatal. But I don't think there's been a more elegant debut made by anyone. People talk about batsmen like Archie Jackson being such an elegant player, but surely Mark was up there with anyone. It was tremendous to watch.

Australia was all out for 386, Matthews the second-best scorer with 65. In reply, England made 229. Craig McDermott took 5–97, and Ian Healy took five catches behind the stumps. Mark was given four overs, finishing with 0–13.

David Boon (121) led Australia's second-innings charge towards a declaration, while Mark was brought somewhat back to reality when he was bowled by Malcolm for 23. Allan Border eventually called the innings closed at 6–314, leaving the visitors with little more than a day to score 472. Captain Graham Gooch (117) and opening partner Mike Atherton (87) inspired a spirited chase, but when stumps were drawn England were 5–335. Mark bowled only the one wicket-less over, but he did leave a slight impression on the final day, taking his first catch to dismiss Atherton off Bruce Reid's bowling.

The teams travelled to Perth for the final Test, which Australia won by nine wickets. In his only innings Mark scored 26 before falling to Malcolm for a third time. Australia had retained the Ashes 3–0, and unlike some of the team's older campaigners, Mark was part of a winning side in his first series. In the years to follow, success would be common. He says:

> I can't remember much about the celebrations. I can remember having a few drinks in the dressing room with Goochie, Robin Smith and some of the other England players. That was a big thing back in those days. There was time to socialise with the opposition.
>
> My strongest memory is going back to the team hotel nearly straight after the match because we had to have needles for the West Indies tour. I was glad I'd made the tour, but once again I didn't really know what to expect.

A fifteen-man squad had been chosen for the tour which was to begin in mid-February. There would be five Tests and five one-dayers against the world's most powerful team in a region where cricket often contradicted the way of life. Off the field, the slapping of hands in high-fives, wide smiles and rum-stained laughter underlined the happy-go-lucky nature of the people. On the field, they called for blood. After a relatively gentle introduction to Test cricket, Mark boarded the plane for the Caribbean knowing he was about to face a much tougher challenge of both character and skill. Violence in paradise was waiting.

CHAPTER TEN

VIOLENCE IN PARADISE

P arty lights. Palm trees. Curried goat. Limbo queens. Rum punch. Surf. Sand. Steel drums. It had to be the West Indies. For the many tourists who holiday among this vast scattering of islands in the Caribbean Sea, there seem to be few cares in the world. The region is poor, yet the people are rich with character and warmth.

Australia's cricketers first fell under the calypso charm when Ian Johnson led his country to a 3–0 victory in five tests in 1954–55. Between then and 1991, four other sides from down under had toured, but only one, Ian Chappell's 1972–73 visitors, had returned home on top.

Ian's brother Greg was the last captain to enjoy success in a series against the West Indies, when Australia hosted and thrashed them 5–1 in 1975–76. That contest is widely regarded as having inspired a remarkable turnaround in Caribbean cricketing fortunes. For the next twenty years, steel wills and unbridled talent changed the face of the modern game. In the 1980s, under the leadership of Clive Lloyd and Viv Richards, the West Indies swatted aside all international challengers with a ruthless efficiency based on furious pace attacks and murderous strokeplay. They were the undisputed masters of cricket.

Allan Border and his troops were under no illusion as to how difficult a conquest of the Windies would be. In only their second warm-up game, against Jamaica at Sabina Park, Kingston, they received a sample of what lay ahead when Mark and Craig McDermott were both felled by bouncers from the captain, Courtney Walsh. Mark recalls:

Being on my first tour, I was pretty nervous. We'd spoken a lot about what to expect, especially from their fast bowlers. They could be pretty intimidating, even if you were an experienced batsman. We knew we were going to get lots of short stuff, and that we'd all get hit at some stage. It didn't help that the crowd love seeing bouncers flying around, and batsmen getting hit. They actually prefer batsmen getting hit than seeing batsmen doing the hitting.

I can remember the groundsman at Sabina Park telling us before the match, 'This pitch is going to be bouncy, man. It's a dangerous pitch; Mike Gatting's nose is still in here.' [England's Mike Gatting suffered a badly broken nose after being hit by a Malcolm Marshall bouncer in 1986. Afterwards, some cartilage was found in the ball.]

I think I was batting quite well before I got hit. I'd made 30-odd and actually felt quite comfortable. Then I just ducked into a short one from Walsh. It hit me in the back of the helmet, didn't split me open, but made me a little dazed. I went off and came back in after Craig McDermott got split open above an eye. There was blood all over the pitch which made me think, 'This is a bit scary, this is only a tour match.'

Walsh was pretty fired up. He bounced me straight away and got warned off for too much short-pitched bowling. It was an intimidating start.

While McDermott was driven to hospital to receive stitches, out on the bloodstained pitch Mark kept close watch on the rows of stitches that were constantly hurled his way at eye level. He was thankful that apart from Walsh, Jamaica's bowling wasn't very strong. Once the captain was out of the attack, runs flowed readily until Mark became the third Australian, behind Mark Taylor and David Boon, to make a century on that tour. His innings of 108 was the highest score in the match Australia won by an innings and 137 runs. It was the last outing before the first limited-overs international three days later at the same ground.

After Border won the toss, Australia batted first, reaching 4–244 off 50 overs. Dean Jones top scored with 88, and Mark offered stylish support with 67 off 66 deliveries before surrendering to Curtly Ambrose. They shared a 136-run stand for the fourth wicket, a pleasing act of defiance in the lead-up to the first Test. The home side folded for 209, Craig McDermott taking 4–34, while Mark chipped in with the wicket of top-scorer Gus Logie for 65.

Although the victory gave the Australians confidence, the players were prepared for a much more hostile and uncomfortable time when the first Test began at Sabina Park. Mark remembers:

Even going to the ground was scary enough. We'd drive past the Kingston gaol, and see all the inmates standing up and yelling at us, saying things like, 'You're gonna get killed, man. There's gonna be blood, man.' And they meant it. It was the same at the ground, the crowd was very aggressive.

I might have played well in the first few matches, but I knew I had my work cut out to make runs in the Tests. I wasn't very confident at all of having a productive tour. The West Indies had a very good side: Ambrose, Patterson, Marshall, Walsh. Facing those blokes at your throat all day wasn't going to be any fun. And then you saw their batting: Greenidge, Haynes, Richardson, Hooper, Richards, Logie and Dujon, a class player coming in at 7. They had an aura around them. They knew they were the best, and wanted to show it.

I was pretty nervous and was quite happy that the West Indies batted first because I could settle in to the atmosphere.

I clearly remember the 39 I got when I did bat because I was thinking to myself while I was out there, 'How am I going to get runs?' I didn't get too many half-volleys. To be honest, I thought I was out of my depth. I didn't feel comfortable at the crease at all.

It was a scary place. The crowd were right behind the bowlers and screaming for blood. I hadn't experienced anything like it. At the end of the match, I remember thinking how lucky I was to only bat once. I think some of the other guys felt the same way. How could you go in and get runs against that attack?

In his book *Caribbean Odyssey*, Mike Coward wrote that Mark showed 'extreme discomfort against the steepling delivery'. Such observations would gain considerable momentum much later in the careers of both Waugh twins.

Mark could thank leaky covers for the much-appreciated absence of a second innings. Heavy rain late on the rest day seeped through the covers' seams, leaving several significant damp spots on the pitch. The bowlers' run-up at one end had also become a bog. In a desperate attempt to dry the pitch, colourful curator Charlie Joseph set fire to sawdust he'd laid on top of the rolled strip, but he couldn't prevent play from being abandoned on the fourth day. The match finished a draw after a stoic 109 not out from David Boon took Australia to a 107-run lead on the first innings. An unbeaten 104 from Richie Richardson ensured the home side had cleared away the deficit by the time stumps were drawn. Craig McDermott took eight wickets in the match remembered by Mark for the short-pitched barrage that saw 'blokes getting hit left, right and centre'. There were bruised and bloodied bodies on both sides — Boon with a cut chin, Logie a split eyebrow and Haynes with a crushed toe were the worst victims.

The resumption of the limited-overs series gave the players limited time to nurse their injuries. Australia won the second match by 45 runs at Trinidad's picturesque Queen's Park in Port of Spain. Mark scored 16 and took 2–6. The following day the West Indies reversed the result, winning a rain-affected contest on run rate. Mark again made a start before falling for 17. Richie Richardson was his only scalp with the ball.

Mark played a vital part in Australia's series-winning victory in the fourth game, at the delightful Kensington Oval in Bridgetown, Barbados. Sent in by Viv Richards, the visitors relished the small boundaries and quick outfield. Geoff Marsh scored 113, Border 79, and Mark 49 off just 37 balls. Chasing 284 for victory, the West Indies fell 37 runs short. Mark capped off a rewarding day, taking 3–34.

Marsh (106 n.o.) was again the hero in the final match which Australia won by six wickets at the Bourda Ground in Georgetown, Guyana. Mark had his poorest return of the tour, stumped by Dujon off Hooper's off-spin for 7, and taking 1–36 off six overs.

He was also third party in a dispute between Australian keeper Ian Healy and Windies opening bat Desmond Haynes that would simmer throughout the tour. Haynes was obviously upset when given out lbw, hit on the front pad lunging forward to off-spinner Peter Taylor. After standing his ground for some moments, he glared at Healy who'd made a vociferous appeal, then walked off the field. As he passed Mark he said with daggers in his eyes, 'Tell Healy he's a thief!' Later, at the presentation, he asked Mark if he'd relayed the message.

Haynes believed Healy was appealing too much and putting too much pressure on the umpires. Their strained relationship would reach boiling point in the Test series.

Personal conflicts aside, the match was in many ways a sad contest because of surprisingly vocal crowd support for the visitors. Guyana is an impoverished country on the north-eastern tip of mainland South America. While cricket offers its people an escape from the hardship of everyday life, different heritages, cultures and political views to those common on the islands of the Caribbean can lead to unrest in the stands. And so it proved during the one-dayer when the primarily Indian crowd voiced its anti-African feelings against players including Viv Richards. It was Mark's first experience of the cultural divides that are common in many of the world's cricketing countries.

Australia's 4–1 series triumph was a healthy tonic for the remainder of the Test series, but as the West Indies soon proved, it is much easier to be crowned for a day than to be king at the end of five.

The teams remained in Georgetown for the second Test. Amidst a downwards spiralling economy, the West Indians displayed a wealth of talent that belied their performances in the limited-overs series.

After winning the toss and batting on a flat wicket in the middle of a tiny ground with a lightning fast outfield, the Australians were given their best opportunity of the tour to put the West Indians under pressure. However, they were trapped by their defensive attitude and a painfully slow over rate of fewer than twelve bowled an hour. Marsh battled to 94 during five hours at the crease, but the most authoritative innings came from Mark, who scored 71 in nearly four hours. His command of leg-side shots drew praise from team-mates and former West Indian captain Clive Lloyd.

'He's the best-looking leg-side player I've seen in my time,' says Mark Taylor. 'You'd probably compare him to Greg Chappell. Anything drifting into his pads is hit beautifully. It's his sort of strokeplay that brings people to the games.'

Australia ground their way to 348 — a disappointing total considering the favourable batting conditions and the West Indians' reply of 569, dominated by Richardson (182) and Haynes (111). Border's men then crumbled for 248 against a relentless pace attack. Mark made 31 in a scorecard headed by Ian Healy's 47. Haynes and Greenidge quickly rubbed away the 28 runs needed for a 10-wicket victory. Despite the dominance of the home team, talk afterwards centred on one of the more bizarre incidents seen on a cricket field. After being bowled by a Walsh no-ball, Dean Jones began walking from the field, oblivious to umpire Clyde Duncan's call of the illegal delivery. Carl Hooper picked up the ball and ran the batsman out. Under the laws of the game, Jones shouldn't have been dismissed, but continued making his exit. Mark remembers:

> I was next man in. All I saw was Jonesy getting bowled, so I got up, put my gear on, and started to walk out. Then there was a bit of commotion. I don't think any of us really understood what had happened. All I knew was that we were trying to save a Test match. The incident didn't affect my concentration because I thought Jonesy was out. Simple as that. It was only after we got off the field that all the rule books came out and Simmo [Bob Simpson] started complaining. It was just one of those things. In hindsight it wasn't good for cricket because the West Indians were criticised for bad sportsmanship, but we didn't know the rules either, and we might have done the same thing.

While not a student of the laws, Mark was at least aware a new chapter in cricket's history was to be written in the third Test, at Queen's Park. Looking to strengthen their batting, the Australians brought Steve back into the team at the expense of Greg Matthews. It was to be his first Test since making way for Mark during the Ashes. The moment had finally come — the Waugh brothers together, the first set of twins to play Test cricket. Mark says:

> It was good to see Stephen back in the team. And it was good to be back together. We didn't speak much about it, but we hoped it would be the first Test in a good campaign together. There were a few photos taken and the journalists made a bit of a deal of it, but I don't think either of us thought that much about it. It probably won't be until a few years after I finish my career that I'll appreciate just how much the achievement really means.

Their moment together in history's spotlight prompted the obvious articles that recalled Australia's other cricketing brothers — Dave and Ned Gregory; Alec and Charles Bannerman; George and Walter Giffen; Albert and Harry Trot; and Ian, Greg and Trevor Chappell. It was inevitable that the forever popular topic of comparisons between Mark and Steve would also be raised. Yes, they were significantly different. In his five years on the international circuit, Steve had shown himself to be a fierce fighter with immense spirit and application. He respected the game's history and traditions, and had such pride in the baggy green cap that he was never seen in the field without it. Off the field he relished adventure. His life as a professional cricketer offered him the chance to explore the world, visiting places that had once been nothing more than names on geography exam papers. Although the media microscope, forever increasing its magnification on players, was still to examine Mark in as much detail as Steve, it considered the younger twin a more casual person than his brother. He was never ruffled, always composed. An extraordinary talent on the field, an everyday bloke off it. He liked a punt, loved hitting a long drive off the first tee, and enjoyed the simple pleasures of touring such as sitting poolside at the team hotel and sleeping in, one of his lifelong pleasures. He was certainly not an explorer like his brother. The trip to the Caribbean had already established a practice Mark has maintained throughout his career — he never packs a camera nor takes a photo for himself.

Back home, Bev Waugh read the comparisons with interest. To this day, she is somewhat amused by the general observations.

I think Mark and Stephen might even play along with the reports that they're so different and not close to each other. They do not appear to be close at times. I think it's fascinating. It makes people think, makes people talk.

We're not a strange family, but we're different in the way that there's not a lot of emotion shown. Yet when it comes down to it, by gee they really stick up for each other. But they won't do it if they don't believe in each other.

Over the years the comparisons in the media have led to judgements that haven't always been favourable to Mark. At times it has been suggested he would have been a more successful player if he'd had Steve's resolve. Or he would have been a more worldly and widely educated person if he'd shared Steve's sense of adventure. Such views were only tiny specks of thought on the West Indies tour, but they'd grow to more damaging proportions in the years that followed.

Despite their differences, the twins have always shared the desire to 'play their guts out', as Mark describes it, for their country. Their passion and determination needed to be accompanied by some good fortune if they were to succeed on their opening day together, 5 April 1991.

Rain washed away hopes of a memorable beginning. Only 31 overs were bowled during the first two days, prompting the teams to shift the rest day in the hope of achieving more play. The Australians, sent in after losing the toss, reached 294. Steve made 26 before falling caught behind to Walsh, and Mark enjoyed some luck, dropped twice in his top-scoring innings of 64. By this stage, Clive Lloyd had become an avid fan, writing in the local paper *Trinidad Guardian* (9 April 1991):

Australia must be delighted to have found such a young and exciting player who is maturing with every innings he plays. I am positive Mark will provide lots of enjoyment to cricket lovers. His talent is rare and we shall be hearing much more about him in the future.

In reply, the West Indies were dismissed for 227. Merv Hughes claimed four wickets, but for Mark the most notable dismissal was that of Ambrose — caught Border, bowled M.E. Waugh, 53 — his first Test wicket.

Neither Waugh batted in the second innings as Australia played out time for a draw, finishing at 3–123. Mark laughs:

Once again it was good to get away with one bat. It was that sort of tour where I was hoping to limit the damage to myself and my batting. It seems strange to say that, but it was like that in those days. We weren't as confident as we are now. We were just trying to hang in there. But I was pretty happy with the way I batted in the first innings. At that stage I was gaining a bit of normality to my batting. There weren't as many bouncers, and there wasn't as much intimidation from the crowd.

The fourth Test in Bridgetown was truly remarkable — the West Indies won by 343 runs after leading by just 15 on the first innings. On a pitch that played a few tricks, including a Marshall delivery that almost ran along the ground to bowl Border, both batting line-ups proved fragile on the opening day. Sent in, the home side collapsed for 149 against an attack led by McDermott and Hughes who took four wickets each. The innings was remembered as much for an ugly exchange between Healy and Haynes as for the sterling efforts of Australia's pacemen. After surviving a confident appeal for caught behind, Haynes was quick to indicate that he believed the ball had flicked his hip. Standing at close range in the slips cordon, Mark watched Healy respond in less than polite terms, suggesting that the batsman should leave the umpire to 'do his job'.

An astonishing outburst from Haynes followed. He tore off his helmet with furious exaggeration, then stormed towards Healy for a toe-to-toe exchange that ended with the wicket-keeper blowing a kiss to his sparring partner.

It understandably caused much interest in the press box. Verbal taunts, or sledging, had long been part of the game, but from the late 1980s, the increased scrutiny of television close-ups and numerous replays ensured the over-analysis of players' behaviour. Haynes later told the *Barbados Sunday Sun* (21 April 1991) that :

Healy used abusive language to me and I'm sorry it looked as though I was protesting because he appealed. It was just a matter of me showing Healy where the ball hit me on my shirt but then he started cursing me.

The Australians considered it an outrageous outburst considering Haynes was one of the most talkative players when the West Indians were in the field. Mark remembers:

Their fast bowlers didn't talk a lot — they lived more by actions than words, but you could always hear the other players yapping away in the slips. Viv Richards and Desmond Haynes were the most frequent, always chirping. They didn't talk at you, but more across you, saying things like, 'Come on Amby, he's your meat. Get him on the step-ladder,' meaning dig in the short balls. It can help do the job because it can be easy to start thinking, 'Yeah, they're really after me.'

But sledging is so overrated. If someone says something to me, it's going to make me more determined not to get out. What's it matter? It's totally irrelevant really. Sometimes it can get into the minds of the players and they lose their concentration, but apart from that it's just like 'Sticks and stones ...'

I don't think I've been accused of going over the top — I wouldn't say I've said nothing in my career because I have. I've chirped, certainly not personal things, but I've tried to break the concentration of players. Plus if three or four other players are saying something, you generally join in.

Since I've been playing, the Australian team has been accused a lot of sledging. But it depends what you mean. If you mean you are attempting to unsettle the opposition players' mental skills, then sure we sledge, but if you mean being immoral, unethical or personal, then we're against it. The whole issue is totally out of hand really. Who cares if someone calls you a name?

I wouldn't say we overstep the mark at all. I'd say it's been overdone by the media. We play hard but fair. Guys like Heals [Ian Healy] were as tough but as fair as you could get.

The Haynes–Healy incident put additional fire in the West Indians' bellies when they took to the field defending their meagre total. Just 50.1 overs later they were back in the dressing room with the pads on after Australia had been humbled for 134. Mark remained unbeaten on 20. He'd been a helpless spectator at the bowler's end, watching his team-mates come and go like postmen delivering mail. They lost their last seven wickets for 35, an appalling collapse that handed the incentive back to their rivals who took swashbuckling advantage in an innings of 9 declared for 536. Gordon Greenidge was the hero, his 226 the fourth double century of his Test career. Mark was the most successful bowler, taking 4–80 off 28 overs, including his most prized scalp at that time, Viv Richards. The fifth player to be given a chance with the ball, Mark wasted no time in bouncing his rivals. His theory was simple: 'Definitely give it, because you're going to cop a lot back. Try not to be intimidated and show them you're going to get right in there and fight.'

Unfortunately the warrior-like attitude didn't transfer to the batting crease as the visitors folded for 208. The dismissal of Marsh off the first ball he faced from Ambrose, was the 'worst lbw decision' Mark had ever seen. He recalls it 'would have missed leg-stump by about 10 feet!' Despite a defiant 76 by Mark Taylor, the Australians never recovered. Mark was bowled by Hooper's off-spin for three, his exit part of a middle-order and tailend capitulation that saw the last six wickets fall for 18 runs.

Amidst the cacophony of blowing horns and beaten instruments, some of which were nothing more than rusting tyre hubs, the West Indians celebrated their successful defence of the Frank Worrell Trophy. Border and his shell-shocked men were left to wonder what had gone wrong. Mark acknowledges:

*The West Indies is a hard place to play because it's so casual, you get in a
relaxed mood and feel like you're on holidays. It always lulls you into a false
sense of security, then all of a sudden you're at war. It's really hard to change
from one to the other.*

*We didn't say it, but deep down we were probably thinking we couldn't win.
Looking back, I think a lot of the players didn't want to be there. We were just
hoping to get through the tour without getting too much damage to our
reputations. We were always going to struggle with that attitude.*

*But having said that, we were playing the best team of the era, and one of
the best teams, if not the best I've ever played against. Most batsmen don't like
it at the best of times when you've got the ball whistling around your ears, but
when you've got four quality bowlers at you all the time, you have to be
switched on because you know you could get hurt. You're not scared, but you
are intimidated. That can wear batsmen down because there is just no let-up.*

*Their bowling was exceptional, especially Marshall, Ambrose and Walsh. I
think Ambrose is the best fast bowler I've ever played against. Even back then he
was relentless. Never bowled any bad balls. If he wanted to stop you scoring, he
could do that; if he wanted to step up and intimidate you, he could do that too.
He could do everything. His first and last ball would generally be as quick as
each other. But then he'd have the off day, occasionally he'd have a patch of
bowling where he wouldn't look interested, but you were never sure when he'd
come back and step up a gear. He could do it whenever he liked. Even when he
bowled badly he was still very hard to play.*

*Walsh was a bit the same. I didn't really see Marshall at his peak, but he had
swing, pace, control — a great bowler, and a good bloke who was friendly off the
field. Generally there was a good mixing between the teams, although Heals and
Desi had their problems. But since then they've developed a great respect for
each other.*

Australia had one final chance to dent West Indian pride and restore some of
their own in the fifth Test at the Recreation Ground in St John's, Antigua, an
island of black power, dreadlocks and more than occasional wafts of smoke
drifting from the mouths of the Rastafarians delighting in the 'magic of the herb'.

It was also home of the King, Viv Richards, who was desperate to see his
side remain unbeaten for the series. Having been humiliated by Australia at the

beginning of his career, he saw every match as a chance to exact ruthless revenge for those early days. However, the Antiguan leader's desire wasn't matched by deed. He fell for a duck and 2 as his side stumbled to a 157-run defeat that was due in no small part to a dashing 139 not out by Mark in the opening innings.

Australia won the toss and batted first on the truest pitch of the series. Half-centuries by Mark Taylor, Allan Border and Dean Jones were the warm-up acts before Mark moved onto centre stage, at first looking like a reluctant shuffling showman unaware of what to do with his cane and straw hat. His routine lacked rhythm, but once he acknowledged that he was being 'hit on the hands from pillar to post', he decided to dance. His view was simple: 'Stuff this, I'm going to play my shots here and get runs as quickly as I can.' Occasionally backing away to the leg side and hitting short deliveries over backward point, he showed the innovation and aggression that Australia's batsmen had lacked throughout the series. His 188-ball innings included eleven fours and three sixes. His dominance was described in the *Sydney Morning Herald* (29 April 1991) by journalist Patrick Smithers:

He sneaked up on his opponents without warning and, before they realised it, struck a telling blow. There are few more fluent or unobtrusive scorers in world cricket than Mark Waugh.

When Waugh came to the wicket Dean Jones was on 20 and in one of his rampant one-day moods, having already dispatched Carl Hooper over the sightscreen and out of the ground for six. For the first time in the series, an Australian batsman was threatening to steal the initiative from the West Indies bowlers.

Yet, by the time Waugh posted his century with a cheeky paddle around the corner to the ultra fine-leg boundary, Jones was, comparatively speaking, dragging his feet on 70.

Mark reached his hundred in two hours, thirteen minutes. Australia compiled 403, and after McDermott and Hughes maintained the momentum, taking four wickets each, the home side were in trouble, trailing on the first innings by 189.

Despite seeing their team in trouble, the good-natured Antiguan supporters continued to treat the game as a carnival. In one stand, heads bobbed and bodies swayed to the periodic blasts of music from 'Chickie's Disco', and in another section of the ground, renowned character 'Mayfield' entertained his followers with his smart one-liners while wearing a variety of costumes that ranged from the most formal grey suits to scuba-diving outfits. Four years later, when the Australians were in the early stages of their successful campaign, Mayfield walked around the ground with a piece of meat attached to a vinyl LP that displayed the words: 'Record at Steak!'

However, Mayfield had serious competition for the title of crowd favourite. In the same stand that housed 'Chickie's Disco', the loose-limbed, dreadlocked figure of 'Gravy' always had something to match his rival. In 1991, he had caught the attention of the masses when he appeared as Father Christmas, but in Australia's second innings he bore no gifts after he changed into a nurse's uniform. Walking to the crease with his side 5–184, Mark was stunned to discover the makeshift Nightingale was at his side checking his pulse. One ball later, he was on his way back to the dressing room after being trapped lbw by Walsh!

However, Mark Taylor (144) ensured his team didn't lose their advantage. Australia was dismissed for 265, leaving their rivals to chase an impossible target of 455. When Terry Alderman trapped top-scorer Gus Logie in front for 61, the Windies were all out for 297. Victory to Australia. Mark believes the West Indians may have 'eased off a bit', and regardless of any reasons the locals may have given for the loss, nothing could be taken away from Border's men who could return home with a spring in their step.

Mark finished on top of his side's Test averages with 367 runs at 61.17 After seven Tests, he was beginning to feel more comfortable in the team. His first Test season had been a success, but just as any premiership-winning football coach will tell you, 'it's harder to defend your trophy than win it for the first time'. Many athletes talk of the 'second-year blues', the time when results aren't as spectacular as during a successful debut season. That was the challenge facing Mark. He had to maintain, if not improve, the high standard he'd set. After enjoying a relaxing three-match tour in Bermuda, he returned home eager for a rest during the winter, but knowing the 'hard yards' were just about to begin.

CHAPTER ELEVEN

DROPPED

A long summer — the only way to describe the 1991–92 season during which Australia would play a five-Test series against India, the Benson & Hedges World Series against the wristy men from the subcontinent, and the West Indies, then back up as defending champions for the fifth World Cup, the first to be hosted in the southern hemisphere. All by the end of March. A very long summer indeed.

Once again administrators decided to stage all matches in the FAI Cup before the Sheffield Shield season commenced. Mark scored an unbeaten 40 and Steve, a man-of-the-match earning 74 to help New South Wales to a six-wicket win in the opening encounter with Queensland at the Gabba.

The two innings were teasers for an exhibition of batting brilliance two days later against Victoria at North Sydney Oval. Short boundaries, especially square of the wicket, and a pitch as flat as busy Miller Street outside the ground ensured it would be a day of heavy run-scoring. Geoff Lawson surprised no-one by electing to set a target after winning the toss, but he had a few extra canyons in his brow after the departures of openers Steve Small and Mark Taylor left the home side 2–9. However, by the time the next wicket fell, New South Wales were 249! The recovery was inspired by twin centuries from twin brothers. Steve (126 from 133 balls) and Mark (112 from 123 balls) demoralised a strong attack which included Merv Hughes, Paul Reiffel, Tony Dodemaide, Damien Fleming and Simon O'Donnell — all Australian players at the time or of the future. Labelled the 'Blues Brothers' by numerous members of the media and fans, the pair set a new state record partnership for the third wicket, a record that had only been established the previous summer by Mark and Trevor Bayliss. Their strokeplay was exhilarating, and on one occasion dangerous, when a six from Steve almost hit an elderly gentleman in the crowd. Their performances drew praise from Lawson and his rival captain O'Donnell, whose simple quote in the following morning's *Daily Telegraph* (16 October 1991) said it all: 'You'd have to go a long way to see guys bat better than that.' They completed a memorable day by taking two wickets each in the 100-run win.

Although Mark and Steve failed to repeat their eye-catching form in the final two matches, New South Wales won the trophy after defeating Western Australia by 69 runs in the final, at the WACA Ground.

The Blues returned to Perth a week later to open their Sheffield Shield campaign. The twins ignited hopes of repeating history when they launched into the bowlers on the second afternoon, but just as it appeared the home side would be staring at another massive partnership, Steve was trapped lbw to Terry Alderman, ending a 98-run stand in only 77 minutes. However, he'd already made 115, and Mark joined the triple-figure club the next day, reaching 136. New South Wales claimed first innings points.

After scoring 19 against Victoria, and 0 and 60 against Queensland, Mark had one final innings before the Test series began. In the unlikely warm-up venue of Lismore, he enjoyed a close look at the Indians who resembled anything but a Test team as they lost to New South Wales by an innings and 8 runs inside three days. Mark enjoyed three valuable hours at the crease, making 79 before playing a ball onto his stumps off wiry paceman Javagal Srinath, whose new-ball partner, Manoj Prabhakar, would prove to be a much more slippery customer off the field a decade later when cricket's corruption scandal erupted. The Indian all-rounder would eventually play a key role in almost bringing Mark's career to a premature end, but in the quiet surrounds of a country town in far north New South Wales, it was impossible to imagine the seedy world of illegal bookmaking was lurking in the shadows.

Despite form that had only returned one win in four matches on tour — the victory was against the New South Wales Country XI — the Indians paraded enough talent to suggest that although success against Australia might be rare, tight contests mightn't be. Led by one of the world's most delightful stroke-players, Mohammad Azharuddin, the tourists had considerable batting strength in Ravi Shastri, Dilip Vengsarkar, Kris Srikanth and an eighteen-year-old destined to become one of the game's greats — Sachin Tendulkar. The team rested much of their pace hopes on Kapil Dev, a bowler of immense class, but they were weakened by a lack of quality spinners, an enormous surprise considering the country's unmatchable reputation for producing slow-bowling magicians.

Australia won the first Test, in Brisbane, by 10 wickets after Craig McDermott reduced the Indians to 6–83 on the first day. The red-headed paceman was man of the match with returns of 5–54 and 4–47. In his only innings Mark struggled to 11 off 37 deliveries. He eventually edged a ball from Srinath to wicket-keeper Kiran More after nearly an hour at the crease. His poor showing and the convincing early season form of Tom Moody prompted selectors to overlook Mark for the start of the Benson & Hedges series.

Returning to New South Wales for a Shield match against South Australia at the Adelaide Oval, he showed his lapse was perhaps only temporary with innings of 94 and 24. They weren't, however, enough to prevent the Crow-eaters from securing a 10-wicket win.

In the second Test, the Boxing Day outing in Melbourne, Mark again only had one chance at the crease. He cruised to 34 off just 46 balls, but was unluckily dismissed, caught behind off Ravi Shastri's gentle left-arm spin after the ball ballooned into the air from the faint bottom edge of a sweep shot. His innings included two fours and one six in an entertaining but all too brief display. Australia won by eight wickets.

The disappointments for Mark continued when he was dismissed for 18 and 5 at the SCG in the third match of the series. The Indians used interesting tactics in both innings when they placed a fieldsman at short mid-wicket and another just forward of square about 10 metres from the bat — moves that made Mark think about the placement of his leg-side strokes.

The drawn encounter is remembered most for Shastri's double century (206) against an attack that included a bulky blond Victorian making his Test debut.

Shane Warne took 1–150 off 45 overs, a harsh introduction for a player who would dramatically change modern cricket's approach to leg-spin.

Despite his indifferent performances, Mark was called into the Australian squad for the second half of the Benson & Hedges series after Bruce Reid tore side muscles that forced him out for the remainder of the campaign. Australia beat India 2–0 in the final — the West Indies had a disastrous series, winning just two games and forcing a tie in a third — but Mark's contribution was weak. In his five matches which allowed just three innings, he totalled 20 runs at 6.67 and failed to take a wicket. However, the worst was still to come in the fourth Test, at the Adelaide Oval, scene of so much joy previously for the younger Waugh twin.

Sent in to bat after losing the toss, the Australians crumbled for just 145. Mark was lbw to Prabhakar for 15 in a decision that could have easily gone the other way.

Under pressure when they took to the field, the Australians were soon frustrated by the rejection of a number of lbw appeals, which Mark believes were just as tight as the one that led to his dismissal. Annoyed after one such shout, Mark ran past umpire Peter McConnell between overs and uttered quietly, but loud enough to be heard, 'How about being consistent with your lbws?'

He repeated his suggestion at McConnell's prompting, then resumed his position in the slips cordon, where he says the umpire 'just stared at me for about half an hour'.

The Indians were dismissed for 225, a first-innings lead of 80. Mark went to the crease with his team in a more comfortable position in the second innings, but they still weren't out of trouble at 4–277. Not only was it an important time for the side, but also a critical moment for Mark who'd scored just 83 runs in five innings. He remembers:

> I didn't know if I was close to being dropped, but I knew it would be a good time to get a few runs. I was facing Kapil Dev. Peter McConnell was the umpire. The first ball hits me on the hip, goes to Tendulkar in the slips, and I'm given out caught. Out! I couldn't believe it.

The night of McConnell's decision, Mark and vice-captain Geoff Marsh were dropped for the next Test. At the time there was no standard procedure to tell an axed player of his fate. Sometimes he was informed by team management, but there were other occasions when radio news bulletins or journalists became the bearers of bad news. Mark and Marsh were told of their demotions by Bob Simpson before play began on the final day of the Test. The rest of the team was informed soon afterwards in an announcement that Mike Whitney recalls left every player stunned:

> *We were doing warm-ups before the day. We got into a circle before we started to do the fielding, Simmo calls everyone in and says, 'Well, we've picked the team for the fifth Test. I just thought I'd tell you that Geoff Marsh and Mark Waugh have been dropped.'*
>
> *The look on everyone's faces was just amazing. We still had a day of the Test to play. The timing was unbelievable. It was as if someone had just walked out and shot someone in front of us, then expected us to continue our warm-ups with no worries.*
>
> *That is the only time I've ever seen Mark Waugh rattled. He just lost it for about five minutes doing the fielding drills. He was throwing wide of the stumps and fumbling. I watched him for a while, he got it back together, but it was the only time in my life that he has looked ordinary when I've been with him.*
>
> *At the time we were a real big family of hard-core cricketers.*

A furious Allan Border stormed back to the dressing room, and with only about 10 minutes remaining before he was due to lead his team onto the field he told twelfth man Paul Reiffel to get his whites on. The surprised Victorian did as he was told after Border said he was not going out with the rest of the team. Simpson suggested the skipper change his mind, but Border was in no mood to listen.

A few moments later, Marsh, in what was to be his final day of Test cricket, led Australia out of the dressing room. Border stayed behind to ring Lawrie Sawle, the chairman of selectors in Perth.

He later returned to the field as Australia won an enthralling contest by 38 runs. There were many occasions when sloppy fielding helped the Indians; several catches were dropped, including one by Mark.

That night, as the team prepared to go to the airport to head for Perth, Border stayed behind. Whitney recalls:

The feeling was really strong, and the guys in the team were pretty angry.
Before we left, I sidled up to Allan and said, 'Need anybody to stay with you?'
He told me, 'That's very honourable, Big Roy, but I don't want to see you out of
the side too.' I told him if I walked onto the bus and asked the players who
wanted to stay, the whole team would have come back. But Allan said, 'No, just
let everything get settled.' We were so much behind him. Allan really stuck up
for them.

David Boon was made vice-captain, and placed on stand-by for the main job, but Border eventually arrived in Perth, still shattered by the removal of Marsh, his close mate, and Mark, widely considered by the players as the most gifted cricketer in the team.

Mark was humbled by the support he was shown by his leader. He acknowledges Border was more concerned with the treatment of Marsh, veteran of fifty Tests, but his staunch backing of a still-developing player showed loyalty beyond the call of duty.

The incident came nearly a year to the day after Mark had made his scintillating Test debut, at Adelaide. In tones of considerable understatement, he says:

Yeah, Adelaide, holds a couple of interesting memories for me. I probably
deserved to be dropped, but then again I thought it would have been easy to give
me another chance. I was very disappointed, but I knew I'd be back.
It made me realise the fine line professional sportsmen walk. One minute
you can be winning a grand slam, then the next you're out in the first round.

Mark was dumped because selectors felt it was necessary to remind him of his responsibilities. It was deemed he hadn't put a high enough price on his wicket throughout the summer. In his widely read articles in the Fairfax press, the 'flabbergasted' Peter Roebuck led a chorus of those surprised by the decision, the following appearing in the *Sydney Morning Herald* (30 January 1992):

Nevertheless he is a splendid player and to drop him in his second season in Test cricket, a time regularly associated with sudden and temporary losses of form, will one day be seen as a mistake of colossal proportions. In losing Waugh, Australia are losing a man who takes wickets, catches superbly at slip, runs people out and can bat with technique and class — qualities never in abundant supply.

His game is not in decline, it is merely suffering from a blip from which recovery could have been expected imminently. Still, this is not the end for Waugh, merely a reminder that no-one can take anything for granted.

In an ironic postscript to Mark's dissatisfaction with the umpiring, the Indians complained loudest about the standard of the men in charge: Peter McConnell in his twenty-second Test and Darrell Hair in his first. Perhaps they had good reason — eight of the 10 lbw dismissals in Adelaide went against the visitors.

The only positive from Mark's dumping came for New South Wales who welcomed back their prized stroke-maker for the Shield match against South Australia at the SCG. The blessing for the home side was the bane of the visitors as Mark regained touch in emphatic fashion, top scoring with 158 from 220 balls in his team's only innings. New South Wales won by 30 runs.

Mark made 13 and an enterprising 76 in the next outing, a draw against Victoria in Melbourne. While his state appeared well placed to push for a spot in the final, Mark left behind his whites to play his role in the first World Cup to feature coloured clothing, white balls and night matches. It was the largest tournament of its kind yet, involving nine teams playing in Australia and New Zealand over a four-week period from late February.

Australia were expected to feature prominently, but never recovered from a poor start after losing their opening match to New Zealand by 37 runs at Auckland's Eden Park. Mark scored just 2, but he was in good company as only David Boon (100) and Steve (38) passed thirty against a thinking attack that used off-spinner Dipak Patel to open the bowling.

Mark was dropped for the next three games — a nine-wicket loss to South Africa in Sydney, a 1-run win over India in Brisbane, and an eight-wicket defeat by England in Sydney — before he returned for the remaining four preliminary matches in which his best return was a contemptuous 66 not out from just 39 balls in Australia's 128-run thumping of Zimbabwe, at Hobart's Bellerive Oval.

In a major shock that inevitably led to questions being raised and fingers pointed at various players and the coach, Australia didn't reach the semi-finals of the tournament that was eventually won by the talented but unpredictable Pakistan, led by all-rounder Imran Khan. Mark has no fond memories of the first and least successful of his three World Cup experiences, which yielded 145 runs at an average of 36.25 with an imposing strike rate of 101.40.

We just played badly from the start, but full credit to teams like New Zealand who worked us out at home. I was really disappointed when I got dropped, I thought I should have at least played one of those games, but as it turned out we lost two of the games, and went right off the boil. It was just one of those times when things didn't work out for us.

Even if we'd played well, Pakistan would have been hard to beat. They had such a brilliant but fragmented side. Ever since I've played against them, I've seen guys come to training in different coloured tracksuits and shirts, they wear different hats and helmets when they play — there's just no consistency to anything in their cricket, but you catch them when they're at their best, and you really have to play well to beat them. They had some great players — Imran, Aamir Sohail, Javed Miandad, Wasim Akram.

They also had Salim Malik, another player who would soon enough invite Mark to visit cricket's dark side.

The tournament over, Mark, Steve, Whitney and Peter Taylor had one last duty to perform before their season was finished — New South Wales had qualified for the Shield final against Western Australia in Perth. Despite the boost to their player strength, the visitors lost by 44 runs. The twins, however, yet again left lasting impressions with their third pair of centuries in as many Shield outings in the west. Mark (163 and 19) and Steve (113 and 68) shared a first-innings stand of 204 for the third wicket. They finished first and second in their team's first-class averages for the season: Mark with 841 runs at 70.86. He was the Shield's second highest run-scorer behind Victorian Dean Jones.

While it was a bonus for New South Wales supporters that he was able to play seven matches, a forever expanding international program meant Mark would play fewer interstate games in the future if he returned to the Test team. Bankstown officials had already seen the catch-22 that the twins experienced. Although Mark and Steve were always keen to play more grade matches, higher commitments made appearances almost impossible. However, the

Waugh name wasn't altogether lost from the suburban playing fields. In the same season that their brothers were taking on the world, Danny made the New South Wales Under–17s, and Dean belted 227 against Hawkesbury, a first-grade record for Bankstown.

After such a busy and, at times, emotionally draining season, Mark had every right to take a break, but no sooner had he played the Shield final when he was packing his bags to renew ties with Essex.

Essex, defending county champions, happily welcomed back one of their favourite imports, who wasted no time warming the scorebooks. Mark scored 120 against Kent in his second championship match, which came just a fortnight after a superb century against Northamptonshire in a Benson & Hedges Cup qualifying game in early May.

However, his season's highlight didn't come until early July when he blasted an unbeaten 219 off only 243 balls against Lancashire at Ilford. He shared a 347-run third-wicket partnership in 64 overs with Nasser Hussain (172), eclipsing the county record set forty-one years earlier by P.A. Gibb and R. Horsfall.

The amicable and productive partnership was in contrast to an incident that happened during Mark's previous stint at Essex, when he and England's future captain crossed swords in the middle of the pitch during a match against Kent at Royal Tunbridge Wells. Mark recalls:

I was bowling just before tea, and I think Nasser thought that I wasn't trying hard enough, but I've never not tried, especially with the ball. He reckoned I just wasn't putting in and told me to bend my back a bit. We had a bit of an argument and I told him, 'Mate, you worry about yourself, and I'll look after me. I'm doing the best I can. How about you shut up and go back to the slips?' He didn't like being told what to do, and I didn't like where he was coming from. He kept it going a bit. I'm not one to argue or get into heated discussions, but I knew he was wrong.

He spat it in the dressing room during the tea-break, and ended up getting suspended for a match after having a blue with Mark Illot.

He was out of order, and certainly rubbed people up the wrong way.

I suppose Nasser had the reputation of being a spoilt brat. He was always ambitious — I don't know if he didn't show enough respect for others, but there was an arrogance there. He knew he was good, and he didn't care who got in his way. He'd rub people up the wrong way because he was so ambitious and also probably lacked a bit of respect for senior players.

He was just a cocky young kid, but I always thought he might go places because he was different from the other guys. He always had that ambition, he wasn't happy to settle back and go with the flow. He was always fairly vocal and had his opinion on things. He had quite a good cricket brain, but some of the other guys didn't agree with what he said because he was so outspoken. They thought he should keep quiet because he was a younger player.

He had a bit of a temper. You had to handle him the right way. He was probably self-centred, didn't worry about anyone else — as long as he got what he wanted was all that seemed to matter. Some people got in his way, he burnt a few bridges, but it probably didn't worry him.

He has definitely matured a lot, and I enjoyed batting with him, especially during the Lancashire partnership. I get on well with him now and respect him as a player. I think he's a good player and a pretty good leader too. He always gives 100 per cent, and he's got a bit of an Aussie attitude — he never gives up and expects that from other players. He wants to see them having a go. If they fail, they fail, but at least they've had a go. He's good for England. He's going to back himself and his players. You've only got to see his demeanour on the field — he doesn't take anything from anybody. If someone has a go at him, he'll have a go back.

He's also willing to do the hard work. I've never seen a bloke bat as much in the nets as him. I'd get to training early, walk out to the nets, and he'd already be there. You sometimes couldn't get a hit because of him. We had our disagreements, but you could never question his hunger.

Nor could Mark's desire be doubted for the remainder of the 1992 season. In all, he scored four county championship hundreds, his last two an unbeaten 125 against Gloucestershire at Southend and 138 not out against Worcestershire at Kidderminster. He totalled 1253 runs at 78.31 from fifteen matches. He also took 21 wickets at less than 30, and snared 25 catches. His all-round efforts helped lay the foundations for Essex's successful title defence. Furthermore, they reached the semi-finals of the Benson & Hedges Cup, their best return in the limited-overs arena. However, Mark was unable to enjoy the celebrations towards the end of the season — he was in Sri Lanka, hoping to win back his Test position.

CHAPTER TWELVE

SRI LANKAN DUCKS

S ri Lanka is an endearing country. It floats alone beneath the south-eastern foot of India, and presents a mix of exotic beauty, rich religious tradition and, sadly, consistent and considerable civil unrest. Since 1983, Sinhalese-led governments have been the target of the largest minority groups, the Sri Lankan and Indian Tamils who make up about twenty per cent of the population. The Liberation Tigers of Tamil Ealam (LTTE) frequently launch violent campaigns aimed at creating their own nation in the north. At times, suicide bombings and assassinations have forced this small country, shaped like a teardrop, to cry for lives lost, buildings destroyed and spirits broken. It's estimated more than 65 000 people have been killed since the conflicts began. Despite the sadness, communities continue to smile with a warmth that hovers well above the temperature in this equatorial and political hot-spot. Visitors are smothered with kindness and hospitality. And when visitors happen to be Test cricketers, the kindness and hospitality is of regal proportions.

After gathering in Darwin for a week-long camp aimed at dusting cobwebs off players who, unlike Mark, had enjoyed an off-season, a thirteen-man

Australian squad headed to the island nation to play three Tests and a limited-over series. The most notable omission was Steve. Victorian Wayne Phillips, Geoff Marsh's controversial replacement for the last Test against India in Perth, had also been overlooked. Selectors had decided to gamble on the elevation of Tom Moody to the opener's spot. The West Australian all-rounder had taken Mark's position at number 6 in Perth, but the reshuffle meant there was a middle-order vacancy. Confident and in form after his successful county season, Mark seemed the logical replacement. He recalls:

I was really looking forward to the tour. There were going to be very different challenges to the West Indies. No real quicks, just lots of good spinners on slow, turning pitches I'd never experienced. I thought coming straight off the back of Essex would be good because I was one of the few blokes who'd had time in the middle. I thought I had a pretty good chance of regaining my spot, and making a few runs against one of the minnows. They had a fair team, but I didn't think we'd have trouble with them.

Mark's county experience showed in the opening tour game against the Sri Lankan Board President's XI in Kandy. Described by Fairfax journalist Patrick Smithers as a 'class above his team-mates', Mark top scored with 74. His innings included seven boundaries and one six off only 96 balls. Allan Border (33) was the only other top-six batsman to pass 20 in the total of 9 declared for 278. The innings offered the Australians their first look at a 21-year-old off-spinner with a most unusual rubber-wristed action that would cause much controversy in the years to follow. Muttiah Muralitharan took 1–79 off 22 overs, not outstanding figures, but his mysterious deliveries were enough to prompt considerable analysis in the visitors' dressing room. Lack of time in the three-day match prevented Australia having a second innings, leaving them significantly underprepared for the first one-day international, held three days later at the Saravanamuttu Stadium in Colombo.

Despite the absence of a solid lead-up, Border's men performed well, reaching 5–247. Mark scored 31 off 30 balls before throwing his wicket away at the death. Earlier, openers Mark Taylor (94) and Tom Moody (54) laid the foundations for the reasonable total. However, Aravinda de Silva (105) steered his side to a four-wicket victory.

The teams moved to Colombo's Sinhalese Sports Club for the first Test, which proved to be one of the most enthralling contests ever played between the countries. Chasing 181 on the final day, the Sri Lankans appeared to be heading for victory when they were 2–127, but in a stunning collapse in the final session they lost 8–27 to hand their opponents an unexpected win. After falling caught behind for 5 in the first innings, Mark looked in formidable touch when he batted again, reaching 56 before edging a ball to wicket-keeper Romesh Kaluwitharana off medium-pacer Gamini Wickramasinghe.

In the following provincial game against the Southern Districts XI in Matara, Mark sent a warning to the Sri Lankans for the final two Tests when he scored a wonderfully composed 118 — his 36th first-class century — in three and a half hours. The Australians' most consistent batsman with 284 runs at 56.80 was seemingly at home on the slow and low damp pitches. His enviable form threatened to be one of the most dangerous obstacles for the Sri Lankans when the second Test began at Colombo's Ketterama Stadium. However, in a match that fizzled to a draw after more than a day's play was surrendered to rain and poor light, the gloomy weather reflected Mark's surprising misfortunes — he bagged a pair, lasting just five balls in the first innings before popping a catch to bat-pad, then falling lbw for a golden duck in the second after playing back to a skidder and presenting Muralitharan with the first of his many hundreds of Test wickets.

The next two one-dayers, sandwiched between the second and third Tests, brought mixed results for Mark and Australia. The Sri Lankans won the first match, in which Mark made only 10, but his mini-run of poor returns ended when he cruised to 52 off 63 balls in his side's five-wicket success in game three.

He remained confident when Australia headed into the final Test, at Moratuwa's Tyronne Fernando Stadium. Rain disruption again prevented any chance of a result, but amidst the downpour there was one humiliating drought — the runs had completely dried up for Mark as he suffered the embarrassment of his second pair. He was bowled by medium pacer Rami Ramanayake after lasting just five balls in the first innings, and was caught behind off the fourth delivery he faced from Dulip Liyanage in the second. Four Test ducks in a row in the space of fifteen balls. An ignominious result for a batsman whose team-mates said was hitting the ball very well at training sessions. Mark reflects:

Anyone can get out for a duck. It doesn't matter who you are. You cop a good ball first up and it's all over. Or you just might react a bit slowly or you're not accustomed to the pitch, or whatever. It can happen. There's nothing the matter with getting the odd duck, but four in a row was hard to take. I just couldn't believe it. Fair enough the pair in the second Test was possible, but to do it again next up was pretty shattering. My head just wasn't right. I began thinking about how I was going to get my next run. Everything was just hard. It's funny how the mind can play tricks on you. All of a sudden you look around and can't find any gaps in the field, every ball seems to be too good for you, and you start thinking, 'What am I doing here?' I tried not to let it worry me, but every batsman likes getting off the mark, don't they?

I remember feeling pretty sort of numb when I got my fourth one [duck]. I couldn't really believe it, but in a way I expected it to happen. It's a bit like a golfer with the yips. Even tap-ins are hard.

There were a number of factors that made it hard to get runs. The practice facilities weren't good, and the pitches could be a real challenge. Richard Hadlee once said Sri Lanka is the best place in the world to bowl because the overnight storms and constant high humidity mean there's always moisture about. I've always had troubles in Sri Lanka. They're my bogey team. It happens in a lot of sports. Tennis players, footy teams all have opponents they struggle against. It's disappointing. You get a few bad decisions, play some bad shots, everything just seems to go wrong.

He finished with 61 runs for the series at an average of 10.17, perhaps his worst return at any level of cricket. Team-mates light-heartedly labelled Mark 'Audi', in reference to the European car manufacturer whose symbol is four circles. They also suggested Mark was lucky there wasn't a fourth Test in the series or he could have been labelled 'Olympics' or 'Rings', after the famous five-ring logo.

He joined in the banter, leaving his inner doubts on the field, a characteristic that impressed his captain. Allan Border says:

If it was me, I'd almost be suicidal. But Mark was taking it all in his stride. He just gave the impression that, 'Hey, it's a game of cricket, let's get on with it.' I always thought I was a bit too tense about my cricket, and I always thought it would be good to have a bit more of the Mark Waugh in me.

Mark's tour could only be described as unsuccessful, and Australia's 1–0 series win as unconvincing. Perhaps the most significant moment of the tour happened away from the field at the Taj Samudra hotel in Colombo, when Dean Jones received a phone call in his room from a former Indian cricketer who said he wanted to discuss a business proposition.

Jones met the cricketer in the hotel foyer, and was introduced to another man who claimed to be a bookmaker. The bookmaker told Jones he had 'narks' in every international cricket side in the world. These 'narks' were paid by the bookmaker in return for providing regular information about team tactics and pitch and weather conditions. The bookmaker discreetly opened a cake-tin full of US dollars, and also revealed a mobile phone, which he said could be used to contact him.

Jones rejected the approach as 'dodgy', and reported the meeting to Border, David Boon, Bob Simpson and Australian team manager Dr Cam Battersby, all of whom agreed with the player's decision.

Mark felt that had this been communicated wider than this it may have had an impact on the events when Mark and Shane Warne were approached by a bookmaker in Sri Lanka two years later.

The Australian Cricket Board's *Player Conduct Inquiry Report* that resulted from inquiries undertaken by Queen's Counsel Rob O'Regan between December 1988 and February 1999 states:

> *No more was thought about the situation and it was not mentioned in the tour manager's report at the end of the tour. However, Bob Simpson stated that all the players were told of what had occurred and of his strong disapproval of any such approaches.*

This is a matter of contention with Mark. He says:

> *I can't remember anything about it, nor can Warney. I was pretty young then and in the background minding my own business. I remember vaguely someone saying something about Dean Jones getting offered some money, but I didn't have a clue what it was for, or what it was about. And I certainly didn't hear Bob Simpson warn the players about this particular incident, yet in the O'Regan report it said that we all knew about it, which in my view is totally*

wrong. I, for one, didn't have a clue. I didn't know anything about it at all. All I
knew about bookmakers was in racing really.

To say that we knew what we were getting into was wrong. Definitely not
right. That disappointed me. If I'd been warned, I would have taken the advice.

There is some confusion as to when Simpson's alleged warning may have occurred. In his autobiography, Shane Warne writes of Australia's 1994 tour to Sri Lanka:

Apparently, Bobby Simpson, our coach at the time, has said somewhere that he
told us at a team meeting to be on guard against people offering gifts. I have no
reason whatsoever to doubt his word, but it certainly didn't register with me.

Whether this reference in fact relates to the 1992 tour is open to conjecture. The passing of time was an obvious problem for Mr O'Regan during his inquiry, which included interviews with 64 players and officials. Among other duties, the Queen's Counsel faced the arduous task of collecting information more than six years after the incidents occurred.

In the context of what would follow in international cricket, it was unfortunate that the approach made to Jones wasn't mentioned in Cam Battersby's tour report. As Mr O'Regan wrote:

... it was to an extent understandable but regrettable that the tour manager's
report did not record the events as it may have been of assistance in briefing
later teams about the dangers of becoming involved in such matters.

The fact that the events weren't mentioned showed administrators had less concern about the corruption issue than they presently do. This adds weight to the argument that Mark could understandably believe he was doing nothing wrong when he later accepted an offer in 1994.

When Mark left Sri Lanka in September 1992, little did he know that four ducks in a row wouldn't be his greatest cause of anguish in the teardrop nation. At this stage he needed only to worry about his on-field form causing a disruption to his career. He returned to Australia knowing that his Test position was surely far from secure for the five-match series against the West Indies.

His preparation began with some rare grade appearances, including a match against Sydney University, which will be remembered for Steve's destructive 141 and Mark's haste to watch the running of Australia's weight-for-age horse racing classic, the Cox Plate at Moonee Valley. Mark had backed the popular chestnut Super Impose, trained by Lee Freedman. Eager to watch the event, and knowing Bankstown were strolling towards victory with Steve in command at the other end, Mark lifted the tempo, but played one aggressive shot too many, and walked from the field with his team in sight of the win. Despite being dismissed, there was a silver lining — he was in time to watch the race. In one of the most eventful Cox Plates in history, the heavily backed Naturalism, stablemate to Super Impose, fell after tangling with Sydeston. Super Impose, brilliantly ridden by jockey Greg Hall, galloped to success ahead of Kinjite and Slight Chance. Mark recalls the winner 'paid about twenty-five dollars' — one way to sweep aside the disappointment of losing his wicket. Eight years later when cricket's match-fixing accusations were at their peak, some critics absurdly used Mark's profitable afternoon in grade to underline his love of gambling and to question his character.

After winning the FAI Cup the previous season, New South Wales, aided by the early availability of their international players, could have been viewed as short-priced favourites to continue their success in the newly-named Mercantile Mutual Cup competition. However, in their opening game they were crushed by eight wickets by Western Australia at the WACA. Mark fell lbw to Bruce Reid for 2. In his following outings before the Sheffield Shield season began, his returns were 55 from 53 balls and 2–23 in a 111-run win over South Australia in Adelaide; 1 and 0–15 in an 11-run victory over Queensland in Brisbane; and 39 off 43 deliveries against Victoria at the SCG in a 'no-result' match because of rain.

The weather also affected the start of the Shield match between New South Wales and Victoria. Mark relished some valuable time in the middle, scoring 88 in the first innings, but failed in the second for 2 when Shane Warne lured his good mate out of the crease for Darren Berry to complete the stumping. The match ended in a draw.

After making 46 and 35 in a five-wicket win over Western Australia in Sydney, Mark was given the tremendous opportunity to show selectors that his Sri Lankan performances were nothing more than a slight stumble when New South Wales hosted the West Indians at the SCG. If there had been any doubts about his form, they were blasted away by an unbeaten 200 in nearly seven hours. Captain Mark Taylor also scored a century, 101, against an attack that was depleted from the mid-afternoon of the first day when Curtly Ambrose twisted his ankle. Nevertheless, the visitors still boasted formidable strike power with Courtney Walsh and Patrick Patterson.

Mark gave three chances after he reached 100, but his blemishes couldn't dampen the style of an innings that included twelve boundaries off 304 deliveries. His elegance prompted one old-timer watching from the Bradman Stand to suggest, 'He could play in a dinner suit, Mark Waugh,' an ironic statement considering Mark's dislike of being in the spotlight at formal occasions.

Forced to follow on 290 runs behind, the West Indies saved the match by making 9 declared for 507, a vast improvement on their first innings of 183. It was their last hit out before the first Test, in Brisbane. Mark had guaranteed his spot, but still faced the uncomfortable prospect of going into the encounter with the possibility of earning the mooted nickname, 'Olympics'. The pressure increased when he walked to the crease with Australia in trouble at 2–21 following the dismissal of Mark Taylor and Steve on the opening morning.

A leg-side flick off paceman Ian Bishop not only dispatched the ball through the mid-wicket field, but took with it the fears of another failure. On a good batting strip, Mark coasted to 39 before occasional off-spinner Carl Hooper took a hot return catch from a scorching drive. Allan Border (73) ensured his team a respectable but not satisfactory total of 293.

An unbeaten 157 by left-hander Keith Arthurton dominated the West Indian reply of 371, a lead of 78. David Boon (111) and Mark (60) provided the starch in Australia's second innings of 308, which left new captain Richie Richardson and his team-mates needing 231 for victory. Their hopes quickly evaporated after Craig McDermott (4–35) and Bruce Reid (2–39) cut through the top order. If it wasn't for Richardson (66) the West Indies would have crumbled to defeat, but they held on to be 8–133 when stumps were drawn. It was a psychological victory to Australia, but the momentum was halted by the start of the Benson & Hedges series, which included Pakistan as the third team.

The Australians began poorly, losing by nine wickets to the West Indies in Perth. Mark top scored with a hard-fought 36 off 80 deliveries in a team total of just 7–160, which had seemed likely to be much less after the score had crawled to 4–50 at the halfway point. The visitors won the match with nearly twelve overs to spare.

Fortunes swung dramatically in the next encounter between the teams, at a rain-sodden SCG. The match was reduced to thirty overs a side. Dean Jones (21) and Mark (17 from 25 balls) were the chief scorers as the home side battled the seaming conditions to finish with 101 all out. In a remarkable run-chase, the West Indians folded for just 87. Mark took 1–13, his wicket, Ian Bishop (11), one of just three batsmen to reach double figures.

Mark wasn't needed to either bat or bowl in Australia's eight-wicket win over Pakistan at the Adelaide Oval, but he soon returned to front-line combat for the final game before the resumption of the Test series. Facing a crowd of nearly 75000 under lights at the MCG, Mark had his best match of the tournament.

He top scored with 57 from 70 deliveries in a meagre team total of 8–198, but unexpectedly his main contribution came in the final stages of the West Indian innings when the visitors held the match firmly in both hands. At 2–158, with Brian Lara and Richardson at the crease, the result seemed inevitable. However, in his most rewarding display of medium-pace bowling in either form of cricket, Mark demoralised his rivals, taking 5–24 off six overs. Lara (74), Richardson (61), Arthurton, Junior Murray and Anderson Cummins were all victims. Australia won by 4 runs, and Mark was an obvious choice for man of the match. Mark Taylor, who was stand-in skipper for four matches during the series when Allan Border was sidelined with a hamstring injury, believes Mark is 'one of those rare blokes who can turn a match by doing anything'. The grinning Taylor recalls:

We'd have some nicknames for him with the ball — ones that I can't say. We used to call him Golden 'something' because he had the knack of coming on and just getting a wicket when you needed one. He was the sort of guy who could bowl you an innocuous delivery to get you a wicket, then he could bowl you a jaffa. Even when he started bowling spin later in his career he had the knack. Shane Warne mightn't have turned one for half an hour, then Mark comes on and turns one a foot that gets you a wicket. Then he'll bowl three overs of tripe, so you get him off. But that's the sort of cricketer he is. Then you add that to the fact he can win a match with his batting, and any bloke like him who can change a game with a bit of fielding is priceless.

The true value of his batting was written in gold three days later when he returned for his final Shield appearance of the season, against South Australia in Adelaide. In the match celebrating the competition's centenary, Mark recognised a century of his own when he batted brilliantly, making 164 from just 186 deliveries. The speed at which he built his innings allowed New South Wales to declare at 5–399 before the end of the first day. The Blues eventually won by 9 runs.

He carried his form into the first two days of the second Test, at the MCG. Border decided to bat after winning the toss, but found himself walking to the crease with his side in trouble at 4–115. David Boon, Taylor, Steve and Damien Martyn had all been and gone, leaving the Australian captain with Mark as his last recognised partner on a pitch that both teams expected to provide inconsistent bounce on the fourth and fifth days.

Knowing another quick wicket or two could send the Australian innings into a tailspin, the West Indies lifted their intensity with some ruthless short-pitched bowling.

The two batsmen, the fearless warrior and his daring follower, refused to be intimidated. The only sign of weakness in the early stages of the partnership came from wicket-keeper David Williams who missed a stumping chance when Mark was 23.

As the partnership grew, so did Mark's willingness to take the challenge to the bowlers. On several occasions he repeated what he had done two years earlier in Antigua by backing away to give himself room to cut and deflect bouncers over the off side, including over the slips. Sometimes his efforts ended in embarrassment when momentum from air swings left him in no-man's-land well outside leg-stump. However, such failures to connect were rare, and only had the effect of increasing the frustration of Curtly Ambrose, Ian Bishop and Courtney Walsh, who struggled for answers against the novel, but risky tactic. When they directed short balls closer to the body, Mark would either hook and pull the ball between fine leg and mid-on, or he'd bend at the knees and sway out of the way. He recalls:

When you bat, most of the time the idea is to score runs as quickly as you can. That's what batting is meant to be about, isn't it? There are some people who thought I was backing away because I was scared, but it was just a way to score runs. It can be pretty hard to constantly hook and pull, especially on an inconsistent pitch like the MCG was, so I thought it was a safer option to sometimes go over the top on the off side. You could see the bowlers were pretty annoyed every time I did it, so why not continue with it while it was working? Yeah, it was premeditated but it worked. Blokes like Ambrose used to get angry if a single was scored off them, so if you could annoy them with something different, you knew you could get on top of them.

By stumps on the first day, Mark (63 n.o.) and his captain (51 n.o.) had added 112 runs. More heroics came the following day against an Ambrose-inspired bowling line-up that relentlessly attacked with a mixture of bouncers and yorkers, but rarely a half-volley or full toss. Border remembers:

We had to face the new ball in the morning. It was probably the hardest hour and a half of Test-match cricket that you'd ever want to face. I can remember talking about it with Mark between overs. We were both saying, 'Geez, how tough is this?'

It was becoming a more difficult wicket, and the bowling made it even harder. It was just typical West Indies — getting into that zone of bowling short of a length. At that stage of his career Mark was hooking, but they had two fieldsmen out on the hook, so the percentages dropped a lot.

When he started playing those backing away shots, improvising as only he could, sometimes I closed my eyes and thought, 'Geez, I hope he gets through this.' And he did. They were giving him a really hard time but it didn't seem to worry him.

Batting with Mark could be pretty funny because generally he wouldn't say that much between overs, and then he'd come up with something like, 'Oh gee, how good a shot was that!' He'd give himself a wrap, or he'd bag the bowling saying something like, 'This bloke's bowling pies.' He'd make some real throwaway, off-the-cuff comment, which was quite good because it could help me relax, and I'd walk away with a lightened load. Sometimes he'd come up and say: 'Oh geez, I got away with that one!' He could be self-effacing as well as patting himself on the back.

He often didn't give the impression to the outsider, but he was as tough and competitive as anyone. That innings against the West Indies took a lot of guts and character.

Mark enjoyed another stroke of good fortune when he was dropped at 71 by the luckless Williams. It was the last chance he gave before raising his bat for his third Test century, which was greeted with a standing ovation from nearly 30 000 fans.

Soon afterwards it was a case of third time lucky when Williams finally held on to a ball Mark edged off Ambrose. He had scored 112 from 234 deliveries after five and a half hours at the crease. Most importantly, the 204-run partnership with his captain had taken Australia from a precarious position to one of considerable strength. Border finished with 110 in his side's total of 395, which proved too great a target for the West Indians to overhaul — they were dismissed for 233 after McDermott again proved the chief destroyer with 4–66.

The 162-run advantage was worth much more on a pitch that was starting to behave as expected. A good indication of its inconsistency came when Boon was first man out in the second innings for 11, bowled by a ball from Phil Simmons that crept through below knee height. The Australians fought hard to reach 196, Damien Martyn top scoring with an unbeaten 67, while Mark took an hour to make 16 before surrendering to Courtney Walsh.

Shane Warne, relishing the conditions at his home ground, exploited the visitors' weakness against leg-spin bowling by taking 7–52. The West Indians were rolled for 219, presenting Australia with a 139-run victory, and a surprising 1–0 lead in the series. After such an irresistible showing, would Border's team dare think of claiming the Frank Worrell Trophy? Mark recalls:

> Obviously we were taking notice of what was being said. But deep down I knew it was still going to be very hard to beat these blokes. We knew there was a lot of work to be done, but we felt the pendulum was swinging our way a bit after the first two Tests, so there was no reason why we couldn't push them all the way.

Their hopes were further lifted by the venue for the next Test — Sydney, a spinner's pitch with a reputation for breaking the backs of even the most persistent pacemen. However, bowlers of all kind and creed struggled on a lifeless surface that rolled out the red carpet for the batsmen. Brian Lara (277), Richardson (109) and Steve (100) all scored centuries in a rain-affected match that saw the completion of only the first innings of both teams. Mark, who scored 57, recalls his missed opportunity:

I really threw away a hundred that innings. I was feeling really comfortable, then hit a ball which I thought had passed Carl Hooper at short mid-wicket, but he stuck out his hand, grabbed the ball and threw the stumps down. I was pretty annoyed with myself. It was one of those things where you can't believe what has happened.

I was pleased for Stephen that innings. He was batting at 3, and had been copping a lot in the press. They reckoned he wasn't suitable in that position and had too many troubles against the short ball. You know, I'd like to count how many times over the years that the media has had a go at Stephen about his handling of the short ball. I reckon he'd come out on top a lot more often than he's failed. It's a bit like the image I have for playing soft shots. You get out once or twice, then all of a sudden you're tagged with a reputation forever.

It was disappointing the match ended the way it did because we knew Sydney should have given us a really good chance. The pitch was just too dead, and there was no way we were going to get on top with Lara batting the way he did. He's great to watch when he gets going. He's one of the best in the game, but not as good as Tendulkar.

For the second time in the summer, any momentum the Australians may have built up through the Tests was halted by the Benson & Hedges series. Mark continued his consistent returns, top scoring with 54 from 72 balls and taking 1–23 in a 7-run loss against the West Indies in Brisbane. Australia won their next two matches against the disappointing world champions, Pakistan. Mark's limited contributions were 12 and 1–24 in Melbourne, and 11 in Sydney.

The first final at the SCG is remembered for an unusual exchange between two players. Not long after coming to the crease, Dean Jones requested that Curtly Ambrose remove a long white sweatband from the wrist of his bowling arm. The annoyed Antiguan reluctantly obliged, then proceeded to take 5–32, wrecking Australia's hopes of reaching the West Indians' tally of 8–239. Mark top scored with 51 before a direct hit from Richie Richardson caught him short of his ground while trying to steal a quick run. Australia were dismissed in the fiftieth over for 214. Many in the crowd of 38 000 left the ground that night wondering if Jones' request had significantly affected the outcome. Reflecting on the incident, Mark simply says, 'You don't get Amby worked up. What's the saying? It's best to let sleeping dogs lie.'

As had been the case throughout the preliminary matches, Australia struggled for runs in the second final, at the MCG. Tight bowling — Ambrose again led the way with 3–26 — restricted Australia to 147 all out, a target reached with considerable difficulty by the visitors who had only four wickets in hand at the finish. Mark had a disappointing game, being run out by Gus Logie for 8 and failing to take a wicket. However, it was a small blip in a series that had been personally rewarding. Mark finished the 10-match tournament with 259 runs at 28.78 and nine wickets at 17.67. His batting strike rate of 68.8, one of the highest among the leading run-scorers, reflects how the limited-overs game has evolved in recent years. Mark acknowledges:

The batting is much more dynamic these days. More risks are taken, especially early on. Back when I started, 200 to 230 was a good score, but these days you generally need at least 250. Right at the very start of my career we had Geoff Marsh and David Boon, who were very good one-day batsmen at the time, but if you look back at their strike rates, they were only in the 60s. Strike rates these days push 100, although the one-bouncer-an-over rule has given the bowler more of a chance, and the scores showed that last summer [2001–02].

Everything is a lot faster. You can't carry fieldsmen like we used to a bit. The fielding is a lot better, and the players are a lot more versatile. Nowadays everyone can do a bit of everything — batting, bowling, fielding. You have to be good at at least two of the three things. I think we had a good one-day side back then, but we would have struggled with the way the game is played today.

Despite their loss, the Australians remained hopeful of pressing their rivals all the way in the remaining Tests. They would win the Worrell trophy if they claimed the fourth match, in Adelaide. Defeat would mean the series would be decided in Perth — a situation that would certainly favour the visitors on the notoriously hard, fast and bouncy surface of a WACA pitch.

So it seemed the city of churches would decide the fate of a contest that had been one-sided for twenty years. Would Border, in the final stages of his career, finally shake his Caribbean rivals' hands as a winner? Sadly for the Australian captain, the match in Adelaide proved that there can be an almost undetectable gap between success and failure.

The West Indies won the Test by one run, the smallest recorded margin in Test history. Mark remembers 'it was not a great game for me personally' — he scored 0 and 26 and took one wicket — but he'll never forget the last day when a 40-run tenth-wicket partnership between Tim May (42 n.o.) and Craig McDermott (18) nearly claimed the impossible.

Chasing 186 for victory in a low-scoring match, the Australians had slumped to 9–144 when McDermott joined his defiant partner. Mark recalls:

We didn't think we had a chance, but then when we started getting closer, the West Indies started to tire. Tim May was frustrating them with a really good defence. By the time we were down to about 20 to get, I started thinking that we might be an outside chance. Everyone was really nervous and sitting in the one spot — it's an unwritten rule that no-one changes their seat in those situations. AB [Border] was really tense, he was playing with a ball. You could tell how much it meant to him. We were on the brink of a great achievement.

Then it was all over. Craig was given out caught behind off a short one from Courtney Walsh. It was a really tough decision for Darrell Hair. One of those decisions that was probably right, but could have gone either way. When Craig first came in we asked him if he'd hit it. At first he said, 'Nah, nah, no way. I missed it.' Then a while later he agreed it might have brushed his glove on the way through. The decision was such a fine line. The thing I remember most is how devastated AB was. He was shattered, probably more than the rest of us because people like myself knew we'd have other chances to peg the Windies back. I really felt sorry for him.

It was really quiet in the dressing room. We were just sitting around not saying much. It was just one of those moments in sport and one of the intriguing things about a Test match — fortunes can change so quickly. You think you've got it, then you have one bad session and the match has swung the other way.

Fortunes not only swung for a session and the match, but for the series. In the decider at the WACA, the Australians were thumped by an innings and 25 runs in just two and a half days. It was a cruel result considering how tight the whole summer had been.

Helped by a green pitch which added to the glint in their eyes that had been evident since leaving Adelaide, the West Indians let their pacemen loose against a line-up that simply couldn't withstand the constant pressure exerted by the world's best attack. Mark scored 9 in a depressing first innings total of 119 in which Ambrose took 7–25. He fared only slightly better the second time around, scoring 21 out of 178, and although he bowled well, taking 2–21, there was no reason for even a thin slice of satisfaction. He recalls:

I remember seeing the wicket before the game. It was really, really green, and I thought, 'Geez, it's going to be hard work playing these guys on this. Their eyes are going to light up!' It was going to be almost impossible getting runs against 6 foot 7 [2 metres] blokes on that pitch. And it was.

We just couldn't handle them. They were just too good. Amby was unbelievable. He's just the sort of bloke who'll put the ball in the right spot. He knew there was bounce there, but didn't get carried away — he just kept that up his sleeve and made us play. Undoubtedly the best bowling I've ever faced.

Those West Indian teams at the start of my career could just grind you down physically and mentally. Every run could be an effort, every ball even.

If we'd got a good batting wicket we could have pushed them. It was disappointing because we were so close to winning the series, then all of a sudden we're not even in the game. We were gone. It was a disappointing way to finish, but we found out then that the West Indies were beatable. There'd been a bit of a changing of the guard, and they didn't look as strong as they had been. That was the good thing to come out of the series. We knew we had a good chance next time we played them.

David Boon had been the outstanding batsman for Australia throughout the series, scoring 490 runs at 61.25. Mark tallied 340 at 37.78, took four wickets at 21.00, and with the exception of wicket-keeper Ian Healy led the way in the field with 6 catches.

There was little time to recover from the gruelling series. Just a fortnight after licking the wounds that were opened in Perth, the Australians were playing in New Zealand on a six-week tour that would have a substantial impact on Mark's career.

CHAPTER THIRTEEN

EVERYTHING OLD IS NEW AGAIN

Heading into his first tour of New Zealand, Mark had amassed 1038 runs at an average of 34.6 in nineteen Tests. He'd scored three centuries and been dismissed for seven ducks. He'd also been dropped from the side, but returned one match later. All in the space of two years. To say the least, it had been an eventful introduction. And more was to come across the Tasman before the Ashes tour beginning in April.

The Australians won the opening Test at Lancaster Park, Christchurch, by an innings and 60 runs, but Mark contributed little to the match, making just 13 before edging a ball to wicket-keeper Adam Parore from off-spinner Dipak Patel. The second Test, at Wellington's Basin Reserve, ended in a draw after rain allowed less than an hour's play on the opening day. Once again, Allan Border's side batted only once, and once again Mark barely had time to settle in the middle. He departed for 12, caught and bowled by Michael Owens.

There had been little joy in Mark's recent stints at the crease. In his last six innings, he had tallied just 81 runs. However, those numbers only indicated part of the story. There was growing concern among the selectors back in Australia, and the tour selectors — Border, Mark Taylor and Bob Simpson — that Mark's figures just didn't add up. How could someone bat so well against the West Indies, yet struggle against the weaker bowlers from New Zealand and Sri Lanka?

Prior to announcing the team for the final Test, at Auckland's Eden Park, Border told *Sydney Morning Herald* journalist Patrick Smithers, 'I think he's smart enough to realise that he's got to start producing against all sorts of attacks on all sorts of wickets and that he's wasting his talent.'

Yet again, the soft dismissal argument had been raised. After that comment from Border, it wasn't surprising that Mark made way for Damien Martyn in a match the Kiwis won by five wickets to level the series. Mark reflects:

I didn't think I was going that badly. Only a few Tests before that I'd scored a hundred and a fifty against the West Indies. I think the selectors both at home and on tour had a different mentality then. If you weren't scoring runs you were out. Simple as that. That made it really hard for me to have a bit of confidence in them because being dropped for the second time in a year made me think selectors weren't going to muck around with me for too much longer. I really didn't know where I stood. Even when I'd first come into the team I was on my own really. No-one sat me down and told me this or that, or what to expect. There wasn't as much communication with team management and players as there is now. Those days you were on your own a lot more, but that's just the way it was back then. Most sports were like that. No-one really knew any different, there wasn't as much team framework, and it was more a case of fending for yourself.

Today, it's a lot different. You have your meeting with Trevor Hohns [Australian chairman of selectors] each year when you get your contract, and you have the chance to discuss any problems or issues. It's changed for the better now. It's a lot more comfortable for a new player to come into the squad. In the early days of my career you certainly didn't get a phone call from the selectors or the captain or the coach. Once you were out of the team, you were out of the team. That was it. So I was very disappointed with what happened in New Zealand. I was still playing reasonably well and thought I deserved more of a go. It was tough to accept, but once again I thought I just had to make runs.

Mark's dumping raised speculation that he'd be overlooked for the Ashes. However, his fightback received a most unexpected boost when he was promoted to open the innings at the expense of David Boon in the first one-dayer, at Carisbrook, Dunedin. As he walked out to bat, it seemed everything old was new again because his former New South Wales Combined High Schools partner, Mark Taylor, was keeping stride with him. It was also a significant turning point in not only Mark's career, but the direction of Australian cricket in the limited-overs arena. Allan Border recalls:

We needed to inject something new into our game. We'd played a very similar game plan since the World Cup in 1987, but it was probably time to inject something new into the mix. I just felt that if we got off to a good start, a bit of a flyer at the top of the order, it was amazing how it could snowball for the rest of the innings. Whether it was good management or good luck, we thought Mark could play that role. He could play all different roles. He could be one of the greatest sloggers you'd ever want to see if he needed to go after the bowling, and he had some opening experience. Because of all that, he fitted the bill.

The decision proved an immediate success as the two Marks launched a change of direction in Australian one-day cricket with a 95-run stand that was dominated by the less experienced of the two openers. Mark raced to 60 from 75 deliveries before falling to the medium pace of Willie Watson. Border, watching from the dressing room, was pleased. Everything he expected could happen, did happen. Mark showed a willingness to go over the top in the early overs when the tight fielding restrictions were in place, and on several occasions he frustrated the bowlers with his inside-out approach of hitting balls directed at leg-stump over and through the cover and long-off region. It was a successful habit that would torment bowling attacks well beyond New Zealand's shores.

Taylor top scored with 78 in a healthy scorecard of 4–258. Led by a four-wicket haul by Tony Dodemaide, Australia tore through their rivals, who at one stage plummeted to 7–52 before the tail added a little respectability in a still miserable total of 129.

It was a much tighter contest at Lancaster Park two days later when the visitors won by just one wicket in a low-scoring affair. Mark gave Border further reason to smile by compiling 57 from 80 balls on a difficult pitch. The innings, the highest of the match, showed another dimension of Mark's game. Border says:

> There's criticism of some players that they don't always play the conditions, even in one-dayers. Sometimes in one-day cricket you play on wickets that might be seaming or turning — they're not always going to be flat belters, although the crowds always want to see runs scored. From his very early innings as opener, Mark showed he was smart enough to adjust his game accordingly. If he recognised it was a flat belter, you'd probably see him going hard at the bowling as early as the second over. But if it was a more difficult wicket, say Melbourne where you can get spongy bounce, he'd rein it back in. He did that in New Zealand too. That separates the real quality players from just the good.

After failing in the third encounter, won by New Zealand at the Basin Reserve — he was bowled second ball by Danny Morrison for a duck — Mark broke through for his first international limited-overs century in the fourth game of the series, at the Trust Bank Park in Hamilton. His 108 from 131 deliveries included seven fours and a six, but the feature of the innings was precise placement. On numerous occasions New Zealand captain Martin Crowe moved players just a few metres in a bid to plug apparent gaps, but no sooner had the field been changed, than Mark would caress deliveries through the new holes where fieldsmen had originally been standing.

Crowe enjoyed some revenge when he was just as impressive and cunning during his innings of 91 from 101 deliveries that sealed a three-wicket victory for his team with just two balls remaining.

Australia won the fifth and deciding game by 3 runs in yet another contest relished by Mark, who top scored with a run-a-ball 83. The nonchalant two-hour innings was far and away the highlight of the Eden Park encounter. For the third time in four games, the result wasn't known until the final over. Chasing 8–232, New Zealand appeared gone after they had scraped their way to 8–175, but an enterprising 52-run stand between Gavin Larsen and Chris Pringle took the home side to within a whisker of winning. Mark says:

Over the years, the New Zealanders have always been very hard for us to beat, especially in the one-dayers. They seem to lift themselves to play us. That team mightn't have been full of stars, but they had some determined players who always seemed to play above their ability. I've always held New Zealand in pretty high regard as a competitive fighting team.

Mark was undoubtedly the outstanding batsman of the series. His return of 308 runs at 61.60 was well ahead of Crowe, the second heaviest scorer with 195 runs at 48.75. The most significant statistic was Mark's strike rate of 82.80. Border's wish to create 'a flyer at the top of the order' had come true.

While Mark's Test performances were still not as consistent as selectors considered they should be, there was certainly no concern over his limited-overs form. Since the beginning of the Sri Lankan tour, he had scored 50 or more in seven of his last seventeen innings, a solid return that was boosted by his elevation to opener. Mark acknowledges:

The New Zealand one-dayers gave me a lifeline. After being dropped from the last Test I was a bit worried about which way I was heading, but then AB came up and said, 'Would you like to try opening? You haven't had much of a hit, and the Ashes are coming up, so it might do you a bit of good.'

I was really keen on the idea because opening is the best position to bat in one-day cricket. I don't like waiting around for too long at the best of times, even in Test matches, so it's good to get going right at the start. It suits me because I can just play at my own pace.

I think changing to opener sealed my spot in the team for the Ashes. If I hadn't had much of a go during that New Zealand series, I really don't know if I would have been fortunate enough to get picked.

Mark's doubts were understandable. His limited-overs form against the Kiwis had obviously enhanced his Ashes prospects, but regardless of how he performed, it would have been a strange move by selectors to leave out a player who'd proven during his seasons with Essex that he thrived in English conditions. As Crowe suggested at the end of the series, Mark and Dean Jones, who was considered another fringe candidate, 'picked themselves'. Crowe was only partly right — Mark was bound for England, but Jones had been cast aside.

Arriving in Sydney after the New Zealand tour, Mark was greeted with the news that New South Wales were on the brink of winning the Sheffield Shield final against Queensland at the SCG. Victory would complete the 'double' after the Blues had beaten Victoria in the Mercantile Mutual Cup final the previous month.

Although Mark had played a limited role in the campaigns — he played three Shield matches and four one-dayers — he shared in the success of his state team-mates. From his earliest days at first-class level, he recognised that one of the frustrating yet insoluble problems of Australia's growing cricket program was the regular absence of the international players from the domestic competitions. He says:

Ideally I'd love to play a lot more games for New South Wales, but it's just not feasible. Unfortunately it has to take a back seat. Even when there have been chances to play, there have been times when I've had to take a break, because if you play too much cricket you won't be fresh enough for the Australian games. You need a break when you can get it. We don't want to be like England where players go into Test matches flat, carrying injuries, and not mentally ready.

Before joining the seventeen-man squad for the Ashes tour, Mark was able to enjoy a rare break from the game, a three-week 'holiday at home' with Sue, his longest rest since Australia had returned from the West Indies in May 1991, twenty-three months earlier.

By this stage the couple had bought a house in Revesby. It was, like their current dwelling in the Panania area, a sanctuary, an escape from life in the spotlight. Mark was and remains very much his own person who needs time and space to himself. Time at home is for simple pleasures — watching sport, especially the races on television; reading the form guide and placing a few bets over the phone; playing with the dogs; sleeping in; swimming; whistling indescribable tunes; and just relaxing in tracksuits, T-shirts and shorts — which have to be constantly culled by Sue because they become prematurely tattered through overuse. Then there are the casual dinner parties after which a bottle of Mark's favourite alcoholic drink, Wild Turkey bourbon, may be opened. An everyday life for an everyday person. Except when he leaves his front door. Mark comments:

Yeah, home gives me the chance to escape. Everywhere else, everybody is always looking at you. With the cricket, obviously the media is always there, but even socially if you go out to a restaurant or theatre, you can feel like everyone is saying, 'There's Mark Waugh,' or 'There are the Waugh brothers!' I get a bit embarrassed by it really, but you just learn to cope with it. I don't like it, but you just have to try and smile and go along with it. It's just the nature of the business. I know when I see someone famous I always look at them — it's just human nature I suppose. It's good that people do recognise us, but there are times when you do want your privacy. Like when you're asked for your autograph. You can be having dinner and someone will come up and say, ' I don't mean to be rude, but could you please sign this?' Sometimes people will think I'm arrogant or rude because there are times when I won't sign autographs, but everyone needs space occasionally. I know we have a responsibility, but we also have to find time outside our jobs for our family and ourselves. That's why home, or friends' places become very important, and it's why I rarely go out when I return to Sydney. I'm not the big social person; I'm definitely not into the big social scene of wanting to be seen at fancy restaurants or big movie premieres. Photos in the social pages just aren't me at all. So I stay at home because there's so much privacy. Obviously the neighbours and the local shopkeepers know who you are, but they respect you. You need to get away from it all and be normal. I'm a fairly private person. Stephen is as well.

Coming and going can be tough, especially on Sue. It's a hard relationship. You do get a little used to being away from your home, family and friends, but at the end of the day it's hard being away for as long as we are.

It really becomes two separate lives. The cricket life is really a false life. You get looked after all the time. Someone organises your transport, your hotel, your bags. When you go out you are treated like a king — it's such a false world. Then obviously when you get home it's so different. You have to do the normal chores that normal people do. I suppose I don't really do much when I'm home, I'm pretty lazy. But I really appreciate the chance to get home. Always have.

Sue laughs when she describes the difference in Mark's behaviour when he first arrives home from a tour.

I say to him, 'You have two weeks grace, then the housemaid dies! I'm not going to pick up your towel off the floor, I'm not going to pick up your dental floss, I'm not going to clean up after you. You've got two weeks!'

All the players are so used to having everything done for them that it takes time to adapt when they come home. When Mark leaves for a tour, I always say that he puts his cotton-wool suit on at the airport and doesn't take it off until he's back home again. It's quite bizarre. They don't have to think for themselves at all. They only have to know where they have to be, and at what time. It's all on a sheet. Their lives are listed on running sheets. So it can be quite a shock for them to come home again.

Then you have the language! I won't tolerate the language. He's not in the dressing room any more when he comes into the house. We do have our arguments, but they work out in the end. Punting is probably the worst thing that we argue over. When he's home for a break or a long period between tours, I have to have a punting-free day once a week. I tell him, 'If that bloody Sky television goes on, I'll kick the TV in.' So Mark will look up the form guides, decide what meetings he doesn't want to bother with, and we'll have a total punt-free day.

He loves his time at home. The privacy is so important to him. He hates being in the spotlight. He doesn't feel he needs the adulation from everybody, but I think he secretly enjoys it — he just doesn't want the commitment or fame that goes with the star syndrome. He doesn't want to do the media, doesn't want to walk the red carpets. He just wants to be happy and comfortable in his life, and away from cricket home can give him both.

He likes to think that he helps around the house, but he's totally useless. Really, really useless. Heaven forbid he's not a handyman. He tried to get up and sweep the gutters one day, but he was making such a mess of it I had to tell him to get off the roof before he broke his neck.

Mark was back in his 'cotton-wool suit' in the final week of April 1993 for the Ashes tour. There was a real sense of excitement and anticipation when the squad gathered in Melbourne two days before flying out. For Mark, a trip to England to play Test cricket was the realisation of a boyhood dream. For every Australian and English player, the Ashes matches are special. For the game's fans and historians, it is easy to be swept away by the names from the past:

Bradman, Bedser, Hutton, Hobbs, Laker, Larwood, Lindwall, Lillee ... Would anyone from the teams of 1993 perform such great deeds that they'd join the Ashes honour roll of immortality?

Appropriately, the team arrived in London on 25 April, Anzac Day. Led by Border, the stalwart-fighter, the Australians were searching for their third consecutive series win against the old enemy. After a hectic four days of social and promotional engagements, Border's troops had seven matches to adjust to the conditions before the first of three limited-overs Texaco Trophy matches against England. In the second warm-up, the traditional festival match against the Duchess of Norfolk's XI at Arundel, Mark showed promising form with the ball, taking 5–32 off 10 overs. However, his early performances with the bat were disappointing until he scored 68 in a three-day game against Somerset, then followed it with 74 in a one-dayer against Northamptonshire in the last warm-up before the international commitments began.

Having suffered only one loss — defeated by Northamptonshire on run rate in a rain affected contest — the Australians were confident heading into their opening Texaco Trophy encounter at Old Trafford, Manchester. Despite his New Zealand form, Mark was re-shuffled to first drop to accommodate the powerfully built left-handed Queensland opener, Matthew Hayden. Sent in, Australia reached 9–258 from their allotted 55 overs. The top three were the leading scorers: Taylor (79), Mark (56 from 63 balls) and Hayden (29). In reply, England fell tantalisingly short by 4 runs.

Later that night the Australians went to a private party with players from the Manchester United football team, another reminder to Mark of how far he'd come from the early days at 56 Picnic Point Road.

Unpleasantly cold conditions greeted the teams for the second game of the series, at Birmingham's Edgbaston Ground. In one of the most explosive innings seen in one-day cricket, Robin Smith smashed an unbeaten 167 from 163 deliveries to dominate England's total of 5–277. Despite facing a daunting chase against an attack encouraged by Smith's assault, the Australians remained composed, overhauling the target with nine balls remaining and six wickets in hand. No-one was calmer than Mark, who drove, flicked and glided his way to 113 off 122 balls — his second limited-overs hundred in four innings.

Australia made a clean sweep when they won the last game of the series by 19 runs at Lord's. Mark made 14 and took a catch in an otherwise uneventful match for him.

However, he was the star in the following three-day game against Surrey, which the visitors won by 174 runs. Coming to the crease with the score 2–35 on the first morning, Mark destroyed the weak attack, scoring 178 from just 174 deliveries. It was a critically important performance because he was in a tight battle for a Test spot with Damien Martyn, who did his chances no harm, making 84 in the same innings. The two candidates shared a fourth-wicket stand of 237 in two and a half hours.

Mark's innings included eight sixes, prompting journalist Greg Baum to write in the *Sydney Morning Herald* (26 May 1993): 'Watching Waugh is like watching fireworks: explosive, spectacular, effortless, graceful, colourful and balanced, sometimes all in one shot.'

In the same article, Baum described Mark as 'the enigma', in reference to his inconsistent performances that previously had 'teased and deceived' selectors.

Adding difficulty to the selectors' unenviable decision was the knowledge that some of the gloss was taken off Mark's century by Surrey's reluctance to include most of their front-line players. In reality, the encounter was farcical. Sadly, it is a common practice of counties when they play a touring team to rest their best players, because there are no championship points on offer. Why risk injury to mainstream players when they can take a brief but refreshing break from the regular grind of the circuit?

While his team-mates enjoyed a more valuable hit out in the following encounter with Leicestershire, Mark was given the match off. It was a good chance to escape the selection worries and play some golf, one of his favourite pastimes on tour. He jokes it is one of his few interests that will get him out of bed early in the morning.

The boys reckon I've got a swing like Tom Lehmann because I dip the knees a bit. I don't think Tom would be too happy with the comparison. I've always loved playing the game. I probably get a bit frustrated because I'm not as good as I'd like to be. I hit pretty long off the tee, but I'm a bit too wristy with my chip shots. I break my wrists. That's probably my weakness.

It's a good game. I love the competition, and I can't play it non-

competitively. Playing with the guys on tour there always has to be some incentive. I think I've done quite well against the boys over the years.

Nowadays, he is a member at Sydney's Liverpool Golf Club. His handicap hovers around 8, the result of obvious natural ability and the practice rounds he has sneaked in on tour, especially during the long three-and-a-half-month Ashes campaigns.

After Australia beat Leicestershire, and Mark packed away his clubs, the tourists headed to Old Trafford for the first Test. The evening before the game the squad gathered for the announcement of the team — Mark was in and Martyn didn't even make the twelve as Border and company opted for both spinners, Tim May and Shane Warne. May was named twelfth man the next morning.

The match launched the career of the effervescent Michael Slater, but Mark remembers the encounter for two other reasons. The first was 'the ball of the century' by Warne. It's likely that in another fifty years television clippings will show Warne's opening Test delivery in England as regularly as it currently shows Don Bradman's flowing cover drives. Mike Gatting was the victim, not only beaten but bewildered by a ball that floated towards leg before biting back to hit the stumps. The perfect leg spinner. Mark remembers:

It was a miracle ball. None of the England side had seen too much of Warney, except on TV, so there'd been a fair bit of publicity about him even before the series began. Then he goes out and bowls a ball like that. He doesn't even know how he did it. It just happened. I didn't appreciate it until I saw the replay on TV later in the day and thought, 'Where'd that come from?'

Mark's other memory is of the incident that swung the match Australia's way when England were fighting to hold on for a draw on the final day. Century-maker Graham Gooch (133), who appeared immoveable, became only the fifth player in Test history to be given out 'handled the ball' when he instinctively knocked a bouncing ball away from his stumps after playing a defensive shot. Australia went on to win by 179 runs — Mark's contributions were 6 and 64.

Australia dominated the second Test, at Lord's, from the very first delivery when Slater hit a slashing boundary off Andy Caddick. For the following five hours, Slater (152) and Taylor (111) dominated England's attack in a 260-run partnership. Mark sat with his pads on watching from the players' balcony. It was a long time to be a spectator for someone who always liked being in the action. Occasionally he walked back into the dressing room behind the balcony and picked up a table-tennis bat and ball from his kit. Having a few hits kept his eye in and stopped him from drifting too far away from what his job would be when he finally made it to the middle. It was a catch-22. If he was kept waiting to bat for a long time, Australia were obviously doing well, but he preferred to go in early, and therefore when his side might be in trouble. He says:

> It's hard sitting around for hours with your pads on watching every ball. You can get drowsy, you can switch off, then all of a sudden you're going in to bat not quite focused or switched on. I actually prefer to go in early when it may be 2–40 or 50. That's probably when I'm a bit more lively, a bit more awake. And you have less time to think about how you're going to go, or if you're going to cop a bad decision, or what type of balls you're going to get. I enjoy watching, but the more you watch the more the mind can play a few tricks, especially when the bowling looks really good and you start thinking to yourself, 'How am I going to get runs out there?' At least if you're in there straight away, you can find out. I guess it just means I have less time to get nervous.

Team-mates say there have been occasions when Mark has fallen asleep waiting for his turn at the crease. More commonly he gives just the occasional yawn, which he believes is a sign of nervousness, not relaxation. By the time he batted at Lord's, he perhaps had reason for a little heaviness in the eyelids because play was about to be put to bed for the day. Only half an hour remained, a difficult period for any new batsman to negotiate regardless of the score or position of the match. When Taylor departed, Mark adjusted his box and thigh pad — would there be another stickman to add by the end of the innings? — then put his helmet on, picked up his bat, walked out of the dressing room, down the stairs and through the famous Long Room, under the penetrating gaze of the greats who stared down knowingly from paintings on the walls. He walked through the doors into open air, putting his gloves on, his bat tucked under his arm, then finally, after the longest but most stirring entry in the game, he trod on the hallowed turf of the home of cricket.

Back in the dressing room, space was being made for two more Australian names on the honour board reserved for century-makers and bowlers who'd taken five or more wickets in an innings. Out in the middle, Mark (6 n.o.) and David Boon (11 n.o.) survived until the close of play.

Resuming the next morning at 2–292, the pair had few difficulties against an attack that included Mark's Essex team-mate Neil Foster, playing what would be his last Test for England. Despite being an opponent, he recognised the 'gorgeous' player he was watching. Mark and Boon followed the trend set by their openers the previous day — runs were flowing freely, England's frustrations were high. In a display that drew typically polite applause from the crowd, Mark strolled to 99, overhauling Boon to be third in line for the honour board.

The Australian team gathered on the balcony for the impending salute to another centurion. Phil Tufnell, the left-arm orthodox spinner who'd caused Mark few problems throughout the innings, began another over. Bowling over the wicket, he offered his opponent the chance to reach triple figures with his first delivery, a fullish ball that Mark hit superbly. It was the type of shot a batsman knows means runs as soon as he has played it. However, this time the ball shot into the shins of Robin Smith fielding at short-leg. No run.

In a most negative tactic, Tufnell had been aiming his attack wide of leg-stump, hoping his opponents might make a mistake through frustration. As Mark recalls, England's wishful thinking became an unfortunate reality in the same over.

The ball was way outside leg-stump. But somehow I managed to get it to hit my pads, go through my legs and onto the stumps. Bowled by Tufnell again. I couldn't believe it. It was a pretty good effort by me!

I was very disappointed, especially with the other guys making tons. Boonie ended up getting one too, so I was the only one in the top four to miss out. It was also the dismay of getting out to such a bad ball. Bowling outside leg-stump is very defensive cricket. The bowler isn't trying to get you out. He's waiting for a mistake, which goes against my way of thinking. The opposition knows that I like to score quickly, so it's a fair enough tactic. If I'd been a bit more patient and waited a bit longer ... but then that's the game isn't it? You can't do anything about it afterwards. It's gone. That's it. These days I'd let the ball hit the pad, but back then I'd always try to hit it. That's what a bat's for, isn't it?

There was only one bloke more disappointed than me. A bloke in Ladbrokes
had bet the first four Australians to bat would get hundreds. The odds were
something like a 100–1. Apparently he knocked on the dressing room door a bit
later and said, 'Mark Waugh has cost me a lot of money!'

The odds were in fact 1000–1, on which the MCC member had waged 100 pounds! A shorter priced offering would undoubtedly have been the odds on Mark being dismissed by Tufnell. His Lord's dismissal was the third time in as many innings he'd been humbled by the Middlesex tweaker. In the following morning's *Daily Mail*, the headline barked: 'Waugh's failure staves off ultimate insult'. If Mark had scored one more run, Australia would have become the first team in Test history to see its first four batsmen score centuries. An insult indeed to England's pride.

It wasn't the last unexpected happening for Mark in the Test. Not long after the tea-break on the second day, Craig McDermott was rushed to hospital after complaining of severe stomach pain, the result of a twisted bowel that needed immediate surgery. In the absence of his lead paceman, Border called on Mark to open the attack with Merv Hughes. He failed to take a wicket, but it mattered little, as Shane Warne assumed the responsibility of strike bowler, taking four wickets in each innings as the demoralised English fell to defeat by an innings and 62 runs.

After the drawn third Test, at Trent Bridge, in which Mark scored 70 and 1, and took two catches, the Australians retained the Ashes with victory by an innings and 148 runs at Headingley, Leeds. Mark made 52, a small return in comparison with Border's unbeaten 200 and centuries by Steve (157 n.o.) and Boon (107). By this stage of the series, England's players looked like lost explorers trudging through the desert without water. Their faces were drawn, their shoulders hunched, their steps slow. They surrendered meekly for just 200 in their first innings, 453 runs behind, and although they fought harder to reach 305 when they followed on, the result was never in doubt. Mark again took two catches for the match. The second — to dismiss Alec Stewart on the final day — was extraordinary. Stewart had tried to cut a delivery from Paul Reiffel that was too close to his body, and succeeded only in edging the ball through the slips cordon before anyone seemingly had the chance to move. Diving low at least two feet [60 centimetres] behind him to his right at second slip, Mark held on to the half-chance to take what remains the best catch he says he has ever taken. The one brief moment that was over in the click of a finger showed how valuable he was to the team. Border, Taylor and Ian Healy were standing nearby at the time, all perfectly positioned to pass comment on their team-mate's brilliance. Border says:

> He makes catches that other blokes can only dream about, and he does it regularly. I've never seen anybody catch the ball as well one-handed as he does. The one thing I really noticed when compared to someone like myself was the placement of his hands. If I didn't get the ball pretty much in the middle of my hands, it would bob out, like the one that smacks you on the heel of the hand, at the base of the thumb. But Mark has soft hands, and that innate ability to not catch the ball flush in the middle but still hang on to it. That's rare. He and Greg Chappell are the best I've ever seen.

Healy agrees: 'He was awesome right from the start of his time in the slips. Just the ease of his movements was incredible. We did hours and hours of practice together, and his control was something I'd never seen before or since.'

Taylor sums Mark up succinctly by saying, 'He's the best all-round fieldsman I've ever seen.'

The Ashes win prompted some rowdy celebrations in the visitors' dressing room. Amidst the incongruous mixture of tunes by Cold Chisel and John Williamson — 'Khe Sanh' and 'True Blue' were the favourites — the Australians, under Boon's passionate direction, shouted the words to the team's victory chant:

> Under the Southern Cross I stand.
> A sprig of wattle in my hand
> A native of this native land
> Australia! You bloody beauty!

There couldn't have been a greater contrast to the sombre mood in England's dressing room where players and officials were coming to terms with the resignation of Graham Gooch from the captaincy. Mark recalls:

> The Poms were in a bit of disarray. They were going through a lot of players, and there was a fair bit of pressure on Graham. He's a pretty gentle sort of bloke,

so he probably wasn't coping too well with all the slagging off he was getting in the media. England's media can be really hard and unfair.

But I think it's great when a team is in disarray. When your opponents, like Graham and Neil Foster are good mates, you might feel a little bit sorry for them, but everybody goes through that stage when they're struggling for form, or the team's been doing badly. You know the opposition isn't going to take it easy on you, so when the boot's on the other foot, you want to play well and keep playing well. There's no softness in professional sport. You have to keep the momentum up because it can change quickly if you happen to ease off a bit. It's always good to beat England — I didn't feel sorry for them.

England have always seemed to have good players on paper, but they lack the killer instinct. They have shown they have a soft underbelly. They need another 'Beefy' Botham, or one of those sorts of players who'll really take it to you. Someone who is very talented and willing to have a go. The greatest mystery to me is Graeme Hick. He is a very good player, but he has never really fired. I don't know whether the system has got to him, which can happen in England, or he just gets overawed. He hasn't performed like he should have. England need players like him to step up.

Hick, who'd been dropped after the first two matches of the series was again a spectator when Edgbaston hosted the fifth Test. Gooch remained in the team under the new leader, Mike Atherton. While the announcement of the new captain had come as little surprise to the Australians, there were raised eyebrows at the reappearance of off-spinner John Emburey, who was approaching his forty-first birthday. Considering his scant regard for slow bowlers, especially finger-spinners, Mark was eager to make his biggest impression of the series. He was extremely confident after scoring an unbeaten 152 in the lead-up game against Glamorgan, but if he was to produce something similar at Birmingham, he had to overcome an apparent jinx. Rodger Waugh had flown over to watch his sons play, and although excited, he was also very nervous.

'Any time I went to watch them, especially in grade cricket, they'd get out. Every bloody time!' says Rodger. 'To this day it still happens in grade cricket with Danny.'

By the end of the second day Mark had dismissed his father's concerns with a wave of the bat acknowledging his fourth Test century (137) in Australia's first innings total of 408. Steve (59) further repaired Rodger's state of mind by sharing with Mark a crucial 153-run partnership for the fifth wicket — the twins' first century stand in Tests. When they'd come together, Australia were in trouble at 4–80 chasing England's first innings of 276. Mark was in wonderful, free-flowing touch. Time and again the bowlers played to his strength, feeding him straight full-length deliveries that were whipped through mid-wicket with a level of disdain that bordered on arrogance.

The innings included eighteen boundaries from 219 deliveries. Although Rodger could be satisfied that the jinx had been crushed, there was a strange twist in the final overs when Steve, batting at the other end, had a premonition that his brother would be caught at backward square leg. The following ball, Mark clipped a delivery from left-arm medium pacer Mark Illot straight into the hands of Graham Thorpe who was fielding in the precise spot Steve imagined. It was at least a better hunch than the last one Steve had — when Mark was on his ill-fated 1992 tour of Sri Lanka his twin had predicted one of his four ducks.

Mark looked in century-making form again in the second innings, but was stopped by the number of runs Australia needed to win. He was 62 not out when Australia reached 2–120 to take a 4–0 lead in the series. Mark's tally of 199 for the match was the most ever by an Australian in a Test match at Edgbaston.

He scored another century, 108, in the final lead-up match to the sixth Test, at The Oval. The innings was significant not only because it was made against his county mates at Essex, but because Mark was dismissed by the overseas professional who'd replaced him — Salim Malik. Perhaps fate had a strange sense of humour considering how the two players would come together only a year later.

The Oval Test provided a disappointing finish for Border's men who spoke before the match about the need to maintain intensity. The incentive was a 5–0 scoreline and immense embarrassment for the home side. However, the return to the England team of erratic fast bowler Devon Malcolm and tireless medium pacer Angus Fraser proved successful. Taking fourteen wickets between them for the match, they were the main reason England could celebrate at last after a comprehensive and thoroughly deserved 161-run win.

Mark scored 10, then in the second innings looked set for a sizeable score, but on 49 hooked Malcolm down to the fine-leg boundary where Mark Ramprakash gleefully accepted the catch.

The tour was over. Under pressure at the start, Mark had proved his worth to the team, finishing third in the Test averages behind his brother and Boon. He made 550 runs at 61.11 and took 9 catches, second behind Taylor of the non wicket-keeping fieldsmen. Mark says:

I was really happy with the series. It was a good series for us, despite the problems in the last Test. I don't know whether we subconsciously eased up a bit, but England deserved their win.

The Ashes tour establishes a really good camaraderie between the players because you spend so much time together on such a long tour. On the bus, playing cards, watching movies. You're just always together, and when you're winning, it just brings everyone together closer.

Back then I thought the Ashes tour was the ultimate tour, but now there are other trips I rate just as highly for prestige. South Africa, the West Indies, and no doubt about India. I really wish we could play a five-Test series over there.

After the Ashes tour, there was another country — not renowned for its cricket — that some of the Australians had to visit. The island with the hair-raising touchdown for plane travellers — Hong Kong — was hosting a cricket tournament that years later would leave Mark's future up in the air.

CHAPTER FOURTEEN

HONG KONG

The first official game of cricket in Hong Kong was played in 1841. From that moment, bat and ball had a role to play in the country caught, like a tentative batsman having trouble deciding whether to go forward or back, between British and Chinese culture.

In 1851 the Hong Kong Cricket Club was formed, and fifty-three years later the neighbouring island of Kowloon followed suit. Matches and tournaments were primarily played between British expatriates, and despite visits from overseas clubs, and occasionally countries, a regular international competition wasn't established until 1992 when Kowloon began hosting the annual Hong Kong Sixes. A series of five-overs-a-side matches between six-man teams from all the major Test-playing nations was played over one weekend.

In October 1993, Australia were one of nine countries, including Hong Kong, vying for the trophy. Mark was part of an experienced team that comprised Ian Healy, Tony Dodemaide, Matthew Hayden, Damien Martyn and Jamie Siddons.

Although the locals considered the tournament to be of utmost importance and prestige, many players regarded it as a social weekend at which the hardest playing took place off the field. For Mark, the trip offered a chance to catch up with long-time friend and former Bankstown team-mate David Thompson who'd moved to Hong Kong for work reasons, but also found himself representing the host nation in the tournament.

After winning two of their three preliminary games, the Australians qualified for a semi-final against Sri Lanka, who, led by Arjuna Ranatunga, claimed the match by the considerable margin of 18 runs. Mark (17) top scored in his team's total of 3–60.

In comparison to the just completed Ashes tour and the upcoming home summer that would involve series against New Zealand and South Africa, the result was of no consequence — unless you were an Indian bookmaker.

Indian all-rounder Manoj Prabhakar was one of the middlemen — not only a player, but also allegedly a paid source of information for the bookmaker Mukesh Gupta.

In December 2000, Prabhakar, who'd retired from the game in 1996, was found guilty of being a 'conduit' for bookmakers, and was banned from playing for five years and from holding any official position in international or domestic cricket. The penalty imposed by the Board of Control for Cricket in India (BCCI), followed the release of a report conducted by the Central Bureau of Investigation in India (CBI) into corruption and match-fixing. In the report, Gupta claimed he'd been introduced to Mark by Prabhakar at the 1993 Hong Kong Sixes. Gupta further stated that he paid Mark A$20 000 in exchange for information about the Australian team. Mark was adamant this did not happen, but the allegations would cause him to face an uncomfortable inquisition in February 2001. However, at the time, no-one could have known what lay ahead. Thompson remarks:

> All I can remember is that everyone in the tournament shared the same dressing room. When we weren't playing, we sat in an area at the top level of the Kowloon Pavilion. I'm sure if anything was going on, we would have known about it. The only real thing I remember about Manoj Prabhakar is that other than when he played, he sat in the room with a towel over his head.

Mark returned to Australia, and immediately slipped into state commitments. Once again, it would be a season of rare appearances for New South Wales. He played just two matches in the Mercantile Mutual Cup, scoring 33 in a 133-run win over Queensland in Brisbane, and a rapid 68 in a 59-run win over Tasmania at North Sydney Oval. His collective strike rate for the two innings was 150.74. Despite missing their international stars for the remaining four matches, the Blues won the competition, beating Western Australia in a rain-affected final that was decided on run rate.

Mark was only available for three Sheffield Shield encounters, but made his presence felt, scoring 370 runs at an average of 61.66. The highlight came in the first innings of his final game when he compiled his forty-fifth first-class century, 119 against Victoria on a turning SCG pitch. It was a brilliant display that boasted 10 boundaries and a six in four and a half hours. From the moment Mark came to the crease, he engaged in an intriguing battle of wits and skill with Shane Warne.

In an article for *Inside Edge* (September 1993) before the season began, Mark gave an insight into how Australia's batsmen could play Warne much better than the Englishmen had during the Ashes in which the leg-spinner had taken 34 wickets.

If I were playing him I would definitely be looking to be positive and upset his rhythm as I'm certain many a Shield batsman would be.

A risk or two would have to be taken, such as hitting him over the infield, but hopefully I could spread his field. Getting rid of the close-in catchers frees things up for singles and you'd still be looking for the boundary as well.

It sounds easy doesn't it?

And easier said than done. In tactics reminiscent of Phil Tufnell's approach, Warne bowled around the wicket outside leg-stump, and waited for Mark to either make a mistake or be beaten by deliveries that bit back sharply. Mark, however, showed a level of patience that had been lacking in some of his battles with Tufnell. Time and again he thrust out his pad, or went back on his stumps and let the ball hit him. When he could, he used his feet, hitting Warne straight or with the spin through the covers. It was as hard as Shield contests could be, and considering Warne's success in England it could easily have been suggested that it was harder than Test cricket. Mark acknowledges:

It's probably the best Shield hundred I've made. And it's up there with any of my centuries. It took me ages to get off the mark, and I had to work for every run. It was tough going.

Warney is one of the best bowlers I've faced. His aggression is one thing that makes him so successful. He's willing to try different things even if he gets hit for the odd four or six. He's always thinking, and always at you. You can never feel as if you're completely on top of him.

I suppose the fact that Warney was bowling made me concentrate harder in that innings than if it was someone else. We'd been ribbing each other for a while about who'd come out on top.

The overall honours were shared because Warne finished with 5–77 off a marathon 40 overs, and in his second innings return of 3–90 enjoyed the belated satisfaction of dismissing Mark for 23. The match was drawn.

While Warne matched his good mate every step of the innings, the same couldn't be said for luckless first-grade off-spinner Bruce Mills, who was the victim of a brutal assault from Mark when Bankstown played Northern Districts in a one-dayer at Waitara Oval in Sydney's north. In one of only three outings for his club that season, Mark slammed 112 from 101 deliveries. Mills bore the brunt of the punishment, his four overs costing 60 runs, including 26 off one over in which Mark clubbed two fours and three sixes.

After his successful Ashes campaign, there was never any doubt Mark would be an automatic selection for the first Test against New Zealand, in Perth. Two weeks before the series began, he and his New South Wales Test team-mates examined their trans-Tasman neighbours at close range during a four-day match in Newcastle. The Kiwis won by three wickets, but Mark enjoyed some valuable time in the middle, scoring 63 in the first innings. Some tidy bowling on the final day was the highlight of Mark's match. He took 1–20 off 13.5 overs, troubling the batsmen with his variety, and suggesting he might be a useful secondary weapon in the Test attack.

The match in Perth, which launched the Test career of stringy paceman Glenn McGrath, was dominated by the stubborn and at times ugly first innings resistance shown by the Kiwis' top-order batsman Andrew Jones, who withstood Australia's attack for nearly six hours while making 143. He eventually surrendered to Mark when he tried one back-foot slash too many and edged a delivery through to Ian Healy.

The game ended in a draw. Mark scored 36 in his only chance with the bat, and dismissed Jones in each innings.

Sadly for New Zealand supporters, the Kiwi players forgot to pack their fighting qualities when they headed to Hobart's Bellerive Oval for the second Test. In a remarkable contrast to the WACA match, the visitors were torn apart by an innings and 222 runs inside four days.

On the flip side, it was an unforgettable time for Mark, who scored his fifth century in 29 Tests: 111 from 139 deliveries in Australia's only innings. After watching Michael Slater (168) and David Boon (106) set the trend for the innings, Mark delighted spectators with handsome front-foot play that led to fifteen boundaries evenly scattered forward of square on both sides of the wicket. He shared a 150-run fourth-wicket stand in little more than two hours with Allan Border (60), and reached his hundred with a sweetly struck cover drive. His ensuing casual wave to all quarters of the ground was a cruel reminder to the sloppy New Zealanders that they'd twice dropped the century-maker. Simon Doull finally held on to a chance at long-on as Mark attempted to lift the run rate, but the damage had already been done. Australia declared at 6–544. The size of the score and the 10-hour battle in the field were enough to demoralise the visitors, who crumbled in each innings for 161. Mark completed a man-of-the-match performance by taking 1–7 off nine overs, and 1–8 off four in the second innings. He also took 3 catches, two while fielding at silly mid-off to off-spinner Tim May. While Mark had already established his reputation as a brilliant slips fieldsman, he lost nothing in the bat-pad position. He remembers:

> I used to field there a lot to the spinners because Mark Taylor was in the slips. I really enjoyed the spot. You'd probably get just as many catches there as slip, but you can't be scared. Anticipation is the key. Wherever I field on the ground, I watch the bowler bowl the ball. At bat-pad I can tell by the flight of the ball what shot the batsman is likely to play, and that helps me anticipate.

The final Test in Brisbane was another lopsided contest that Australia won by an innings and 96 runs. Mark scored 68 and claimed a wicket in each innings, finishing the series with 5 scalps at an average of 18.8, and 215 runs at 71.66.

It was a pleasing series for Mark, who showed for the first time in his career that he could make runs against the weaker attacks in international cricket. However, he still had his critics who pointed to the significant difference between his returns in first-class cricket and the Test arena. His century in Hobart had pushed his Test average into the 40s, well below the mid-50s mark he'd set for New South Wales and Essex. As a result, he continually found himself subject to the 'underachiever' tag.

He gave little reason for the label to be applied to his limited-overs form when the Benson & Hedges series began in December. After minor contributions in the first two matches, he showed his ability to bat to the conditions in the third contest against South Africa, in Sydney. An unbelievably green seamer's pitch made batting extremely difficult, as shown by Australia's lowly total of 9–172 off 50 overs. Coming in at number 4 to accommodate the inclusion of Michael Slater at the top of the order, Mark worked hard for his runs, hitting only two boundaries in an innings of 36 from 75 deliveries. Only Ian Healy (38) scored more. In reply, the South African total of 69 showed just how difficult the conditions were. In the following match, the last before a three-week break in the competition, Mark returned to his free-flowing style, hitting 53 from 78 deliveries in a 3-run win over New Zealand at the MCG. He also took 2–42 off nine overs.

Unfortunately Melbourne's weather had no sense of occasion 10 days later when rain ruined the first Test between Australia and South Africa since 1969–70. Play didn't start until five o'clock on the opening day, no play occurred on the second, and the third day hosted only two hours of cricket. One of the few highlights of the drawn encounter was a fourth-wicket partnership of 169 between Taylor (170) and Mark (84). When he was trapped lbw by medium pacer Craig Matthews, Mark was not only within reach of a century, but 1000 Test runs for the calendar year. In what was his last innings for 1993, he left the field with a tally of 987 at 49.35.

His new year didn't start as well as the old one had ended. He was dismissed for 7 and 11 in a Sydney Test that will be remembered for a twelve-wicket haul by Warne, and a remarkable final-day collapse by Australia that handed South Africa victory by 5 runs. Needing just 117 to win, the Australians surrendered to some intelligent bowling by popular paceman Fanie de Villiers, who finished with 6–43 off 23.3 overs.

As the champagne spray sprinkled the camera lenses that were pointed towards the visiting team's balcony, the home side quietly assessed their reputation of having trouble chasing small targets. Mark acknowledges:

> It was really disappointing. Warney had bowled us into a winning position, then we let ourselves down. The South Africans played really well, but we allowed them to. We were probably overconfident because we'd been on top the day before, but then we gave them a sniff and they lifted.
>
> Damien Martyn copped a lot afterwards for batting the way he did [he scored 6 in 106 minutes before hitting an Allan Donald delivery straight to Andrew Hudson in the covers], but it wasn't his fault. We all stuffed up but it was a bad wicket to bat on. It was dry and powdery and going through the top.

Post-mortems quickly made way for the resumption of the Benson & Hedges series that brought no notable returns for Mark to the extent that the media speculated he would make way for Martyn for the eleventh match of the tournament, against South Africa in Perth. In his only two outings since the Sydney Test, he'd scored 10 in a 48-run win over South Africa at the Gabba, and 15 in a 13-run loss to New Zealand at the SCG. Yet again there was concern in the Australian camp that his form was drifting. He was also troubled by a heavily bruised hand.

He overcame the injury and survived the sharpening knives to play at the WACA, but there was no reason to celebrate after the Australians slid to an 82-run defeat. Although Mark impressed with the ball, taking 2–26 off seven overs, he struggled with the bat, hitting 14 from 26 deliveries. Amidst growing rumours that his place was in jeopardy for the final, he answered his critics to some extent with a timely 45 off 53 balls in a 51-run win over New Zealand on a two-paced MCG pitch.

His return to form continued in the the final against South Africa. The Australians lost the first match, in Melbourne, by 28 runs — Mark scored 36 from 51 deliveries — but they hit back strongly to claim the second game by 69 runs, at the SCG. In a match-winning performance that kept the critics at bay, Mark caressed and thumped 107 from 111 deliveries, and along the way shared an entertaining 175-run partnership with Dean Jones (79) for the fourth wicket. Mark frequently stayed leg-side of the ball and drove through the off side, while Jones walked across his stumps to glide deliveries to fine leg. Two inventive stroke-makers at full pace, and eleven fieldsmen shaking their heads in a mixture of frustration and wonderment.

Defending 6–247, their biggest total of the series, the Australians dismissed their rivals for 178 after Warne and Craig McDermott took three wickets each.

Mark maintained form in the decider two days later at the SCG, scoring 60 from just 53 deliveries in a respectable tally of 8–223. The South Africans never recovered from losing three quick wickets, and despite some hopeful batting in the middle order only managed to reach 9–188. Australia won the series 2–1, and in a satisfying finish to the campaign, Mark was named player of the finals. He was also the tournament's leading scorer with 395 runs at 39.50, and a strike rate of 75.38. Not a bad comeback for a player on the verge of being dropped.

However, the third Test, in Adelaide, provided a disappointing finish to his international summer. Australia won by 191 runs, but Mark had a poor game with scores of 2 and 12. His brother was the undoubted hero, smashing 164 in the first innings, then following it up with 4–26 off 18 overs.

By this stage of the summer, there was growing speculation in the media that Border was nearing retirement, but he shied away from the topic and occasionally snapped at journalists who pestered him for a definite answer. Mark recalls that when the team left for three more Tests and a one-day series in South Africa no player really knew what their captain was thinking, but concedes there were enough hints to suggest that the end was near.

AB was pretty snappy at times during the tour. I remember one incident in particular in Cape Town when he came into the dressing room after batting for a session, but hardly scoring a run. Heals took AB's bat and put it in an esky full of ice, just joking around that AB was on fire, but AB just blew up. He was saying things like, 'It's all right for you blokes back in here, but I've been out in the middle playing my guts out for this team. It's about time some of you blokes did too.' Heals was just trying to have a bit of fun, but AB took it the wrong way, and that made the situation very tense. We obviously all wanted to do well on the tour, but not knowing what AB was going to do made us try that extra bit harder. If it was going to be his last trip, then we wanted to make sure that he finished a winner.

AB had helped me so much during my career. He gave me the chance at Essex, got me to open the batting in the one-dayers, and just taught me so much about the game itself. I didn't have to ask questions. I just watched. He was as tough a competitor as I've ever seen. He just didn't know when to give up or how to give up, but sometimes he could be a bit negative. Especially when he was waiting to bat. You could see him in the dressing room watching the cricket and talking himself down, saying things like, 'I won't be able to get runs out there. Look at how well they're bowling.' He was okay once he actually went in to bat, but he was pretty tough on himself while he was waiting.

The tour itself was a real eye-opener. Obviously it was very important because we were the first official Australian cricket team in South Africa since apartheid had finished. I was amazed by the level of poverty. Black people just lived by the roadside in tin huts with no water or electricity and not much food. In South Africa, poverty and wealth sit side by side. You hear so many people say it, but it made me realise how lucky I was to live in Australia. You tend to take things for granted until you see how other people live.

The Australians arrived in early February, just two and a half months before South Africa's national elections after which African National Congress leader Nelson Mandela would become President of the country. Mandela met the visitors during the lunch-break of their first match against Nicky Oppenheimer's XI. Once again Mark realised how lucky he was. If it wasn't for cricket, he certainly wouldn't have had the chance to talk with one of the world's most respected figures.

The mood in South Africa at the time was tense. Border's squad were under heavy security and had been warned that trouble could erupt without notice. Thankfully there were no serious incidents during the two-month tour, and predictions of mass riots at the 27 April elections did not eventuate.

Considering all that could have happened, the trip was relatively quiet. The eight-match limited-overs series, split into an even amount of one-dayers and day-nighters either side of the Tests, was drawn 4-all. Mark endured an inconsistent campaign that was highlighted by a man-of-the-match performance in the third one-dayer, at St George's Park, Port Elizabeth, a ground that four years later would host one of his greatest cricketing moments. He blasted 60 from 55 balls, including four boundaries and two sixes, then took a wicket in Australia's 88-run win. In all, he made 199 runs for the series at an average of 28.42.

Mark reserved his best displays for the longer games. In the final hit out before the first Test, he scored 154 in a 60-run win over Orange Free State at Bloemfontein. He and Steve (102) signalled the South Africans a formidable warning with a fourth-wicket stand of 242 in just 155 minutes. However, the innings and the partnership weren't Mark's main memories of the match. He recalls:

It was a really important game for Merv Hughes. He'd had a back injury and was struggling for form and fitness. We'd just come out onto the field after lunch, Merv had the first over, and all of a sudden after bowling a ball he went halfway down the wicket and crumpled over, hands on his knees and yelling a bit. Everyone immediately thought, 'Oh shit, his back has gone. We're in trouble.' We all ran up to him, and as soon as most of us were there, he let out this almighty fart! He was one of Australia's great characters.

These days personalities like Merv have gone out of the game a bit because you can't get away with what you used to. There are so many cameras, so many rules and regulations that in some ways the fun has gone out of the game. If Dennis Lillee played now, he'd last one game or two, then he'd be suspended or fined. Even though it can be good-natured fun. It's not only cricket either. I used to love watching John McEnroe play. I'd love to see that sort of player again in tennis, but you just can't get away with it now. There's just not enough leeway for that sort of character in many sports these days, which is a real shame.

Merv's antics on tour were always something to look forward to, for us and the crowd.

Even back in 1994 when the rules and regulations weren't as tight as today, Hughes still managed to find trouble, or trouble found him. Johannesburg's imposing Wanderers Stadium lived up to its nickname of 'the Bull-Ring' when Hughes had an altercation with a spectator while walking along the players' race on the final day of the first Test. The Victorian fast bowler thumped his bat into the fence dividing the players from the crowd, then stopped to single out the spectator who'd abused him. Already fined $450 for sledging in the match, he was penalised a further $4000 by the Australian Cricket Board. Warne copped the same punishment for giving opener Andrew Hudson an animated send-off in the second innings. Back in Australia, the incidents, combined with a 197-run loss, didn't make pleasant reading at the breakfast table. As was his way, Mark preferred not to be drawn into the media hype surrounding the incidents. Not known as a troublemaker, he simply wanted to play cricket because that's what he enjoyed and that's what he was paid to do. The simplicity of his approach balanced the more intense and aggressive personalities in the team. As Ian Healy says, 'Mark was rarely ever ruffled.'

Border's men found the perfect way to retaliate when they won the second Test by nine wickets at the beautiful Newlands Ground in Cape Town. Steve was named man of the match after scoring 86 in his only chance with the bat, and taking 5–28 in the second innings. Mark stayed in the shadows, scoring 7 and failing to take a wicket, leaving him with little else to do than offer quiet encouragement from the slips to his team-mates.

Much louder applause was directed his way in the final match, at Kingsmead, Durban, when he became the only Australian to score a century — the sixth of his Test career — in the series. His unbeaten 113 came from 222 deliveries in nearly five hours. By Mark's standards, it was a subdued display, but as Steve later wrote in his *South African Tour Diary*, the man-of-the-match winner's innings was 'character building'.

It was also quite possibly a match-saver, because when Mark went to the crease Australia were in trouble at 3–109 on the final day, still trailing by 44 runs overall. When Border joined him at 4–157, the visitors were effectively 4–4. At that stage, a few quick wickets could have led to defeat. However, Mark and his captain (42 n.o.) guided their side to a draw by sharing an unbroken fifth-wicket stand of 140. Mark's performance was undoubtedly timely, as journalist Phil Wilkins suggested in the *Sydney Morning Herald* (29 March 1994):

Mark Waugh is a frustration and a joy. While his position was perhaps not in jeopardy, it did come up for review, having had a sequence of eight Test innings without a half-century.

While Mark could look forward to future battles, what about his captain? At various times throughout the partnership, Mark was told by Border, 'I'm not gonna get out here. It might be my last dig.' It was as big a hint as Mark had received that the end of an era was fast approaching.

As the players walked from the field at the end of the match, Mark dropped a few steps behind his leader, who clutched his helmet in one hand, his bat in the other. He didn't announce his retirement for another six weeks, by which time he was back in Australia, but nearly everyone at Kingsmead who saw AB walk off felt they were farewelling a champion.

The 1–all draw was a fitting result for the series. Mark finished second to Steve in the batting averages with 233 runs at 58.25. Furthermore, he led the tour averages with 573 runs at 71.63.

After the Tests, Mark and about half the team travelled to the Phinda Lodge game reserve for a two-day break — no visit to South Africa would be complete without the wildlife experience. About nine months before, a tourist had been killed by a lion at the reserve, so there was considerable apprehension among the players when they went to their huts on the first night. Mark says:

We were told it was pretty safe there, but it was still bloody nerve-wracking. The next morning we were to go on an early morning safari at about six o'clock, and were told group leaders would come down to our huts and escort us to the main reception area about 100 metres away. But they didn't turn up at my place, so I had to walk to reception in the dark. All I could think about was the lion and the tourist. I sprinted up — it was the fastest I think I'd ever run — but then I realised I'd forgotten my jumper, so I had to sprint back again with the thought a lion may jump out. Up and back two times. Luckily I made it.

Although he had escaped, Mark had been given a brief taste of what to expect later in his career when mauled by a different pack of beasts — the media. By then, the reason wasn't a forgotten jumper, but a man from the land of the tiger — John the bookmaker, who was about to change Mark's life.

CHAPTER FIFTEEN

JOHN AND SALIM

Nowadays, one-day matches are like confetti — the brilliance they offer for a fleeting moment or two generally becomes nothing more than scraps flicked from the memories of the players. There are simply too many encounters for all of them to be recalled by cricketers, fans or administrators. As Mark acknowledges, 'One-dayers can all become a bit of a blur.'

However, administrators the world over talk about the financial importance of the shortened version of the game. Capacity crowds and lucrative television and sponsorship deals mean big money for controlling boards. Nowhere is this more evident than on the Indian subcontinent and in Sharjah.

At the end of the South African tour in April 1994, an Australian team under the leadership of Mark Taylor — Allan Border had returned home, but was still to announce his retirement — travelled to Sharjah to compete in the six-nation Australasia Cup.

After winning their two preliminary matches, in which Mark's best score was an unbeaten 64 against Sri Lanka, Australia were beaten by India in a semi-final. Pakistan beat New Zealand in the other semi-final, then celebrated a 39-run victory over the Indians in the final.

It was an insignificant tournament. Just another piece of confetti to the players. However, for the illegal bookmakers and punters following the tournament, the honeymoon was just beginning. Gambling on cricket — everything from results to individual scores could be bet on — had become a multi-million dollar business. Clandestine meetings in hotel rooms between bookmakers and targeted players, subtle phone conversations and negotiations in US dollars were becoming more frequent, though still far from public knowledge.

In September 1994, everything began to change. By this stage Mark Taylor had officially assumed the Australian captaincy following Border's retirement four months earlier. En route to Pakistan for a three-Test series, the new captain took his players to Sri Lanka for the Singer World Series limited-overs tournament that involved the host nation, India and Pakistan.

Mark's opening experiences of the two-week tournament are more comical than controversial. He recalls:

We had to go a sponsors' function at the start. It was really hot, so the organisers gave us these bottles of water, but for some reason the bottle they gave me was full of vinegar. It looked like water for all money, but the first mouthful told me the truth real smart. The organisers were so ashamed and apologetic — they treat you as such important people in those countries that they try too hard sometimes.

Sri Lanka is a really friendly place to visit, but the security is always so high. There were guards with machine guns outside our rooms, and we weren't allowed to leave our hotel in Colombo without guards looking after us. It led to some amusing but scary moments. One day when we were going to the ground, we saw a bus with all the curtains closed heading in the same direction. We asked our security guys who was on it, and they told us it was simply a decoy bus for us. We also used to travel different routes to the ground each day.

The funniest story was when we wanted to get out of the hotel one night to go to a Mexican restaurant about fifty metres up the road, but officials wouldn't let us walk there. So we had to get in a bus to go there with a huge police escort. A bus to go fifty metres! It created more attention than if we'd walked.

In such eventful surroundings, the cricket could have become little more than a support act in what was basically another meaningless tournament, but with the benefit of hindsight it is clear that the spotlight was very much on the on-field activity.

The Indians won the competition, defeating the host nation in the final. In Australia's three matches Mark tallied 108 runs at an average of 36.00. His highest score of 61 against India was the best by an Australian for the tournament.

He also made 24 against Sri Lanka and 23 against Pakistan in a match that drew public speculation and whispers in the dressing room. Chasing 180 for victory off 50 overs on a slow and low pitch that wasn't conducive to quick run-scoring, Pakistan managed only to reach 9–151. As time passed, the Australians had their suspicions, but as Taylor wrote in his autobiography, *Time to Declare*, 'That day we won in Colombo we probably won fair and square, and they probably lost fair and square. But I don't really know … and I guess I never will.'

It was during this tournament that Mark made a decision that would affect not only his future career but his life outside cricket. At the team hotel in Colombo he was approached by an Indian who introduced himself as 'John', but gave no surname. The Indian revealed he was a bookmaker who wanted Mark to provide general information about pitch and weather conditions and the Australian team's mood, tactics, and selections in return for US$4000. The arrangement was to continue until the end of the Australian 1994–95 home season. Mark accepted the money, but told John he would not under any circumstances talk about team tactics or line-ups. He recalls:

I treat people the way they treat me. In that regard I'm probably a bit naive. I don't see the bad side in people, so obviously when I met John I took him at face value. I thought someone was going to give me a bit of money to give a bit of information on pitch and weather conditions. I didn't know it was illegal or against the code of conduct. I thought there was no problem with it, otherwise I wouldn't have done it. Even back in my school days I always hated getting into trouble and doing the wrong thing.

I didn't see it as a deceitful thing. I just saw it at face value — he's going to give me some money to tell him about the pitch and the weather, and the general

feeling in the team. I think if a lot of people were offered that I'm sure they'd do
the same thing. To me it's no different from doing a radio interview before a
game. You talk about how you're going, whether the pitch is going to keep low
or seam a bit, whether it's good to bat on first. It's the same thing you do in a
radio interview — that's how I took it.

Mark's view that he accepts people at 'face value' is supported by his family
and friends. Peter V'landys recalls a time when his close mate and harness
racing partner wanted to buy a horse that was 'an absolute shocker' because he
believed everything he was told by its owner. V'landys says:

Some people call Mark naive, but I prefer to say he's an innocent person. I can
imagine him doing it [accepting the money from John] because of his total
innocence. I can just picture a bloke coming up to him and saying, 'I'll give you
a few grand for some weather and pitch information.' I can just see Mark
saying, 'Yeah, I'll do that for you. Is that all you want?' He'd be wiser now, but
a few years ago, he wouldn't have read anything into it.

After accepting the arrangement with John, Mark agreed to introduce the
bookmaker to Shane Warne. The meeting took place at a casino near the team's
hotel; Mark told Warne that John was someone who 'bets on cricket'. At the
time Warne was down US$5000 after an unsuccessful run on the roulette wheel.
The following day, John sought a meeting with Warne at the hotel. After
initially rejecting a 'gift' of US$5000, Warne took the money with 'no strings
attached'. In his autobiography *Shane Warne*, he wrote:

He [John] said that he was a very wealthy man and wanted to give me something
as his way of saying thanks for the number of times he had won on Australia in
the past.

At the time, it was known that players on the subcontinent sometimes received
extravagant presents from extremely rich individuals, but there was no
evidence to suggest such gifts were linked to corruption in the game.

Later, John did seek general pitch and weather information from Warne
three times over the phone during England's 1994–95 Ashes tour of Australia.

Mark's and Shane's meetings with John weren't spoken about in the team environment, but the O'Regan report acknowledges that:

> Mark Waugh had been warned in 1994 by a senior player rooming with him that providing information over the telephone about conditions, games and teams was unwise as it was likely to come back and haunt him later in his career.

Considering Mark can't recall who the player was, it's highly likely the comment was just a casual observation that was passed over quickly.

Bob Simpson, still coach at the time, says he didn't know of the approaches, suggesting, 'The boys would have known my attitude, so they weren't coming near.' Mark, however, told his partner, Sue, who recalls:

> He rang up and we spoke about it, and decided it couldn't be any different from talking on the radio about the same sorts of things. I'm a fairly honest person, and if I'd have been worried, I would have told him, 'No, don't go near that.' I really didn't think it was all that bad.

Whether it was 'all that bad' is a matter of personal opinion. However, when compared with what followed less than a month later on 1 October 1994, the provision of general information was certainly a minor matter. At about 10.30 p.m., Warne and team-mate Tim May were in their hotel room at Karachi's Pearl Continental Hotel when they received a phone call from Pakistan captain Salim Malik. At the time, one day remained in the first Test match, at the National Stadium. Chasing 314 to win, the Pakistanis were to resume in the morning at 3–155. Malik invited Warne and May to his room in the same hotel. May turned down the invitation, saying he was too tired, but Warne went. He came back soon afterwards and told his room-mate that Malik had offered them US$200 000 if they bowled wide of off-stump to ensure a draw. Pakistan's captain said the money could be delivered before midnight, but Warne rejected the offer.

The final day led to one of the most thrilling finishes in Test history. Pakistan won the match after Inzamam-ul-Haq (58 n.o.) and unlikely hero Mushtaq Ahmed (20 n.o.) added 57 in a record-breaking final-wicket stand. The winning runs came from four byes after Ian Healy missed a chance to stump

Inzamam off Warne, who finished with five wickets, and eight for the match. Mark had a solid match, scoring 20 and 61. He remembers:

> It was a good game of cricket. We had a few injuries that didn't help us. Glenn McGrath only bowled six overs in the second innings. We should have won. We really thought we were home when we got the ninth wicket. Mushie's not a bad player, but you wouldn't expect him to hang around that long. There were a couple of close lbw shouts — it was pretty similar to the West Indies game we lost by one run in Adelaide. We thought we were there, then it was taken from underneath us.
>
> We were devastated after the game, especially Ian. The chance was a real tough one to take because the ball kept low and just missed the stumps. There's no way we'd ever blame Ian, but Ian would have blamed himself because he would think he could have won us the Test match. In the dressing room we sat around stunned for a good hour or so. Everybody was sitting in their own spots not saying anything.

The remaining two Tests were drawn. Mark batted only twice more, both times impressively, making 68 and 71. He also took two wickets in the second Test and showed he still had surprising pace when he hit left-handed opener Aamir Sohail in the lip with a bouncer that hurried on to him. Salim Malik scored 237 in the same match, and Victorian swing bowler Damien Fleming became the third bowler to take a Test hat-trick on debut.

The series was also notable for Warne's outstanding bowling (18 wickets at 28.00) and the success of pacemen Waqar Younis (10 wickets at 25.80) and Wasim Akram (nine wickets at 22.22) who showed their incredible, albeit controversial, ability to move the ball on lifeless pitches. Mark says:

> They're both great bowlers. If you look at their records, they're phenomenal, and to do it bowling in the conditions they do in Pakistan where the wickets are good for batting. Certainly the thing that has helped them is the reverse swing. They're the masters of it.
>
> It makes a big difference, but you still have to bowl the ball in the right spot, which is what they do. It's a big advantage — they've worked out how to do it the best of anybody. They're great bowlers, no doubt about it.

Wasim is very hard to face because he has a quick action, and the ball hits the bat before you know it. He runs off a short run, and when he bowls around the wicket he runs from behind the umpire, so it's hard to line him up. He can do everything. He can intimidate and swing the ball both ways. Because he is so fast through the air, he is just as quick when he bowls short, or pitches up. That's unlike many bowlers who can't maintain the same pace when they vary their length.

Waqar has a better strike rate. Those blokes will clean up the tail for a living. Bowl at the stumps. Bang! They're a deadly pair. And they compete against each other — there's always been a bit of rivalry, so they try to outdo each other.

They're an amazing team, Pakistan. They're so segregated. They're individual players and that's it. They're not a team at all. They really just want to worry about themselves. It makes it hard when they seem to have a different captain every series too. They can be very fragmented, but sheer talent keeps them in a lot of games.

We knew they were talented, but we thought if we put the pressure on them they would crack and start arguing with one another. I think they're quite selfish players — maybe it's the way they're brought up, they've just got to fend for themselves. On their day they can beat anybody. We just tried to be consistent and ruthless against them, hoping they'd fragment, which is what usually happens, but they held together for the Test series. They played well.

Earlier, Australia had enjoyed success in the limited-overs series that also involved South Africa. It was during this competition wedged between the Tests that Mark became the third Australian to be approached by Salim Malik. It happened on 21 October at a reception for the teams in Rawalpindi, the night before a game against Pakistan. Mark recalls:

I was stunned. I already knew about the offer to Shane and Tim — the team had spoken about it, not in a formal setting but just among ourselves in the dressing room. Everyone was a bit taken aback, thinking this sort of stuff couldn't happen. I was stunned that he would have the guts to do it again after he'd been told in no uncertain terms by Warney and Maysie they didn't play that way.

He said, 'I'll offer you US$200 000. I'll have it in your hotel tonight if you
get four or five players and you throw the game tomorrow.' He put the offer
forward, and then we separated straight away. I knew straight away I wasn't
going to think about asking anyone else. It was categorically no, but Malik had
already walked away and was speaking to somebody else.

About an hour and a half later I went up to him and told him that we didn't
play the game that way. That's it. End of story.

The following day Mark, batting at number 3, scored a brilliant unbeaten 121 from just 134 deliveries in a total of 6–250. However, Pakistan reached the target in 39 overs for the loss of only one wicket after Saeed Anwar scored 104 not out, and Inzamam-ul-Haq flayed an explosive and unconquered 91 from 80 balls. It was an extraordinary batting display, almost as though the home side needed to catch an early flight. After the game Malik approached Mark and half-jokingly said, 'See, you should have taken the money.' It was the last time Mark ever spoke with him.

Although there remains some conjecture as to when exactly the team management of Col Egar and Bob Simpson became aware of Malik's offers, it's likely to have been after the one-dayer when Mark joked in the dressing room that he would have been better off taking the bribes.

It would take another four months before the issue became public.

The Australians went on to win the tournament, beating Pakistan by 64 runs in the final, at Lahore's Gaddafi Stadium. Mark made 38 from 50 balls and took 2–43, ending a successful tournament for him in which he'd made 243 runs at an average of 48.6. However, he says it wasn't a tour to remember, primarily because of boredom.

I find it [Pakistan] the toughest tour because there's nothing to do, there are not
a lot of distractions. The hotels are okay, but there are not the social activities
where you can let your hair down like there are in other countries. Very few golf
courses, you don't really go to the pub or the movies, so you find yourself
spending a lot of time in the hotels, and you get a bit sick of it. But the people
are very friendly. There were a few highlights. We went up to the Khyber Pass,
which was quite interesting, and Lahore isn't a bad city — they've even got
McDonald's there now!

Such a view again illustrates Mark's desire for simple pleasures. This is the man who has been to the Taj Mahal once, but 'wouldn't do it again'. In England he has said, 'Seen one castle, seen them all.' To him, a good time on tour is playing golf, going to a restaurant, shopping, passing some hours in Ladbrokes, or going to the trots or gallops with Ricky Ponting. Most probably, it was this well-known love of gambling that contributed to Mark becoming a target of cricket's match-fixers.

A family get-together.

Some of the Australian cricket team's biggest fans — rock group INXS. Tim Farriss in centre of picture with bandanna is currently President of the Manly Cricket Club.

The international pastime. Wherever he is, Mark enjoys going to the racetrack. Mark and Ricky Ponting in Barbados, 1995.

A win for Oblico at Albion Park in Brisbane. The trainer-driver is Vic Frost. Earlier in the day Mark scored 100 against Pakistan in the first Test at the Gabba (1999–2000).

Mark and Allan Border celebrate their match-winning efforts after the second one-day international against England at Edgbaston during the 1993 Ashes Tour. Mark scored 113 and his captain, an unbeaten 86.

Mark and Stephen after appearing on the Nine Network's popular 'This is Your Life' program. Sue Porter is to Mark's right, and Stephen's wife Lynette is holding their first child, Rosalie.

A night out on tour for the 'girls'. Sue is between Jane McGrath *(left)* and Tracey Bevan *(right)*.

Golf is one of Mark's favourite ways to relax when on tour. He says it is one of the few reasons to get out of bed early. (PHOTO BY CRAIG PRENTIS/GETTY IMAGES.)

Aiming for the clock-tower on top of the SCG Members Stand. Mark has hit some of the longest sixes in the game's history. (Photo by Adam Pretty/Getty Images.)

'There is nothing better in cricket than crunching a cut.' (Photo by Niels Schipper/Getty Images.)

A special moment for the Waugh family. All four brothers played for Bankstown in the 1995–96 Sydney first grade final. Unfortunately they were beaten by the Glenn McGrath-inspired Sutherland.

Shane Warne and Mark have shared good and bad times throughout their careers.

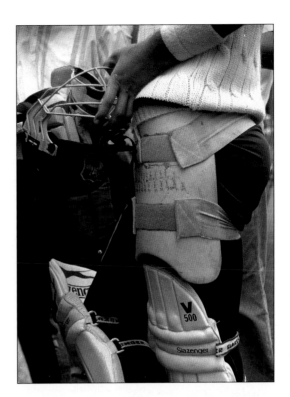

Mark's unique honour board.
The thigh-pad with stick-men
recording each first-class century.

A trademark flick through mid-wicket. (Photo by Nick Wilson/Getty Images.)

Mark will be remembered as one of the greatest limited-overs cricketers of all time.

A unique team photo of Australia's successful 1995 Caribbean tourists.

CHAPTER SIXTEEN

GRANDSTAND DRIVER

The 1994 advertising campaign was an outstanding success — Mark Waugh, famous international cricketer, promoting the Miracle Mile, Australian harness racing's most prestigious sprint. It swept Mark back to his childhood, when he and Steve were about 10. Deciding his boys were old enough to learn one of the ways of the world, Rodger Waugh began taking the twins and Dean to the Bankstown trots. Mark loved the 10-minute drive from Panania because he knew what was waiting at the other end — harnesses glinting under bright lights; men with whole lifetimes etched on their faces, form guides in back pockets; lathered sweat glistening on fine horseflesh; thundering hooves, flying manes and tails, rustling silks; flashing bulbs past the finishing post ... and no night would be complete without sneezing, reddening eyes and a running nose. It is one of the ironies of Mark's life that he is passionate about harness racing, but is allergic to horse hair. He jokes that every time he goes to the track he has to take about '58 million tablets'!

In those early days at Bankstown, Rodger used to give his sons a dollar each to have a bet with. The thrill of driving home a winner was cause for great banter on the trip home. Mark recalls:

Then in our teenage years we got into the greyhounds. We used to go to Harold Park or Wentworth Park with our junior cricket coach, Glen Russell.

I remember getting caught one night jumping the fence at Wentworth Park. We used to say we were younger than we were and try to get in for free because we wanted to save our money for punting purposes. Either way we were contributing to the sport. We went every Saturday night for a time. I remember Stephen backing a 100–1 winner on the dogs at Harold Park, but I don't think he or Dean ever enjoyed the nights as much as I did.

While Steve drifted away from the races as he grew older, Mark found the outings irresistible. He also enjoyed thoroughbred racing and was only seventeen when he backed the longest priced winner of his career, 150–1 chance Long John Silver at Canterbury. He only backed it because he saw one of his favourite rugby league players, Australian halfback Peter Sterling, with the horse in the stables not long before the race.

At about the same age, he discovered his junior representative team-mates Brad McNamara and Mark Patterson were also devotees of punting.

In the early 1990s the three wise men bought a share in a horse through renowned thoroughbred trainers Tommy Smith and his daughter, Gai Waterhouse. It was named Drivetime, but Drive-Slowly would have been a more apt description. 'It was a slow gelding with nothing to offer,' remembers Patterson.

Mark was 'turned off the gallopers a bit' by the experience. And he much preferred the down-to-earth nature of the harness-racing people. 'Most of them are battlers,' he says. 'There's not the money there is in the [thoroughbred] racing game. They're mostly knockabout people.'

Peter V'landys, the chief executive of the Harold Park Paceway, is one such person. A gregarious man who is passionate about his sport, he recognised Mark — 'a bit of a punter' — would be a high-profile drawcard for the Miracle Mile. In mid-1994, he proposed using Mark in an advertising campaign to promote the race that would be held towards the end of the year. After negotiations were completed with sports agent Leo Karis, who'd only just signed Mark to his books, arrangements were made for the shooting of a television commercial which involved Mark, dressed in his Australian limited-overs uniform, walking through the crowd at Harold Park telling people he'd witnessed a miracle. V'landys recalls:

I'll never forget the first time I met him. I get the message that, 'Mark Waugh is
at reception.' So I go out to meet him, and there he is in his full one-day outfit.
He'd come in totally dressed up and ready to go. I remember saying, 'Jesus,
mate, you're keen!' He just said, 'Well, what's the use in getting changed? I
may as well come in this way if that's what I've got to wear.' We've been close
friends ever since.

After that, he started coming as a guest to the Directors Room at Harold
Park every Friday night. He loved it. He just fitted in perfectly to the culture.
Harness racing hasn't got a very wide demographic, and most of the people
are from working-class backgrounds. I think Mark's upbringing in the
western suburbs really helped. He might have met the Queen and so many
important people, but he's never forgotten his roots, never forgotten he's a
Bankstown kid.

The next stage of Mark's development took place one Friday night when
V'landys and colleague John Dumnesy introduced their new friend to leading
trainer–driver Glenn Frost, whose father Vic owned one of pacing's most
popular horses of the 1990s, Westburn Grant.

'That night we tipped Mark one of our horses, Very Tricky,' says Glenn. 'Old
Trick came out and won, and that set us off on the right leg, and at the end of
the night I told him he should think about coming in on a horse.'

Mark needed no persuading, and contributed $10 000 to a five-man
syndicate, including Frost, who was responsible for buying horses on his
frequent trips to New Zealand. The first two buys had mixed fortunes. Clever
Kiwi was as successful as Drivetime, but Oblico won seven races despite
having bad legs that Frost recalls 'ended up going amiss before we could get
the best out of the old bugger'. Vic Frost believed Oblico would have been an
Inter-Dominion (one of Australia's most prestigious harness races) horse if he
stayed fit and healthy.

Since those early days, Mark has been involved with more than a dozen
horses. Among his latest horses, Chip Machine and J-B-Dean won thirteen races
in six weeks at the beginning of 2000. In his typically optimistic style, Mark
holds high hopes for one of his most recent purchases, a filly called Expedience.
He also part owns New Energy and Clifton Chief with Australian team-mate
Ricky Ponting.

His passion for harness racing is never-ending. When in Sydney, there's no place he'd rather be on a Friday night than in the Directors Room eating oysters and prawns while quietly summing up his chances for the evening. Occasionally he will be asked for an autograph, or will have a cricket question fired at him, but most people recognise it is Mark's time away from duty. There is no better example of its importance than at the end of Australia's Test tour of South Africa in March 2002 when Mark, amidst tremendous speculation about his future, went to a meeting at Harold Park the day he arrived home. Going to the 'trots' is an escape, even a therapy. However, when one of his own horses is racing, there's no chance he'll sit back quietly and watch the race. Sue Porter describes her partner 'moving with the horse, and taking every step'. In contrast to his undemonstrative demeanour on the cricket field, the Mark Waugh driving from the grandstand is almost as animated as Jason Gillespie at the height of an appeal. Mark agrees:

> Yeah, I'm a great driver from the grandstand. I get pretty excited and worked up. It's funny actually because I get bloody nervous before the start. The first thing I hope is that the horse and rider don't get hurt, and then I just hope they win the race. I probably get a bit biased. My horses are always a bit unlucky, or the best in the race, even if they don't win.
>
> I don't like tipping my horses to people because I feel bad if they don't win. Owners are always biased. They always think their horses are better chances than they actually are.

Despite his yearning to be trackside whenever any of his horses race, Mark's profession simply makes it impossible. However, there's no chance that when out of sight the horses are out of mind because on many occasions on tour Mark has risen in the earliest hours of the morning to ring home and listen to a race call. At the other end of the line, either V'landys or Sue is perfectly positioned, holding the phone up to a television, while Mark listens intently to the broadcast. On one occasion V'landys remembers having the phone to the speaker for most of the evening, allowing Mark to hear the entire program of races while at dinner. He also remembers being woken by Mark on trips they've had together:

There'll be a knock on my door at five o'clock in the morning, and it will be Mark saying, 'Come on, the race is on.' So we'll ring up Australia, listen to the race, Mark will go back to bed for a sleep then do it all over again for the next race an hour later.

As with anyone who has backed a horse from Harold Park to the Bong Bong Picnics, Mark relishes the thrill of fattening the wallet. He isn't a gambler who backs numbers, pretty names or colours. Instead, he is a keen student of the form, an avid reader of racing publications, and when at home he'll surf the internet for information on breeding and bloodlines, results and upcoming meetings. He is a serious follower of the horses, recognised by his various racing colleagues, including Australian team-mates, as a good-natured punter who shies away from short-priced runners. V'landys acknowledges his friend is a 'very astute punter'.

He makes a habit of getting all the high-priced horses. Really long-on winners. He does it all the time. If there's going to be a roughie that will win, Mark will back it. He has an unbelievable strike rate. Never backs a favourite.

What amazes me about him is that there'll be no form on the horses, and yet he'll still back them thinking they're sure winners. He gets this feel for them. Reads up on them, and is confident to follow them. He's just so confident when he backs a horse, like no punter I've ever seen. Everything he backs, he's sure will win.

But he's a good loser. He won't take it out on anyone. He'll just shrug his shoulders, say, 'Okay,' and move on to the next race.

Patterson describes his mate as someone 'who never dies wondering. He bets on most things to go around. If you go to the races and there are thirty races, he'd be struggling to miss one.'

Ponting, Shane Warne, and Darren Lehmann are the few members of the Australian squad who share Mark's racing passion. Ponting says with a laugh that he's not sure how Mark has gone over his entire punting career, 'but he always seems to have a fair bit of money in his wallet!' It's common to see Mark or any of his three gambling team-mates flicking the dressing-room television to the races, but it's even more common to see other players hurriedly changing the channel or turning the television off altogether.

Somewhat surprisingly, Sue 'absolutely hates' punting. The most she's ever won is $75. She remembers going with Mark to the races in the early days of their courtship. She'd take a rug, sit on the ground with a book and become lost in the words while Mark would take his already well-thumbed form guide and become lost in the numbers on his way to the betting ring or the mounting enclosure. She says:

He'd forget I was there. Then suddenly he'd realise, come racing across and say, 'Oh my God, do you need anything to eat?' He'd actually forget I was there. It was his little escape in life. Geoff Marsh said to me once he was amazed how Mark could switch everything else off in the world when he went to the races. He just goes off with the fairies. His grandfather and father were exactly the same. I can remember the three of them at Lismore races one afternoon. They were all the same, walking along, hands in their pockets jingling their change, while whistling these inane tunes. All the same. Same hair. Same walk. Same everything.

It's highly likely this third-generation racing Waugh will become more heavily involved in harness racing when he retires. Perhaps he'll become a board member at Harold Park, or a breeder with his own piece of dirt near the Frost stables at Exeter in the New South Wales Southern Highlands. It would be yet another escape for Mark, watching sapling-legged foals develop into 'athletes' with potential. And perhaps their routines, although very different to a cricketer's, would remind Mark of his own days and years of practice. He comments:

Being an owner has given me a much better appreciation of the sport. So much just goes into getting them to the barrier even before a race. They have to be fit and healthy, but it doesn't take much for something to go wrong. It can be really frustrating at times — the horse is ready to race, then it will do something, like kick its stall or do its foot in the paddock or get the flu.

All most people do is see the horse at the races, but to see how much work goes into the preparation is amazing, and gives me a real appreciation of what they have to go through. It's like practising batting. You work that hard in the nets that you want to see the results in the middle. It's good when it actually happens and you get a winner. And I think to breed that winner, actually start the whole process, would be the ultimate feeling.

When asked what he would choose if he had the chance to achieve anything in sport, Mark throws up several possibilities. He would love to play soccer for Australia at a World Cup, win a grand slam tennis tournament, or maybe play in a rugby league grand final for his beloved Bulldogs. However his list is topped by dreams of breeding or owning an Inter-Dominion or Melbourne Cup winner. Because of cricket commitments he has never been to Cup Day at Flemington, but has backed more than his share of winners. Among those he remembers are Black Knight (1984), What a Nuisance (1985) and Subzero (1992).

When visiting Mark and Sue's home, you need not look far to see the influence of racing. In the same room in which Bradman memorabilia has its own cabinet, there are pictures of Oblico flashing past the post. Mark's favourite gallopers Super Impose and Kingston Town also stride across the walls.

Kingston Town, one of Australia's most popular horses, died several years ago, but his memory lives on in the black labrador that quietly patters across the room and sits at Mark's feet. He is much more reserved than his play-mate Jezabeel, the excitable chocolate-coloured labradoodle named after Flemington's 1998 two-mile champion. And then there is Bonecrusher, named for the big-hearted 1986 Cox Plate winner, who follows the sun and curls up to do what cats do best — sleep. He's not alone; Gammelite the ginger 'pacer' with dainty paws keeps him company.

This stable of cats and dogs — given free rein from pool to patio, bedroom to bar — is just one indication of Mark's love of racing. How many people are fanatical enough to name their pets after their passion?

CHAPTER SEVENTEEN

REVERSE SWEEPS AND POINTED FINGERS

At the Singer World Series tournament in Sri Lanka in September 1994, organisers left no-one in any doubt as to which Waugh was which, presenting the twins with playing shirts that were labelled simply 'Mark' and 'Steve'. There was no hint of a surname anywhere.

By the end of the 1994–95 home summer, the names would no longer be merely on the backs of shirts but firmly at the front of Australian cricket-lovers' thoughts, albeit for very different reasons. Steve would be named Test player of the year for his performances against England, while Mark would incur the wrath of officialdom for his involvement with 'John the bookmaker'.

Mark began the season impressively. In his first outing he scored 80 and 0 in a four-wicket win by New South Wales over England at the Newcastle Sports Ground, and was then in commanding touch, making 113 against Queensland at the SCG. An easy 10-wicket win by the Blues prevented Mark having a second chance with the bat, and one last hit out before the first Test, in Brisbane, the following week.

The lack of preparation didn't affect him as he cruised to 140 from 215 balls. His innings, which included fourteen fours and one six, was majestic, and a fascinating contrast to the ebullient power displayed by Michael Slater (176) in a highly entertaining third-wicket stand of 182 in just 154 minutes. Mark was at his regal best, driving, cutting and occasionally pulling his way to his highest Test score at that stage of his career, and his best total in Australia. Marooned on 98 for nearly half an hour, during which he was dropped by second slip Graeme Hick off a Phil DeFreitas delivery, Mark displayed the composure that had been lacking in his game at the start of his career. He eventually reached his fiftieth first-class century with a seemingly effortless cut off Darren Gough. Back foot easing across the stumps, gentle hands and a swing of the blade urged the ball to change direction just as flowing water in a creek can be deflected around a stone.

The home side were dismissed for 426, and after Craig McDermott took 5–53 in England's disastrous reply of 167, Taylor's side had the match by the scruff of the neck. Choosing not to enforce the follow-on, the Australians sought quick runs in the second innings to set up a declaration, and it was amidst the haste that Mark, on 15, suffered the most extraordinary and perhaps embarrassing dismissal of his career. Appropriately the bowler was Phil Tufnell. Mark recalls:

Again Tufnell was bowling over the wicket with a lot of men on the on side. It was pretty hard to score runs that side of the field, so I thought I'd try the reverse sweep. I'd never practised it before in my life. It was some ungainly sort of effort, and I managed to chop the ball back onto my stumps.

I couldn't work out how the hell I got bowled. I wasn't worried about getting out — people say it was a soft dismissal, but in the context of the game we were that far in front I was figuring it didn't really matter if I got out. We needed quick runs, and I thought that was the best option.

It was a premeditated shot that I didn't think I'd get out to. I thought I might miss it and it would hit me in the pads, but I thought it was worth having a go.

I keep hearing that 'Tuffers' gets me out a lot but the thing is how many runs I've scored against him. I like facing him. My theory is that I'm always going to attack him, so he always has a chance of getting me out. But I think it's the best way to play because if you attack him, he can go on the defensive, and it puts him off his game. I suppose when he comes on, there's a chance he's going to get me out, and there's a chance I'm going to score runs, so it's good attacking cricket. Good for the crowds.

The dismissal was a source of much amusement in the Australian dressing room. Mark Taylor recalls:

I could see Junior was getting the dirts with Tufnell because it was fairly defensive bowling, then in typical Mark Waugh fashion he decides to play a shot that none of us has ever seen him play before.

Simmo went berserk; I couldn't look at him because I was laughing so much. I rushed inside to watch the replay, and we all waited inside to see exactly what Mark would do when he came back in. He walks in, looks at us and just says, 'How did that get back onto the stumps?' That was it for me. I couldn't hold it in. Neither could half the side. It was just the way you'd expect Mark to handle it. It was his way of saying he had no luck. I asked him how many times he'd tried the shot. And he was just so straight-faced when he said, 'Oh that's the first time.' It never would have occurred to him to practise the shot before giving it a go. But that's the way he was. I'm sure he wouldn't have played it if we were 5–93, but we were well placed, looking to set a total, so he tried something.

People are always saying that he has to cut soft dismissals out of his game, or it's time to find someone else. Well if you find someone else, we're going to have the most boring cricket team you've ever seen. The way Mark plays has always been great for the game.

Australia won the match by 184 runs, an ideal platform on which to build an assault for the rest of the series. The team won the second Test in Melbourne by 295 runs, Mark contributing 71 then battling in the second innings for 29 in two hours. The encounter is remembered for a hat-trick by Shane Warne.

The Ashes were retained by the end of the rain-affected third Test that was drawn in Sydney. Mark had a quiet game, falling for 3 and 25, and he also showed his fallibility in the slips when he dropped Darren Gough. It was such a rare sight that more than one spectator was prompted to utter, 'You don't see that very often.'

Nor have the past few Ashes series seen many Test victories by England. However, the visitors showed they could be successful when they won the fourth Test by 106 runs, at the Adelaide Oval. Despite the loss, Mark had a memorable outing, taking his best Test haul of 5–40 off 14 overs in England's second innings. His victims were Mike Gatting, John Crawley, Phil DeFreitas, Angus Fraser and captain Mike Atherton. Three of the five fell to the short ball after Mark adopted his favourite 'Lennie Pascoe tactic' of digging the ball in. After scoring 39 in the first innings, he was dismissed by Tufnell in the second for 24, the next best tally behind Ian Healy's unbeaten 51 in a disappointing total of 156.

Australia returned to the winner's circle with a 329-run triumph in the final Test, in Perth. It was an eventful match for the Waughs, who showed their alleged sixth sense had a wiring problem after a mistake running between the wickets left Steve stranded on 99 in the first innings. Mark, who'd made 88 earlier in the day, was back at the crease acting as runner for Craig McDermott who was struggling with a back injury. He recalls:

It was a big mix-up. I don't think Stephen has sent me a Christmas card since. The over before it happened, I was at the non-striker's end when Stephen hit a ball which almost could have been a single, but I said no. At the end of the over he was on strike again but still hadn't got his hundred. He came up to me and told me to get ready for the single. So, first ball from Chris Lewis he knocked one down at his feet. I thought it was a single, so I took off and got about halfway down before he sent me back. Lewis got to the ball, threw it back to Goochie [Graham Gooch] who underarmed it into the stumps. I reckon I must have been out by about a tiny bit of hair.

I felt pretty ordinary. I was to blame I suppose, but I was just trying to get Stephen's hundred.

Apparently he scattered the dressing room and the room attendant when he came off. I was a little behind him, so I didn't see it, but the guys reckon he walked in, and someone said, 'Look out, here comes Stephen.' The room attendant dived and a bat went whistling over his head into the lockers. It wasn't a great feeling.

Steve went close again in the second innings, hitting 80 before falling to Lewis. Mark was caught behind off DeFreitas after making only 1, but he played a handy role with the ball, claiming three wickets for the match to take his series haul to 10 at 19.63, the best average on either side. He also collected 435 runs at 43.5.

England's fourth straight Ashes series loss prompted the predictable response in the English press. What had gone wrong with the team? Why were the 'colonials' considerably better? Mark reflects:

> *Since I started playing, people always seem to have asked, 'What's the problem with English cricket?' No matter where we are playing them, or when, everyone is feeling sorry for English cricket, but we certainly don't. We just like beating them.*
>
> *I think we've got a mental edge over them. They don't think they can beat us, and once you have that attitude, one thing is for sure, and that is you're not going to win too many games. I've always thought England have had good talented players, but for some reason they just don't put it together as a team. I think the players are always worried about their positions in the team. That holds them back. Plus they play a lot of cricket, so injuries are a problem. Their fast bowlers carry injuries into Tests and you just can't do that.*

England suffered further dents to their reputation by failing to make the final of the Benson & Hedges series. Zimbabwe, the other touring side, also fell short in a tournament that included a fourth, controversial team — Australia A. The inclusion of a squad of fringe players wasn't only considered an insult to England and Zimbabwe, but drew fierce criticism from Taylor who neither liked playing against his countrymen in an international series nor was he pleased by the level of support the 'underdogs' received from the crowds. On several occasions Taylor firmly told the media, 'I don't like it when the Australian cricket team is not supported when we are playing at home.'

Just a year out from the World Cup on the subcontinent, administrators considered it a positive move to give every possible candidate the chance for exposure and experience at the top level. It wouldn't be the last time that preparations for the most prized trophy in limited-overs cricket would stir strong and often angry reactions. Taylor, Ian Healy and the Waugh twins can all testify to that.

The strength of Australian cricket was illustrated when both home teams made the final. Faced with a potentially embarrassing situation, Taylor's players breathed a collective sigh of relief after they won the best-of-three decider 2–0. It was the end of an inconsistent campaign for Mark, which was highlighted by a sparkling 93 off 102 balls against the A side in Brisbane during the preliminary rounds. On the flip-side, Mark was dismissed five times for less than 20 in a relatively lean competition that yielded just 175 runs at an average of 25, and three wickets at 37.67. Throughout the series, he found it difficult to 'lift myself up mentally to play against fellow countrymen. It just wasn't right.'

In a very rare occurrence, Mark had been forced to miss one game because of a thigh injury. His resistance to major breakdowns has been a significant feature throughout his career. Allan Border comments:

> It wasn't so long ago I asked Mark how he was travelling. And he said, 'AB, any tougher, I'd rust.' And I actually thought that was about right because if you look at his cricket both at home and on tour, he's one of those uncomplaining blokes who rarely misses a game. Stephen's got different problems with his body whereas Mark is so resilient because he plays all the Test matches and invariably he's up near the top of most matches played on tour. You don't think of it too much, but he just doesn't miss much cricket.

For New South Wales, injuries didn't cause as much damage as international commitments. In 1994–95 Mark was unable to play any Mercantile Mutual Cup matches, and managed just three Shield games, returning 312 runs, including two hundreds, at 62.4. After two very successful seasons, the Blues slid to second-last in the Shield and failed to win a one-day game. The season is best remembered for Queensland's breakthrough triumph, claiming the Shield for the first time since entering the competition in 1926–27.

Throughout the summer Mark continued his communication with 'John the bookmaker'. Irregular phone calls by the Indian were met with standard answers about pitch and weather conditions. Mark continued to think 'nothing of' the relationship.

However, the landscape changed dramatically in February 1995 when the *Sydney Morning Herald*'s Phil Wilkins broke the story that an unnamed Pakistani player had tried to bribe Mark, Warne and Tim May during Australia's tour of Pakistan the previous year. Within days of the first article, the finger was pointed at Salim Malik. By this stage, the Australians were in New Zealand for a limited-overs series with the Kiwis, South Africa and India.

It was during this campaign that tour manager Ian McDonald was told by a journalist that there was speculation an Australian player had received payments from a bookmaker in Sri Lanka. After contacting Graham Halbish, the chief executive of the Australian Cricket Board (ACB), McDonald began investigating the claim. On 20 February, Mark and Warne acknowledged their involvement in unsigned handwritten statements taken by McDonald that were immediately faxed to Halbish.

The players continued to take part in the tournament which Australia won six days later after beating the host nation by six wickets in the final, at Auckland's Eden Park. Mark returned home the leading batsman with 179 runs from four matches at an average of 44.75. After failing with just 11 in his first outing against South Africa, he scored 74 against the Kiwis, 48 off just 32 balls against India, then 46 in the final.

His performances, and those of Warne (five wickets at 28), meant little to Halbish and ACB chairman Alan Crompton when they interviewed the players the following day upon their arrival in Sydney. The meeting took place at the Parkroyal Hotel where the Australians were staying for the night before flying to the West Indies. After again admitting their association with 'John', Mark was fined $10000 and Warne $8000. Although the ACB's directors and the International Cricket Council were informed, the matter was considered a private one between the board and the players — a decision that nearly four years later would be the subject of immense criticism throughout the cricket world. In his 1998 report, Rob O'Regan QC said the punishments imposed on Mark and Warne were 'inadequate', and suggested: 'A more appropriate penalty would, I think, have been suspension for a significant time.' He also wrote:

> They [Mark and Warne] must have known that it is wrong to accept money from, and supply information to, a bookmaker whom they also knew as someone who betted on cricket. Otherwise they would have reported the incident to team management long before they were found out in February 1995. In behaving as they did they failed lamentably to set the sort of example one might expect from senior players and role models for many young cricketers.

Once he'd been fined, Mark considered the matter was over. End of story. He says, 'I made a mistake, they fined me accordingly. As far as I was concerned that was the end of it. At the time I didn't think it was too big a deal at all.'

However, the developing controversy surrounding Malik ensured no matter involving bookmakers and cricket would die peacefully. Bob Simpson, who had been pushing the ACB to take action over the Salim Malik affair, was among the first to vent his anger. He says he was 'furious' with the ACB when he only found out about Mark and Shane's association with 'John' and the subsequent fines when the Australians were just about to board the plane to the West Indies. He recalls:

> If I'd known 24 hours before I wouldn't have gone because I'd been trying to push the board into action into what happened in Pakistan. I felt, 'Here am I, the man leading the push in the hotel where there's a meeting going on about something that mightn't have been connected to Pakistan, but was still obviously serious, and I'm not being told.' My initial reaction when on the plane was, 'What am I doing here if these people don't trust me?'

When the Australians arrived in the West Indies in early March, Mark was keen to concentrate on nothing but cricket. He was contacted by 'John' prior to the first Test, but he told the bookmaker the relationship was over.

The 1995 trip to the West Indies was not to involve John, but by the end of the tour the Australians had welcomed another stranger into their camp — a long-lost trophy they affectionately called 'Frank'.

CHAPTER EIGHTEEN

WELCOME BACK, FRANK

Apart from bats, balls, pads, gloves and all sorts of protective paraphernalia, the Australians arrived in the West Indies with a vital piece of equipment that they hoped would deflect the physical and mental challenges that lay ahead — they'd come with a ready supply of 'attitude'.

By this stage, Mark, as one of the senior members of the team with forty-four Tests behind him, was one of the players who wanted his team-mates to adopt a rugged 'let's take 'em down' approach to the Test series. He recalls:

Right at the start of the tour we said, 'Stuff these guys. Their tailenders, their bowlers have bounced us for years, now let's get our own back. Let's get stuck into them. Let's get up them. Don't worry about what might happen. They might get the shits and bowl quicker. Who knows? But one thing's for sure, and that is they're gonna bowl us bouncers and intimidate us, so let's get them before they get us.'

Stephen and I were really part of that. I think teams in the past had been scared, but we weren't going to give up. It's always tough going to the West Indies, but we thought we had a side that was equipped to do well. We thought the Windies had lost a bit of their aura of invincibility, so we thought we were a chance.

The early signs weren't positive as Australia lost the limited-overs series 4–1. After missing one game with a slight leg strain, Mark had a moderate time with the bat, tallying 125 runs at an average of 31.25. His highest score of 70 from only 58 deliveries came in the final game. He also took four wickets, his best return of 3–42 coming in the first encounter.

The losses weren't the worst news to strike the Australians — bowlers Craig McDermott and Damien Fleming both suffered injuries that ruled them out for the remainder of the tour. The bowling attack had suddenly gone from being threatening to threadbare. It would have been hard to imagine a more troublesome start for the visitors, who only had two matches after the one-dayers to settle on a combination for the first Test, in Bridgetown. They cruised to an innings and 61-run victory over Bourda in Georgetown, Guyana (Mark slammed 75 off 65 balls before being caught and bowled by off-spinner Roger Harper), and drew a rain-affected match with a West Indies President's XI in Castries, St Lucia (Mark was run out for 73). It was one night during the latter encounter that Bob Simpson stimulated the thoughts of his players by handing out a sheet of questions and answers suggesting why performances hadn't been up to expectations, how the team could improve, and the sacrifices that would have to be made. Many of the players considered this a critical moment of the tour because they were really encouraged to think deeply about the position they were in. The discussions that followed during an intense meeting motivated the players as individuals and as team-mates. The timing was perfect.

Three days later the much awaited Test series began. On the morning of 31 March the Australians left their base at Club Rockley Resort and travelled for twenty minutes through the charming narrow streets of Barbados. Past numerous churches. Past the racecourse. Past hundreds of neat and tidy chattel houses with window shutters open as wide as the mouths of the grinning children sitting in the shade outside. Past numerous small liquor stores. Past old men on bikes, young men on foot, and women of all ages with babies on their hips. Then into a narrow laneway at the back of Kensington Oval, a tiny ground heaving with anticipation, and in some sections already reeking of Cockspur rum. The locals expected nothing other than the continuation of West

Indian supremacy. In five attempts, no Australian team had won a Test at this ground. Why would these Aussies be any different?

When Taylor walked out with Richie Richardson for the toss, horns screamed, the fans yelled and a swarm of Australian flags waved furiously. In the dressing rooms, two teams of anxious players watched. As Mark suggests, there is nothing quite like the first morning of a Test series — no matter where it is played in the world.

The first morning you can be a bit unsettled. You don't know how the wicket is going to play, and you want to get off to a good start. I think it's okay for the bowlers because if they make a mistake they can come back, but the batsmen get a bit more nervous. It's a much more nerve-wracking game for batsmen overall, it's more cut-throat because one mistake can be the end of your game. So you can feel that in the dressing room before the toss.

Everyone is doing their own thing. I keep it pretty simple. I might have a hit in the nets, or just get my gear ready. I get my whites on regardless of the toss because either way I'm going to be involved. I put the sunscreen on, and just get everything ready.

The toss is the most nervous time. Everyone watches it. The bowlers of course always want to bat. And the batsmen, usually nine times out of 10, want to bowl unless it's a flat wicket.

Then when it happens, if we happen to win the toss and bat, the bowlers can carry on a bit, joking with things like, 'You beauty, a day off in the sheds, get a bit of a massage, have an easy day.' But the batsmen are in their corners getting their gear ready and are thinking, 'Am I going to get runs today?' You never know. You just never know. As much as you prepare, and as well as you are hitting the ball, you just don't know what's going to happen. It's hard. There can sometimes be a bit of scrambling for the toilet. Nerves just affect the guys in different ways.

All we can do then is get on the field and perform. We've had our meetings, we know what has to be done. Occasionally someone like Warney, with a bit of the AFL mentality, will yell out, 'Come on boys, first session is real important. Let's get into them.' If we're bowling, a few other guys might say a few words like, 'No loose balls, let's keep the pressure on.' If we're bowling, I'm generally a lot more relaxed. Overall, the room is pretty quiet.

But that first morning of the West Indies series there was a lot of noise. We lost the toss and were getting ready to bowl. Everyone was pretty excited. Our team CD machine was going, and the guys were just really keen to get going. Mark [Taylor] said a couple of things, then out we went.

Heading into the series, we all talked about just how important that first session could be. We wanted to dictate terms from the start because if we could put the Windies on the back foot, we thought we could unsettle them. They were always at their strongest if they took control early and were allowed to dominate.

As it turned out, the session was a wonderful bout of heavy blows and counter-punches. On what appeared a run-making strip, the West Indies were soon back-pedalling at 3–6, but Carl Hooper and Brian Lara repaired the damage in a free-flowing, and at times daring, stand that took the home side to 3–116 by the lunch-break. The Australians talked during the interval about how the next session was just as important as the last. One of the teams not only had to assert authority, but keep it. By tea, Taylor's men had done exactly that. The home side had been dismissed for 195, left-armer Brendon Julian the chief wrecker, taking 4–36.

The innings was scarred by controversy after Lara (65) was given out, caught by Steve on the fourth attempt in the gully. After assessing countless replays, television commentators questioned whether the ball had touched the ground. Lara and the Kensington crowd had no doubts — in their minds it was simply not out. Mark recalls, 'Stephen said he caught it, so that should have been good enough. You should go by the word, but it's not really done these days. I was standing in slips and didn't know whether it was out or not, but Stephen's word was good enough for me.'

While the incident remained a talking point for the rest of the Test, there was no room for dispute over which team grabbed hold of the match and wouldn't let go. Australia's first innings reply of 346 set up a 151-run lead. Ian Healy (74 n.o.), Steve (65) and Taylor (55) were the major scorers. Mark contributed a handsome 40, half of which came in boundaries. He was in such control that his dismissal was a surprise to nearly everyone except his brother standing at the other end. Just as Curtly Ambrose was about to bowl what proved to be the fateful delivery of Mark's innings, Steve had one of his unfortunate premonitions that the ball was going to be edged to wicket-keeper Junior Murray. The hunch was correct. Yet again. Later, when Steve told his twin what had happened, Mark replied, 'Why don't you bloody well tell me when you're thinking those thoughts!'

At stumps on day two, the West Indies were 0–15 in their second innings. While they'd survived without mishap, the same couldn't be said for the Australians who were one short in their dressing room after Bob Simpson had been rushed to hospital in the morning with a serious blood clot in his left calf. His illness somewhat surprised Mark who believes 'Simmo is as tough a bloke as I've ever seen.'

Simpson would eventually recover, but the same couldn't be said for the West Indians, who tripped and stumbled their way to a miserable 189 all out. Glenn McGrath claimed his first five-wicket haul in Test cricket (5–68), taking his game tally to eight scalps, a return that deservedly earned him man-of-the-match honours.

Taylor and Michael Slater wiped away the 39 runs needed to launch some rowdy celebrations that continued late into the night on the *Bajan Queen*, a boat that rocked with both teams at an official sponsor's party in the middle of Bridgetown Harbour. During the evening when Mark and Michael Slater, both a little the worse for wear, sat down to enjoy some dinner, Mark looked across at his team-mate and said, 'We can win this, we can really bloody do it.' This wasn't alcohol talking. These were words from a player who had a growing belief that a change in the power base of world cricket was approaching. Mark says:

I think the West Indies took us a bit easy in that first Test. Their batting was a bit loose. Sloppy really. They gave us a chance to get into the game and we did. We had our setbacks, but we came back every time. The guys were gelling together really well. We were becoming a really tight team.

The Recreation Ground in St John's, Antigua, hosted the second Test. Twelve months earlier, Lara had smashed a world record 375 against England. As Gigi Fernandez, a taxi driver and charismatic local identity suggested, 'Brian may be the prince of Trinidad, but in Antigua he is the king.' However, not even royalty could overcome the rain. Despite using a helicopter to dry the ground during a frustrating final day, both teams ran out of time to push for victory. Just like the weather, Mark's innings were a mixture of gloom and sunshine. He fell for 4 in the first innings and 61 in the second.

In the context of world cricket, he fulfilled a much more important duty off the field when he, Shane Warne and Tim May talked with the then ACB solicitor Graeme Johnson about Salim Malik's attempted bribes during the tour of Pakistan. All three players signed sworn statements in front of Johnson that were immediately forwarded to the ACB and ICC.

The ACB then issued a statement, declaring that the trio would not go to Pakistan to appear at a planned inquiry into the incident and the wider issues of bribery in general. It was no surprise considering Pakistan cricket chief Javed Burki had already questioned the validity of the claims, and defended his players, despite news that some former and current members of the team, including Imran Khan and Aamir Sohail, were publicly acknowledging there was illegal betting going on. In such a volatile environment, the ACB had every reason to protect its players, citing concern for their safety in Pakistan.

Protection was also an issue during the third Test, at Queen's Park in Port of Spain, Trinidad. A grassy pitch — so underprepared that it could barely be differentiated from the rest of the playing surface just two days before the game — spat violently at both teams throughout a contest that only lasted two and a half days. Neither team reached 150 in conditions that were custom made for the pacemen, especially Curtly Ambrose whose nine wickets for the match cost only 65 runs. The home side won the Test by nine wickets. Mark had a disappointing time, scoring 2 and 7 in Australia's meagre totals of 128 and 105. Steve was the only batsman on either side to record a fifty when he made a courageous unbeaten 63 in the first innings, which included a toe-to-toe confrontation with Ambrose.

The result swept the series momentum towards the West Indians. Was it going to be a similar story to the 1992–93 campaign in Australia where it had been a case of 'so close, yet so far'?

The 1995 Australians' hopes weren't helped by the final Test venue of Sabina Park, Kingston, a hostile environment for visiting teams. Was part of Mike Gatting's nose still in the pitch? Maybe not, but it was possible to see other noses, faces and bodies in a surface so shiny it could have been a mirror. In the days leading up to the encounter, curator Charlie Joseph buffed and polished his pride and joy by sprinkling water on the muddy strip, then spinning a roller in circles. It was an intriguing and unique technique that was accompanied by Charlie's gleeful repetition of, 'Shine, shine, I want my pitch to shine.' Perhaps it was the Jamaican adaptation of the famous witches' incantation:

> Double, double, toil and trouble;
> Fire, burn; and cauldron, bubble.

Both teams realised that as the match wore on, the pitch in the middle of the cauldron of Sabina Park wouldn't bubble, but would undoubtedly cause trouble for the team batting last, as the rolled mud would inevitably break into tiny pieces.

The fall of the coin was set to play a decisive role, and for the fourth time in the series the silver smiled at Richie Richardson, who had no hesitation in batting. However, his decision wasn't followed by a treasure chest of runs. Although Richardson (100) and Lara (65) threatened to steer their side to an imposing total, the rest of the team contributed just 100 between them. Paul Reiffel, the quiet achiever, took 3–48, including Richardson's valuable scalp.

The second day was critical. The Australians knew they needed to post a score that would put the Windies under pressure. An innings of at least 450 was the aim, but when the top three of Taylor, Slater and Boon fell cheaply, Australia were struggling at 3–73. What followed was one of the most significant partnerships in the recent history of world cricket. Steve (200) and Mark (126) combined for a 231-run stand in 233 minutes. Copping as many as four shoulder-high deliveries each over, the brothers built their scores on cheeky running, aggressive strokes and spirited mid-wicket chats that defied the perception that the twins rarely spoke. Mark says:

It was probably our best partnership ever. And I'd say it's as good an innings as I've played anywhere. When I went in we were 2–50, and the West Indies had their backs up. I wasn't overly confident with my memories of Kingston from the matches I'd played there in 1991. It was one of those days when I walked out thinking, 'Yeah, I'll be happy if I get some runs.' But I certainly wasn't confident.

I started well, saw the ball well and was lucky enough to get into my stride. I hardly missed a ball all day. My shot selection was good, just the way I struck the ball felt great.

There were two shots I really remember off Courtney Walsh. I actually hooked one right out of the screws for four, and I hit another one over second slip. He was bowling short, I just stood my ground and guided it over. It was a special feeling just to have that control to do it against one of the best bowlers going around who was trying 100 per cent. You could see he was fuming when he ran down the wicket.

You know when you are in full control, when everything goes right for you, just happens for you. It doesn't matter how well the opposition bowl or try to unsettle you, you are just in your zone. That doesn't happen too often because normally every run is bloody hard work.

I didn't feel good at all going into that Test. I didn't feel in form at all, but everything just happened. I can't offer any explanation. They say preparation is really important, but I've been through a lot of things where to me it hasn't mattered at all. Like that innings. I didn't have any great practice, I hadn't been hitting the ball well, and wasn't confident just watching the bowling before I went out to bat, and yet I went out and batted the best I ever have. And yet there have been other times when I've felt like I'm going to go really well, but don't. It's one of the things that is really attractive about cricket, the uncertainty of it all.

That partnership put us on our way. Stephen was great. He just gutsed it out and showed the bowlers that he just wasn't going to give in. I actually thought I batted the better, but it didn't matter because as long as someone was doing it we were going to be in a good position. But being together with Stephen for such an important partnership made it really special. It is one of my biggest highlights of our time together playing cricket.

At the end I was really disappointed to get out. I got a ball from Carl Hooper that jumped out of the rough and I was caught by Jimmy Adams at bat-pad. I actually had something in my eye that ball. I was going to back away but thought, 'No, it doesn't matter. It's only Hooper bowling, and I should be able to get through it.' But I honestly couldn't see out of one of my eyes.

Only the most one-eyed of West Indian supporters couldn't have appreciated the batting brilliance of the Waughs. Mark's innings, which took him past 3000 Test runs, lasted 276 minutes and included twelve fours from 192 balls. Steve's 555-minute epic included seventeen boundaries and one six from 425 balls. Steve recalls:

> Throughout the partnership we realised the significance of what it was setting up. We both peaked at the right time, we were ready for that challenge. We'd put a lot of work into playing for Australia, all those years of practising and sacrificing things to make it — we knew it was going to be our time. When we started the partnership I felt good about it. I felt comfortable out there and could feel a big partnership coming on. It was a big moment. We enjoyed it. We wanted that challenge.

An aggressive Greg Blewett half-century was overshadowed by the performance of the twins, but was also a significant contribution in Australia's total of 531, a lead of 266 with more than two days remaining. By this stage, the pitch was beginning to crumble. It needed grass to hold it together, but the only grass available was in the reefers that hung from the lips of dejected locals in the stands, who watched their heroes finish the third day at 3–63. Reiffel had taken all three wickets, including Lara lbw for a duck with a ball that almost sneaked along the ground.

After a storm hit Kingston on the rest day, the Australians were relieved to wake to sunshine on day four. Outside Sabina Park, before play began, a crying local said to an Australian television reporter, 'See what you do, see what your team do.' When questioned, the middle-aged man informed the reporter that a friend had suicided the previous night; the death was blamed on the impending loss and the inevitable shattering of Caribbean pride.

It was all over by the end of the day. When Kenneth Benjamin edged a Warne delivery to Taylor at first slip, Australia were celebrating their first series win in the West Indies since Ian Chappell led a team to victory in 1972–3. Taylor was presented with the Frank Worrell Trophy, named in honour of one of cricket's most respected leaders, who'd captained the West Indies during their tied Test campaign down under in 1960–61. The trophy had been missing for some years, but had been discovered recently in a cupboard in the home of the mother of former West Indian fast bowler, Wes Hall.

In the dressing room, the Australians passed the trophy around and posed for photos with the silverware that quickly became known as 'Frank'. Mark remembers:

It was a great feeling. After so many years of coming up empty-handed, we'd finally turned everything around. It was the start of a new era for us. It gave us new confidence. We knew we could start setting the benchmark in world cricket. We wanted to take cricket to a new level.

In a series dominated by the bowlers, Mark, with 240 runs and an average of 40, finished second behind Steve (429 runs at 107.25) on Australia's run-getting list. Lara (308 runs at 44) was the only other player on either side to average above 40.

En route back home, Taylor's men stopped off in the rich man's playground of Bermuda for two social games and some well-earned relaxation. The island made a lasting impression on Mark, who considers it one of his favourite destinations. A 'fantasy island with crystal-blue water, magnificent houses and a lot of great golf courses'. At the expense of the ACB, many of the players were joined by their wives and partners for the week-long break. Despite it being Mark's favourite cricket tour destination, he had cause for concern when Sue crashed a scooter into a hedge in the team's hotel car park.

Only her pride was hurt, and she managed to have the last laugh when a number of Australian players, including Mark, David Boon and Ricky Ponting, who to this day doesn't have an Australian driver's licence, had 'stacks'.

While most of the team could afford to ease off the throttle during the winter, Mark headed back to Essex for his fifth county season. This time Sue would travel with him. After weighing up her future with her globetrotting partner, she quit her job at the Kingsgrove Sports Centre, telling her boss, Harry Solomons, 'I'm being ripped apart here. My loyalties are with you as a friend, but I can't keep my relationship going with Mark.' She acknowledged she hadn't been fair to Harry, herself or Mark. It was time for Harry's first employee to call it a day.

Sue and Mark set up base in Colchester. After the excitement of the Caribbean, it took a little time to adjust to the 'real world' again. He scored just one half-century in his first twelve county championship innings, and did not hit triple figures until early July when he made 126 against Surrey at The Oval. Mark admits:

I struggled at first. It was tough to go from the beautiful warm weather of the West Indies and winning the series to fronting up to play county cricket where it can be cold and damp with nowhere near the same atmosphere.

The first bit of the season I just wasn't there mentally. As much as you try to do your best, there can be times when you're just not with it. I think I needed a rest. I probably didn't enjoy it as much as I should have. It's hard when you're mentally fatigued to lift yourself. There just isn't the energy there.

It's easy to get questioned about your level of commitment. When you're a professional player in a team you have no history like I have with New South Wales or even Bankstown. To me, there's no difference in attitude between playing for New South Wales or Essex. It's exactly the same. Once you're with a bunch of guys for about a month, you just feel part of the team no matter where you are. I've got a lot of good friends at Essex and immense respect for the county. They were a great county to play with. We had great team spirit, and a lot of good players. I always tried to give 100 per cent, but was disappointed I didn't do as well as I should have.

It was more than coincidence that Essex struggled near the bottom of the table while Mark's returns were poor. However, by the end of the season the county was sitting fifth in the championship after Mark had come home strongly with 1347 runs at an average of 51.8. He made five hundreds in fifteen matches, his top score 173 against Somerset at Southend. He also took 17 first-class wickets at 46.41. However, for his team-mates, there were much more telling impressions than cold statistics. Ron Irani recalls:

That year 'Waughry' had this aura about him. A world-class cricketer, and a world-class individual — and the individual really brought more to the club. The performances on the field still ended up being great — he got a shed-load of runs — but what he brought most to the Essex dressing room was himself as an individual.

I don't mean to say that off the cuff. I genuinely mean that. He used to put . people in their place if they needed to be, but he wasn't real interested in that.

He was more interested in having a laugh, but playing hard on the field and always playing hard to win.

He was tough on the field. Even though he was a jolly Jack-the-lad off the field whom everyone warmed to — not just the players, but the members and supporters as well — he was a real win-at-all-costs player. He just wants to win. He gets up in the morning, gets to the ground, and all he thinks about is winning. And the guy has had plenty of practice — he's been a winner throughout his career. He was fantastic. He had total respect from everybody on and off the field.

As a player he was sheer class. Just watching him whip the ball through leg side off off-stump was fantastic. Just a total natural. Natural eye, natural flair. And he did it all simply. He said to us a lot of times, 'If a ball comes down and I fancy hitting it, I will.'

He was very confident and he used to say, 'I'll give these blokes a touch-up. I'll get a hundred today.'

But it didn't always happen the way he wanted. I can remember this one match where I think there was a batsman called Greenfield. He was playing and missing, playing and missing, and Mark got stuck into him from slips. He started saying, 'Oh this Greenfield is an impostor!' We were all having a bit of a giggle. Getting to 10 he must have played and missed about thirty times. Waughry kept on calling him an impostor, and saying how useless he was. Well, in the end Greenfield got about 120! We decided then and there it was time for Waughry to keep snot regarding the sledging stakes because the batsmen were always getting runs!

He used to get carried away a bit with his bowling too. He fancied himself a real quickie — he bowled good pace. I remember one game down at Hove against Sussex in the county championship. It was an all-time classic, we still talk about it now in the dressing room.

He was getting a bit of pace up, but he was struggling a bit with the front line was Mark, and he was bowling a few no-balls. He dropped in a few short ones which the batsman fended away past his nose, then he pitched one up and hit this batsman bang in front. We all went up for lbw, but the umpire called, 'No-ball.' Waughry came down the wicket, he was absolutely spitting and frustrated, he turned and looked at the front line, then went back to his mark. He was a bit more angry, had a bit more pace, and shoved it up the batsman

again. He pitched one up and the batsman was stone dead in front again, and
we all went up. The umpire went, 'Not out.' Well Waughry came down towards
the umpire, and said, 'Mate, is there any chance of concentrating on the far end
rather than this end?'

    The umpire looked at him in disbelief, but Waughry got away with it. That
was the beauty about it all. The umpire just laughed in the end. Waughry didn't
abuse the umpire, he just said it totally off the cuff. Everyone just cracked up.
Even though it pains me to say it, he is quite a funny bloke, but I wouldn't tell
him normally! He's definitely by far and away the best overseas player I've
played with at Essex. All the members relate to Mark Waugh, even now. We
miss him.

That was Mark's final county season because Australian commitments were making it increasingly difficult to commit enough time and energy to the English circuit. He'd made runs and mates in abundance, but not everyone who played at Essex was fond of him. In 1991, the season after Mark had finished a three-year stint on the English circuit, he was replaced by none other than Salim Malik. Four years on, there was considerable doubt whether the embattled Pakistani batsman would follow in Mark's footsteps again by heading to Australia for the 1995–96 summer.

CHAPTER NINETEEN

JUSTICE AND BOMB BLASTS

C oncocted. If the word is used in a kitchen, it's more than likely referring to a cook's attempt to mix ingredients into a culinary masterpiece. If used in a classroom, it may refer to a child inventing a story to avoid trouble: 'Honestly sir, I didn't kick him, I just tripped and fell.'

But what happens when the word is uttered by Fakhruddin G. Ebrahim, a former Pakistani Supreme Court judge? On 21 October 1995, the Pakistan Cricket Board's independent inquiry headed by Judge Ebrahim cleared Salim Malik of the bribery allegations contained in sworn statements by Mark, Tim May and Shane Warne. After questioning Malik and examining the Australians' statements in their absence, the judge concluded the allegations 'are not worthy of any credence and must be rejected as unfounded'.

Criticising the ACB for not making its players available for the inquiry, Judge Ebrahim, in closing his report (Pakistan Cricket Board, Independent Inquiry Report, 21 October 1995), declared:

Having given my most anxious consideration to the whole case, the conclusion is both obvious and inevitable. The allegations made against

Salim Malik cannot be believed and appear to have been concocted for reasons best known to the 'accusers'.

Concocted. Just add a bit of spice and wait for the issue to boil into a controversy. Could Mark, Warne and May really invent such a story?

Perhaps the most farcical suggestion to come from the inquiry was Salim Malik's claim that Mark may have held a grudge because he'd been replaced by Malik at Essex. The ACB condemned the findings, and contended the International Cricket Council should have conducted its own inquiry. However, throughout the early days of the corruption issue, the ICC preferred to act as a middleman, and in doing so revealed its weakness and powerlessness to control the game.

Although disappointed and perplexed by the outcome, Mark didn't want to be drawn further into the issue. Some journalists would later suggest the quiet approach was an attempt to hide his association with John the bookmaker. These comments angered Mark, and contributed to his dislike of certain scribes and reporters later in his career.

At the time, it seemed unlikely Mark could avoid being dragged into the controversy in some way. Just days after Judge Ebrahim's report was made public, the Pakistan team arrived in Perth for a three-Test tour. Days later, all attention focused on the belated arrival of the man who'd been under suspension until the outcome of the inquiry — Salim Malik.

On the other side of the country, all Mark wanted to do was 'get on with playing cricket'. He'd scored 16, 18 not out and an unbeaten 43 in the opening three Mercantile Mutual Cup matches that New South Wales won against Queensland, Western Australia and Victoria, and at the time of Pakistan's arrival, he'd already had a Sheffield Shield outing, making 48 and 33 in a rain-affected draw with Western Australia in Perth.

In his following matches before the first Test, in Brisbane, his returns were 44 and 17 not out in a 214-run win over Tasmania at the SCG and 1 and 10 not out in a six-wicket victory against Victoria in Melbourne. He took one wicket at the MCG, but he was being increasingly hampered by a bulging disc in his back that he had first felt in the final weeks of his season with Essex. Sharp shooting pains down his left leg told him that his time as a medium pacer was coming to an end. However, his bowling career wasn't.

He'd long toyed with tweaking off-spinners at New South Wales and Australian net sessions, and had even claimed some Shield scalps with his slow deliveries. He recalls:

> There was only one downside about taking up off-spin — I couldn't have that aggression. If someone was going to hit me for four or six, I wouldn't have an aggressive comeback. That's one of the reasons I always loved bowling medium pace, because I could bowl bouncers and put it up the batsmen!

Mark took his first Test wicket as a spin bowler in the opening encounter against Pakistan, in Brisbane. In the second innings, the heavy-footed Inzamam-ul-Haq shuffled down the pitch with the aim of lofting the ball over the cover infield, but he managed only to sky it straight to Craig McDermott at mid-off. Mark finished with 1–6 off five very tidy overs as Pakistan slid to an innings and 126-run defeat. Earlier, he had scored 59 in Australia's total of 463, more than enough to ensure the home side didn't need to bat again. An unbeaten 112 by Steve was the cornerstone of the innings, but the performance was overshadowed by Warne's match haul of 11 wickets. None gave the leg-spinner greater pleasure than Salim Malik's second innings dismissal. After failing to bat in the first innings because of a gash he'd suffered while catching Mark Taylor on the opening day, Salim walked to the crease in the lowly number 8 spot. Four balls later he walked off without scoring after hitting a catch to McDermott at mid-off. Mark recalls:

> I was at silly mid-off when he [Salim] walked out. You could feel the tension. I don't think anyone really knew what to say. We were all really quiet. We'd spoken about what could happen in the team meeting before the match, and all of us just wanted to put the bribes issue out of our minds and just play cricket. When Salim was out, we all got pretty excited. We all wanted him out really badly. The fact that Warney got him made it pretty sweet.

A week earlier against South Australia, Salim had fallen victim to Tim May. In the eyes of the accusers, some justice had been served.

After winning the second Test by 155 runs, in Hobart — Mark scored 88 and 3 — the Australians sought a clean sweep of the series at the SCG. In his four previous Tests at his home ground, Mark had tallied only 126 runs from seven innings. However, one innings later the tally had almost been doubled after Mark scored 116 on a pitch that was biting and spinning considerably.

The performance stood alone, dominating Australia's first innings total of 257. In 206 balls Mark hit eight fours and one six, the latter a powerful hit over mid-wicket off off-spinner Saqlain Mushtaq. Throughout his stay, Mark engaged in a captivating battle with jaunty wrist-spinner Mushtaq Ahmed, who took 5–95. It was the most fascinating duel of the match. Mark's resistance finally ended when Mushtaq held on to a chance in the gully from the bowling of captain Wasim Akram. The century-maker walked from the field, satisfied that he'd finally performed well on his own patch of turf. Mark says:

> Sydney is one of my favourite grounds. The SCG, Adelaide and Lord's would be my top three. Obviously being my home ground makes it special. The size of it is perfect for cricket, there's great tradition, the stands create a great atmosphere, and you can sit outside the dressing room and soak it all in. Obviously with your friends and family there, the occasion is always important. But in some ways it's actually harder playing there because you always want to perform well for them. Plus, you're always organising tickets for friends, someone always wants to say hello to you, there are always more distractions than elsewhere.
>
> Scoring the ton was a great moment. It's always good to do well in front of your family, isn't it?

In the second innings, Mark's dismissal in the final minutes of the fourth day was the turning point of the match, according to Australian captain Mark Taylor. Chasing 247 for victory, the home side were well positioned at 2–117 when Mark was the victim of a dubious decision by Steve Randell. He was given out, caught behind off Wasim Akram's bowling after playing forward to a delivery that only flicked his pad. Mark was 'shitty' with the decision. At the time, the first innings century-maker was in complete control, strolling to 34 from only 46 balls.

Resuming in the morning at 3–121, the Australians collapsed to be 172 all out. Mushtaq took 4–91 to finish with nine wickets and the man-of-the-match trophy.

Despite the disappointment, it had been a good series for Mark who finished with 300 runs at an average of 60. His two wickets from off-spin had come at 48.50 runs each, and as the Pakistanis returned home, Mark was also pleased that he'd managed to avoid any further 'incidents' with Salim Malik.

However, he had far from a clear mind when he walked out to bat in the first Test against Sri Lanka, in Perth. The memory of his four successive ducks on the 1992 tour was impossible to dislodge. They had been raised in the newspapers, and even Shane Warne questioned his mate about them in his match preview for Channel Nine. Mark admits there have been few times in his career when he has felt more nervous. Until he scored a run, the ducks were at the forefront of his thoughts. But such feelings didn't last long as he pushed to a century in four hours, finishing with 111 from 223 balls.

After reaching triple figures, he used his bat to gesture rudely to a group of spectators who'd been sledging him from the scoreboard hill. It was a rare show of displeasure from the century-maker.

The innings wasn't a typical Mark Waugh display full of grace and charisma. For once, it could be seen that Mark wasn't making batting look easy. He worked hard, an aspect that really pleased him, together with the knowledge that he'd scored centuries in successive Tests for the first time in his career. It was his tenth Test hundred, in his fifty-second match. Significantly, all but one of his tons had come in the first innings. Michael Slater was the star performer, blasting 219 in Australia's victory by an innings and 36 runs.

However, individual performances were soon overshadowed by controversies and confrontations as the Sri Lankan visit degenerated into one of the most unsavoury campaigns in recent history. After facing accusations of ball-tampering in Perth, the Sri Lankans were decidedly wobbly, but the wheels didn't fall off until the opening day of the second Test, in Melbourne, on Boxing Day. In the space of three overs, umpire Darrell Hair, officiating at the bowler's end, no-balled off-spinner Muttiah Muralitharan for throwing seven times. Mark, who was batting at the time, recalls:

It was very off-putting to bat in those circumstances because just about every second ball was being called. It was pretty well impossible to concentrate. You could see the Sri Lankans obviously weren't happy. They were talking in their own language, wondering what was going on. All I could do was try to concentrate. It was a very strange situation.

I can't tell if Murali throws the ball or not because he has such an unusual action, an unusual wrist. I've always found him the hardest spinner to face because of his action. He's got the off-break that turns a mile, then he's got the top-spinner that goes the other way. It's almost like playing a leg-spinner because he's almost got a wrong 'un, and that puts doubt in your mind. He just gets so much spin on the ball and pace off the pitch.

As far as whether he should be called? Well, it's up to the individual umpire, and they have to call it the way they see it. The bottom line is that he's been cleared several times by the ICC since Darrell called him, so we just have to accept that he has an unusual action and get on with it.

Murali is a good fella, a bit of a character, like a clown in a circus the way he jumps around with those big eyes. He's a very likeable sort of fella. I don't wish him any bad luck.

Despite Mark's charitable view, the Boxing Day incident would have ramifications for the rest of the summer and beyond.

Australia won the match by 10 wickets. Mark scored 61 in his only chance at the crease, but was disappointed he 'didn't go on with it'. He was bowled by Muralitharan, the topical spinner's only success.

The Benson & Hedges series, involving the West Indies as the third team, had begun in the fortnight before the Melbourne Test. The Australians won all three of their opening encounters in which Mark's highlight was a man-of-the-match return of 53 from 65 balls, and 1–26 off 10 overs against the Windies in Adelaide.

It had been an incident-free start to the tournament, but the Muralitharan controversy ensured there would be considerable unrest when the matches resumed. On New Year's Day, Australia won their fourth game after Michael Bevan hit West Indian spinner Roger Harper for a boundary off the final ball of a thriller in Sydney, then four days later Muralitharan was called for throwing again, this time by umpire Ross Emerson while the Sri Lankans were playing the Windies in Brisbane.

As the protests of Sri Lankan captain Arjuna Ranatunga and company became louder in the remaining preliminary matches, Mark made a telling statement of his own. After a run of low scores, Michael Slater was dropped, and once again Mark was elevated to open with Taylor. In and out of the role since his first taste of it in New Zealand, Mark indicated his latest promotion had a ring of permanence to it when he hit a belligerent 130 from 144 deliveries against the dispirited Sri Lankans, in Perth. At the time it was the third-highest one-day innings by an Australian, and the partnership of 189 with Taylor (85) was the seventh best of all time. The innings ended in unusual fashion when Mark was run-out going for a quick single off a wide. Australia won by 83 runs and confirmed a spot in the final where they again met Sri Lanka.

The first encounter of the championship decider, in Melbourne, had several controversial umpiring decisions that further affected the visitors' mood. However, they retained their composure, despite losing by 18 runs. Mark scored 4 and took 1–23 off six overs.

The second match in Sydney proved a bitter finale to the tournament. Batting first, the home side again received a tremendous start when Taylor (82) and Mark (73 from 82 balls) shared a 135-run partnership that laid the foundations for a formidable total of 5–273. Rain during the interval almost forced the abandonment of the contest, but play finally resumed with the Sri Lankans chasing the modified target of 168 off 25 overs.

In a strange but successful move, Mark (1–31 off five overs) opened the bowling with his off-spin and claimed the dangerous Aravinda de Silva. However, the most notable incidents weren't dismissals or boundaries, but a series of confrontations, including a mid-wicket collision between Glenn McGrath and Sanath Jayasuriya, and a brief but animated exchange between Ranatunga and Ian Healy when the Sri Lankan captain, complaining of cramps, called for a runner. Healy and the rest of the Australians had good reason to believe that the overweight Sri Lankan was overexaggerating the seriousness of his injury as a ploy to get a faster set of legs to the wicket. Mark says:

I'd be lying if I said he didn't get under our skins. He is tactically very astute. He pushes the rules of the game to the limit. There is no doubt he has a different approach to the game than the Australians.

The way they play can be irritating, but you can't let it get to you. They also talk a lot. There's just constant banter. We never know what they're talking about. It's the same as the South Africans because they can speak in Afrikaans. But they all seem to be able to swear all right in English!

The Australians had the final say when they restricted Sri Lanka to 8–159, six runs short of the target. The last unfortunate incident occurred when many of the losers failed to shake hands with Taylor and his men at the end of the match, an incident which Mark remembers as 'one of the worst' during his career because 'no matter what happens in the game, we've always been taught to shake hands afterwards. It was an insult.' It was a sour end to what had been a consistent series for Mark, who amassed 357 runs at an average of 35.5 and a strike rate of 73.46. His six wickets came at 35.83 apiece.

He completed a profitable international summer when he scored 71 in the third and last Test, in Adelaide, which the Australians won by 148 runs. Although he made only 12 in the second innings, he finished third (255 runs at 63.75) behind his brother and Michael Slater in the series aggregates. He also took two wickets at 36.50. Muralitharan, who'd sat out the Adelaide match, finished with three scalps at 116. It was a sad and humiliating return for one of the most popular players in the touring party.

By this stage, the Australians' minds were wandering beyond the cricket field to the approaching World Cup on the subcontinent. The Sri Lankan controversies had already led to alleged death threats against Shane Warne, Bob Simpson and Craig McDermott during the summer. When combined with the Salim Malik affair the fourteen-man squad had every right to be concerned about security.

Three days before the Adelaide Test in the final week of January, players met to discuss their worries with ACB officials, including the chief executive, Graham Halbish. A number of proposals were put forward. Could the team boycott the Sri Lankan leg of their campaign? Or would it be a 'wait and see' approach before every match? On the morning of the final day of the Test, the players voted unanimously to continue with the tour as scheduled.

But then a suicide bomber struck. On 31 January, a Tamil man drove a truck laden with explosives into a nine-storey bank building in the commercial heart of the Sri Lankan capital, Colombo. About 100 people were killed and hundreds more were injured.

The Australian cricketers' fears were very real. Suddenly, Australia's opening World Cup match, against Sri Lanka, was in jeopardy.

CHAPTER TWENTY

BEATEN BUT NOT BROKEN

After intense discussions about the bomb blast in Colombo, the ACB's Board of Directors made the only sensible decision possible — to abort the Sri Lankan leg of their team's campaign. Mark Taylor's squad were scheduled to play all their remaining preliminary matches in India, and under the rules of the competition they could still qualify for the semi-finals, despite forfeiting their contest with Sri Lanka. The West Indies soon followed the Australians' lead, but the two other teams in Pool A, Zimbabwe and Kenya, decided not to withdraw, and later played games at Colombo and Kandy without incident. The Australians and West Indians' actions angered the World Cup's organising committee, PILCOM, and countless fans across the subcontinent, particularly in the teardrop nation. Mark says:

It wasn't a hard decision for the Board to make. Cricket is obviously an important part of life, but it's not worth risking your life for. If the opposite decision had been made, I still would have gone, but I wouldn't have been too comfortable.

By the time we got there [the team went straight to India], we tried to put everything behind us and concentrate on what we were there to do. There was heavy security everywhere, but it wasn't the first time. If you look at some of the cities we've played in like Kingston and Karachi, you soon get used to that way of life. After a while you don't really notice it. At the start of the tour it's a bit off-putting having a bloke standing next to you with a gun, but you accept it before too long. You do get used to it. Actually, their body odour is more unsettling.

It was hard because we were copping a bagging in the Indian papers, and some locals were coming up and asking us why we weren't going to Sri Lanka, but most of them accepted the reasons. It was really only the officials who had a problem with it. The fans were different. Most of them didn't really seem to care, they were just really excited that we were there.

India has the most fanatical cricket fans in the world. There are just so many people — that's the first thing that hits you when you arrive. It's hard to comprehend from the moment you get there, everyone is staring at you at the airport like you're not human. It's a bit off-putting. They'd win a gold medal in a staring competition for sure. All they want to do is touch you, and get close to you. It can get a bit overbearing.

You can't really walk out on the streets without security or some sort of formal party because the people just mob you, and they'll do anything for you. They want to take you to their restaurants, show you their carpets for big discounts. For them just to say hello or for them to tell their friends that they've met us is a big thing in their lives. Occasionally they can get a bit annoying, but they're not meaning to be rude. Many of them haven't got much in their lives except for religion, movie stars and cricketers. We know we're in a privileged position when we go there because people just want to worship us and treat us like kings.

It was in this contrasting environment of public adulation and official anger that the Australians conducted their campaign. They based themselves in Bombay, nowadays Mumbai, before the tournament began. Mark showed he was in ominous form when he scored fifty in a practice match, which prompted Ian Healy to suggest to him afterwards, 'Mate if you bat like that, you'll get three or four hundreds on your ear.' Their belated first match was against one of the minnows of the cricketing world, Kenya, in Vishakhapatnam. In his *World Cup Diary*, Steve referred to an article in the *Hindu* newspaper (21 February 1996) the day after the Australians arrived in the east coast city.

In all, five Assistant Commissioners of Police, twenty Circle Inspectors, forty-eight Sub-inspectors, 130 Head Constables, 431 Constables and eight Armed Platoons, equivalent to three companies of Andhra Pradesh Special Police (APSP), besides an anti-sabotage squad and a pack of sniffer dogs specially requisitioned, will guard the Australians from the time their plane lands till they fly out to the venue of their next match.

When added to the team of sari-clad women in charge of rolling the pitch, the hundreds of men and boys who were clambering up and down the makeshift scoreboard that was held together by bamboo sticks, the hundred or so more who were painting advertising boards, myriad other ground staff doing nothing in particular, the relentless rolling maul of local journalists who hung on every word or movement of the Australians, the massive outside broadcast television crew, and last, but certainly not least, the players, it was almost impossible to imagine there would be any room for paying spectators.

After winning the toss, Kenyan captain Maurice Odumbe sent his opponents in on what would prove to be a painfully slow-paced pitch. The night before, the Kenyans had spoken excitedly about playing Australia, in particular the Waughs. By the end of the fiftieth over, the African cricketers had perhaps seen enough of the twins. Mark scored 130 from as many balls, and Steve made 82 from 92 deliveries in a third-wicket stand of 207, the first double-century partnership in World Cup history. Australia reached 7–304, and although Kenya were spirited in reply, they finished at 7–207. In a blow for Taylor's side, Craig McDermott tore a calf muscle while bowling, and was ruled out for the tournament.

The next outing was a special occasion — the first day-nighter to be played in Mumbai, home of Sachin Tendulkar, who the locals boasted would tear Australia apart single-handedly. As it turned out, their predictions weren't too far from the truth. However, Australia managed to win by 16 runs after Mark became the first player to score successive hundreds in a World Cup. His innings of 126 from 135 balls was a stunning exhibition of batsmanship. Aided by some wide bowling at the start, he moved quickly into stride, time and again hitting over the covers or through mid-wicket. He batted as though the attack consisted of schoolboys, and in a sign of rare class changed his mind mid-stroke on several occasions.

Mark's array of shots, however, was matched by India's pocket-sized hero, Tendulkar, who rocketed to 90 off 88 balls. His one six and each of his fourteen boundaries made the capacity crowd delirious. Every possible object, from miniature drums to empty plastic bottles were banged each time Tendulkar scored a run. Surely there has rarely been a more exhilarating atmosphere in world sport than that at Wankhede Stadium on the night of 27 February 1996. Just as it appeared he would guide his side to the winning target of 259, Tendulkar danced down the pitch to Mark, who summed up his rival's movements quickly enough to toss the ball out wide. Tendulkar missed it, Ian Healy completed the stumping, Australia had made it two wins from as many games, and Mark had the same number of man-of-the-match trophies. He says:

> The Indian game was a really big game. The win showed we were in the tournament with a really big chance. It was a great start. Personally, I was obviously pretty happy with the way I was hitting them. I was probably in as good a form at that tournament as I've ever been in. Everything just felt right.

It's likely Mark would have also made a century in the next game in Nagpur if Australia had been chasing a bigger total. However, a four-wicket haul by Warne destroyed the Zimbabweans, who scrambled to make 154. Mark was 76 not out when the target was reached.

His runs finally dried up in the desert city of Jaipur when the West Indies beat Australia by four wickets. Mark struggled to 30 off 63 balls before the frustration of his slow strike rate prompted him to try to hit Roger Harper over the top. The result was a stumping by Courtney Browne.

Despite the loss — it was effectively the team's second loss because of the forfeit to Sri Lanka — Australia qualified for a quarter-final day-nighter against New Zealand in Madras. Mark clearly remembers the match for several reasons.

> There were only two blokes in the New Zealand side that we didn't really talk about at the team meeting. Chris Harris and Lee Germon. We just brushed over them, we didn't think they'd worry us too much. But they just creamed us. Germon got 80 odd [89 off 97 balls], and Harris took us apart [130 off 125 balls].

I remember thinking they were going to get about 350. I thought: 'We're gone. That's it. It's over.' We just couldn't stop the scoring, but we ended up doing all right to pull them back to what we did [9–286].

The weather made it worse for us because it must have been the hottest day of all time! I bowled a few overs [1–43 off eight overs], and I just kept cramping in the calves. I was cramping up just from fielding too. It was about as uncomfortable as I've ever been on a cricket field.

In the interval between innings I could feel my calves cramping up again, and I thought, 'Geez, I don't know how I'm going to bat here.' I took some tablets, but was still cramping up when I went out. Harris was as well. After his hundred he had to bowl 10 overs, and he hardly looked as if he could walk. He was cramping up everywhere. When he started bowling, he'd run a few steps then have to pull up with a sore calf. It was exhausting for all of us.

I don't know how, but I got another 100 [110 off 112 balls]. When I got there, I thought, 'I've got to get out of here.' I had nothing left, we needed fresh players at the crease. It was the hottest I've ever been. Madras must be the most uncomfortable place I've ever played cricket. It even felt as if my pads were on fire. So I just decided to have a slog. If I got runs, I got runs; if I got out, then good because someone fresh could come in.

When Mark departed, Australia still needed 74 runs from 70 balls, a task that Steve (59 n.o.) and Stuart Law (42 n.o.) achieved with 13 deliveries to spare. It was a remarkable run-chase, a thrilling match and a showcase for extraordinary individual performances, none of which shone brighter than Mark's. In just five innings, he had amassed 472 runs, eclipsing Graham Gooch's tournament record of 471. Those cricket-lovers who were fortunate enough to see the display will never forget it. Bob Simpson says, 'If I could watch an hour of anyone batting, I would want to see Normie O'Neill at his best, and Mark is in that category. I can't give a batsman higher praise.'

O'Neill was a dashing stroke-maker who played forty-two Tests for Australia in the 1950s and 60s, scoring 2779 runs at 45.55. Over the years Mark has also been compared with Doug Walters and David Gower, but in the early rounds of the 1996 World Cup his name deserved to stand alone.

Unfortunately, Mark couldn't maintain his form for the final two matches. The first, the semi-final against the West Indies, in Chandigarh, was one of the most remarkable limited-overs games ever played. Australia started disastrously, slumping to 4–15 — Mark was lbw to Curtly Ambrose for a second ball duck — but Stuart Law (72), Michael Bevan (69) and a late order flurry from Ian Healy (31) dragged the team to 8–207.

In reply, the Windies looked in no trouble at 2–165, but in a dramatic collapse they lost their last eight wickets for 37 runs, six short of qualifying for a spot in the final, against Sri Lanka at Lahore's Gaddafi Stadium. Mark recalls:

My first memory of the match is my batting. That might be strange seeing that I only lasted two balls, but I remember not being able to see the ball. The sun was right behind Amby, and there was a real glare on the wicket. A white wicket and white ball made it pretty hard. First ball I didn't see, I let it go, and it went past off-stump. Then the next ball — bang, out lbw.

The win was one of the most amazing I've ever been a part of. We bowled well, but the Windies basically just stuffed it up. They should have walked it in. In the dressing room afterwards we were stunned, thinking, 'How the bloody hell did we win that?' We went back to the hotel that night and had a bit of a party. It was as though we thought we'd won the whole cup. Looking back we played our big game one game too early.

We didn't prepare as well as we should have for the final. We actually had to go to a function the night before the game for some reason. And while we were there, Sri Lanka were out training. There was a heavy dew at the ground, which Sri Lanka obviously knew about, but we didn't. They were smart getting accustomed to it.

The next day they won the toss and bowled first. They knew what to do because by the time we started bowling under lights the dew was there, and it was almost impossible to grip the ball. You just couldn't do well bowling second in those conditions. But the bottom line is we should have made more runs when we batted. Halfway through our innings we were looking at at least 20 to 30 more than we ended up getting.

Perhaps it was a fitting revenge for the Sri Lankans who were still stung by the memories of their recent tour to Australia. Their captain Arjuna Ranatunga took immense pleasure from the result — victory to Sri Lanka by seven wickets.

The Australians were beaten, but not broken. After their initial fears over security, their campaign had been relatively trouble free. They received warm hospitality wherever they went, and apart from the occasional travel bungle that no trip to the subcontinent would be complete without, the team generally had few reasons to complain.

Despite his poor finish to the tournament — he made 12 in the final — Mark was the tournament's second-leading run-scorer with a tally of 484 runs at an average of 80.67 and a strike rate of 85.36. The figures of the leading player, Sachin Tendulkar, were very similar: 523 runs at 87.17 and a strike rate of 85.32.

The Australians returned home in time for the final weeks of the Sheffield Shield. The Waughs, Taylor, Bevan, McGrath and Shane Lee all played for New South Wales in a drawn match against South Australia at the SCG to end a disappointing summer in which the Blues failed to figure prominently in either the first-class or one-day arena. Mark scored 57 and 26, and took 2–19 in the second innings. In all, he played five Shield games in the season, scoring 250 runs at 31.25 and taking three wickets at 16.33. A glance along the averages list reveals the name of Dean Waugh, who wore the baggy blue cap once while his brothers were on the subcontinent. He was also involved in two Mercantile Mutual Cup games. But one of the most enjoyable moments for the brothers came in the final of the Sydney grade competition when Dean captained all three of his brothers. Mark believes both his younger brothers 'had the talent, if not the desire, to have gone all the way to the top'. Unfortunately for the family and Bankstown, opposition club Sutherland had some special talent of their own — Glenn McGrath dominated the decider and ensured the Belvidere Cup had a new home after spending the previous two seasons at Bankstown. Nevertheless it was a memorable occasion for the Waugh family. From Lahore to Lord's, Bankstown to Balmain, Mark, Steve, Dean and Danny were leaving their mark in cricket, and forever filling their parents with immeasurable pride. Rodger Waugh comments:

There are a lot of times I pinch myself and think, 'God, how lucky are you to have four very talented boys, and two just happen to be Test cricketers?'. You've got to be blessed. Every time I see them now I think it's a bonus. It's phenomenal. I get asked about them and I talk to people about them, and it quite often goes over my head, but when I have a quiet moment to think about it, I know we're very lucky.

The end of the 1995–96 season gave Mark some valuable time away from cricket because Australia's next commitment was a Singer Series limited-overs tournament in Sri Lanka in late August. The four-month break was Mark's longest period out of the game since he'd received his initial call-up to Essex in 1988. The years had passed quickly.

Although neither Mark nor Sue can remember exactly, it was at about this time that they became engaged while having a holiday in Hong Kong. Shrugging his shoulders, Mark says:

It just happened I suppose. I'm no romantic bloke, just a simple bloke who likes his sport. It was a mutual decision really, but we still haven't made the next step. Maybe we never will. Marriage might be a bit overrated you know. So many people end up divorced anyway. I think as long as you enjoy each other's company and love each other, that's the main thing.

Sue laughs when she says:

The ring has been changed about eight times since then. It was something we did to keep Mum and Dad happy. People can't keep saying I'm Mark's girlfriend, but there's no reason to get married. I can't have children any more, and that would be my only reason to marry. Why fix something that isn't broken — we're happy the way we are. I've been there and done that with marriage. We might change our minds in six months time, we might change our minds in six years time. It's just not a priority at the moment. It doesn't worry us. It's only others who are fascinated.

During the winter, apart from the regular Friday night trips to the Directors Room at Harold Park and the days at home watching Sky Channel or reliving any of his horses' winning races on video — 'Even when you've seen them 100 times it still feels good' — Mark relished the chance to follow his favourite rugby league team, the Bulldogs, formerly Canterbury-Bankstown. Mark acknowledges:

I'm a mad Bulldogs supporter. I fire up at big games. I can actually see how people can get carried away cheering for Australia at cricket. When I'm playing

I can never see how they can get that excited, but when I'm in the stands I get a completely different feel. I can relate it to me at the rugby league. I get a bit down if the Bulldogs lose or suffer a bad decision. I'm not aggressive, but I do get into the game. I'll yell at the ref, tell him to get 'em back 10 metres. I love it.

Mark's close association with the Bulldogs began during the reign of the club's most famous administrator, the late Peter Moore, who Mark remembers fondly as a 'man who loved his club and his district. He earned immense respect of players both at club and international level.' To this day Moore's widow, Marie, continues the habit established by her late husband of sending good luck faxes to Mark and Steve before most Test matches. She is also often seen sitting by herself at Bankstown Oval watching grade cricket.

The Bulldogs current chief executive, Bob Hagan, was introduced to Mark by Moore several years ago. He acknowledges football is an outlet for Mark, but realises the relationship is not just a one-way street. He says:

Mark's a very good judge of rugby league, and the players pick that up. You get some people who try to talk the talk and are way off the pace, but when Mark comes in he knows what the players are going through, and he understands and appreciates the ferocity of the game and the knocks the players take. He's faced the same things with Allan Donald and Waqar Younis, and the players respect that.

He's one of the icons of the district. We see Mark as a role model so that we can get our younger players to aspire to the things that people like Mark have achieved. We like to make sure that people who come in the front door go out the front door as better people. Whether they've achieved great heights in the game or not, they've at least learnt more about themselves and life, so that they go out and are ready for the outside world. That's how people like Mark help. He's a role model to so many players in this club.

In honour of his all-time favourite players — rugged five-eighth Terry Lamb, who led the Bulldogs to a Premiership in 1995, and Laurie Daley, a Canberra, New South Wales and Australian legend — Mark chose to put the number '6' on the back of his national one-day uniform. Upcoming Bulldogs star Braith Anasta is the latest five-eighth to win Mark's admiration. It is just another example of a simple man's passion for sport.

The four-month lay-off passed quickly, and Mark was soon back chasing greater numbers on the cricket field. In a replay of the World Cup, Australia reached the final of the Singer Series, but were again beaten by Sri Lanka. Mark had a quiet tournament, scoring 100 runs in four innings.

Little more than a month later, the Australians, without Shane Warne, lost by seven wickets to India in a one-off Test match at the Feroz Shah Kotla Ground in Delhi. The contest lasted just three and a half days. Mark made starts in both innings, scoring 26 and 23, but found the going extremely slow on the 'driest Test wicket' he'd ever seen. He remembers:

> It looked like it was a week old before the match even started. We were under strength with our spinners. It was only Peter McIntyre's second Test, and Brad Hogg's first. But that was no excuse. We should have done better.
>
> There were a lot of suggestions that the wicket had been doctored. I accept that pitches will be tailored to suit home teams but they still have to be of a suitable standard. This one was on the suspect side of too dry. I'd never seen anything like it. But I suppose it was their way to get the home ground advantage. You play in the conditions you know best. The Indians would be stupid to produce a green-top, wouldn't they?
>
> And if you're a good player, you have to learn to adapt — that's the challenge of being away from home. But we just didn't adapt; we batted poorly in the first innings and that cost us the game.

The Australians were dismissed for 182 and 234. Steve, with a stubborn 63 not out in the second innings, was the only batsman to notch a half-century against an attack inspired by fast leg-spinner Anil Kumble, who claimed nine wickets for the match.

Afterwards, the new coach of Australia accused some of his team of 'playing like millionaires'. Geoff Marsh had replaced Bob Simpson during the winter. Whether or not the players deserved the criticism, a daunting schedule over the next two years certainly meant they were going to be working hard for their money.

CHAPTER TWENTY-ONE

STAYING ON TOP

If only it were possible to be a fly on the wall at an Australian team meeting. What would be overheard? How will we bowl to Tendulkar? Watch Waqar's inswinger. Don't give Lara any room. Play Mushie as an offie. Let Cullinan know he's our bunny. Remember to bat in partnerships. Rotate the strike. Don't lose concentration at the end of an over. Switch on before the start of a new one.

To an outsider, a team meeting wouldn't only be an intriguing example of the workings of a professional sporting unit, but it would also tell much about individual personalities. There are the players who are keen to contribute as much as they can, the motivational types who seek to stir the emotions of their team-mates; then there are others who sit quietly, soaking in what is said, offering occasional words of their own. When these players speak, everyone listens. Mark is generally a member of the quiet brigade. He analyses the subject, then chooses his words carefully. His comments are precise and precious; sound, succinct and above all else, simple. Mark Taylor says:

We'd be sitting in a meeting, and we might be discussing the same point for half an hour about how we're going to face Ambrose, then Mark will say, 'Well, if he bowls a good ball, you play defensively, and if he bowls a bad ball, you hit it for four.' And you tend to think it's a pretty simple comment, but it's true. You can over-analyse the game, but Mark is definitely not a bloke who does that; he tries to keep it pretty simple, he definitely enjoys it, and that's why he's been so successful.

One of the points Mark stressed at the start of the 1996–97 series against the West Indies was, 'We've got them down, let's keep them there.'

After working so hard to regain the Frank Worrell Trophy in 1995, the Australians felt it would be just as difficult to keep it. Under captain Courtney Walsh — Richie Richardson had retired since the 1995 series — the Caribbean visitors may have appeared to have lost some of their sparkle, but to take them lightly was akin to walking along a tightrope in gumboots.

Because of the one-off Test in Delhi, and the ensuing Titan Cup limited-overs tournament in which Mark Taylor's team failed to reach the final, the Australians had only light domestic commitments before the first Test against the Windies, in Brisbane. Mark made 18 and 69 not out in a draw against Queensland at the SCG, then in what would be his last appearance for New South Wales for the summer, he scored 72 and 2 in another draw with Victoria at North Sydney Oval.

Australia won the opening encounter of the Worrell Trophy series by 123 runs after an unbeaten 161 by Ian Healy put the home side into a commanding position by the end of the second day. Mark made 38 before falling caught behind from a Walsh delivery. Earlier in the innings, he'd suffered a knock to the side of his head when he ducked into a short ball from Kenneth Benjamin. Mark was rarely to play a hook shot throughout the summer, a decision commentators and journalists turned into a considerable talking point.

He top scored with 57 in the second innings as the Australians reached an overall lead of 419. Despite starting strongly, the visitors folded after lunch on the final day, succumbing to Glenn McGrath (4–60) and the left-arm wrist-spin of Michael Bevan (3–46).

The home side won the second Test, in Sydney, by 124 runs. Mark contributed 19 and 67 in a game he remembers most for his unfortunate mid-wicket collision with opener Matthew Elliott while going for a second run off Carl Hooper's bowling in the second innings. At the time Elliott was closing in on a century, but instead of leaving the ground with a raised bat, he farewelled the match and the series on a stretcher, retired hurt (78) with a torn cartilage in his right knee. Mark recalls:

> I still don't really know how that happened. I remember thinking, 'I'll change sides to get out of Matthew's way, but he changed sides at the same time while we were both looking at the ball. The last thing I expected was to run into anybody and get hit as hard as I did. Then, after the hit, I looked around and saw Matthew. All I remember was being flat on my back and trying to get up, sort of like in those bad dreams when you're fighting to get up or get away from something. But I couldn't get up, and all Hooper had to do was flick the bails to get me out, but for some reason he threw it to Matthew's end where Herb [Elliott] managed to scrape home. How one of us wasn't run out, I'll never know. I thought it was a bit of a joke, so I started laughing, then I saw Herb was in big trouble with his knee.
>
> It was a sports blooper. He said I cost him his hundred. I didn't realise how serious it was until I got off the field. I felt pretty bad, but what could I do? It was just one of those mistakes that happen.

The whole Australian team tripped and fell in the Boxing Day Test, at the MCG. The third match of the series lasted only three days as Curtly Ambrose took full advantage of an inconsistent pitch, finishing with nine wickets. Mark was lbw to the man of the match in the first innings for a duck, then battled to 19 in 81 minutes in the second before Courtney Walsh trapped him in front with a shooter.

The six-wicket triumph lifted the Windies' hopes of a comeback for the remaining two matches of the series, but as quickly as their spirits had risen, they slid again, at the Adelaide Oval, after Australia won by an innings and 183 runs. Against an attack that was without the injured Ambrose, Mark was in classic touch, scoring 82 from 150 balls, but was overshadowed by Matthew Hayden (125), Greg Blewett (99) and the stand-alone performer Michael Bevan, in a purple patch at the time, who added an unbeaten 85 to his bowling hauls of 4–31 and 6–82.

The visitors had one final chance for revenge on their favourite Australian ground, the WACA in Perth. And they succeeded on a pitch with incredible canyons that opened up to such an extent that it was possible to stand a bat upright in the cracks. Ambrose, returning from injury for his last match in Australia, proved unplayable at times, taking seven wickets, including Mark for 79 in the first innings.

Mark wasn't at the crease long enough in the second innings to make an impression — he was dismissed by Courtney Walsh for 9 as Australia crumbled to 194 all out, leaving the visitors just 54 runs for victory, a target they achieved without losing a wicket.

Unfortunately the encounter was soured by some incidents on the second day when West Indian batsman Robert Samuels, who'd already offered his fair share of lip in Australia's first innings, was sledged by the home side. He was continually called a 'loser', and his cricketing ability came in for some harsh judgement from the slips cordon. Brian Lara went to the defence of his young team-mate, and afterwards in a media conference, he condemned the verbal taunts he'd heard. Mark acknowledges:

Yeah, we were having a few words to Samuels. It wasn't anything personal. I've played Test cricket for a long time, and I can't remember any of us getting personal with anybody. It was just our view of his batting.

I don't know why Brian stepped in when he shouldn't have. He was probably just trying to protect his own player, or maybe he just wanted to get into the limelight, I don't know. But he does like getting involved when he shouldn't, he gets a bit carried away. For some reason he always seems to be in the middle of it when something happens on the field. I don't agree with him having a go at us in the press conference. Our philosophy is, 'What happens on the field, stays on the field, then that's the end of it.'

I don't know Brian particularly well. I don't ring him up when we're not playing, but we've had a few drinks with him after games or on the odd night out. He's always been very friendly with me, Shane [Warne] and Stephen. He keeps to himself a fair bit, even within his own team.

In a series dominated by the ball, Mark finished the leading scorer in either team, gathering 370 runs at 41.11. Despite the retention of the Frank Worrell Trophy, the Australians were under fire after a disappointing limited-overs tournament in which they failed to reach the final for the first time since

1979–80. Just one man was absorbing the pressure — Mark Taylor, whose form throughout the summer had prompted headlines that the Australian captain was facing the sack. He scored 153 runs at just 17 in the Tests, and 143 runs at 17.87 in the newly named Carlton & United series. Mark says:

> *I suppose being captain, he got a few more favours than another player got. But because he was such a good captain and leader, the selectors didn't want to disrupt a team that was going well. Sure, we didn't perform well in the one-dayers, but that can happen easily enough. We were just a bit stale, then lost concentration. Mark hadn't had a very good run at Test level, but there were thoughts that he would come out of it. To me, there's nothing worse than not playing to your true ability. It can be very frustrating when you know you can be letting the team down. It can be very hard.*
>
> *You have to give credit to him. When you're struggling for form it can wear you down a lot, but Mark's demeanour and the way he handled the side didn't really change at all. He would have been getting more frustrated innings by innings, but most of the time he didn't let it show.*

At times later in his career, Mark would know exactly what his captain would have been feeling when he too was at the centre of some savage criticism over a run of low scores. However, in 1996–97 he had few worries. In contrast to his team's fortunes, he had enjoyed a successful Carlton & United series, gathering 385 runs at 59.66 and a strike rate of 71.60. His highest score, 102 from 114 balls, in a seven-wicket loss to the Windies in Brisbane, was his ninth limited-overs century. It continued a remarkable run for him as opener. The 1996 calendar year had returned 1059 runs, which swept him past the 4000 mark in 123 matches. It was an imposing record.

The end of the international home summer brought no rest for Mark and his team-mates who headed to South Africa for a three-Test campaign and seven limited-overs matches. In two lead-up games, Mark hurried to 101 from 93 balls before retiring in a 50-run win over Boland in a one-dayer, then hit an aristocratic 124 in Australia's eight-wicket success over Natal in a four-day match at Durban. His innings included thirteen fours and four sixes, three of which came off off-spinner Pat Symcox, who was renowned for 'chirping' against batsmen. On this occasion he decided applause for each shot was a more sensible action. At one stage, rival captain Dale Benkenstein had five men on the fence in a bid to counter the onslaught. Mark eventually threw his wicket away, his performance prompting journalist Malcolm Knox to write in the *Sydney Morning Herald* (25 February 1997):

> In many ways it was typical Mark: aggressive, imperious, effortless and terminated by a shot that led watchers to conclude that he had simply grown bored with batting.

Boredom was only an issue for South African fans during the first Test, in Johannesburg. After winning the toss and making 302 on the opening day, the home side spent the next two and a half days in the field as Australia demoralised the attack, eventually declaring at 8–628. The highlight was unquestionably the 385-run fifth-wicket stand between Greg Blewett (214) and Steve (160). The pair had batted through the entire third day on their way to the highest ever partnership against South Africa. Just like the crowd, Mark was a spectator, somewhat annoyed after making only 26. His all too brief appearance included four boundaries, and his demise, caught behind off an Allan Donald delivery, surprised many. It wasn't the first nor last time a Mark Waugh innings of promise would end in disappointment.

Trailing by 326 runs, Hansie Cronje and his men collapsed for just 130 in the second innings. When Daryll Cullinan walked out to bat, Shane Warne eagerly told Mark, 'I'm going to have this bloke for breakfast.' The leg-spinner's notorious bunny delivered his wicket on toast — caught behind with a half-hearted prod that showed a lot about his state of mind and the mental dominance the Australians have long tried to assert over their opponents. Mark comments:

> When we first played Cullinan we worked out fairly quickly that he didn't play spin particularly well. The way cricket has gone over the past few years, teams have plans now for every player, but a plan is only good if you can implement it. If you can't carry it out, there's no use doing it. You have to have the ability to back it up. That's why Cullinan is a great example because Warney seemed to get him most of the time with a flipper, or a quicker one. It was a pretty obvious thing to do against him.

At our meeting before the match we'd watched a lot of videos of South Africa's players, and Hansie Cronje was one bloke we had a definite plan for. We wanted to try to unsettle him with the short ball. It worked a bit throughout the series, but not all the time.

People talk about how important it is to get on top of the other captain. It has a bit of relevance because if you can take down the leader of the pack in sport, business, even warfare, you're more of a chance of defeating the opposition. He's the decision-maker, so if you put him down and get him off his game, he mightn't be as effective in running the side, and making those decisions.

But I think the targeting of captains and players is a bit overrated really. You know each batsman's idiosyncrasies, strengths and weaknesses. If you just basically keep pressure on a player with good line and length on top of off-stump, that's a pretty good plan for everyone. What more can you do really? It's only a ball isn't it? It's not as if you can bowl two balls to a batsman at once. You're still bowling one ball. The game doesn't change. You can't put obstacles on the pitch, or have an extra fieldsman. A lot of it is mental, and that's where the Australians have a big advantage. We can worry teams just by them thinking we have special tactics for them. You might stick two blokes back for the hook, but it doesn't mean you're going to bowl a bouncer. But it does immediately get the batsman thinking about what's coming up. It just gets into his mind.

A good example is when Warney bowled Basit Ali with the final ball of the day when we played Pakistan, in Sydney in 1996. We stopped play before that ball, and had a bit of a chat. It was bluff. Nothing much was said except for, 'It's been a good day hasn't it?' We said nothing, but we made him think that we were thinking something. As it turned out, he was bowled around his legs.

We talk among ourselves and discuss tactics all the time. The captain quite often gets the plaudits. He either gets the glory or the bagging, but a lot of the time different tactics come from different players which you don't really know about. It's only common sense. You've got eleven different people in the team, so you have eleven different ways of thinking. Or if you discount the fast bowlers — they don't think too much — you have eight or nine ways of thinking. You'd be silly not to use that experience.

But really, plans are no big deal. You just have to overcome them. It's not as if you're going to go out there and bowl half-volleys and full tosses. It's a hard game.

The second Test, at Port Elizabeth, was indeed a hard, and fluctuating, game of cricket. After stumps on the second day, a tired and sunburnt Taylor, under growing pressure over his batting form, walked through the foyer at the team hotel. As he passed a couple of journalists he muttered, 'Not a good day that one, not a real good day at all.' It was a considerable understatement. South Africa had gone to stumps at 0–83 in their second innings, an overall lead of 184, after dismissing Australia for a miserable 108. Matthew Elliott (23) and Mark (20) were the only two recognised batsmen to make starts. As the scores suggested, the St George's Park pitch was proving very difficult to bat on. Green, inconsistent and seaming, it was the type of surface no batsman could ever feel 'in' on, even if he had runs next to his name.

The trend continued on the third day when Jason Gillespie (3–49) triggered a dramatic collapse that saw the home side dismissed for 168, leaving Australia 270 to win — by far and away the biggest total of the match.

As he watched Taylor and Matthew Hayden leave the dressing room to begin the chase, Mark began his familiar routine of only putting his pads on, then finding a place to sit and watch the early overs. The players' viewing area at St George's Park is surrounded by glass, not the preferred way for Mark to monitor the game because of the stuffiness of the enclosed environment. Once seated, he followed the game closely. The home side had been hampered by the loss of Shaun Pollock with a hamstring injury, forcing Allan Donald to carry the attack's hopes, but all-rounder Brian McMillan claimed the first breakthrough, trapping Taylor lbw for 13. While Elliott walked to the crease, Mark put on his thigh pad and protector. He felt more comfortable being wholly prepared than waiting for another wicket to fall before collecting his gear. He says, 'It's a recurring bad dream for a lot of players that they're not ready when they're going in to bat.' He was only caught short once, when playing for Essex. A wicket fell, Mark was next in, but was forced to rush his preparation because he was sitting on the toilet. Since then, he's never risked addressing the porcelain while waiting to bat.

When Taylor returned to the dressing room, everyone was quiet. Australia were in an uncomfortable position that was soon made worse when an almost comical mix-up between Hayden and Elliott resulted in both batsmen running for the same crease. Hayden was run out for 14, with the score 2–30.

Mark picked up his bat and gloves, put on his helmet, walked out of the dressing room, down an external flight of stairs, along a pathway, then on to the field of play. At a team meeting after the disastrous first innings, Mark had boldly said, 'We've got to be positive. The wicket's not that bad.' It was now time to prove it.

The rest of the day was hard-nosed Test-match cricket. Just as it seemed the visitors were getting on top, Elliott (44) returned a catch to left-arm spinner Paul Adams. Mark and Steve then had to survive a final burst from Donald before stumps. The battle was captivating. The twins survived until the close, reaching 3–145. Mark was 54, Steve 11. Were the odds slowly swinging Australia's way?

The following morning Steve fell to Jacques Kallis for 18. The score was 4–167. Too close to call.

Mark remained defiant. Always confident he would bat well, he received a sign it was going to be his day after he 'feathered' an Adams delivery to wicket-keeper David Richardson when he was in his sixties. Only Cullinan offered a slight appeal. Not out.

There was no such fortune for Greg Blewett, bowled by Adams for 7.

At 5–192, Mark found a valuable ally in Michael Bevan, who replaced his natural tendency to attack with imperturbable defence sprinkled with cautious aggression. Mark was just as watchful. As the runs were whittled away, South Africa took the second new ball, and soon afterwards Mark acknowledged his eleventh Test century, described by *Sydney Morning Herald* writer Malcolm Knox as 'nerveless'.

Every day of the Test, schoolchildren had crowded the stands and sung almost ceaseless renditions of 'Bohemian Rhapsody' and 'Stand by Me'. Although they eventually wore on Mark's nerves, another song could have easily been performed about the century-maker — 'Killing Me Softly' — because that is what Mark had done to the home side.

At 105, he gave his only chance, a shot off the toe of his bat flew knee-high to Cullinan who couldn't hold on to it at first slip. Donald, the bowler, crouched in despair. Two balls later Mark cut the fast bowler for four, leaving Australia less than 20 to win.

However, the match had more twists to come. After a 66-run stand with Bevan, Mark was bowled by an inswinger from Jacques Kallis. His 116 off 228 balls had taken 323 minutes, but the following half-hour seemed just as long as Australia lost Bevan (24) and Warne (3) in the nervous hunt for the last twelve runs. The final line to this extraordinary match was written in the boldest of print when Ian Healy hoisted Cronje over square leg for six. That night, the television news footage sent back to Australia showed Taylor barely able to watch the final few deliveries before Healy's magical stroke sent Greg Blewett leaping into his captain's arms. A priceless moment. Australia had won by two wickets. The series was won. And Mark, having earned the fourth man-of-the-match award of his Test career, had won new respect from the critics who had previously questioned his seemingly casual attitude. He says:

> *I rate that up there with my top couple of innings. The wicket was a bit of a seamer, but I always thought it wasn't that hard to bat on. Everybody just got a bit carried away with it.*
>
> *Some of the press said it was a turning point for me, but I thought I'd proven I could bat under pressure when Stephen and I scored centuries in Kingston. But I suppose this was a bit different because we were chasing. I just managed to keep pretty calm and still play my shots as much as I could.*
>
> *At the time Aussies weren't great chasers. We'd had a few problems when we were in good positions, so I don't think many people gave us much of a chance. In some ways it's probably easier chasing 270 than 115 because you're expected to get 115, and you often don't concentrate as well as you should. When you're chasing a bigger score, you plan your innings a bit better.*
>
> *The only disappointment was getting out when I did, but I did get a good ball. We were under pressure at the end. Heals hitting a six was the best way to win the match. It's one shot I'll remember out of all of them during my career. It was a great win, one of the best I've been involved with.*

Whether or not the display of stoicism was a defining moment in Mark's career is open to debate; however, for those watching, the innings highlighted one of the most sought after qualities in any sportsman — the ability to be a match-winner. Taylor, undoubtedly one of Mark's most loyal fans, says:

> *The frustration for some people is that Mark averages in the forties, but his value can't be written in statistics. His value is that he often makes runs exactly when you need them, but people tend to forget that. Port Elizabeth was a great innings, so was his century at Sabina Park. If you look back at that one, Stephen*

was the one who in typical Stephen fashion gutsed it out, gritted it out hour
after hour. While Mark was the one, along with Greg Blewett, who scored runs
quickly to put the Windies on the back foot. People tend to forget those sorts of
innings, which is an absolute shame because they win you games of cricket.

Mark has the ability to change the context of a game. In the space of two
hours we can go from being in trouble to having the game by the throat. That's
what he did in Port Elizabeth.

Steve was also full of praise, suggesting it was a 'breakthrough innings' in which Mark 'stabilised things, was very solid and people batted around him, which is not normally his role'.

And Geoff Marsh remembers the performance was 'definitely the best innings I've ever seen him play. It was a tough wicket to bat on, no doubt about that, but it was more the pressure of the game that he had to conquer. Mentally he's very tough when it comes to competition.'

While the Australians had dispelled their reputation as bad chasers, they couldn't rid themselves of the tag of being dead rubber sleepers in the final Test, at Centurion Park, Pretoria. With the series decided, Taylor's team performed below their best, losing by eight wickets. Mark scored 5 and 42, and took 1–34 in the first innings of a match that was marred by several controversial umpiring incidents.

Mark finished as the third leading run-scorer for the series with 209 at 41.80.

Injuries forced him to play a reduced role in the limited-overs campaign. After missing the first game because of a flare-up of his back problem, an inflamed disc pressing against a nerve, he returned to Port Elizabeth for the second game of the series, and again showed his liking for the St George's Park pitch, scoring an unbeaten 115 in Australia's eight-wicket win. He showed no signs of the nervous nineties when he went from 91 to 103, blasting two sixes in a row off Pat Symcox.

However, in the following game at Newlands Stadium, Cape Town, Mark suffered more damage than he caused after he dropped a hot chance in slips off Jason Gillespie's bowling. The split webbing that needed six stitches was incredibly the first major hand injury of Mark's career. He missed two games, but despite still being in discomfort, he returned for the final two. He failed in both, scoring 0 and 3, but Australia won the series 4–3.

In many ways the South African trip had been a demanding tour for Australia because not only did it continue a non-stop schedule that had begun in India six months earlier, it also had players feeling the tension of a captain under siege. Mark Taylor had gone twenty innings without scoring a Test fifty. He led his team to England for the Ashes, knowing knives that had already been sharpened were being raised for the kill.

CHAPTER TWENTY-TWO

A BAD GUT FEELING

Perhaps this is a question for a trivia competition at the local on a Friday night: After leaving Australia for the 1997 Ashes tour, where did Mark Waugh score his first century and who was he playing? Answer: He made 116 from 66 deliveries in a four-wicket win by Australia over a World XI at Hong Kong's Kowloon Cricket Club.

The steamy lushness of Asia seemed a world away by the time the Australians arrived in a cold, wet and gloomy London a day after the match. Mark soon found some heat when the local media seized upon comments about the English team he'd made in the *ABC Ashes Tour Guide*. His views were typical of his character — direct and to the point.

I look at the team on paper and think they are good players, but they aren't tough enough or hungry enough on the field ... They don't play as a team; they worry about themselves.

When you're out there, you don't feel that you've got eleven guys up against you; they just haven't got the toughness you need to win Test cricket consistently.

Mark further endeared himself to the English team by suggesting there wasn't a quality spinner in the squad. He described his old nemesis, Phil Tufnell, as a 'fairly weak sort of player', and predicted Australia could win the Test series as easily as 4–1.

His words were used as motivation by the home side at the start of the campaign when they surprised Australia by winning all three Texaco Trophy one-day matches, the result prompting premature newspaper headlines that the Ashes would soon be back in English hands. Mark scored 11, 25 and 95.

He made 66 and 32 not out against Gloucestershire at Bristol in his only other game before the first Test, at Birmingham. The Australians were 'underdone' for the start of the series, and it showed at Edgbaston in a performance that had the English press gleefully writing off the visitors, while searching for new superlatives to describe their own players.

Although Mark Taylor finally lifted some pressure from himself by scoring a much awaited century, Australia were simply outplayed in a nine-wicket loss, and were suddenly in the unfamiliar position of being the followers, not the pace-setters. It was a forgettable game for Mark, bowled by Darren Gough for 5 in the first innings, then suffering acute stomach pains that forced him to watch two days of the Test from a hospital bed. Originally it was feared he had appendicitis, but the problem was later diagnosed as a severe viral infection. He recalls:

> It was quite weird. Here I am playing a Test match, but watching it in bed a couple of miles from the ground. I saw Tubby's [Taylor] century while in hospital, and that was the only good thing to come out of the game for us. Everybody was really relieved his pain and anguish were over. Spectators, selectors, team-mates, everyone. It's hard to enjoy your cricket when you're not performing at your best. There's nothing better than making runs when you're having a bad trot.

Mark left hospital in time to bat lower than usual at number 6 in the second innings. Gough claimed him again, caught behind for 1. Once again he was reminded by the press and English fans of his pre-tour comments.

Mark was hopeful of a longer stay at the crease in his following match, against Nottinghamshire at Trent Bridge. However, for at least a few minutes of the game, his thoughts were very much elsewhere when he was caught in a dilemma while waiting to bat. He remembers:

> I had a horse, Clever Kiwi, racing back in Sydney. I was next in to bat, and I told Ricky Ponting, who was ahead of me, that he couldn't get out early because I had to listen to the race. So I've gone out the back into the toilet with the mobile phone — you're not meant to use mobile phones in the dressing room — and I hear this big 'Howzat?'. Ricky's out. There's about 600 metres to go in the race, the horse is doing well, and I have to go out to bat with 200 metres left.

Not only did the pacer fade to finish out of the placings, but Mark didn't last a significant distance when he was dismissed for 29. He also found time in the middle hard to come by against Leicestershire, making 6 and 16 not out — not the most heartening of warm-ups to the second Test, at Lord's, three days later.

Rain ruined the encounter, but not before Glenn McGrath took 8–38 in England's abysmal first innings of 77, and Matthew Elliott scored 112 in Australia's only innings. Mark made a short but rapid 33 as the Australians sought quick runs in their only chance with the bat, hoping to force a result against a dispirited rabble that looked nothing like the team that had won in Birmingham. An indication of Mark's aggression was his mode of dismissal — caught by Devon Malcolm at third man while trying to cut paceman Andy Caddick for six.

Ian Healy won high praise during the match when, after taking an apparent catch from Graham Thorpe in the first innings, he told umpire David Shepherd that he didn't think he'd taken the ball cleanly. Thorpe was given not out, and Australia's wicket-keeper was openly clapped by Shepherd who later said, 'That's what cricket needs.'

While Shepherd, too, could be applauded for his actions, the incident again brought attention to the issue of umpiring standards and the use of technology. It's a subject Mark feels needs to be urgently addressed by administrators. He says:

> I don't think you can use third umpires for caught behinds because sometimes edges can be deceiving. It's all right to use it [camera evidence] on line decisions for run-outs and stumpings, and also whether the ball has carried, but even that can tell lies.

To be honest, I'm not really sure how much we should use technology. In any sport you have the human element, and although we should try to reduce that by improving the umpires themselves, I'm not sure if more decisions going to the third umpire would make things better.

It would obviously help if the teams cut back their appealing. There's definitely excessive appealing in the game. It's a problem. If I think it's out, I appeal. If I don't, I won't — it's just the way I play, but there are some other teams who know when it's not out, but still appeal.

Throughout the 2001–2 Australian summer, Mark's fair approach to appealing was acknowledged on ABC radio. As former Test leg-spinner Kerry O'Keefe observed during the final Test against South Africa, in Sydney. 'If you want to know whether it's out or not, look at Mark Waugh. If he's excited, then the odds are it's out.'

However, Mark admits there have been times when his judgement has been astray. He says:

There have been occasions where I've appealed, and so has Heals or Gilly [Adam Gilchrist] who are both as honest as anybody. We genuinely think it's out then look at the replay and see that it's nowhere near it. Sometimes it just happens and you get it wrong.

It's not only technology, but the way umpires are treated that needs to be addressed. There have to be some pretty big changes. Because of the TV coverage nowadays, umpiring is highlighted more than ever before. The TV replays are definitely hurting umpires. I think lbw replays shouldn't be shown in slow motion — just show them at the normal speed because that's what the umpire sees. With modern TV, everything is over-scrutinised. Every ball is replayed, even the no-balls. It puts more pressure on the umpires. I don't think television broadcasts should show no-balls. To me, if a bloke is over by a couple of centimetres, it doesn't really make any difference at the other end. You're better off concentrating on getting the decision right at the important end.

By the same token, the umpires can improve a hell of a lot. The main thing is that you need to have young people. Blokes like Simon Tauffel. I reckon he's the best umpire in Australia by a fair way. Younger people have better hearing and eyesight. I remember one Test umpire who was deaf in one ear. How could he be umpiring? He told us that he couldn't hear properly in one ear. If you talked to him on that side, he didn't acknowledge you!

Younger umpires are also fitter, so they should be able to concentrate better for longer periods in hot conditions. I think they all need to pass fitness tests to be on the international panel. It has to help them. Physically you look at most umpires and they don't look particularly fit, do they? Most other sports — soccer, rugby league, tennis — have officials in their mid-thirties whereas in cricket you've got blokes in their sixties. Generally speaking, it stands to reason that younger umpires would have more alert senses and be fitter than older umpires.

The age has to be brought down, but the only way you're going to do that is by making it an attractive career. So you have to pay them properly. If they're paid better, obviously they're going to be full-time, so they can train a lot harder. They can work on things more than they do. Like going down to the nets sometimes. Simon Tauffel does it occasionally. Just to get used to the deliveries that the bowlers bowl. Umpires get it wrong with Warney a lot of the time. They still think he's a big turner of the ball, but mostly his balls go straight on. But the umpires don't know that because they don't watch enough.

You need to try to get more players involved because the more cricket awareness the umpires have, the better decisions they'll make. For example, a bump ball — you can tell by the flight of the ball whether it's gone into the ground or straight up.

Umpires should also have a dossier on each player, so they can research the way each cricketer plays. They have a rough idea but I don't know if anything is officially marked down. Knowing the players is critical. For example, someone who uses their pad all the time while they're batting. Someone like Jimmy Adams. If I was an umpire I'd say, 'Listen mate, you keep doing that, I'm going to give you out because I know you're not playing at the ball. It looks like you are, but you're not.'

I used to get a bit dirty sometimes with lbws. Someone like Boonie — to me he was lbw a lot of times but because he was playing straight, umpires wouldn't give him out, whereas someone like me who plays across the line a bit more won't get as much benefit.

In some instances I think the umpires are too well protected. They make the mistake, and yet the player gets penalised. The umpire should be open to criticism from players. A player can't make a comment on an umpiring decision. Why not?

I know umpiring is a hell of a tough job that I wouldn't enjoy, but I really think mistakes can be limited.

Mark gave the men in black plenty of time to formulate a Waugh dossier when Australia played Hampshire between the second and third Tests. After an indifferent start to his tour, he showed signs of his best form, hitting 173 in the visitors' victory by an innings and 133 runs.

The winning momentum was carried into the third Test, at Old Trafford, when Australia levelled the series with a 268-run win in an encounter highlighted by Steve scoring magnificent twin centuries on a difficult pitch. His first innings of 108 is rated by Mark as one of Steve's greatest 'knocks'. Mark made 12 and 55, the latter display the first time he felt he'd 'really got going' in the series. His returns had been disappointing when compared with the 1993 tour and his seasons at Essex. Ian Healy, one of Mark's closest friends in the team at the time, offers a fascinating insight.

Although he was very hard to ruffle, I knew he worried about things like being out of form. What he'd said about England and Tufnell bugged him — it was an Ashes series that he didn't particularly enjoy. While on the outside he looked as cool as a cucumber, he did worry about things, but he never let that affect his role as a team player.

In the slips he'd always be coming up with good ideas for Tubby [Taylor]. 'Why don't we try this or that?' Some would be outrageous, others would be genuinely good tactics. He was nearly always thinking cricket, and although he was more of a listener than a talker, once a session he'd say something funny. He was a good balance for me because I suppose I could be too intense at times.

Throughout our careers, he would always be there for me. He'd be very direct, not pampering. He just gave direct comments that put the issue in perspective. He might say something like, 'I think you're making a bigger thing out of this than it really is.'

Direct and conscious support — that is Mark Waugh. I don't think he'd ever go over the top, go up and put his arm around anyone and say, 'Now let's see what you're thinking.' He'd think: 'Stuff that.' He'd say his piece, then step back and let you take it in.

That's the way he treated himself too, but there were times, like during that Ashes series, he did get worried.

However, Mark appeared to have few worries about his form after scoring an unbeaten 142 against Middlesex in his final innings before the fourth Test, at Headingley. The following day the Australians met Queen Elizabeth II at Buckingham Palace. Four years earlier when he'd bowed to royalty for the first time, Mark admitted being 'bloody nervous', but on this second occasion he had the courage to ask Her Majesty if 'she enjoyed a flutter on the horses'. The Queen smiled politely and suggested punting wasn't a correct pastime for a person in her position.

If she had been a betting lady, she wouldn't have been backing England after the early shots were fired at Headingley. Sent in by Taylor, the home side were humbled for just 172 in 59 overs. In reply, Australia declared their only innings at 9–501, after Elliott (199) and Ponting (127) led the way. Mark was caught and bowled by paceman Dean Headley for 8.

England fared better in the second innings, reaching 268, but it was a long way short of avoiding an innings defeat.

Taylor's players were joined in their victory celebrations by the Canberra Raiders rugby league squad who were in England for the Super League world club challenge. After some drinks in the dressing room, the footballers were in full swing by the time the party flowed back to the bar at the Australian team hotel. During the revelry, Mark and Steve tried to tackle Canberra coach Mal Meninga, a former Kangaroo centre who tipped the scales at about 110 kilograms. Mark laughs:

We brought him down. But he just got over the line. I'd hate to tackle him in a real game because this was only in a bar with a three-metre run-up. I know I chose the right sport when I was growing up! Those blokes knew how to party. They were all pretty lively, dancing, carrying on. I remember Alan Crompton [ACB team manager] running round the bar cleaning up after them. He was worried it was a bad reflection on the team, but it was just good fun. At one stage Crommo went to Mal Meninga and asked if the boys could settle down a bit, and Mal said, 'You tell them!'

Rugby league had already made a much more significant impact on Australian cricket than a three-step charge from Meninga with a can of Foster's in his hand. At this stage, momentum was building towards a showdown between cricketers and administrators over payments and conditions. It had been partly prompted by the absurd escalation in salaries to league players as a result of the establishment of the Rupert Murdoch backed Super League, a breakaway competition from the traditional Australian Rugby League premiership.

Towards the end of the Ashes, the cricketers would meet secretly with Tim May, by then the President of the recently formed Australian Cricketers' Association, and shrewd businessman James Erskine. There would be far-reaching effects over the months ahead. Mark recalls:

That was a big meeting with James Erskine. We didn't know what we were getting into really. James just explained what his thoughts were, where he thought the players could go in relation to payments, and what our rights were. It was an important step for cricketers because in the past we had no input into decisions made by the ACB about money, fixtures, the scheduling of tours. The Cricketers' Association was an important move so that we could stand up for ourselves, and put our views across in the right way. The guidelines started to be put in place while we were still on tour.

The Australians gave themselves more ammunition for the upcoming battle with the ACB when they retained the Ashes with a 264-run win in four days in the fifth Test, at Trent Bridge. Mark continued his inconsistent form with scores of 68 and 7, but also took the series-winning catch at second slip to dismiss Devon Malcolm off McGrath's bowling. Afterwards, Shane Warne was criticised for his celebratory hip-wriggling, stump-wielding dance on the players' balcony. He has always endured a love–hate relationship with the English crowds and media that certainly helps take the spotlight away from other players. Mark says:

He's a character — larger than life. You do sympathise with him sometimes because the spotlight is on him wherever he goes. But he'd be the first to admit he's brought some of that on himself. The responsibility that goes with the profile is probably one he has to accept a bit more I think.

He's a knockabout bloke — you're not going to change him, and if you did,
he probably wouldn't be the cricketer he is.

The sixth and final Test, at The Oval, was an unsatisfactory finish for Australia's three and a half month campaign. Mark had to 'eat humble pie' one last time when, on a biting pitch, he was dismissed cheaply in both innings by Tufnell who was playing his only match of the series. Chasing just 124 to win, the Australians exposed both their small target and dead rubber frailties by capitulating for just 104.

It completed a frustrating series for Mark, who tallied just 209 runs at 20.90. Some rumblings in the press box were slowly becoming louder: was the younger Waugh twin on thin ice? After sixty-nine Tests, he was about to begin a new stage of his career.

CHAPTER TWENTY-THREE

UNDER PRESSURE

At first, they were nothing more than murmurings. Quiet conversations between fans, officials and, most notably, journalists. The theme of the discussions was common: 'It will be interesting to see how Mark Waugh goes. He'd better get a few runs before too long.'

At the start of the 1997–98 home summer, Mark was under pressure. It was not yet at a critical point, but certainly was sufficient to make people think about his future should he be unable to lift his Ashes form. To the player in the spotlight, there was no need for alarm. His returns in England hadn't necessarily been the result of poor form — he'd received a few good deliveries that perhaps would have missed his bat instead of finding the edge if more luck had been running his way. In hindsight, his most disappointing performances were the starts he didn't capitalise on, a cardinal sin for a front-line batsman. As a result, he had no reason to doubt himself when he fronted for New South Wales duties in early October. However, he knew he was being watched.

He smashed 76 from 58 balls against South Australia in his first Mercantile Mutual Cup appearance, at North Sydney Oval. New South Wales won by 37 runs after 599 runs had been scored in a day that rained sixes. The following week, Mark took 2–32 and scored 20 off 27 balls in a one-wicket victory over Queensland at the Gabba. The Blues stayed in Brisbane to inflict a nine-wicket defeat on the Bulls in their opening Sheffield Shield match. In his only innings Mark found the going difficult, scoring 20 in a painstaking hour and a half at the crease.

The next match, against Victoria at North Sydney Oval, was overshadowed by developments in the Australian Cricketers' Association's (ACA) push for better pay and playing conditions. The day before the game started, Tim May and James Erskine handed ACB chief executive Malcolm Speed a twenty-page document with a log of claims that included the distribution of a greater percentage of the ACB's total cricket revenue among the twenty-four contracted Australian players and all first-class cricketers. The ACA wanted a fund of at least $12.5 million, which would increase by a minimum of $5 million within three years. Other claims involved medical cover, input into tour schedules, the attendance of ACA representatives at ACB board meetings, and better ticket arrangements for the families and friends of players.

The ACB rejected the claims. May consequently told the media that strike action by the players was possible. This led to an extraordinary sight the following morning at North Sydney Oval when the New South Wales and Victorian teams stood shoulder to shoulder on the field before play in a move that players' representative Greg Matthews called 'an act of solidarity'.

As the dispute raged, a common line from the ACA to the players was that 'no player will be worse off'. Arguments, meetings and finally resolutions continued for eleven months. Thankfully, no strike took place, but by the time an agreement was signed in September 1998, a number of Australia's high profile players, including Mark, were indeed worse off. In his book, *Taylor and Beyond*, Malcolm Knox wrote: 'The senior men also had to pay up to $80 000 each in fees to the ACA, but only Mark Waugh, effectively a non-contributor to progress during the pivotal periods of the dispute, complained publicly.'

There was no malice in Mark's complaints when they were stated in the media. It was simply an honest appraisal of the situation. Throughout the dispute, he and his peers had been advised by the ACA, and a council of senior players including Steve, Mark Taylor and Shane Warne. Although the dispute led to the establishment of much better conditions for domestic players, Mark had every reason to be confused with the initial outcome for the Test players. He recalls:

> *The first couple of years, the actual contracts went down, and I couldn't work that out for the hell of me. I just remember Greg Matthews saying at the time that no-one would be worse off, then the next year our contracts are cut. We went through all that drama for what? For the life of me I couldn't work out how the hell I'd lost money. But the bottom line was that everyone else was better off. But it's all turned around now.*
>
> *It wasn't only about the money — we wanted to have a voice, have a foot in the door with the decisions made by the ACB.*
>
> *It was a pretty uncomfortable time. I suppose the ACB saw it as a threat and didn't quite know how to handle it. We needed the ACA — we were hell bent on not backing down, but at the same time we didn't want the game of cricket to suffer. Strikes were our last option by a long way. I don't think it was ever going to get to that situation.*
>
> *It seemed like we were going around in circles for a while, but everything has come out well.*

During the most turbulent period of the dispute in the early stages of the 1997–98 season some players found it difficult to concentrate on their cricket, but Mark was able to divide the off-field issues from his performances at the wicket. After scoring 72 against Victoria in a draw, he made 57 off 58 balls in the ensuing Mercantile Mutual Cup match against the Bushrangers at North Sydney Oval. It was his last domestic one-dayer for the season, and he played only two more first-class matches for New South Wales, including one against New Zealand at Newcastle. He scored 44 in his only innings, his last before the first Test against the Kiwis in Brisbane.

Under their former New South Wales coach Steve Rixon, the New Zealanders adopted an aggressive approach at the Gabba. Mark remembers the first morning was full of verbal taunts and intimidation. Australia won by 186 runs, but Mark failed twice, caught in the gully for 3 off all-rounder Chris Cairns in the first innings, and dismissed by left-arm spinner Daniel Vettori for 17 in the second. He also dropped a relatively easy catch, a sign to some observers that he was losing focus. The pre-season murmurings had suddenly become a bit louder. In an article in the *Age* (16 November 1997) examining whether Mark's Test spot was in danger, Fairfax journalist Mark Ray suggested that it seemed 'excessive' to drop the batsman who 'often needs a swift kick behind the thigh pad to get him working harder ...'

Ray also wrote:

That sort of kneejerk reaction to a temporary lack of big scores does not address any number of factors. Factors such as team balance, the player's seniority and the experience that he brings, the quality of the man in question compared with the quality of the likely replacement and the next few games the team has to play.

Over the following months, not all journalists were as supportive as Ray. Although it is difficult to define a moment, it is reasonable to suggest that this period began the decline in Mark's respect for certain commentators.

He went into the second Test, in Perth, under mounting scrutiny, but his fortunes changed in a flash on the first day when he was fielding at mid-wicket. After hammering a Shane Warne delivery, and seemingly sending the ball hurtling to the boundary fence, Chris Cairns watched in disbelief as Mark launched himself horizontally to take a spectacular right-handed catch at full stretch. It was one of those moments that defines a gift that leaves everyday people shaking their heads in wonder. It was also a moment that 'flicked a switch' in Mark, who returned to his elegant best at the crease the following day when he scored 86 and shared a fourth-wicket partnership of 153 with Steve (96). His innings included an on-drive that sent a Vettori delivery an estimated 130 metres onto the roof of the Lillee–Marsh Stand. There have been few bigger sixes hit anywhere in the world. Mark had answered his critics in the most emphatic way. He remembers:

I wouldn't be human if I hadn't felt some sort of pressure going into the Test because you hear things, see things. Deep down you know how you're playing, and you go back to that and have faith in your ability.

It seems I've been under pressure ever since then. Sometimes maybe it's justified, but not all the time. I seem to be able to produce when I'm under a bit of pressure. Mum's a believer in that — whatever happens is meant to happen.

I batted really well, and I suppose the Vettori hit was just a nice bonus.
Every time I play in Perth I look up there [The Lillee–Marsh Stand] and think
how bloody hard it is to hit it up there. Even in practice you probably couldn't
do it. I don't know what happened really. I went down the wicket, didn't
actually swing that hard, but got the ball on the up — you have to hit it on the
up to get the height — and I just hit it at the right time and it kept on going. It
just came out of the sweet spot like a good golf drive.

Australia cruised to victory by an innings and 70 runs, and headed to Hobart where Mark was forced to work much harder for his runs, scoring a patient 81 in the first innings and only 9 in the second when he was promoted to opener as Australia sought quick runs for a declaration. The match ended in a draw. After his troublesome start, Mark finished the series with 196 runs at 39.2, not brilliant figures, but enough to force the daggers of his critics back into their sheaths.

By this stage, the media had found a much better source of good copy after the ACB announced during the Test that Mark Taylor and Ian Healy had been dropped from Australia's one-day team. It was the end of an era and the start of a new controversy as selectors reasoned it was time to look to the future and begin the build-up to the 1999 World Cup campaign. Steve was named the new captain. Mark says:

People say the teams were split when it happened. But they just picked the best
eleven Test players and the best eleven one-day players. It was common sense.
You don't run a sprinter in a staying race, do you? I actually can't believe it
didn't happen much earlier. It was stupid picking an out and out Test player in
a one-day game.

Who could have forecast that the cyclical clean-out of senior players would affect Mark and his brother soon enough?

Mark believes Australia took a different approach to one-day cricket under Steve's leadership. He says:

With all due respect to Tubby [Taylor], he wasn't as worried about one-day
cricket, and saw it as a bit of fun, and a bit of a Mickey Mouse game. I don't

think we really put in as good an effort as we could have in one-day cricket.
Stephen made it just as important as Test matches.

Australia won just three of their preliminary games of the Carlton & United series against New Zealand and South Africa. With Taylor gone, it seemed Mark barely had time to acknowledge a replacement opening partner before he was shaking hands with another new one. Dashing Tasmanian left-hander Michael Di Venuto, Tom Moody and Stuart Law were all tried in the early stages.

Mark's best performance came in the second game when he scored 104 off 113 balls — his eleventh limited-overs century — in Australia's three-wicket win over the Kiwis under lights at the Adelaide Oval.

The South Africans' world-class pace attack of Allan Donald and Shaun Pollock made life for Australia's batsmen much more difficult when the much awaited 'unofficial world championship' over three Tests began at the MCG on Boxing Day. As against New Zealand, Mark began the series with a double failure, falling to Donald for 0 and 1. He'd looked particularly uncomfortable in the first innings, battling for eighteen deliveries before edging a ball to wicket-keeper David Richardson. The match was drawn.

The glorious uncertainty of sport was underlined by Mark during the second match, in Sydney. If he'd translated his Melbourne returns into racing form, perhaps he would have stayed away from backing himself to make runs. However, in his brother's hundredth Test, Mark made the century, an even 100. Along the way he shared a 116-run partnership with Steve (85) in a tick over two hours. The incomparable highlight of their stand came in gloomy conditions nearing stumps on the second day. The lights were on, but there was a greater sense of electricity on the field as Donald launched a brutal assault with the second new ball that left both twins searching for ice packs in the dressing room afterwards. The brief half-hour period offered some of the fiercest cricket seen in Australia since the West Indians were at their peak. Mark recalls:

We were hit from pillar to post. Allan was world class. Definitely the quickest
white bowler in the world, probably as quick as anybody. He was bloody quick
that day on a flat wicket. Some of the best bowling I've ever faced. Every ball
was a test of your instincts.

Mark finished the day with 78, and added another 22 the following morning before Pollock trapped him in front. The innings lasted 211 minutes and 186 deliveries. The match had one other significant celebration of triple figures — Shane Warne collected his three-hundredth Test wicket when he bowled Jacques Kallis in the second innings. He claimed 10 other victims, undoubtedly deserving man-of-the-match honours after Australia took only four days to win by an innings and 21 runs.

The South Africans reversed their fortunes when they beat Australia by six runs in the first final of the Carlton & United series, at the MCG. Mark was run out for 3 after a brilliant piece of fielding from his good friend Jonty Rhodes at backward point. In this match, Mark had his fourth opening partner for the series, Adam Gilchrist, who destroyed the visitors in the second final with a century off 104 deliveries at the SCG. Mark scored 25 off 31 balls in Australia's seven-wicket win. He then made 21 off 38 in the decider, which the home side won by 14 runs. For Mark, it was the end of a profitable series in which he led the team aggregate with 320 runs at 35.55.

However, his season didn't reach its climax until the final day of the international season on the ground that had already offered so many diverse experiences during his career — the Adelaide Oval. After making 63 in the first innings of the third Test, Mark took guard in the second innings late on the fourth evening with his side in trouble at 2–17, chasing 361 for victory. At stumps, he was 11 not out already, having been dropped at bat-pad.

Resuming the following day at 2–32, the Australians had little chance of winning on a pitch that was behaving a little inconsistently, as could be expected after three innings of wear and tear. The South Africans were desperate to salvage something from the tour. To return home without a trophy or a win in the Test series would be a wound to the proud sporting nation.

It was a tough day of Test cricket. Hansie Cronje's men shot the arrows, and Mark deflected them.

By tea, the home side were 4–162, with Mark unbeaten on 78 against an attack that was without its main strike weapon, Allan Donald, who'd been ruled out after suffering a buttock strain in the one-dayers. Shaun Pollock and Lance Klusener pushed themselves to the limit, and although they both met with success — Pollock took nine wickets for the match and Klusener claimed five — neither could find a way past Mark as they lifted for one last effort in the final session.

The innings and the match revolved around Mark, who reached his thirteenth Test hundred in the final hour — however, there was still work to be done. And more than enough time for a controversy to be born.

With Mark resolute at 107, there were 51 balls and four wickets remaining. Pollock bowled a short delivery that hit Mark's arm and lobbed into the slips. He was not out, but then the South Africans noticed something that excited them — the bails were on the ground. Mark had hit his wicket. But how? And when?

While a heated argument began on the field between Hansie Cronje and the umpires, Doug Cowie and Steve Randell, third umpire Steve Davis replayed the incident in the grandstand. Yes, Mark had indeed hit his stumps, but only after he'd completed the shot and was walking away. The verdict was not out, and Cronje was angry. Mark, remaining calm throughout the incident, insisted the delivery had numbed his arm, forcing him to briefly lose control of his actions.

He survived until stumps, finishing unbeaten on 115 after 404 minutes and 305 balls. It was the first time he'd batted through an entire day of a Test. Australia finished at 7–227. The match was drawn, but the series was won by Australia. In an unfortunate incident after the players left the field, the furious Cronje speared a stump through the door of the umpires' room. He maintained that, 'If somebody gets hit on the head, and he's a bit wobbly, and he walks onto his stumps, he's out. That's all I want to say.'

Mark saw the incident differently. He remembers:

The ball hit me right on the elbow. It hit a nerve. I just couldn't feel my arm at all. The ball ballooned away. As far as I was concerned, that was it — the ball was dead, so I started to walk away. By this stage I couldn't feel my arm at all, had no control over what it did. Then all of a sudden my bat flicked the leg-stump and knocked the bails off. I don't think a lot of the South Africans actually saw me hit the stumps. They would have been watching the ball, then the next thing they know they see the bails on the ground and would have immediately thought, 'He's trodden on his stumps.' They all blew up. I explained to them what had happened.

I suppose there is a grey area when you get hit in the head, and you actually stumble onto your stumps and are out. I suppose the same thing could be said about hitting the arm. But I thought I was definitely not out.

The feeling came back into the arm straight away. The South Africans kept carrying on — Pat Symcox was there mouthing off as usual, but that was the end of it. Not out was not out — time to move on.

It was one of my better innings — saving the game rather than trying to win it was different for me. I prefer players who win matches. There are a lot of players around who can save matches, but there aren't many who can win them. Ideally you should be able to do both. That's where Stephen is so good. It was something I'd never really been good at, but this maybe was a turning point.

Mark was the leading run-scorer for the series with a tally of 279 at an average of 69.75. For the second time in his career, he scored centuries in successive Tests. Surely speculation about his position was over.

Once again, he had little time to reflect on his performances because the Australians immediately headed to New Zealand to play a four-match limited-overs series during which Mark passed 5000 one-day runs. The contest was drawn 2–all. Mark's highlight came in the first match at Christchurch when he and Gilchrist slaughtered the attack in a 146-run partnership off just 25 overs. Mark finished with 65 off 78 balls, and Gilchrist slammed 118 from 117 deliveries. It seemed a stable opening partnership had been found. It meant a slight change in roles because during his time with Taylor, Mark was frequently the more aggressive batsman, but with Gilchrist, a natural tornado, he found himself playing the support role. Gilchrist acknowledges the early days as a vital part of his development as a cricketer.

I've learnt a lot from Mark, he's brought a lot to my game. His relaxed approach rubbed off and settled me. It's been a wonderful part of my career to have been able to forge such a strong partnership and friendship with him. I respect him a great deal, and to bat with him has been great fun. I think that's the major word in my thoughts when I think about batting with him — it's fun.

The Australians about-faced after their Tasman crossing and travelled to India to win a limited-overs tournament that included Zimbabwe as well as the host nation. However, nearly all attention focused on three Test matches. Taylor's men had developed a formidable away record, with victories in the West Indies, South Africa and England, but success on the mystical subcontinent had eluded them. They began the quest for the Border–Gavaskar Trophy, aiming to become the first Australian team to win a series in India since Bill Lawry's 1969–70 tourists beat the home side 3–1 in a five-match campaign. Hopes were high, but so too was the standard of the opposition, in particular one diminutive man stood tall above friend and foe alike — Sachin Tendulkar. Mark says:

> He's definitely the best batsman in the current era. When you play against Tendulkar, you almost want to see him get a few runs just to see him bat. He loves batting against us. It's amazing how hard he hits the ball. If the ball is a foot wide of you in the field, it's four. I can't believe how much power he has. He is a great player. Most of his innings are outstanding. When he's going, it's hard not to stand in slips and think, 'How good is this?' I hate blokes who don't play shots, whereas blokes who have a go make it exciting.

Tendulkar amassed 446 runs, including two centuries, at 111.50 for the series. India won 2–1, wrapping up the trophy after the second Test, at Calcutta's imposing Eden Gardens Stadium.

It was an eventful tour for Mark. In the opening match at Chidambaram Stadium in Chennai, formerly Madras, he was one of a number of Australians disenchanted with the standard of umpiring. After making a graceful but patient 66 in the first innings, in the second he was given out to a dubious bat-pad decision off Anil Kumble's bowling for 18. The visitors lost by 179 runs. Mark recalls:

> I didn't go anywhere near the ball, but these things happen. The only problem was that we copped about four bad ones in the first hour on the last morning. If we hadn't got them we would have drawn the Test. It was frustrating because we hadn't played too badly, we deserved a draw.
>
> I think it's fair to say that umpiring in India is a bigger challenge than anywhere else in the world. It's just the conditions you play in, it's so humid and hot. It's easy to feel off colour, even for umpires. Concentration and the pressure of overappealing can be a real problem.

The second Test was disastrous. Mark fell for 10, lbw to Javagal Srinath in the first innings, and when the chance came for redemption he had no answer to a spitting Kumble delivery that he hit to short-leg before he'd opened his account. Australia slid to defeat by the incredible margin of an innings and 219 runs inside four days.

Before the match, respected writer Mike Coward suggested in the *Australian* (18 March 1998) that, 'The peerless, not the plain, Mark Waugh is required at Eden Gardens these next five days.' In an article heavily supported by statistics, Coward also wrote: 'He would never say so publicly, but Mark Waugh is irritated his name is not automatically offered when discussion turns to the pecking order of the world's finest batsmen.'

Coward recognised Mark's ability, but also questioned the 'vast disparities' in his performances. Over the following years, one of the cricket world's most acknowledged members of the Fourth Estate would be placed on Mark's list of least liked journalists.

Although the 'plain' not the 'peerless' Waugh had been seen at Eden Gardens, Mark finished the series brilliantly, reaching his highest Test score, 153 not out from 267 balls in six and a quarter hours at Bangalore's Chinnaswamy Stadium. After overcoming the steamy conditions and a frustratingly slow pitch, Mark was unbeaten on 58 at the end of the second day. Only then did the toughest part of his innings begin. He remembers:

I was sick as a dog. That night I was vomiting and had diarrhoea — I didn't think I was going to live. I had to call in our manager, Cam Battersby, who was also a doctor. He gave me some needles, but I still didn't think I was going to get out of bed and down to the ground. I did get there, but didn't warm-up. I was that crook I just thought I'd go out there and play some shots because I didn't think I could hang around for too long.

I think it was the first time I batted without a helmet on in a Test match. I was just that hot and cooked. I couldn't sprint between the wickets, but ran very slowly. I just tried to conserve energy. It's funny how a lot of people can perform better when they're sick or injured. Maybe it's because you think you have nothing to lose.

Mark's performance and a five-wicket haul in the second innings by tireless fast bowler Michael Kasprowicz led the Australians to an eight-wicket triumph. Mark was the only Australian player to top 200 runs for the series, finishing with 280 at 70.00. However, the hoodoo of the subcontinent continued. Mark says:

> *I thought 1–all might have been a fair result in that series. It really shouldn't be that hard for us to win over there. We've changed our attitude a lot on recent trips. If you go over there thinking you're not going to enjoy it, then you won't. And that will affect your performance.*
>
> *We really try to look forward to the tours there now. I quite enjoy it. There are a lot of different sights, the people are just so cricket mad and you can always have a laugh because it's just so different. I can remember one time over there when I'd been booked on a plane, but the organisers couldn't find my ticket. They looked everywhere, but they eventually found it under Mr Mark.*
>
> *There was another time when a fan was in the foyer of our team hotel and was continually trying to get to Stephen and some of the other players for autographs. He shouldn't have been there, he'd already been told to go a couple of times, but he eventually made it to Stephen and said, 'Mr Wog, Mr Wog, can I be having your autograph now, or should I be fucking off?'!*

India can abuse the senses and yet touch the emotions as vividly as any place on the planet. For Steve, one of the most important off-field moments of the tour occurred when he visited a home for boys whose parents suffer from leprosy. He was so moved by the scenes at Udayan, just an hour's drive from Calcutta, that he helped raise funds for the development of a wing for girls. Nowadays, he and Mark both sponsor girls at Udayan, which in translation appropriately means sunrise.

A new dawn in Australian sport occurred six months later when for the first time cricket was played at the Commonwealth Games in Kuala Lumpur, Malaysia. After a rare winter's break that followed eighteen months of continuous touring, the high profile Australians approached their new campaign with fervour. The team with a five-star reputation surprised many observers by staying in the athletes village. Mark says:

That was great fun. I really enjoyed it. I think some people expected us to be more aloof. We were asked quite often, 'What are you guys doing here? Shouldn't you be in a hotel somewhere?'

We had four in each room — Stephen, Gavin Robertson, Tom Moody and myself were in one, and we made a point of inviting people up for drinks and a chat. We had netballers, swimmers, hockey players. It was interesting to see how they trained and prepared, how they peaked.

We had a better time than the other athletes — we had the chance to have a few beers and go to a few events. We seemed to be the only ones in the hall who used to eat the ice cream from these huge barrels. I remember talking to Daniel Kowalski [an Australian swimmer] and he warned me I'd better watch what I was eating because I had a game to play the next day. I joked that we were actually better athletes because we could eat that sort of stuff and still perform. We were a little bit embarrassed because we weren't as fit as many of the athletes. I'd never seen so many sets of good legs as there were in the dining hall.

It was great to be there. The cricket tournament itself was pretty ordinary. We were playing on sub-standard pitches against some teams that weren't even up to club standard, but the overall atmosphere made up for it. We went to a lot of events, and a lot of people came to watch our final.

We were disappointed when Manchester didn't put cricket in for the 2002 Games.

Surprisingly, Australia only claimed silver after losing the final to an understrength South African team. However, it wasn't long before journalist Malcolm Conn struck gold when he joined the Australians on tour in Pakistan after the Games. Some intense digging brought to the surface some long-buried secrets that would stain Mark's image, perhaps forever.

CHAPTER TWENTY-FOUR

TOUGH TIMES

Readings from the Koran echo through the streets via crackling loudspeakers that stir before dawn. Barefooted boys dig their hardened heels into donkeys laden with baskets of vegetables. Men with flowing beards kneel in prayer. A bus belches filthy black smoke, every panel of its body resembling crushed aluminium foil. The streets are as active as an ants' nest scuffed by a foot. And blue eyes are as rare as silence. This is Pakistan, the toughest country for an Australian cricketer to tour.

Mark Taylor and his team arrived in September 1998 with the knowledge that not one of the players had been born when Australia last won a Test in this country in 1959–60. The 2–0 victory by Richie Benaud's side in a three-Test series had proved impossible to emulate.

Could these Australians do something the previous four teams from Down Under couldn't? Shane Warne was out, recovering from shoulder surgery, but his absence was countered by a Pakistan team that was unsettled by the government's ongoing judicial inquiry into match-fixing. The inquiry, conducted by Justice Malik Mohammed Qayyum, was much more thorough than the initial investigation by Judge Ebrahim, who'd determined Salim Malik had no case to answer against the bribery allegations raised by Mark, Shane Warne and Tim May. This time, Justice Qayyum was examining a number of issues concerning Pakistan's cricketers. Accusations of poor performances and illegal betting had been levelled by former and current players including Imran Khan and Aamir Sohail. Fingers had been pointed at Wasim Akram, Salim Malik and Ijaz Ahmed, but they were still in the side. While Australia missed Warne, Pakistan missed unity.

After just one lead-up match, which resulted in a 333-run win over a Karachi Selection XI, the visitors entered the first Test, in Rawalpindi, determined to take advantage of the cracks in Pakistan's team. Four days later, there were celebrations as Australia won by an innings and 99 runs. Leg-spinner Stuart MacGill took nine wickets for the match, wicket-keeper Ian Healy set a new world record for dismissals (356) while Steve (157) and Michael Slater (108) led the way with the bat. Mark was dismissed for a duck. The day after the Test, he, Taylor and ACB chief executive Malcolm Speed flew to Lahore to face the judicial inquiry.

Taylor recalls there was considerable reluctance to go:

Majid Khan, the CEO of Pakistan cricket at the time, had a chat to me and Mark, and wanted us to go to the hearing even though statements had been signed by Warney, Maysie [Tim May], and Junior [Mark] as to what had happened with Malik. In Pakistan, being there face to face in front of a judge carries much greater weight.

After much convincing from Malcolm Speed and Majid Khan, we finally decided to go. All I had was second-hand information told to me by Mark, Maysie and Warney, but I was told as captain of Australia my story would carry great weight. And of course they wanted to hear Mark's side of the story.

We travelled with an armed guard, which I didn't enjoy. We didn't tell any of our journalists — they were all a bit dirty afterwards because of that. But when we got there we were ambushed by every Pakistani journalist who'd been tipped off. We tried to do the right thing, but the powers that be couldn't keep a secret. I certainly don't blame Majid Khan [he had nothing to do with the leaking of it].

Mark and I said our piece, then Salim Malik turned up to cross-examine us. But he didn't have anything to say, which was probably a good thing. If he had any queries he had the perfect opportunity to find out, but he didn't do that.

It was one of those days that I didn't enjoy, but looking back I'm glad we did it because it was our way of saying, 'We've done everything we can to clear up some very ordinary business.'

Mark and I were both bloody relieved when it was over. We were tossing up after we finished in the early afternoon, about two o'clock, whether we'd drive back the four or five hours to Rawalpindi because the plane wasn't leaving until about six. We wanted to get out of Lahore really badly. They said they'd give us a police escort, but in the end it was all too difficult.

I remember the plane landing in Rawalpindi, getting into a car and heading to an official function. I had a headache like you wouldn't believe, but at least it was over. We were both bloody relieved.

Mark has similar memories to his captain. He had questioned why he had to attend, but remained calm under very difficult circumstances. In many ways he was alone among a sea of people. He recalls:

We snuck up from Rawalpindi in the morning because we didn't want too many people to know about the trip. We'd been guaranteed by Pakistan cricket officials that the hearing would be secret, but we turned up and saw photographers everywhere. I couldn't believe it. I thought, 'Here we go.' I wasn't nervous, but there was no way I wanted to be there. Warney and Tim May weren't there, so I was sort of left there by myself. I had a simple statement to make that Malik had offered me a bribe and that was it. It was a statement that I'd already made. I didn't know why I had to go and rehash it again.

The hearing was in a really dingy room with a lot of people who all seemed to be staring at me. There was hardly meant to be anyone. That annoyed me. The officials said they'd guarantee our safety, but how could they when they couldn't even keep the hearing a secret?

The judge began asking me questions about the affidavit I'd signed, then about halfway through, Salim Malik turned up. That was really uncomfortable because the judge was still asking me questions while Malik was sitting right behind me. I don't know if he was looking at me or not. There was nothing hard about the questions. I just told the judge what was already in the statement, but I was glad when it was over. It must have lasted about forty minutes.

*We went back to Majid Khan's afterwards because we had a few hours to
wait before the plane trip. Majid was the one who really wanted to clean up
Pakistan cricket. He was quite influential in getting us there. When we left I
just couldn't wait to get back to the team. It was a day I'd rather forget.*

But could it be forgotten? Perhaps it was briefly brushed aside amidst the
euphoria surrounding Taylor's monumental 334 in the second Test, in
Peshawar. The innings equalled Don Bradman's Australian record set sixty-
eight years earlier at Leeds. Not surprisingly, nothing else seemed to matter in
the drawn match. Mark scored 42 and 43, comparative failures in an encounter
on a benign pitch that saw four centuries and two batsmen, including Taylor in
the second innings, dismissed in the nineties.

Mark could have been excused for having his mind elsewhere during the
game because of revelations from the Pakistan Cricket Board that it had
received a letter accusing Mark and Dean Jones of involvement in betting and
match-fixing. However, the PCB refused to disclose the source of the letter,
giving rise to speculation that the accusations weren't credible.

Malcolm Conn, the journalist covering the tour for the *Australian*, saw the
letter without discovering its author. After speaking with Mark, Conn
dismissed the accusations in an article, but was surprised two days later when
he was asked by Mark what he'd written. Conn's instincts told him there was
more to the story, and his digging began.

In the meantime, Australia moved to Karachi for the last Test. After winning
the toss, Taylor hoped to bat the home side out of the game, but his side made
only the moderate score of 280. Mark made 26 before falling to debutant all-
rounder Shahid Afridi, caught by Inzamam-ul-Haq at first slip. In reply,
Pakistan managed 252.

When Mark came to the crease in the second innings Australia were 2–135,
not yet in a position from which they couldn't lose, but the indications were
that more runs could be made against a tiring attack. Mark made the most of
his chance, reaching 117, his fourth Test century for the year. He finished the
series with 228 runs at an average of 45.60.

Australia were dismissed for 390; in reply, the Pakistanis batted out time on
the final day to finish at 7–262, still 156 in arrears. The draw ensured the end of a
long wait — Australia had won the series. Benaud's men were no longer alone.

After a clean sweep of the three limited-overs matches — Mark scored 11, 19 and 13 — the Australians headed home for an Ashes series. By the time he arrived more than a month into the domestic season, Mark was only able to play one game each in the Sheffield Shield and Mercantile Mutual Cup competitions between his national commitments for the summer. He made 64 and 126 in a draw against Victoria in Sydney, but failed to score in an eight-wicket loss to Tasmania in Hobart.

He made starts in all four innings of the first two Ashes Tests, scoring 31 and 27 not out in a draw in Brisbane, and 36 and an unbeaten 17 as the home side recorded a seven-wicket victory in Perth.

Throughout these matches, Malcolm Conn was methodically piecing together a story that would lead to him winning a prestigious Walkely award for outstanding journalism. By Tuesday 8 December, just three days before the start of the third Test, at the Adelaide Oval, Conn informed ACB chief executive Malcolm Speed that he was going to reveal details of the 'cover-up' concerning the fining of Mark for his association with John the bookmaker. At this stage Conn didn't know of Warne's involvement. Forced into action, the ACB released a brief statement that evening saying two unnamed players had been fined in 1994–95 for receiving money from an Indian bookmaker. Later that night, former Test cricketer David Hookes named Mark and Warne on Melbourne radio station 3AW. Conn's article ran the following morning.

Before the ACB released its statement, Speed contacted Mark's manager Leo Karis to inform him of what was going to happen. Mark's initial reaction to the news was, 'So what? I got fined. I paid the price. What's the big deal?' Karis contacted Warne's manager at the time, Austin Robertson, to discuss the likely repercussions. The next morning, the day of Conn's article, Karis flew to Adelaide, and contacted Mark's sponsors — to allay their fears and let them know that a media conference would be held after training that afternoon. Karis remembers: 'It was a crazy morning. But Mark went about his business. He trained that morning, then I spoke with him after that about the type of reaction he was likely to get at the press conference. Yes, he was down — the reaction really got to him.'

At the Adelaide Oval, in a room bursting with clicking shutters, camera flashes and rolling tapes, Mark and Warne read prepared statements. Both said their actions were 'naive and stupid'. The final lines of Mark's statement read:

I regret them [his actions] entirely and wish to restate in the strongest possible manner that I have always given my best for my country in every match I have played and I believe my record, particularly in the last three years, fully supports this statement.

I must emphasise that I have never been involved in match-fixing or bribery on cricket matches in any stage of my career.

Mark recalls:

I was obviously feeling very nervous. I don't like the spotlight at the best of times, let alone when it's bad. I felt very uncomfortable all the way through the affair, starting with the press conference. In some ways we were naive even in our press statements. Warney's and mine were very similar. I thought no matter what we said people were going to have their own opinions and people were going to write it up in a bad light. It was just snowballing so much. The fact that it had been hidden for so many years immediately made people think there was something more to hide. The thing I wanted to stress was that I was proud to play for my country, and we got that across in the statement. That was the main thing.

Afterwards, Mark played a round of golf at Kooyonga with brother Dean, who'd just moved to Adelaide to further his first-class career. Dean remembers: 'There were news helicopters hovering over us. There was no way Mark was going to be left alone, but he told me he'd done nothing wrong and that was it.'

Unfortunately for Mark, public opinion was not as dismissive. Not only were the players attacked, but the ACB was condemned for its cover-up. Prime minister John Howard said he felt an 'intense feeling of disillusionment'; outspoken former Test player Neil Harvey called for the banning of both players; Salim Malik said he was 'delighted'; and Pakistan's judicial inquiry questioned the credibility of the players and called for them to re-present their stories in Lahore. On the opposite side, ACA President Tim May pledged the Association's support for 'outstanding servants of Australian cricket'.

May also wrote privately to Mark. In part, the letter reads:

Mate, you made an error of judgement which was completely innocent and honest. The subsequent media outrage I believe is more directed at the ACB and their 'cover-up' as it's been titled. Do not let it get the better of you. You are a decent and honest bloke. You made an error of judgement. We all make them. Hold your head high. Everyone I know respects Mark Waugh as a player and a man. Nothing has changed. You are still the same player and still the same man.

Hang in there, learn from it and continue on being Mark Waugh.

The letter was one of just hundreds Mark received from friends and complete strangers alike. Among others, support came from radio commentators Alan Jones, Andrew Moore, and David Lord, journalist Phil Wilkins left a handwritten note at the team's hotel, and rugby league star Laurie Daley sent a fax that read: 'Just a quick note to let you know my thoughts and support are 100 per cent behind you.'

However, in the public domain of newspaper editorials and 'letters to the editor', there was a much more razor-edged response. In a letter to the editor of the *Australian* on 10 December 1998, Queensland reader Rob Ryan reflected one of the most common themes:

If Mark Waugh is as obsessed with punting as portrayed in the sports pages, then naivety is not a reasonable description of his action. Indeed, as a horse owner he would be intimately aware of the influence track conditions can have in determining outcomes. After all, isn't this the reason Australia has struggled on the subcontinent? Simply stated, Mark Waugh and Shane Warne must be stood down immediately for providing bookies with insider information. Otherwise, it will be a case of the pot calling the kettle black.

Furthermore, the *Australian*'s lead editorial on that day stated:

Waugh and Warne said yesterday they had been naive and stupid. Put the emphasis on the second adjective — and add greedy.

Similar views were presented in all the main newspapers across the nation. On the same day as Ryan's letter was published, the *Sydney Morning Herald* ran a page of reader comments under the headline 'A sad day for the baggy green cap'. Hugh Darling from Lake Conjola West wrote:

To ensure that the right message is given to players at all levels of the game, Mark Waugh and Shane Warne should have their contracts with the ACB cancelled immediately and they should never represent their country again.

They should also be joined by those within the ACB management who sanctioned the cover-up and the imposition of the fines, a paltry amount for the players concerned.

In Sydney's *Daily Telegraph*, columnist Miranda Devine condemned Mark and Warne when she commented:

The coolest, most street-wise big name cricketers in Australia are naive. Who buys that?

However, not all reaction was negative. In the *Sydney Morning Herald*, other readers supported Mark and Warne. Garth Clarke of Kirribilli suggested the players were 'guilty of little more than putting their hands up for Tony Greig's Channel Nine job,' and on 12 December, *Daily Telegraph* writer Peter Lalor wrote in a very balanced report that 'Shane Warne and Mark Waugh are likeable larrikins with competitive natures and a fondness for a bit of easy money.'

It seemed every Australian had a view. The unfortunate reality for Mark and Warne was that sport, in particular cricket, was so firmly woven into Australian culture that very few controversies could be dismissed with just a short tug of a loose thread. Whether the media unfairly portrayed the players during this issue is a matter of personal opinion, however, it is indisputable that such an emotive issue would affect any individual placed in the same position.

The worst was yet to come. While Warne, still mending from surgery, missed the Adelaide Test, Mark was in the brightest possible spotlight — the playing arena. When he walked out to bat on the first day, there were jeers and boos from sections of the crowd, primarily members of the English 'barmy army' of fans. In thirty-six drawn-out minutes at the crease, he struggled to make 7 runs before returning a catch to off-spinner Peter Such.

He recalls it was the toughest day of his career:

It was very hard. I didn't want the guys in front of me to get out when we won the toss. All I wanted to do was stay in my hotel room, go to sleep, and hopefully wake up the next day to no front-page news or headlines on the TV. That obviously wasn't realistic, but I just wanted to distance myself from it all. I just wanted to sleep, it was the only chance not to think about anything.

Going to play cricket was the last thing on my mind, the last thing I wanted to do was get out there in front of people and have them booing at me, yelling I shouldn't be playing for my country. It was hard to take. I'm only human, so I did take it in. It definitely affected me. I was in a dream-like state for that whole game. It was overwhelming.

I managed to get a fifty in the second innings (51 not out off 83 balls). I don't know how really. There was a bit of booing from the crowd. Not a lot though. I think most people were pretty good, but there were a few people having a go, and that really hurt me because I'd played for so many years, giving my best for my country, but people were willing to forget all of that.

It was a difficult time. Sue was there with me. We just sat in the hotel room every night. We didn't go out, we couldn't be bothered facing everybody. Just all the media, the fans, the cricket experts all with their opinions on what I thought was a little thing.

I was disappointed how it was portrayed because I couldn't understand how such a simple thing could become such a big deal. People were drawing conclusions left, right and centre. I was surprised how big an event it was.

One thing for sure is I worked out who my friends were at the time. There were not too many friends from the media. Of course the media generally likes bad news over good news because it sells papers, gets people to watch TV or listen to the radio. So the media jumped on this. They thought, 'Great! This is big time for us. It's a big story. We'll drum it up as much as we can. We don't really care if we exaggerate a bit, or distort the truth. This is big stuff for us. It's a bad news story, so it's good news.'

I started to get headaches. I felt sick all the time and lost weight. It was distressing. It was the same for Sue, my family, my parents, my grandmother. They were upset by what they read in the papers and people said on the radio. It was really hard for Dad because he owned a newsagency, and every morning he was coming in to work seeing me on the front page. It was a nightmare really that snowballed from something I didn't believe to be that bad.

Sue Porter was Mark's staunchest supporter, but her unyielding belief in her partner came at considerable emotional and physical cost. She began losing her hair in 'big clumps', and she'd been drained of her usually cheerful personality. She recalls the period was 'really, really really tough'.

> Adelaide was horrendous. It was awful. All the girls [the players' wives and girlfriends] were around me in the stand. There was a photographer sitting below watching us when Mark went out to bat. I just wanted to wrap Mark up and take him away from it, get him away from all the troubles. It was fairly emotional. When he got out, I just felt, 'Oh God, oh no.' How he went out there I don't even know. It was amazing. I was in tears. I just felt so helpless and sad.

Rodger Waugh was in the stands during Mark's first innings in Adelaide. Despite the turbulent day, he didn't feel the full effect of the controversy until he returned to his newsagency in Revesby. He says 'the hardest part was seeing the headlines first thing at six o'clock every morning', but he was boosted by the support of the local community. He remembers:

> People were very good around here, there weren't many cheap shots. Mark was worried about how it would affect us, but we got through it all right. Just certain people in the media seemed to have it in for him. They went overboard, and that upset me. I thought it would have affected his cricket more than it did.
>
> I was over in Adelaide when he had that first innings, and that was pretty tough for him. It was just one of those things that happen in life. We were upset, but we accepted it.

Each member of the Waugh family is critical of the media's handling of the issue. It's human nature that a family protects one of its own, and under the circumstances, it would have been impossible for the Waughs to remain impartial. Their son, their brother was being criticised, and it was their duty to support him. Yes, he had made a mistake, but surely it was only a small blemish in an otherwise trouble-free career. Bev Waugh says she 'always had great belief in Mark. You've got to stand by them and take the criticism, see the rubbish in the papers and know you can't do anything about it.'

Mark's greater family extended to the Australian team. Steve recalls:

All the Australian side was behind Mark and Shane. You never really know all the details — I still don't know them all. I just know they were treated pretty harshly, and it just kept going on and on.

It seemed as if the press just wanted a scapegoat, and Mark, and Shane to a lesser extent, were the people that were going to cop it.

He stayed strong, showed good character throughout that period, and played good cricket.

Leo Karis believes Mark simply made 'an innocent mistake'. As Mark's manager, he adopted a slightly different position to Mark's family. He says:

Not once did I think, 'Am I standing by someone who has done something wrong and my professional reputation is on the line?' Not for one second did I think that. I believed him. I sat down and spoke to him about it for many hours, and sat down and probably played the role of investigator myself in trying to determine what had happened. I walked away from every discussion thinking, 'This man is an honest, good bloke. And he just wants to play cricket.'

I tried to put myself into Mark's position when he first met John. I can understand how he entered into such a relationship.

The issues were very serious ones, and I don't think Mark trivialised his involvement in them. He regrets the day he entered into an agreement with John. He certainly didn't enter any agreement with deceit in his mind.

Despite the tide of opinion seemingly against him, Mark enjoyed a rare moment of widespread support in Adelaide. After scoring his unbeaten half-century, an innings described by his brother as having 'poise and grace', he walked from the field to a standing ovation from some sections of the crowd. He then took three catches in England's second innings. Australia won by 205 runs to take a 2–0 lead and retain the Ashes. For Mark, one of the worst moments of his career was over.

The visitors claimed revenge in the fourth Test, the traditional Boxing Day encounter in Melbourne, winning by 12 runs. Mark fell to a dubious lbw decision for 36 in the first innings, and passed 1000 runs for the calendar year in the second before his dismissal for 43 had an obvious bearing on the result. When he played back to a full-length Dean Headley delivery and edged the ball to Graeme Hick in the slips, Australia were 4–130, needing a further 45 for victory. The final six wickets fell for 32, and the visitors had secured an unexpected win.

Although Alec Stewart's players had a chance to square the series in Sydney, they couldn't overcome the nemesis of leg-spin, this time from Stuart MacGill who took 12 wickets for the match.

Mark began 1999 in the same way he'd christened the previous year — by scoring a century, 121, in nearly five hours. The innings was blessed with some belated festive spirit when John Crawley dropped a chance in the slips before Mark had made a run. He and Steve (96) shared a blistering fourth-wicket stand of 190 in 202 minutes.

Mark posted another ton in England's first innings when he softly took an edge from Nasser Hussain off a delivery from medium pacer cum off-spinner Colin Miller. It was his hundredth Test catch; only five other Australians had reached the mark.

Despite falling for 24 in his second innings, he had a profitable series, finishing second in the team's averages with 393 runs at 56.14. In the face of immense public scrutiny and ongoing questions over the strength of his personality, Mark had shown what he believes is one of his greatest qualities — resilience. His ability to handle the pressure and separate the bookmaker controversy from his on-field performances drew admiration from team-mates. Ian Healy says:

> I take my hat off to him the way he got through it. Whether he just shelved it or not I don't know, but he was mostly able to divide his cricket from the hoo-ha around him, and that was a big sign to me that he'd toughened up, or the skin had thickened, because I don't think he would have got through that as well as he did if it had happened in the early years of his career. He only went from strength to strength during that period.

Mark also had some prominent critics. After his Adelaide media conference, his relationship with certain journalists continued to slide. He makes special mention of the *Australian*'s Mike Coward, who was beginning to state that the younger Waugh twin was receiving preferential treatment from selectors. In an article in the *Weekend Australian* (12–13 December 1998), primarily about Justin Langer, Coward wrote during the Adelaide Test: 'Batting toffs like Mark Waugh don't just get the applause and the accolades, they get security of tenure. Mind you, the selectors will deny it, but it is a fact of this sporting life.'

These types of comments angered Mark as much as the ones calling for his head. While the seeds of diminishing respect for journalists had been sown before the season, 1998–99 provided the watering can and fertiliser. To Mark, it was a point of no return. Nowadays, nothing has changed; Mark's relationship with several journalists is infamous. He says dealing with the media, in particular the press, has been one of the biggest 'negatives' of his life.

To say that I get favours from selectors is bloody rude. I can't see where he's [Coward] coming from. I think it's unfair.

I think Coward, Conn and Robert Craddock [News Limited] have had some sort of bee in their bonnet about me for whatever reason for about three years. I don't know why. I haven't done anything to them.

They criticise you at the drop of a hat, they don't give you credit when you do well. They only see what they want to see.

As soon as you have a go back at them, they go all defensive. They say you're thin-skinned, they blow up about it. It's all right for them to criticise you day in or day out, but when you have a go at them they get upset. The thing with those guys is that they've never played the game, so I find it hard to accept that people who haven't played the game are criticising you all the time when they haven't been there and done that.

I think you have to have played some sort of sport at some level to understand the pressures, the whole set-up. It's not necessary, but it would definitely help you get insight into the game. Just how things unfold, whether it's on the field or off the field. There are good journalists who haven't played, but I think it definitely helps if you have.

The other thing is that they [the media in general] turn a simple comment into a headline a lot of the time at press conferences or at the airport — that's happened to me a few times. You make some off-the-cuff comment and it's a headline. Or some footage will be taken for TV one day, then used in a different context the next day. The next time they get upset when you don't want to do an interview with them. I think the media think the world revolves around them and their stories a lot of the time. It doesn't matter what gets in the way, or who gets in the way.

There should be more respect shown. People always say it's part of the job, but at the end of the day you're dealing with other people, their families and their emotions. It has to weigh on their minds a bit. We shouldn't be there for the beck and call of the media all the time.

I don't read half the rubbish in the papers because I know a lot of it isn't true. It's just there to sell the paper. It goes with the territory, but you just have to try to cope with it and ignore it as best you can.

From 1998 on my relationship with the media has definitely changed. There's a few guys I respect. I think Peter Roebuck writes pretty good stuff. I like Phil Wilkins, and Mike Horan when he was writing. The rest I won't say hello to. I won't give them the time of day. I don't think they deserve it. Even now. I won't yell at them, shout at them or abuse them, but I won't acknowledge them either. If I'm in a lift with them I'll just stand there and say nothing. If I walk past them I might say good morning, but that is all. There are just too many people who have burnt me.

Even now they don't see any harm in it. They want to come up and say hello, ask you how you're going, ask for interviews thinking you're a good bloke, but from 1998 on they really crucified me there. And I won't forget that. No way. Because a lot of them put me through a lot of pain, put the family through a lot of pain just for the sake of selling papers. I know who my friends are, and there's no way I'm going to do favours for many people in the media. No way.

Since 1998 I haven't really enjoyed my cricket career. There has always been something nagging there — I've felt the media has always been nagging away, keeping a close eye on me and my form. I don't think I hate anything more in my career than dealing with the media.

After the Ashes series, Mark and Warne were the subject of fresh headlines when the Australian team was named for the Carlton & United series against England and Sri Lanka. Steve was expected to miss the first two matches because of a hamstring injury. (By the end of the series his troublesome muscles had allowed him to only play two games.) Who would be the stand-in captain? Warne received the honour, and Mark was named vice-captain in a sign the

ACB had forgiven its players. Although Australian leadership at a senior level had never fallen Mark's way — he was also vice-captain to Steve on the 1998 limited-overs tour to New Zealand, and eventually captained a World XI against Asia in April 2000 — many of his peers were confident he had the natural flair, instinct and aggression to be successful. Geoff Lawson says he 'wouldn't separate Mark from Steve as far as cricket brains and knowledge went', while Mark Taylor believes 'Mark would have made an excellent captain because he wouldn't have over analysed.' It is one of Mark's greatest disappointments that first-class or Test captaincy haven't fallen his way. However, the leadership of New South Wales remains a possibility. Mark says the chance to help return the Blues to the top of Australian domestic cricket is a 'challenge I'd enjoy'. It all depends on his immediate Test future.

Before the limited-overs tournament began, the new skipper and his deputy had a pressing engagement to attend. On Friday 8 January they fronted a specially convened sitting of the Pakistan match-fixing inquiry in Melbourne. During the hearing conducted by Lahore High Court Registrar Abdus Khawar, Mark drew more unwanted attention to himself when he said in a statement that since the news conference the previous month in Adelaide, he'd given more thought to his dealings with 'John', and believed he had spoken to the bookmaker on 'approximately 10 occasions' as opposed to the 'handful' he had mentioned in Adelaide. The difference was pounced upon by the media, but in the context of a hearing about Pakistani match-fixing, it had little bearing, and no new evidence about Salim Malik came to light.

Mark refused to be distracted by the issue on the field. In a remarkably consistent Carlton & United series, he had innings of 23, 63, 83 not out, 85, 65, 57, 65, 12, 27, 19, 42 and 1. His tally of 542 runs at 49.27 was the highest in the competition, and along the way he and Adam Gilchrist (131) established a record-opening stand of 151 in an eight-wicket win over Sri Lanka at the SCG.

Australia beat England 2–0 in the finals. For at least a few weeks during the competition the bribery issue had been shoved behind the curtain by other unfortunate happenings on centre stage. Muttiah Muralitharan was again called for throwing, and Arjuna Ranatunga was up to his old tricks in a series that simmered, spat and occasionally boiled over with tension.

However, once the international teams had gone home, cricket corruption moved back into the spotlight in February when the ACB released the findings

A rare shot of Mark with his helmet off after scoring a century against Sri Lanka in Perth, 1995–96. (Photo by Shaun Botterill/Getty Images.)

Brian Lara congratulates Mark after reaching his century at Sabina Park, 1995.

(PHOTO BY CLIVE MASON/GETTY IMAGES.)

Mark Waugh hooking during his innings of 126 against the West Indies, 1995.

(PHOTO BY SHAUN BOTTERILL/GETTY IMAGES.)

Mark and Stephen cooling off after their match and series deciding 231 run partnership against the West Indies, 1995. Mark scored 126 and Stephen 200.

Mark was forced to turn to bowling off-spin after suffering back problems in the mid-1990s. He has become known as a 'partnership breaker'.

(Photo by Getty Images.)

The brothers in arms after Australia regained the Frank Worrell Trophy in Jamaica, 1995.

(Photo by Shaun Botterill/Getty Images.)

Mark and Shane Warne the day they fronted the media (9 December 1998) in Adelaide after revelations they had been involved with 'John the Bookmaker'. ACB CEO at the time, Malcolm Speed, is in the background on the right next to Mark's manager Leo Karis *(left)*.

Mark is described by Mark Taylor as the 'best all-round fieldsman I've ever seen'. Here, he flies through the air at mid-wicket to catch Chris Cairns during the second Test against New Zealand in Perth, 1997–98.

Mark rates this catch as one of the best three he's ever taken, dismissing Wajahatullah Wasti during the 1999 World Cup final against Pakistan at Lord's. (PHOTO BY ADRIAN MURRELL/GETTY IMAGES.)

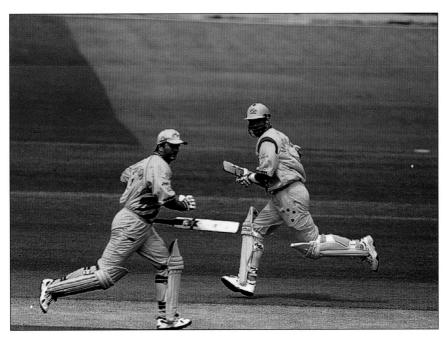

The twins compiling a 129 run partnership against Zimbabwe at Lord's during the 1999 World Cup. Mark scored 104, his record fourth World Cup century.

On the balcony at Lord's with Stephen and Shane Warne after winning the 1999 World Cup.

(Photo by Clive Mason/Getty Images.)

Mark and Sue at Lord's after Australia's 1999 World Cup triumph against Pakistan. This was the first time the players' partners were allowed in the dressing room.

Mark and Stephen with one of their proudest supporters, Bev, after the ticker-tape parade in Sydney celebrating Australia's World Cup success.

The hardest-earned century of his career. Mark before his 100th Test, January 2000 against India at the SCG.

Mark enjoying time out of the spotlight with a beer and one of his best mates, Kingston.

The opening of the Stephen and Mark Waugh Pavilion at Bankstown Oval, 8 February 2000. The author, James Knight, is on the far left.

Mark and Sue at dinner in Nottingham, August 2001, the day they were told there was no evidence to support Mukesh Gupta's claims in the Indian CBI report.

of the Player Conduct Inquiry undertaken by Rob O'Regan, who'd been appointed after Mark and Warne's fines were made public.

At a meeting in New Zealand, the ICC executive stated that there would be no further punishment for Mark and Shane because they couldn't be tried twice for the same offence.

Mark hoped that the issue was finally 'dead and buried'. The 1998–99 season had been the most draining period of his life, yet he quite remarkably prospered on the field. Even his harshest critics had to acknowledge his irresistible will to fight and succeed under circumstances that would have crippled other players.

It was time to concentrate on the road ahead. The road that led to the top of the world.

CHAPTER TWENTY-FIVE

COURAGE UNDER FIRE

Courage Under Fire is the name of one of Mark's all-time favourite pacers. To Mark's most loyal fans, it's also an appropriate way to describe a quality their idol displayed during the troublesome 1998–99 season. And as the Australians left Sydney in mid-February for the World Cup in England via a four-Test series in the West Indies, 'Courage Under Fire' was going to prove a recurring theme.

It was the start of a new era in Australian cricket — Mark Taylor had retired and Steve Waugh was the new Test captain, the logical choice according to his younger brother.

After two warm-up matches, in the latter of which Mark scored 106 against a President's XI at Point-a-Pierre, Trinidad, the tourists launched into their defence of the Frank Worrell Trophy with what could only be viewed as an annihilation of the home side in the first Test, at Port of Spain. The contest was over inside four days, Australia won by 312 runs after the Windies collapsed in their second innings for a paltry 51. Mark scored 2 and 33, trapped lbw in both innings. After the game, he thought, 'How much are we going to win this series by?'

However, in one of the most dramatic turnarounds imaginable, the Windies won the second Test, in Jamaica, by 10 wickets. The reason was simple — the genius of Brian Lara.

After winning the toss and batting, Australia were dismissed for 256 late on the opening day. Steve (100) led the way and Mark (67) also threatened a big score before he suffered one of the cruellest dismissals of his career — bowled by off-spinner Nehemiah Perry, whose delivery shot along the ground, bouncing twice before it hit the stumps. By the end of the day, the West Indians were 4–37, with Lara unbeaten on 7. That night at dinner, Mark thought, 'We're going to win easily here as well.'

But, for the next day and a half Lara flayed the Australian attack in a brilliant, belligerent innings of 213, dominating the team total of 431. He had gone to the crease facing growing pressure to step aside as captain; he departed as the undisputed hero of the Caribbean. Mark says:

He, Tendulkar and Adam Gilchrist are the three batsmen who can tear attacks apart, and really turn it on. When Lara's going, he hits the ball so hard that it's almost impossible to stop the run flow. You try to limit the boundaries and work on the other guy, but you've sometimes got to accept he's too good for you on the day.

Australia folded for just 177 in their second innings. Mark fell to Curtly Ambrose for 21.

The rejuvenated home side needed only three runs for victory. The series was alive, and Mark was no longer thinking how easy it all was.

He had a miserable third Test, in Barbados, bowled by Ambrose for a duck, and trapped lbw by Courtney Walsh for 3. Although Steve scored 199 in the first innings, the match again belonged to Lara, whose unbeaten 153 in the second innings guided the Windies to a thrilling one-wicket win. Mark simply says of Lara's performance: 'It's the best batting I've ever seen.'

Australia's grip on the Worrell trophy was weakening — Steve's men needed to win the final encounter in Antigua to keep hold. It was a task they achieved by 176 runs despite an explosive 100 from just 84 balls by Lara. Mark made 11 and 65, caught behind in the second innings, the fifteenth and last time he'd be dismissed by his old adversary, Ambrose.

No bowler has enjoyed more success against Mark. Despite all the battles he'd had with the Antiguan paceman over the years, Mark says he barely knew the real man behind the ball:

I don't really know if I got on with Amby because I never really spoke to him until that last tour. He seemed a good bloke because whenever the teams were having lunch, you'd see the Windies chatting and laughing around him. His team-mates obviously liked him a lot.

But if you were an opponent it was different. He'd walk past you in the morning going to the nets, going to the ground, or back to the hotel, and he'd just nod at you. That was all he did. He wouldn't say anything, but towards the end of his career he started to say hello and mellowed a bit.

Mark had shown indifferent form throughout the series, finishing sixth in Australia's averages, with 202 runs at 25.25. He did, however, pass a statistical milestone in his final innings — 6000 Test runs. But questions were being raised in the press box. How many more would M.E. Waugh score? Yet again, his Test position was under scrutiny. There was little time to dwell on the issue as attention quickly turned to a seven-match limited-overs series, a critical warm-up for the World Cup.

Mark played in all the games, finishing as Australia's second-highest run-scorer with 217 runs at 31.00. His best performance came in the third encounter, in Trinidad, when he made 74 off 100 balls in a five-wicket loss.

The series was marred by several unfortunate incidents. The fifth contest, in Georgetown, Guyana, had a most unexpected ending when Steve and Shane Warne attempted to steal a third run off the final ball to ensure the match ended in a tie. By this stage, the field was flooded by crowd invaders. Before the West Indians had the chance to effect a run-out, all six stumps had been stolen by spectators. After nearly an hour's deliberation, match referee Raman Subba Row declared a tie.

In the final game, at Bridgetown's Kensington Oval, local hero Sherwin Campbell was run-out after colliding with bowler Brendon Julian in the middle of the match. Replays showed Julian had impeded the opener's path by thrusting out an arm. Campbell inflamed the crowd by making an animated protest, which led to the ground being showered in bottles. After huddling in the middle, the Australians decided to sprint to the dressing rooms. They were reluctant to return, but were told by officials that their safety couldn't be guaranteed if they didn't. Mark recalls:

> I'd been in a match once in Bangalore when the crowd started throwing chairs after Aza [Mohammad Azharuddin] was given out lbw, but this was worse. Someone could have easily been seriously hurt. Stephen nearly collected a bottle in the head when we ran off, and some of the other guys were nearly hit.
>
> I was lucky because I'd been in the inner circle, but when I was running off, I expected to be hit at any time. With a bottle, or you never know, even a spectator. You could see the anger in their faces. They were just staring at us, throwing stuff, looking as if they really wanted to hit some of us and hurt us.
>
> What made it worse was having all the girls [wives and partners] at the ground. They were pretty nervous, but were ushered out.
>
> There was just no control at all. Sherwin's run-out did look bad, but a similar incident happened to Michael Bevan earlier. It was no big deal — Sherwin should have accepted it. It was just ridiculous.
>
> For years crowd control hasn't been good enough — someone will eventually get badly hurt. It wasn't what you expected in Barbados, which is such a friendly place.

Campbell was eventually recalled as the West Indies chased a modified target, which they reached with three overs to spare. The series was drawn 3–all, and after enjoying a week's break in Barbados, the Australians headed to England.

The favourites for the twelve-nation World Cup began with an unimpressive four-wicket win over Scotland at Worcester. Mark was one of three players to drop regulation catches, but he switched on when batting, compiling 67, and winning man-of-the-match honours.

It was a lethargic performance by the Australians, who suffered losses in their next two outings against New Zealand and Pakistan. Mark scored 2 and 41. Australia were suddenly on the verge of making an embarrassing first-round exit from the tournament. Despite speculation in the media, Mark says there was 'no disunity' in the team, and their batting against Pakistan — they were dismissed for 265 chasing 276 at Headingley — gave them 'more confidence'. To win the tournament, they would have to win every game from that moment on. Seven in a row. Was it possible? Many followers had already written them off.

Their chances of advancing to the Super Six round were boosted when they beat Bangladesh with 30 overs to spare at Chester-le-Street. The pace at which the win was achieved proved critical in final net run rates. Mark scored 33 off 35 balls, but failed with only 3 in the following win by six wickets over the West Indies, at Old Trafford. The game ended in controversy when the Australians, knowing they would win and qualify for the next stage, batted slowly — Steve scored 19 off 73 balls and Michael Bevan 20 off 69 — to boost the Windies' net run rate. Under the rules of the competition teams that qualified for the Super Six round would take points forward from the preliminary matches, but only those obtained from victories over other sides in their group that also advanced. By lifting the Windies' run rate, Australia hoped to push Lara's team into the final qualifying spot ahead of New Zealand. This would mean they would carry two points forward, as opposed to none if the Kiwis advanced. Their tactics were heavily criticised as 'unsportsmanlike', but Mark disagrees.

> We were winning the game, but just deciding to score slowly — we were playing by the rules. We didn't make up the rules, but the rules weren't right that's for sure. I suppose it was an example of how hard we play the game. Our actions were compared to New Zealand losing a game against the South Africans in Perth last season (2001–2) to keep us out of the one day finals. That was totally different because we were winning our match. To me, you can do what you want when you're winning, but when you're not even trying to win is something totally different. There was no comparison between the two situations.

As it turned out, New Zealand still qualified ahead of the West Indies.

Driven by the need to win every game, the Australians outplayed India by 77 runs in the first Super Six game, at The Oval. Mark dominated his team's scorecard, compiling 83 off 99 balls in an innings of typical ease and elegance. In their eagerness to keep the ball away from Mark's pads, the bowlers pitched too short and wide, offering Mark the chance to repeatedly cut stylishly for four. His innings defied the trend of the competition in which early-order batsmen had been struggling against the white balls.

The hunchbacked figure of Old Father Time — the famous weathervane overlooking Lord's — watched Australia's next match, against Zimbabwe. Mark always enjoyed playing at the home of cricket, and although he disliked statistics, he was on the verge of a record-breaking achievement — he was just 35 runs away from overtaking Allan Border (6524 runs) as Australia's greatest run-scorer in limited-overs cricket.

As he walked out to bat, prominent in Mark's thoughts was his grandfather, Edward, who was dying at home in Australia. Before the end of the tournament, Mark wanted to achieve something special to acknowledge one of his greatest fans. In a most memorable innings, he flowed past Border's record and kept going with such ease that it seemed the Zimbabweans had joined Old Father Time as spectators. Mark's driving in particular was delightful, although on one occasion a nearby spectator was not impressed — Steve, who was thankfully wearing a helmet at the bowler's end, was hit by a powerful straight shot he had no time to avoid. It was the only blatant act of violence of the innings — Mark proved a soft and almost silent killer, destroying the attack with seemingly gentle touches that nevertheless inflicted deep wounds.

He made 104 from 120 balls to become the first batsman to score four World Cup centuries. It was the twelfth limited-overs hundred of his career. At the end of the match, which Australia won by 44 runs, he dedicated the innings to his grandfather. Mark remembers:

He'd been sick for a while. I really think the cricket kept him alive — seeing us play at the World Cup was important to him. I'm sure that century kept him going a bit longer. The fact that I'd made a century for him at Lord's, and broke AB's record made it a very special day.

The next match will forever be regarded as one of the greatest contests ever played in one-day cricket. Australia beat South Africa by five wickets at Leeds in the final Super Six game. Chasing 271 for victory, they slumped to 3–48 — Mark had been run out for 5 in a poor mix-up with Ricky Ponting — before Steve played one of the most inspirational innings of his career, finishing unbeaten on 120 off 110 balls. Mark recalls:

By this stage, the three best teams were Australia, Pakistan and South Africa. When we were 'three-for' I thought we were gone, we were heading home. We'd done okay, but we just hadn't been good enough. Then Ricky Ponting and Stephen started to look all right, but we still needed 8 an over. The wicket wasn't great and against a really good bowling side the odds were stacked against us.

But Stephen played his best one-day innings and had great support from Ricky, Bevo [Michael Bevan] and Moods [Tom Moody]. The turning point was the Herschelle Gibbs catch. [When Steve was 56 he hit a catch to mid-wicket where Gibbs prematurely tried throwing the ball into the air before having control of it.] If Gibbs had held onto it, we would have been struggling. The unbelievable thing is that Warney mentioned it the night before at the team meeting. He told us not to walk on a Gibbs catch because Herschelle had a habit of throwing the ball up really quickly. Warney does speak some good stuff, but most of the time you don't really listen to it. He raves on and you think, 'Oh yeah, good one Warney,' but this time look what happened. It was definitely not out. And the turning point.

It was quite strange really. Ever since we'd had a team meeting the night before we played India, we were confident we could go all the way. We knew we had to win all the matches, which was going to be really hard, especially at a World Cup, but we knew we could do it. We broke it down by thinking only about winning our next game. We didn't look any further ahead than that. Belief is what got us home. And after the win at Leeds I think we all felt that nothing could stop us.

If the Headingley match was a top-shelf memory for the Australians, the following contest, the semi-final against South Africa at Edgbaston, deserved a whole cabinet to itself. It was a game that had a more dramatic ending than the Tooheys beer commercials of the 1980s in which Steve Rixon and Mike Whitney were final-ball heroes, hitting a six or sliding to safety to win. However, if the finish at Birmingham had been scripted as an advertisement it would have surely been rejected as too far-fetched.

After making a disappointing 213 — Mark was caught behind off Shaun Pollock's bowling for a duck — the Australians fought back, Warne leading the way with 4–29. In the final overs, South African all-rounder and player of the tournament Lance Klusener was brutal, reaching 23 off 12 balls, including a six that deflected through the hands of Paul Reiffel at long-off. Heading into the last over, with Klusener on strike to Damien Fleming, nine runs were needed for a South African win, while Australia were chasing just one wicket. Mark recalls the telling moments of what is widely regarded as the greatest limited-overs game in history.

When Paul Reiffel dropped the catch in the second-last over, I thought that it was all over. Klusener hadn't mis-hit a ball all tournament. I thought he'd win the game for them.

The next over I'm fielding at deep mid-off. First ball, Flem [Damien Fleming] bowls a yorker. Klusener crushes it through the covers for four. Next ball, the same thing. I've never seen balls hit that hard. It was unbelievable. No-one had a chance to even move. I thought, 'We're gone here, gone.'

Obviously we had to bring the field in. In those situations everyone is pretty nervous, and you don't really want the ball to come to you. Next ball, the ball is hit to 'Boof' Lehmann at mid-on. Allan Donald is out of his ground, Boof underarms at the stumps but misses. By this time I'm thinking, 'Well, that's gotta be it. No more chances now.'

Then remarkably Klusener and Donald didn't even have a chat. Klusener seemed that confident he'd hit the winning runs, there was no need to communicate. He hits the next ball to me at mid-off, and for some reason he decides to run. The ball was a bit of an awkward one to take just off the square. I came round, picked it up and did the backhand flick that I'd practised for years. It was an unusual thing to do, but with the angle I was running on I thought it was the quickest way to get rid of the ball. It would have been a dream if it had hit. You visualise those moments when you do something brilliant to win a game. But I just missed the stumps, the ball goes to Flemo, and he underarms it along the pitch to Gilly. By this time, Klusener's at Flem's end, and Donald without his bat is running to Gilly's end. Everyone was yelling: 'Keeper, keeper.' The ball seemed to travel in slow motion. Then Gilly gets it and it's all over. That was the most exciting moment I've had in any form of cricket. I just remember everyone jumping in the air and racing in to hug each other. There was so much yelling and screaming going on. It was a tie, but we were through to the final on a count-back system because we'd beaten South Africa in the Super Six round.

None of us could believe that they'd tried to run — there were still two balls to go. It was just meant to be.

The South Africans were stunned. The girls had been sitting near them, and Sue reckons they were just cock-a-hoop after Klusener hit the two fours. By the time of the run-out they were in tears. Shattered, they were.

We'd had the wood on them in the past, and Stephen threw in a bit of gamesmanship before the match when he said the South Africans couldn't handle the pressure. I think it does get in their minds a bit. In the end though we both cracked a bit, with Pistol's [Paul Reiffel's] dropped catch, and Boof missing the run-out. We cracked a bit, but they cracked under it worse.

Critics say one-day cricket isn't proper cricket, but those two games against South Africa showed they can be as good as anything anywhere. They were two miracle performances, especially Birmingham.

The Australian coach at the time, Geoff Marsh, has one story about Mark that sticks firmly in his mind when he talks of the Edgbaston match.

In our last team meeting before that semi-final we discussed how we were going to bowl to Klusener because he was having a magnificent series. Nearly the whole team was saying we had to bowl yorkers around the wicket to him, not give him any room.

Mark popped up and said, 'That's rubbish. We've got to bowl over-the-wicket yorkers straight at off-stump.'

If you go back to that final over, we started bowling around the wicket, then after Klusener belted those two balls for four, Flem went back over the wicket and cramped Klusener. I always remember Mark coming off the ground and saying, 'See, I told you we had to bowl over the wicket to him!'

Australia returned to Lord's and Old Father Time for the final against Pakistan. For Mark, an important part of the build-up happened the day before when he and Steve rang their father to see how 'Pop' was. The 89-year-old Edward was only just alive.

The following morning, Mark rose early to ring home at six o'clock and listen to one of his horses, New Energy, race at Menangle. It was a good omen — New Energy won.

A few hours later, Mark was standing in the slips cordon watching Glenn McGrath unsettle the Pakistani top order after Wasim Akram had won the toss and decided to bat. With only one run next to his name, Wajahatullah Wasti edged a delivery well wide of Mark, who flew sideways to take a catch that he rates nearly as highly as his snare of Alec Stewart during the 1993 Ashes.

It was the start of Pakistan's slide. By the thirty-ninth over, they were all out for 132. Australia reached the target in the twenty-first over, with eight wickets to spare. Mark remained unbeaten on 37 from 52 deliveries. He finished second behind Steve on the team's run-scoring list, with a tally of 375 at 41.66.

In the midst of the celebrations, Mark and Steve dedicated the victory to their grandfather. Late that night, when few people remained at Lord's, Ricky Ponting led the team onto the pitch for a raucous rendition of 'Under the Southern Cross'. Old Father Time had never before seen anything like it on the hallowed turf.

A few hours later, Mark and Steve were enjoying the celebrations at the team hotel when manager Steve Bernard received a phone call from Lynette Waugh — Edward Waugh had died. The twins slipped quietly away from the revelry for some quiet reflection.

'It was like he wanted to see us through,' says Mark. 'He lived to watch us play. He was a good man. A real good man.'

With the World Cup theirs for a second time, the Australians returned home for a ticker-tape parade in Sydney. Considering their start to the tournament — which came in for heavy criticism — it is fair to say they showed courage under fire.

CHAPTER TWENTY-SIX

NEW MILLENNIUM

During the final months of 1999, mathematicians agreed to disagree on whether the world was approaching a new millennium; information technology experts agreed to disagree on the possible effects of the Y2K virus; and not for the first time, cricket followers agreed to disagree on the future of Mark Waugh.

Mark had just returned home after enduring contrasting fortunes during a 10-week tour of Sri Lanka and Zimbabwe. He began the trip with solid performances — 174 runs in 5 matches at 34.8 — in a one-day tournament in Sri Lanka. However, his form wilted in the three-Test series, which the home side won 1–0. Mark failed in every innings with scores of 6, 0, 10 and 13.

After watching Mark's dismissal in the second Test, in Galle, Mike Coward wrote in the *Weekend Australian* (25–26 September 1999): 'Agreed, it is hard to imagine an Australian team without him. At best he has few rivals in world cricket. But the truth is he's finding it increasingly difficult to produce his best.'

Mark acknowledges criticism of his form was warranted. The truth was simple — 'Yeah, I just wasn't batting well. I just couldn't make a run.' In at least one innings, the second in the opening Test when he was dismissed for a duck, he admits his mind wasn't on the game. But with good reason. At that stage Steve and fast bowler Jason Gillespie were recovering in hospital with the respective injuries of a smashed nose and a broken leg after a horrendous fielding collision.

Mark had been the first to reach his crumpled brother. He remembers: 'He was in a pretty bad way. There was blood everywhere. If Jason had collected him in a different spot Stephen could have been killed. I was pretty shaken up. I found it hard to concentrate for the rest of that day and my head just wasn't there for the rest of the match.'

Steve recovered in time to play the two remaining Tests, and then headed to Harare where he scored an unbeaten 151 to lead his team to a 10-wicket blitzing of Zimbabwe in a one-off Test, the last of Ian Healy's career. Mark found the going easier than when in Sri Lanka, compiling 90. At the time of his dismissal, caught and bowled by part-time off-spinner Grant Flower, he didn't realise he was within reach of becoming the first batsman to score a hundred against the eight other major Test nations.

He did reach three figures in the first of three one-dayers against Zimbabwe, blasting 106 from 97 balls. He followed with an unbeaten 54 in the second game, his final limited-overs innings of a phenomenal year that yielded 1468 runs at 44.48 — the best return of Mark's career. Australia won the series 3–0.

Less than a fortnight later, he forced the critics to take another step back when he scored 100 against Pakistan in the opening Test, at the Gabba. He shared a 123-run stand with new cap Adam Gilchrist (81), who had replaced Healy as Test wicket-keeper. The renowned author David Frith wrote in the Australian edition of the 2000–01 *Wisden Almanack*, 'Quietly, elegantly, but by no means slowly, Mark Waugh stroked a century in his best dream-like manner. The curiously contrasting duet brought a double ration of reassurance to the selectors.'

Mark believes he hit the ball in that innings as well as he ever had, while Gilchrist was relieved to have a familiar face at the wicket when he walked out to bat.

Having Mark there certainly had a huge bearing on me. It was a familiar scene because I'd already batted so many times with him in one-day cricket. It was a

comforting environment to walk in to. He just has this natural ability to put
ease into a situation, and he does it in a confident manner which instils
confidence in others.

Not surprisingly, Gilchrist will never forget the second Test, in Hobart, after he [149 n.o.] and Justin Langer [127] shared a sixth-wicket stand of 238 that ensured Australia an inspirational four-wicket victory when the side appeared down and out after being 5–126, chasing 369. 'It was tremendous for JL [Justin Langer],' remembers Mark, 'because he'd been under tremendous pressure going into that match. The result also gave us the belief we could win from any situation.' Mark had a disappointing match, scoring 5 and 0. However, he produced one of his special blink-of-an-eye moments in the field that changed the context of the game. In the Pakistan second innings, Izamam-ul-Haq looked likely to steer his side to a total that would have taken the contest out of Australia's reach, but after making an attractive 118, he swiped at a Shane Warne delivery, and sent the ball flying to Mark's left at first slip. Gilchrist recalls:

Some people may say when the batsman flashes like Inzamam, the ball either
sticks in the middle of your hand or you don't catch it, but Mark at least gives
himself more of a chance to catch them by his reaction and anticipation.
    It was a wide, quick delivery from a spinner, Inzamam swung fairly lustily,
as he tends to do, and Mark reacted by taking a step back and going where he
thought the ball would go if it came in his direction. And in it went. He read it
beautifully. A lot of people tense up in those situations, but Mark always
remains calm. It was just a freak catch.

Mark rates the catch in his top three.

Australia completed a clean sweep of the series after claiming the third Test, in Perth, by an innings and 20 runs. Mark fell for his second duck in a row. In the press box, the obituaries were being dusted off — the pressure was building as quickly as a southerly change.

In his regular article for the monthly publication *Inside Edge* (December 1999), Mark wrote: 'You don't lose your ability in three games. In Australia last summer, I averaged 50 in the Tests and scored the most runs in the one-dayers. That's not long ago, is it?'

Others thought differently. A week before the Test series against India began in Adelaide, Fairfax journalist Greg Baum wrote in the *Sydney Morning Herald* (4 December 1999): 'Mark Waugh is not over the hill, but he is seemingly past his peak. It is both safe and sad to say that we have seen the best of him.'

The topic had added emotion because Mark was approaching the hardest earned century of his career — 100 Tests. He was due to reach the milestone in the third match against India, in Sydney. Would he make it? Or would he, like his brother had been so many times at the crease, be stranded in the nineties?

His chances decreased after a double failure in Adelaide. Australia won by 285 runs, but Mark fell for 5 and 8. His performance prompted News Limited journalist Robert Craddock to write in the *Daily Telegraph* (14 December 1999):

> To see Waugh painfully squeeze out eight runs in just under an hour yesterday, almost being caught at square leg and slip along the way, was like watching one of the three musketeers trying to win a sword fight with a carrot.

Craddock also suggested Mark's demeanour had changed, as he became more 'insular and less good-humoured'.

'How could he have known that?' asks Mark. 'I never saw him except at training. He was just putting himself in my position and thinking how he'd feel. That type of reporting really annoys me.'

For people who determined success and failure purely by reading statistics, 1999 had been a most unsatisfactory year for Mark, who'd scored 584 runs at 27.81. However, for those who took a wider view, Mark remained a valuable member of the Test team. He was still catching well, offering tactical insight and, as was shown by his catch in Hobart, he still had the ability to help turn a match with an act of untouchable brilliance.

Bob Simpson suggests: 'If Mark fails three times in a Test series, but wins you one out of the next two, he's done his job. He's the type of player who's going to be noticed when he fails. How many people are capable of winning matches the way he does?'

In the build-up to the second Test, in Melbourne, Mark had his one outing of the season for New South Wales in the Pura Milk Cup, formerly the Sheffield

Shield. He scored 1 and 25 in an easy victory over Western Australia in Perth. The innings weren't cause for optimism. However, Steve, National selector Allan Border, Mark Taylor and Greg Chappell all threw their support behind Mark. Even the Prime Minister, John Howard, said, 'I would certainly like to see Mark have another couple of opportunities.'

And so it proved.

He received an overwhelming reception from an MCG crowd of nearly 50 000 when he walked out to bat against India on Boxing Day. Loud cheers saluted him after he scored his first runs, a gentle push through the covers for two. Although he was at times tentative, he showed glimpses of the batsman the supporters longed to see. After two hours at the crease, he was dismissed for 41, lbw by a sharp off-cutter from paceman Ajit Agarkar. The crowd again applauded, and the following day, Mike Coward, one of his strongest critics, wrote in the *Australian* (27 December 1999): 'You've got to give Mark Waugh his due: he's got some ticker.'

He showed further signs of recovery in the second innings when he remained unbeaten on 51 before a declaration gave the home team enough time to bowl out India and record a 180-run victory. The nervous nineties were over — Mark had guaranteed his place for his hundredth Test, the first of the new millennium, beginning on 2 January.

Before the game, the Prime Minister presented the Australians with special skull-caps, replicas of the vintage cricket headwear worn 100 years earlier. When they took to the field for the start of the match soon afterwards, they walked back in time. Many hoped Mark would do likewise when he batted. He made 32 in his only chance at the crease as Australia stormed to victory by an innings and 141 runs — their seventh straight win. Mark finished the series with 137 runs at an average of 34.25, behind Ricky Ponting, the series leading scorer with 375 runs at 125.00. It was the end of a tough home summer. He admits:

It wasn't a good year for me personally. I knew I needed runs, but I honestly didn't feel as though I was that far away from a big innings. It was only at the start of the Pakistan series that I was hitting the ball really well. I suppose the media were justified in questioning my form, but it annoyed me when they started analysing what I was doing wrong. I wasn't moving my feet, I was taking my eye off the short ball. Batting's not easy you know. I think they tend to forget that. They expect you to play the same way all the time. If we all did that, the game would be pretty dull wouldn't it?

Playing my hundredth Test was special. I was only the sixth Australian to have done it [Allan Border, David Boon, Ian Healy, Mark Taylor and Steve were the others], so it was good to be up there with some of the greats. When you look at it, that's a lot of cricket. It means you've been a consistent player. You've obviously had highs and lows and learnt to cope with the pressures of Test-match cricket. It's an achievement to be proud of. It's a hell of a lot of cricket when you think of all the things that can go wrong. It's good to have been part of a winning team for most of that time. If I was someone like Alec Stewart or Mike Atherton who played a lot of Tests, but won very few, I don't think I would have lasted as long.

Australia's ability to win was proven during the Carlton & United series when, after losing their first game to Pakistan, they won every match through to the end of the competition, including a 2–0 win over the Pakistanis in the finals.

After a worrying start to the series, Mark finished with 305 runs at 30.5, including a wonderful 116 off 131 balls against India at the Adelaide Oval. From the moment he cover drove his first ball for a boundary, he was in complete command. He and Gilchrist (92) put on 163 runs for the opening stand, the foundation of Australia's biggest-ever score at home, 5–329.

The world champions' dominance of the one-day game continued in New Zealand where they extended their unbeaten run to a world-record fourteen matches before losing the final encounter of a six-game series. Only weeks earlier, there was speculation Mark wouldn't be selected for the tour, but once aboard, he enjoyed a profitable campaign, finishing with 206 runs at 41.20. He and Gilchrist recorded two more century partnerships, the latter of 189 saw Gilchrist at his most destructive in a murderous innings of 128 from 98 balls. Mark says:

If Adam Gilchrist bats out the full fifty overs of a one-dayer, he'll make 200 easy. Even forty overs would be enough. He'll do it if he settles down a bit. He just goes 100 miles an hour the whole time. I've never batted with anyone like him. He gets runs that quickly. I sometimes told him to 'bat time' and the runs will come quickly anyway, but he just keeps going because that's the way he plays. I really enjoyed batting with him.

Despite his success in the one-dayers, Mark entered the three-Test series against the Kiwis knowing fingers would be twisting on binoculars and twitching on keyboards in the press box.

After winning the toss and batting in the first match, at Auckland's Eden Park, Australia struggled to 214 on an unusually brown pitch, that although moist gave most of its assistance to Daniel Vettori, who troubled the visitors with his searching loop and spin. Mark, however, wasn't rattled during a three-hour stay in which time and again his soft hands and ability to play later than his colleagues nullified the attack. His unbeaten 72, the most valuable innings of the Test, and arguably a match-winning performance, was reminiscent of his century against South Africa in Port Elizabeth in 1997. Only he and Justin Langer (46) passed 20. It was innings such as this one that confirmed Mark had matured since his flamboyant youth. Steve says:

I think his game has changed and evolved over the years. He's realised that you can get through the tough periods, look ugly and still get runs. In his first six or seven years in the Australian side he just didn't like looking ugly and would probably rather have got out than make a scratchy 30 or 40. But he realised he could play that way as well and be successful, so I think he's become a better player as a result.

Vettori claimed revenge in the second innings when Mark was caught behind for 25, but the Australians maintained a slender advantage to win a tense and intriguing contest by 62 runs.

The visitors won the series 3–0. In the final two Tests Mark scored 3 and 44 not out, and 28 and 18 for a return of 190 runs at 47.50.

By this time, a significant change was occurring in the Australian team under the direction of former Queensland player John Buchanan, who'd taken over as national coach, following the resignation of Geoff Marsh for personal reasons. Buchanan, with the bespectacled look of an academic, was a keen supporter of statistical analysis and of thinking 'outside the square'. Together, he and Steve not only thought outside the square, but were moulding entirely new shapes.

Buchanan introduced report cards, euphemistically referred to as 'Player Feedback Sheets' which he handed out after every Test. Innings are broken down into scoring rates, the percentage of singles and boundaries, the number of partnerships, the times a batsman plays and misses, and how many appeals he survives. Bowling is addressed in a similar fashion, and fielding is a matter of touches, dive-stops, assists, throws, poor throws, misfields and errors.

This is the era of dressing room contracts in which players pledge support for each other and their individual goals. Personal development is highly regarded to the extent that team-mates are encouraged to express their feelings and thoughts on pieces of paper stuck to dressing room walls. Sometimes there has been a poem or two. Team values are broken down into tradition, honesty and integrity, hard work, innovation, upholding the spirit of the game, 'raising the bar', and being a partner in the development of Australian cricket. Aggression is a positive factor, but only when used within the rules of the game. There must always be the desire to improve mentally, physically, technically and tactically. The players must ask themselves: can they change the game? And when they fail, they must always be gracious in defeat.

This is the era of bowlers and batsmen arriving in different buses at the ground. It's the era of psychologists. Of ice-baths. Of occasional 'power-naps' before a player goes out to bat. It is a vastly different approach from when Mark began his career. He acknowledges:

It can give you a new freshness. But you have to be willing to go with it because you can't teach an old dog new tricks. I'm from the older school, even the physical side of it. We go to the gym nearly every day now, and I'd never been to a gym in my life until the past two or three years. You've got to change, otherwise you'll get left behind. In some ways it's refreshing, in other ways it's hard to change. There's definitely a lot more work and commitment these days.

There is always room for improvement. We're all working on things, even little things like throwing right and left-handed. I think you'll find in the next 10 years there might be an ambidextrous cricketer.

As far as the playing side of it goes, cricket really hasn't changed a lot. I think you can get carried away with making it too complex. The basics of a good team are still about batting, bowling and fielding well. It's a simple game. A bloke is bowling a ball at you, and you have a bat in your hand, so you just have to keep the good balls out and hit the bad balls. That's cricket in its simplest form. Obviously a lot more goes into it. I think we still try to keep it simple. That's what has held me in good stead for all these years.

Complete with laptop computer, and the more traditional coaching aids, Buchanan and the Australians had one final task before they could enjoy a break over the 2000 winter. They had three one-dayers to play in South Africa. Would Hansie Cronje's men reverse the World Cup result? Or would Hansie Cronje's men be without Hansie Cronje?

CHAPTER TWENTY-SEVEN

THE RIGHT TO DECLINE

The announcement came the night before the Australians left for South
Africa — Indian police had taped phone conversations of South African
captain Hansie Cronje conspiring with an Indian bookmaker to fix matches and
individual performances. Cronje was stood down from the limited-overs series,
but despite the turmoil, the home side won the series 2–1. Mark scored only
11 runs in his three innings, the end of almost two years of continuous cricket
for him.

He returned home in mid-April to be fronted by a large media contingent
eager for his comments on the latest development in cricket corruption. He
simply told the scrum of journalists, 'I'm going home, the season's over.' The
media turned its attention to team manager Steve Bernard. 'Was Mark still
feeling pressure over the ongoing issue?' Bernard thought not. After all, what
could Mark say? The accusations of match-fixing against Cronje were on a
different playing field to the misdemeanours committed by Mark and Shane
Warne. Mark's greatest disappointment about the media's handling of the
corruption issue is that his name was frequently used in the same sentence or
breath as 'match-fixing'. To provide information about pitch and weather

conditions should never be considered in the same disgraceful league as throwing a game. Nor should the two issues be linked together by speculation. Sadly, they were.

When he pushed his trolley out through the sliding doors of Sydney's international airport, Mark was simply off duty. No more cricket for three months. It was time for Friday nights at Harold Park and screaming for the Bulldogs on Sundays.

A fortnight later in London in early May, the ICC announced the establishment of an independent anti-corruption unit that would have wide-ranging investigative powers. The former Commissioner of the London Metropolitan Police, Sir Paul Condon, was later appointed to head the unit.

By late May, the Pakistan Cricket Board had banned Salim Malik for life following recommendations by Justice Qayyum whose investigations supported the evidence given by Mark, Shane Warne and Tim May that Salim had attempted to bribe them. Fast bowler Ata-ur-Rehman was also outed for life for perjury during Pakistan's Judicial Commission. The corruption issue was beginning to gallop.

In July, former Pakistan captain Imran Khan claimed on ABC television's 'Four Corners' that there may have been more involvement by Australian players than had been revealed. The following day at the announcement of Shane Lee as New South Wales captain for the 2000–01 season, Mark fronted the media, and under constant questioning said he'd offer his bank statements to investigators if required.

In August, Australia and South Africa created history by playing three day-nighters indoors at Melbourne's Colonial Stadium. The series was drawn — the teams claimed one win apiece and a tie. Mark scored 17, 48 and 1. At about the same time, speculation began building for the third consecutive year that Mark wouldn't see out the summer as an Australian cricketer. Former Test leg-spinner Kerry O'Keefe wrote in the August–September 2000 issue of *Inside Edge*: '... there are a few who have observed a diminishing of his touch over recent times. And when touch players lose that gift, it is often a quick slide out of the top level.'

Just before the home season, the Australians travelled to Kenya for the ICC Mini World Cup. They were knocked out by India in the quarter-finals. Mark made 7. By the time the team returned home, Hansie Cronje had been banned for life after admitting to South Africa's King Commission that he had accepted money from bookmakers and had offered team-mates money to underperform.

Underperformance was a theme heavily pushed by the media in relation to Mark. It was not in any way linked to the game's sinister side, but a matter of apparent poor form — he had tallied just 98 runs from his past nine limited-overs internationals. These figures seemed only a faint memory when he opened his season with an unbeaten 108, steering New South Wales to a seven-wicket win over Queensland in a Mercantile Mutual Cup match. The 134-ball innings included eleven boundaries, and had added significance for Mark because he played it in front of his home crowd at Bankstown Oval. Only eight months earlier, his name was married to the ground when the imposing Stephen and Mark Waugh Pavilion had been officially unveiled — a tribute to two brothers who've never forgotten where they come from.

Mark followed the century with innings of 53 and 46 as New South Wales launched their Pura Cup campaign with a 117-run win over Victoria in Melbourne. The Bushrangers enjoyed revenge in the Mercantile Mutual Cup match — Mark scored 17 in the two-wicket loss.

The Australians then moved into a four-day training camp at Mooloolaba, on Queensland's Sunshine Coast. On the final day, Friday 3 November, the story broke of a staggering report into cricket corruption by India's Central Bureau of Investigation. In it, Indian bookmaker Mukesh Gupta claimed that he'd paid Mark US$20 000 during the 1993 Hong Kong Sixes in return for team information, weather and pitch conditions. The allegations were supported by disgraced Indian player Manoj Prabhakar, who said he'd introduced Mukesh to Mark. Other high-profile players named in the report included Alec Stewart, Brian Lara, Dean Jones, Hansie Cronje, Aravinda de Silva, Arjuna Ranatunga, Martin Crowe and Salim Malik.

At an impromptu news conference Mark denied the unsubstantiated allegations against him and pledged his co-operation to the ACB. He knew he was in for yet another tough ride.

The Australian Cricket Board was placed under considerable pressure to launch another inquiry of its own. The media's call for immediate action was intense, and there was no greater voice in the editorial push than the *Australian* newspaper, which called for Mark and Lara to step aside from the upcoming Australia–West Indies Test Series until investigations were complete.

At the beginning of the season, Mark was a man whose form was being questioned; now it was his integrity. He was suddenly facing a battle for survival on two fronts, but retaliated in the way he knew best — by performing on the field. Less than a week after the allegations surfaced, he slammed 152 from 205 balls in a drawn Pura Cup game against Tasmania in Hobart. Australia's chairman of selectors, Trevor Hohns, was a most important observer, and although he suggested the bowling attack was understrength, he was nevertheless impressed by Mark's performance. A few months earlier Hohns had issued Mark a one-year ACB contract. The message from that was easily understood — perform or you're gone.

Mark's only other two outings before the first Test, in Brisbane, were one-dayers in which he made 22 in a seven-wicket win over Tasmania and 5 in a 6-run loss against South Australia.

Despite the lapses, he was confident heading into the Frank Worrell Trophy campaign, and was further motivated by the desire to be part of a team that was on the brink of creating history for the longest run of consecutive Test victories. The West Indies had set a mark of eleven wins in the mid-1980s; the Australians equalled that record after winning by an innings and 126 runs in Brisbane. Mark made 26, batting well, but finding it hard to score in two-and-a-half hours at the crease before he offered a return catch to fast bowler Mervyn Dillon.

The second Test, on Perth's bouncy WACA strip, promised the visitors better fortune, but they struggled after being sent in to bat, and were dismissed for 196 in just 61 overs. In reply, Australia finished the opening day at 2–72. Mark was still waiting in the dressing room after Jason Gillespie had been sent in as a nightwatchman. The next morning, Matthew Hayden's dismissal brought Mark to the crease under intense scrutiny. However, there was no sign of the pressure that was tormenting his game and his life. In what he rates one of his best-ever innings considering the circumstances in which it was played, he scored 119, giving just one chance when he was 21. It was a mostly uninhibited display that only struck trouble when Mark was in the nineties facing the second new ball. He survived a confident lbw appeal from a Mervyn Dillon delivery, and copped a heavy barrage of bouncers, one from Courtney

Walsh collecting the side of his helmet. However, nothing proved enough to stop him pushing a ball forward of point to the boundary for his seventy-fifth first-class hundred, taking him ahead of Greg Chappell on Australia's all-time list. Only Don Bradman's mark of 117 is higher. It took a spectacular leaping catch by Jimmy Adams in the covers off Dillon's bowling to end the performance.

His 271-minute innings off 175 balls included thirteen boundaries, and set up Australia's declaration (8–396) before the close of play. By stumps the Windies were not yet in ruins, but at 2–16 they were crumbling.

A five-wicket haul by paceman Brett Lee led the way on the third day as the visitors surrendered for 173, 28 runs short of making the home side bat again. Australia won the match and a page in the record books for their twelfth straight win. As they walked off, Ricky Ponting called his team-mates together for a spontaneous rendition of 'Under the Southern Cross'. Mark recalls:

I'm not sure everyone knew what was going on, but it was a great idea. The song has always been a celebration. It shows just how much playing for Australia means to us. It was a good feeling to break the West Indies' record, against the West Indies. I'm sure there would have been some former players sitting back at home feeling pretty unhappy about the performances of their boys. They had good motivation to beat us, but we were just too good.

The West Indies have gone downhill the most of any country during my career. They've always had naturally gifted players, but the supply seems to have run out now. They just don't have the infrastructure or the facilities, or the juniors coming through. Plus they've lost their aura.

A month later at the SCG, the Australians were celebrating a 5–0 drubbing of their Caribbean rivals. In his remaining innings after Perth, Mark scored 63 and 5, 25 and 78 not out, 22 and 3. He was disappointed he didn't make more runs, especially in the first innings of the Sydney Test where he felt he was hitting the ball as well as he had all summer before he was run out in a mix-up with Michael Slater. Nevertheless, he'd enjoyed a satisfying return of 339 runs at 48.42, third highest of the Australians.

Better performances soon followed in the Carlton series limited-overs tournament, which included Zimbabwe as the third team. From the moment he took guard in the opening day-nighter against the West Indies in Melbourne, Mark not only looked in complete command of the bowlers, but he also appeared comfortably in control of his own destiny. His first return of 51 off 67 balls slipped into insignificance when he made an unbeaten 112 from 128 deliveries against the Windies three days later in Brisbane. However, there were looming complications. On the eve of the next match in Sydney, it was announced the ICC's Anti-Corruption Unit would seek to interview Mark in early February, together with ACB Special Investigator Greg Melick, who'd just returned from India to examine the claims made in the Central Bureau of Investigation report. Melick, a barrister and former member of the National Crime Authority, had been appointed by the ACB in May 2000.

Mark shrugged off thoughts of the impending interview, scoring 58 off 91 balls as Australia recorded their third straight win over the West Indies in the competition. Under the controversial rotation policy, which rested players even when they weren't injured or out of form, Mark didn't play the next game against Zimbabwe, in Melbourne.

The following day, Monday 22 January, can best be described as the day all hell broke loose. It began when Mark's manager, Leo Karis, issued a statement which read:

Mark Waugh's lawyer, Raff Pisano of Maddock Lonie Chisholm, today informed the ACB that their client has presently declined its request for him to be interviewed by ACB and ICC investigators in early February.

Pisano says Waugh has co-operated with previous ACB and ICC inquiries and is continuing to co-operate with their present inquiries.

The ACB and the ICC have not provided Waugh with any evidence about the unsubstantiated allegations made by M.K. Gupta in the CBI report.

He has already denied those allegations.

Waugh's focus is on his commitment to cricket and to ensure the game's reputation is not further tarnished by endless inquiries and speculation.

ACB chief executive Malcolm Speed expressed his disappointment, stating in a media release:

These investigations are an important part of dealing with this issue once and for all and reassuring those who follow cricket that nothing inappropriate has occurred.

I continue to hope that Mark will take this opportunity to address any issues that the ACB Special Investigator, Mr Greg Melick, and the ICC Anti-Corruption Unit may wish to resolve with him.

It was headline news all over the country, with the vast majority of media organisations condemning the stance taken by Mark's camp. In an outspoken piece in the *Australian* (23 January 2001), Malcolm Conn wrote:

> For a man who has played some of cricket's great modern day innings, it is one of the most cowardly acts ever perpetrated in 124 years of international competition.
>
> If Waugh has nothing to hide, as ACB chief executive Malcolm Speed claimed only a few days ago, then why can't he take one simple step for the good of the game?
>
> Instead he continues to slaughter the reputation of Australian cricket. It smacks of a selfish, greedy, narrow-minded cricketer putting himself ahead of one of this country's most loved institutions.

According to the Melbourne based Pisano, there were two key words that were overlooked during that first day of drama — 'presently declined'. She says at no stage did Mark ever refuse to be interviewed.

> *What happened was that a request was made for him to be interviewed in the ambit. There was no indication at all of exactly what the scope of that interview would be, what it was that they would ask, what they wanted to know, what the areas of particular interest to them were. It's very important to properly advise a client there is certain information that you need to have. Now through legal advice what Mark said to the ACB was, 'I've got your request for an interview. Before I agree to go to an interview' — he actually had, despite what people think — 'could you tell me exactly what it is you want to interview me about, and what it is you're interested in knowing?' So we ask some questions of the ACB. And until we get the answers to those questions we decline to be interviewed, 'presently'.*

To the outsider, it's easy to be bewildered by the operations of the legal world. Put simply, Mark was entitled to ask the ACB for information, and did so through Pisano. On Tuesday 23 January, Pisano again told the ACB that she needed answers to the questions that had been submitted the previous day. In turn, Malcolm Speed, with a legal background himself, consulted the ACB's lawyers.

In the meantime, Mark was all but walking death row in Sydney. In the eyes of the public, the media's portrayal of a man refusing to co-operate led to the unfortunate, but immediate presumption of guilt. Mark's manager Leo Karis acknowledges the uncomfortable position that his client was in. He admits that he and Mark 'constantly questioned some of their [the legal team] tactics and advice, but they were lawyers, and the law is an arena that has its own rules and procedures. Looking back I certainly wouldn't change our approach because we did it to make sure Mark was protected.' Nevertheless, the process scarred Mark, who recalls:

It really hurt me that so many people thought I was hiding something. I had to have legal advice because I was out of my depth. I'm just a cricketer. I couldn't make a decision myself, so I had to be guided by the people around me: Raff, Michael Shatin [Mark's barrister] and Leo. Nothing was easy. Every decision was tough because everything had to be analysed. There were lots of things to juggle in every decision that was made. The commercial effects, personal issues, the media's response. I was happy to be interviewed, but it was thought that I needed to know what I was going in to. That's fair enough.

But what the media did just wasn't justified. First, they didn't give me a chance to show I was innocent. Then to have cameras and people from the papers out the front of my house for two days on end was a sickening feeling. I felt like a murderer who was a prisoner in his own home.

It didn't only affect me, but it also affected my neighbours. TV crews were blocking their driveways. They showed no respect. When Sue and I were coming home one day we even kept on going past the driveway, and Sue dropped me down in some bushland where I could walk up the back way into our house without being seen. It's a pretty silly way to have to do it, but they just wouldn't leave us alone.

One of the craziest things was when I had to fly to Adelaide for the next one-dayer. We knew there'd be problems at the airports, so I was ushered in a back *entrance at Sydney. It was like being a movie star. Not that I had anything to hide. I just didn't want the hassle of a free-for-all at the airport with media all over me. In Adelaide we'd organised again for me to be taken out a back way to the team hotel to avoid the media. We were going to front the media, but in a controlled way, not at the airport where you have no control. So we had organised that before I arrived in Adelaide, but for some reason the door I was meant to go out was crawling with media; somehow they'd found out.*

So this guy who was just working at the airport said, 'I'll take you to the hotel.' So we got in this Ansett van and went out this back entrance again. I don't know whether it was bad luck or the media knew about this as well, but just as we were coming out the airport gate, a Channel Seven camera crew in their four-wheel drive spotted us, and that was the end of that secret. They followed us all the way to the hotel. The van driver thought it was his big day out with the media following him, so he tried going different ways. He was getting pretty carried away saying, 'No fuck 'em, we'll go a different way, we'll escape. They're not going to follow us.' So he put the foot down, then he turned a sharp left, speeding along. I told him not to worry and to just take me to the hotel the normal way, but this driver went, 'Nah, fuck 'em, they're not getting us.' So the next street he tried a sharp turn again trying to lose them, but they followed us all the way. It was ridiculous. I felt like O.J. Simpson. I kept telling the driver not to worry, but it was his day out.

Eventually we got to the hotel and there were cameras left, right and centre. I didn't say too much. I just couldn't believe it. I thought, 'What's the world coming to? This is a joke. What am I? A murderer?'

On the afternoon of Wednesday 24 January (the day Mark arrived in Adelaide), the ACB issued an ultimatum — Mark had until four o'clock the following afternoon to inform the ACB he would front the investigators or he would be dropped from the team. Pisano received the ultimatum together with a letter providing the answers to the questions she'd asked on Mark's behalf. That evening, while media outlets quoted Speed's comment that, 'No-one should doubt the resolve of the Australian Cricket Board to deal with these issues', Mark and his legal team made their decision after a teleconference — yes, Mark would appear. Despite it being widely reported over the following days that Mark had 'backed down' as a result of the ACB's threat, the ultimatum hadn't dictated the decision. It had been a matter of Mark's legal team waiting to receive the information they had been asking for from the ACB. According to Pisano, once that was received it was a 'no-brainer that Mark would front the investigators'.

'The tragedy is,' says Pisano, 'that the answers came with the ultimatum. It was quite extraordinary. The whole thing was very, very sad. It was a very sad day in Australian cricket. It could have all been done without the world having to know about it.'

At a news conference on Thursday 25 January, Speed announced that he'd received official confirmation Mark had agreed to meet with anti-corruption investigators. He added that the ACB had gone beyond its duty in providing information to Mark about the five areas on which he'd face questioning. Speed told the media: 'Investigators don't normally telegraph their punches and they're not required to send a form listing all the questions and say tick the box.'

Mark remains critical and disappointed with the way the way the ACB handled the issue. He says:

The Cricket Board had their own agenda. They wanted to come out as transparent and as clean as possible. To be honest, I don't think they worried too much about me, they were looking after their own image.

I had my people looking after me because I knew the ACB wouldn't look after me. But to some extent I can understand the ACB protecting the interests of the game instead of the individual.

Having said that, I didn't hear the ACB come out once and say that Mark has been a great player for Australia, he's played 100 Tests, we're fully behind him. They never once said that. They didn't really ever show any support for me, so I was on my own, apart from my legal people and Leo. I was number one, we were going to look after myself first of all, but at all times we were aware of the ramifications for the Australian team and my own career.

There was no-one else I could really turn to for support because no-one else really knew what was going on. Obviously Sue, and Alan Jones [Sydney radio commentator] was there when I needed him. Even with Mum and Dad, family, close friends, I told them only the basics. I had a good talk with Stephen in Adelaide. He was right behind me.

The handling of the issue raised a number of discussion points. First, should unsubstantiated allegations have been widely published in the first place? (Some allegations made in the report were later withdrawn.) Did Mark have an obligation to co-operate considering the nature of the allegations, and the fact no charges had been laid? What were Mark's rights as an individual? As an employee? What were the ACB's rights and obligations as an employer? As a controller of the game? How far should the ACB's obligation of disclosure have gone? Should Mark's legal team and management have handled the matter better? Did they misjudge the mood of the media and the public?

The ACB was in a difficult position. It was facing a so-called crisis at a time when cricket was experiencing arguably the darkest period in its history. Malcolm Speed and his board had to be seen to be taking a firm stance for the good of the game. The fact that the ACB had been heavily criticised for the 'covering up' of the fines imposed on Mark and Shane Warne in 1995 emphasised the need for transparency.

However, when all was thrown into the public domain at a very sensitive time, it was obvious that reputations and behaviour on either side of the issue would be questioned, criticised, sometimes applauded. For Mark, it was a no-win situation. His innocence would be questioned no matter what he did.

He found refuge on the cricket field, a place where somehow he managed to forget his worries. After four days of conflict he returned to play the West Indies at the Adelaide Oval on Australia Day, 26 January, but wasn't needed to bat. He continued his impressive form in his two remaining appearances during the preliminary rounds, scoring 36 against Zimbabwe in Sydney, then finishing with an unbeaten 102 from 113 balls against them in Melbourne.

'It was incredible how he kept going through it all,' says Adam Gilchrist. 'I don't think many blokes could have coped better. Deep down he was obviously hurting, but he just kept on going. I was amazed.'

Mark played little role in Australia's 134-run win in the first final against the West Indies, at the SCG. He'd only made 10 when he edged a ball from Cameron Cuffy to Brian Lara. The teams then moved to Melbourne, and although Australia were on the brink of penning another line in history by completing a whole season undefeated, Mark was distracted because he had to front Greg Melick and the ICC investigators the morning after the second final.

The significance of the occasion wasn't lost on the knowledgeable MCG fans, who perhaps cheered more loudly than usual when Mark and Gilchrist walked out to have first use of a shiny pitch that looked full of runs. After a few tentative early moments — he believes the first five overs are generally the most difficult — Mark launched himself into the attack, time and again leaving his crease to hit the bowlers straight over mid-off. In a mixture of elegance and old-fashioned slogging, Mark demoralised the bowlers in a display that encouraged the *Sydney Morning Herald*'s Peter Roebuck to suggest (10 February 2001): 'This summer has seen the reawakening of a dormant gift.'

And a most destructive one. For 49 overs Mark blasted, belted, bruised and belittled the bowlers. It was simply his day. When he finally departed, victim of occasional trundler Marlon Samuels, he walked alone from the ground with 30 000 people sharing every step in a standing ovation worthy of a player who'd just made Australia's highest individual one-day score — 173 off 148 balls, including sixteen fours and three sixes. Mark recalls:

I wasn't in a particularly good frame of mind that day. I was obviously thinking about the meeting the next morning. I started off fairly poorly in that innings. I didn't feel good at all. I played and missed a couple of times early, I was battling. Then I seemed to get going, but I actually didn't hit the ball that well. Batting is a funny game — some days you can bat really well and not get the runs you should, then other days you're lucky. I really struggled to time the ball that day. Even when I was going for big hits at the end, the ball was just getting to the rope. I was mis-hitting a lot of balls. I just couldn't get out — some days you can't even get out if you bat as badly as you can. I'm not saying I batted that badly, but I've batted a hell of a lot better.

I couldn't have picked a better time to score it because it took the focus off the hearing. It was a good day to prove myself.

The home team's total of 6–338 was also a record. Despite a willing chase, Jimmy Adams and his players fell 39 runs short.

At the trophy presentations on the ground straight afterwards it seemed obvious Mark would be awarded the slick Honda Fireblade motorcycle for player of the series, judged by sections of the media. However, the announcement triggered a rush of booing — Brian Lara had won the award instead. The embarrassed West Indian accepted the prize but said what so many were thinking: 'I don't deserve this award. One of the Australians deserved this prize.'

Mark had been beaten by one vote — he'd missed a game and didn't bat twice because of Australia's rotation policy during the preliminary rounds. It's likely if he'd had more opportunities he would have reversed the result, which Mark considers 'horrendous. Only the media could have been so far off the mark.' However, there was some consolation when he was named player of the finals. His season had been brilliant: 540 runs, including three centuries, at 108. While his team-mates launched into celebrations, Mark quietly departed because the day wasn't yet over. He recalls:

I virtually went straight from the ground after the match. The meeting in the morning was at the Hilton Hotel, so it was common sense for me to stay there after the game instead of going from the team hotel in the morning. That way I could also avoid any problems with the media. So I just walked across to the Hilton from the ground. It was a strange feeling — I was on a high, but I also felt low because I was worried about the meeting.

I met Leo and my legal team to run through a few things. It was a late night. I can't remember what time we finished up, but after that I didn't get much sleep. The next morning we fooled the media — they were either standing outside the Quay West, the team hotel, or were waiting outside the Hilton. No-one knew that I was already inside.

The questioning went well, and I told them everything I knew. The bottom line was that the allegations simply weren't true. All I could do was deny them.

I was really glad when it was over. There were times during that period when I thought, 'Is it all worth it? I might just as well retire now, give it all away and get out of the limelight.' It was the closest I'd come. I definitely thought about it. I thought of going and playing county cricket, or just retiring from the game altogether. I was getting to the point where I couldn't stand all the pressure and all the hassle. There's only so much you can take.

Thankfully my legal people, Leo and Sue hung in there with me and encouraged me to keep going.

The thing was I was performing pretty well on the field, so I kept thinking that if I was performing like I was while all the stuff around me was happening, surely when it was over there was still a lot of cricket left in me. I think that swayed me to keep going, but it was only natural that I lost some interest in the game. I didn't like even turning up to a game and seeing some of the journalists there. It made me feel uncomfortable. I dreaded Murgers [Brian Murgatroyd, team media manager] coming up to me and saying, 'This is going to be in the papers tomorrow', or 'This is happening'. I was always on edge, the whole way through.

Sue Porter was 'really concerned' for Mark during that period. Would he be pushed too far and throw his career away? She says his character increased her worries:

If things get on top of him, he'll basically just tell you to where to go. I felt he might have got to the point where he said, 'I'm out of here.'

We did discuss retirement, and I told him, 'Don't do anything drastic. It will work out in the end.'

I would have been happy to see him go, but I thought he still had so much to give to cricket. He'd never forgive himself if he left too soon. As it turned out, he had a brilliant year. It was basically: 'Stick it in your ear!' If he was a guilty man he couldn't have played cricket the way he did.

The player who disliked waiting in the dressing room for his turn to bat was now forced to mark time in public while the ICC's Anti-Corruption Unit and Greg Melick reviewed all the material they'd gathered. It would be a long wait.

CHAPTER TWENTY-EIGHT

A REMARKABLE SERIES

Jalandhar is a town in the Punjab in India's north. It's here that cricket bats and balls are made by hundreds of sets of hands in dim, dust-filled factories, and then displayed for sale on a stretch of road that has more sports stores within a kilometre or two than there are Union Jacks flown in London on the Queen's birthday. Whichever way you turn there is leather and willow. There are also shoe-shiners, fruit-sellers, rickshaw-wallahs and men sitting cross-legged making shirts with ancient hand-driven sewing machines. There is a touch of 'The Man from Ironbark' about Jalandhar, for in this Sikh town 'flowing beards are all the go'. So too the brilliantly coloured turbans that are matched only by the dazzling smiles of the people.

In the small, crowded lounge room of a green concrete house on a back street just a few hundred metres from the town's heartbeat, the train station, a young Sikh spins a ball through his long, supple fingers. His mother and two sisters chat quietly, cups of tea in hand. A picture of the children's late father holds pride of place above a cabinet that contains what will become a family heirloom — a trophy acknowledging the first Test hat-trick taken by an Indian cricketer.

A few months earlier, Harbhajan Singh was the hero of millions, no, hundreds of millions, of people when he took 32 wickets in a three-Test series against Australia in March 2001. Such was his dominance that the other 10 bowlers used by India took just 17 wickets between them. Mark says:

> *He caught us on the hop. We played him before in a warm-up game and we knew he was different because he was like Muralitharan with his top-spinner. We knew he was dangerous, but we just played really dumb cricket. The shots we played against him — cross-bat shots, and pushing at the ball — just dumb cricket. He just destroyed us.*

Australia had gone to India in February 2001 — just three days after Mark fronted the ICC investigators — with high hopes and even loftier determination. Despite the absence of Brett Lee, out with a broken arm, the world champions put much faith in speed. It proved a successful formula in the first Test, which the Australians won by 10 wickets in Mumbai. After falling to Harbhajan for a duck, caught at leg slip, Mark had a useful second innings with the ball, taking 3–40, including the golden wicket of Sachin Tendulkar who was brilliantly caught by Ricky Ponting at mid-wicket. The match signalled the start of a magnificent series for Matthew Hayden, whose 119 was a small taste of what would follow.

The second Test, at Calcutta's Eden Gardens, will be remembered as one of the most remarkable ever played. Forced to follow on 274 runs behind, the Indians ended up winning by 171 after V.V.S. Laxman (281) and Rahul Dravid (180) combined for a 376-run fifth-wicket partnership that not only swung the match but the series the home side's way. Laxman's innings, the highest ever by an Indian in a Test, was one of the greatest performances in cricket. His strokeplay was incomparable, especially against Shane Warne — he continually danced down the pitch and drove deliveries that had been aimed at the rough from around the wicket.

Harbhajan was just as dominant, taking 13 wickets for the match, including his first innings hat-trick to remove Ricky Ponting, Adam Gilchrist and Warne. Mark had a disappointing match, falling to Harbhajan for 22, and trapped lbw by left-arm spinner Venkatapathy Raju without scoring. The loss meant Australia's world record winning streak of sixteen matches — a phenomenal achievement — had ended.

The final Test in Chennai was a thriller. Despite a belligerent double century by Hayden (203) and Mark's best performance of the series, a fluent 70, the visitors trailed by 110 on the first innings.

Confessing to only 'working out' how to play Harbhajan by the last match, Mark top scored with 57 in the second innings as Australia reached 264, setting India a target of 155. The home side stumbled over the line with just two wickets to spare. Fittingly Harbhajan, who'd taken 15 wickets for the match, was in the middle when the winning runs were hit. Mark recalls:

We really should have won that series. If you look back to the follow-on in Calcutta, India looked like shot ducks. Their body language said it all. They were gone. That's why Stephen made them follow on because we don't normally do that. And then we had them 3–115, including Tendulkar, and I thought, 'Game over.' It was only a freak innings by Laxman that saved them. He was just unbelievable. One of the most enjoyable innings I've ever watched. We just never looked like getting him out. All of a sudden the game changed, and we were under pressure to save it on the last day, but we weren't good enough. We batted very poorly.

But it was a great Test match. Every match in the series was a great Test match to watch regardless of the result, so we went away with that thought. Although we'd lost, we contributed to a very special series, and that's what Test cricket needed at that time after all the match-fixing dramas.

The last two Tests were two of the best Tests I've ever played in, even though we lost them both. As far as Test cricket goes, that's what it's all about — really tight matches. Realistically we should have won that series, we let ourselves down. Having said that, you have to give it to India. No other country has ever played cricket like they did in that series. It's a real pity we couldn't play five matches.

In a difficult series for Australia's batsmen, Mark tallied 149 runs at an average of 29.80. He played a small role in the following five-match limited-over series which Australia won 3–2. After making just 5 in the opening game in Bangalore, he scored an unbeaten 133 off 138 balls to ensure Australia an eight-wicket victory in the second encounter at Pune. It was his eighteenth limited-overs hundred, ranking him third behind Saeed Anwar and Sachin Tendulkar on the all-time list of century-makers. However, it had come at a price. During the innings Mark's right-hand little finger was fractured when crushed between the bat handle and a ball from Javagal Srinath. At first, local doctors didn't think the injury was serious — after reading X-rays they couldn't even find a break — but Australian team physiotherapist Pat Farhart had more acute eyes, and ordered Mark home to Sydney for treatment. (Perhaps it was an omen — it was to be the last time Mark reached triple figures in the one-day arena.)

Two months later, he left with the Australian team for his third Ashes tour. The trip had added significance because the players went via Gallipoli, the Turkish peninsula that played a tragic role in defining the character and spirit of the Australian people. Mark and Steve laid wreaths at Anzac Cove in memory of the thousands of men — most of them younger than Australia's cricketers — who died over eight months of conflict in 1915 during the Great War. Mark recalls:

It's hard to understand what Anzac Day [25 April, commemorating the day the Australian and New Zealand Army Corps landed at Gallipoli in 1915] means until you go to this place. It surprised me because it was so peaceful. To think thousands of men were killed giving everything for their country. They never really stood a chance, but they never gave in. All the team was struck by that message. We should never forget that spirit, no matter what we do.

Incredibly, the visit was criticised in some sections of the media as a publicity stunt. Mark bluntly suggests such views were 'just terrible pieces of journalism. How could they make a trip like that negative? That upset the players.' However, the Australians remained inspired by what they'd seen when they arrived in England. Their campaign began with victory in a limited-overs series against the host nation and Pakistan. In his four matches, including the final against Pakistan, Mark made 47, 46, 0 and 36. It was an encouraging start.

The Test series promised to be a much tighter affair than recent Ashes contests. England, under the forceful leadership of Nasser Hussain, were confident after recent Test series wins on the subcontinent against Pakistan and Sri Lanka. Although acknowledging their rival's achievements, the Australians felt they could dominate the contest if they could 'reopen old wounds'. The

English team basically had the same nucleus of players who had suffered in recent Ashes series. Mark remembers: 'We didn't think anything had really changed with them.'

The first Test, at Edgbaston, suggested the great divide between the countries hadn't been narrowed as Australia won by an innings and 118 runs. Mark scored 49, but that was overshadowed by his four catches that left him only one snare behind Mark Taylor at the top of the world list. In the lead-up to the series, he'd been constantly reminding his mate Taylor that it was only a matter of time before a new name stood alone.

He didn't have to wait long. On the opening day of the second Test, at Lord's, left-handed batsman Mark Butcher edged a Glenn McGrath delivery low to second slip where Mark casually wrapped both hands around the ball. Taylor and Waugh: 157–all.

He had to wait until the final wicket of England's second innings before he had the record to himself. The scorecard read: Darren Gough ct M.E. Waugh b Gillespie 1. Mark was on top of the world, a long way from the satellite tennis tournaments of his childhood when Rodger and Bev used to hit their sons catches off their racquets. Mark says simply:

The record means two things. It means you're a good catcher, and secondly it means you're in a good team with quality bowlers as well. It's amazing, some catches I think are a lot harder than other ones, but the media make out the other ones are better. I find fielding in slips to the spinners the hardest of all. Even a simple edge is hard because you haven't got the same amount of time to react. When Stuart MacGill gets an edge, the ball comes really quickly. Catching off Warney to left-handers when the ball slides across past Gilly is also hard — sometimes you don't see the ball until the last moment.

Then you have bowlers like Gillespie and Brett Lee who are quick, and the ball hits your hand quite hard. It's just a matter of practice and trusting your own ability.

The hardest thing in slips is the concentration. There are some days where you might only touch one or two balls, but you have to be ready every time. You can also have problems picking up the ball. People don't understand how hard it is to see the ball out of the crowd or against a dark backdrop. It's half the battle. Sometimes you can look really stupid. I remember I got hit in the shoulder in

Adelaide in 2000. I ducked and the ball hit me. It's a position that can make you look really stupid.

Since I moved into the cordon I've more or less been second slip my whole career. When Tubby retired, there was no chance of me moving across. It made sense for Warney because he'd been a first slipper with Victoria. I think first slip is an easier position as far as sighting the ball because there's less angle. But the hard thing there is that I feel enclosed between second and the wicket-keeper.

I've become a slipper, but I still like having a run around — it can get quite boring in the slips. I really enjoy fielding. I've maybe lost a bit of pace over the ground, but I'd like to think I'm an all-round fieldsman.

The record will be broken one day — I reckon Ricky Ponting will go close.

Record aside, Mark had another reason to remember the Lord's match when he made one of the most attractive centuries of his career to join Steve on the dressing room honour board. He had taken guard with his side in trouble at 2–27 in the first innings, but quickly launched the recovery with a series of on-side boundaries that swept him to 20 before anyone had seemingly noticed. It was a performance that belonged at the home of cricket, although the shot that took him to three figures, an inside edge, had no sense of the occasion. After sharing a 107-run fourth-wicket stand with Steve, Mark fell for 108, run out by a brilliant piece of fielding by Darren Gough. Australia went on to win the Test by eight wickets.

Afterwards, two pieces of tape with the words 'World's Record Fieldsman Catches' and 'Mark Waugh 158 Catches' written across them, were noticed on the honour board. Mark had quietly placed them there.

Australia retained the Ashes with a seven-wicket victory in the third Test, at Trent Bridge. After scoring 15 in the first innings, Mark was 42 not out in the second when the winning runs were scored. Three days later, on 7 August, he had additional reason to celebrate — ACB Special Investigator Greg Melick could find no evidence over which Mark could be charged in relation to the accusations contained in India's CBI report. In part, Melick wrote:

Many players and officials were interviewed and all (apart from those involved with the investigation and resolution of the Colombo incident) were adamant

that they had not heard anything (including dressing room banter) about any
Australian player or official taking money from bookmakers prior to the
publicity in 1998 relating to Mark Waugh and Shane Warne.

In a strange twist of coincidence during his investigations, Melick discovered that the Indian Bookmaker, Mukesh Gupta, who'd made the claims against Mark in the CBI report, was sometimes known as 'John'. However, he wasn't the same 'John' who Mark accepted money from in 1994 in Sri Lanka. In his report Melick acknowledged that some of 'Gupta's allegations relating to Indian players have been corroborated', but when speaking at a media conference at the release of the report, he said he'd been 'unable to locate any credible evidence' relating to the claims against Mark. The drama was finally over. Mark says:

I'd like to say the book is shut, but there will always be people who will bring it
up. You never know what might be around the corner. It was a great relief when
it did happen in England because my career could have been finished if it had
gone the other way, or if the Board thought I'd broken my code of conduct. All
my sponsors would have evaporated pretty quickly.

Hopefully it's all finished now, and people will remember me as a damn good
cricketer who played his best for Australia. We all make mistakes. Yeah, I made a
mistake, but I'm not alone. It was only a small part of my career. I've played
100-plus Tests, 200 one-dayers — there are some pretty good memories in there
that are a lot more important than the bad times.

It's a weight off my shoulders. I'm not as stressed as I was. Obviously I'm
sleeping better, eating better, and I'm a lot more relaxed.

I've learnt things. I've learnt that I was a bit naive to think that most people
have got good in them and you treat them how they treat you. I'm a lot more
wary of people now. I'm a lot more wary of the media. If I don't want to do
something for them, then I'm not going to. Most didn't do me any favours.
When the news came through there was no hoo-ha then. No front-page stories
about my innocence. To think there are wars, people dying, you look at what
happened in New York [the 11 September terrorist attacks], and people want to
make such a big deal over what I did do, and all the other things I was meant to
have done in some people's eyes. It's strange really.

I check people out a lot more than I used to. And I know who my friends are now, so a lot of good things have come out of it. It was something that made my life a misery for a long time.

In hindsight I would much rather have never met John. I certainly regret it because it and everything that followed has caused so much grief to myself, my family, and in some ways put an unwanted focus on the Australian team. But it's over now.

With his mind completely clear of the dramas that had been leaking into his thoughts every day since December 1998, Mark looked forward to a new start, but England denied him a memorable one, when a brilliant unbeaten 173 by Mark Butcher single-handedly carried the home side to success in the fourth Test, at Headingley. Australia, without Steve who was sidelined with a torn calf muscle, had been on top for much of the match until stand-in captain Adam Gilchrist offered a sporting declaration that Butcher capitalised on. 'It was a fantastic innings,' says Mark. 'One of the best I've seen against us.' Chasing 315 to win, England achieved the target only four wickets down, and redeemed some lost pride after a disappointing summer.

The final Test, at The Oval, gave English cricket a lasting reminder of two reasons they'd failed against Australia for more than a decade — the Waugh twins. Playing their last matches in England, Steve (157 n.o.) and Mark (120) combined for a third-wicket partnership of 197. Steve, at times almost reduced to a hobble because of his injury, and Mark, as light-footed as he'd been throughout the series, played with the mixture of determination, aggression and flamboyance that had underlined their careers.

Mark's 176-ball innings included sixteen boundaries and a six. It was a graceful farewell to his second cricketing home.

Justin Langer (102 retired hurt) was the other century-maker in Australia's massive first innings total of 4 declared 641. The home side fought hard, replying with 432, but it wasn't enough to avoid the follow-on, and on the final day of the series they surrendered meekly for 184, failing by 25 runs to make their opponents bat again. Mark says:

Everything clicked for us. They'd been pretty confident before the series, but we were just way too good for them. Even the Test we lost we were on top and gave them a chance through a declaration. 4–1. It could have been 5–0. I thought we were back to our best.

Our bowling was mostly good, and I thought our batting was exceptional. I thought Andy Caddick bowled well against us. Darren Gough did sometimes as well, but he tends to get down in the dumps. People say he's got a big heart, but I think sometimes he gets down a bit mentally when he's on the field, and that can affect his team-mates. I think it's a cover-up sometimes when he's jumping around and pretending everything is happy. I thought Caddick put in more during the last series, but he just didn't get the support.

The dominance of Australia's batsmen was reflected by the scores — not once did England bowl their rivals out twice in a match. Mark finished as Australia's leading scorer for the series with 430 runs at 86.00. His place in the team was sound and secure. Steve had the handsome return of 321 at 107.00.

In the early stages of the tour, they'd both celebrated their thirty-sixth birthday, an occasion too good to waste for their team-mates, who presented the twins each with a walking stick. It was a light-hearted gesture, but Mark and Steve knew that the perceived entry into 'old age' had a much more serious side.

CHAPTER TWENTY-NINE

GOODBYE?

Old age in its truest form brings wrinkles and grey hair. On the cricket field, it is different and the issues are not easily defined in black and white. When is a player too old? When does his value become less? How does he know? How do selectors know?

Allan Border says he knew it was time to step aside when he began leaving balls alone that once he'd have taken to with his 'bread and butter shot', the cut. He says, 'I was just fractionally short of being in position to play them. Once that happened, the run-scoring opportunities started to dry up, and all of a sudden getting 50 was harder than it was a few years earlier.'

Ian Healy talks of the mental side:

I don't think your skills or reflexes drop off that dramatically if you don't let them. This is what senior players can have trouble with because you have to work as hard at the end of your career as you did at the start, but you don't like to, you haven't got time to, and you don't think you should have to. They're the things that can eat away at your motivation when you are a senior player.

At the beginning of the 2001–2 season, Mark wasn't troubled by a lack of motivation. For the first time in three years he was clear of corruption scandals, and after his successful Ashes series there could be no queries over his form. However, he knew how quickly it could all change. For the second year running he'd only been given a one-year contract by the ACB, and at his age he was aware that there was little room for error. He had to keep scoring runs, a task he was looking forward to, and confident of achieving.

'It was the first series for some time, about three years, that I started without the media putting my position under a question mark,' he says. 'It made a bit of a change going in with the pressure off. In a way I was more relaxed.'

He started the season in formidable touch. After scoring 21 in the Blues' 123-run win over Victoria at Bankstown Oval in an ING Cup match (formerly the Mercantile Mutual Cup), a week later at the same ground he hammered 123 from 103 balls against Tasmania. The highlight was a whirlwind 228-run opening partnership with Brad Haddin (120) in 28.4 overs. The two innings set the platform for the biggest total in Australian domestic one-day cricket — 4–397. In a rain-affected match, the brave Tasmanians fell just 35 runs short of a revised target.

It wasn't the last the Apple Islanders would see of Mark. Three days later at the SCG, he made 168 in his only innings of a drawn Pura Cup match. Further scores of 12 and 51 against South Australia were signs that there was no need to worry about Mark heading into the three-Test series at home against New Zealand.

However, runs proved difficult to find against the Kiwis who had worked hard on developing plans for each batsman. They attacked Mark with short-of-the-length bowling, rarely giving him opportunity to play aggressively off the front foot either side of the wicket. He was dismissed lbw by Nathan Astle for a duck in the first Test, in Brisbane, and was bowled for 12 after dancing down the pitch and playing outside a Daniel Vettori delivery during the second Test, in Hobart. Media speculation about Mark's future began to bubble again. He recalls:

It's amazing. Two weeks in cricket and a lot of things can change in people's minds. All of a sudden I come off England where I batted really well, and two games later I'm too old and have lost it. People get carried away, especially when you get to a certain age. It's ridiculous. Common sense says you don't lose your ability or your awareness within a couple of weeks or games.

The media were making a really big deal of our [Mark and Steve] ability to play the short ball. These days teams are a lot more prepared than they used to be. It wasn't hard to work out what the plans would be for me and Stephen. Because we don't hook or pull, short balls first of all stop us from scoring, so that puts us under pressure. Although sometimes it doesn't look like we play the short ball well, it rarely gets us out. It's something I knew I had to work on to get a few more scoring chances.

Short bowling is frustrating really because it's so hard to score off it. I don't think anybody likes short-pitched bowling to be honest. Some guys play it better than others, but I don't think anyone enjoys it — maybe Matthew Hayden and Ricky Ponting are the exceptions. If the opposition has the firepower, they're going to use it.

People say otherwise, but I was never a big hooker or puller really. I've seen a few tapes when I played it, but it's just sort of faded out of my game. I might have to bring it back because it's no fun ducking and weaving all day. It got a bit frustrating seeing Justin Langer playing all those cover drives, and yet I hardly had the chance to drive all summer. In a way, I'd like to think it shows the opposition rates you as a danger man. It's not an easy game, Test cricket.

In the final Test, in Perth, he only partially broke free of the critics, scoring 42 and a spirited 86 that included some rare pull shots. His second innings ended ingloriously when he was bowled after backing away to give himself room to hit the ball through the off side off medium pacer Craig McMillan. At the time he was trying to lift the run rate in a bid to help Australia to an unlikely victory.

Afterwards, Mike Coward wrote of the twins' performances to that stage of the summer in the *Australian* (5 December 2001): 'Time waits for no man and on the evidence before us the brothers are finding the going significantly more challenging this summer.'

The three-Test series was drawn. In four innings, Steve had tallied 67 runs at 19.50, while Mark tallied 140 runs at 35. He admits it was a frustrating start to the season.

The series was a non-event because of all the interruptions. It was hard for our guys in the middle order because they spent a lot of time in the dressing room with the pads on because of either rain, or Matthew Hayden and Justin Langer doing so well at the top. [The openers shared four double-century stands during the summer.] It was a hard series to gain any momentum in.

New Zealand played well. They pushed us all the way. People were writing us off saying that we'd lost our intensity and focus, but occasionally the opposition are allowed to play well and you've got to give them credit.

Under the captaincy of all-rounder Shaun Pollock, South Africa tried similar short-ball tactics against Mark and Steve in the final three Tests of the summer.

In the first match, at Adelaide, both brothers were attacked by 'chin music' from Nantie Hayward, who claimed Mark caught behind for 2 in the first innings. The shot was described by News Limited journalist Robert Craddock as an 'airy half-cut, half drive'. He batted with more conviction in the second innings, scoring 74 before he unluckily top-edged a sweep shot into his helmet, then into the gloves of wicket-keeper Mark Boucher off left-arm spinner Claude Henderson. Australia won by 246 runs in a match that was one of those special family occasions for the Waughs — it was Mark and Steve's hundredth Test together. Bev Waugh says:

There have been times when the enormity of it all has hit me. That's emotional. The best feeling I get about both of them is the enjoyment they've given so many people. Old people. Young people. That makes me feel good. Sometimes when things are going badly and they're getting negative press, it's good to have someone say to me how much they love watching them play. That makes me feel quite pleased.

The Waugh family had another reason to puff their chests during the second match when Mark celebrated his hundredth Test in a row, an achievement he didn't know about until he walked out to field and noticed his name in lights on the MCG scoreboard. He batted only once, bowled by Allan Donald for 34, as the home team won by nine wickets.

The series that was seen as deciding the rightful world champions was completely one-sided, a trend that continued in Sydney when the home team claimed the third Test by 10 wickets. Again Mark only had one chance at the crease, scoring 19. His dismissal, caught behind from a half-hearted shot outside off-stump off Allan Donald, came in the final over of the opening day. He'd scored 129 at 32.25 for the series and Steve tallied 141 runs at 35.25 — hardly figures to roll out the red carpet for, yet also returns that didn't warrant the carpet being pulled from under them.

The limited-overs and Victoria Bitter series loomed as a critical time. If, as suggested by some journalists, Mark was out of touch and succumbing to his years, he would surely be found out during the helter-skelter environment of the one-day game. As it turned out, the majority of the squad was off-key — Australia lost three of their first four games, and despite returning to form in the latter stages of the competition, missed out on the finals for only the third time in twenty-three years. There were many areas of concern pinpointed by the media, not least the opening spots, which Robert Craddock described at one stage as a 'dog's breakfast'.

Because of the controversial rotation policy, Australia's opening partnership was changed four times in as many matches. Mark scored 1, 0, 15, 55 not out, 0, 21 and 34 for a return of 126 runs at 21.00, and a strike rate of 70.78. In form Test opener Matthew Hayden was given only two games, scoring 10 in each of them, and was dropped for the second half of the competition when an oversized fourteen-man squad was cut to thirteen. By that stage, Mark knew he was in trouble. He says:

I thought I'd be a chance of getting dropped. It was either Matthew or me. But I hadn't had any communication from selectors, so I assumed I might still be in the team. I felt for Matthew because he only had two innings. I was sure he'd be back though.

It's strange how the media would forget about the bowlers — some of them hadn't done very well either. A bowler can go for 0–50 and not get mentioned, but if you get a low score the media seems to focus on it.

A lot of people have very short memories in the media. A bloke has played well over a five or 10-year period, then he has two or three bad games, and all of a sudden he should be dropped or just can't play any more. They don't even look at the circumstances of how you fail. I got run out by a couple of inches in one game, and got caught on the fence hooking in another. You just can't look at the statistics. You have to look at the state of the game, how it happened.

We also weren't helped by the rotation policy. At the top of the order you need to be settled. The wickets helped the bowlers, and the new rule of allowing one bouncer an over definitely helped the bowlers. It was a good rule though because it gave the bowlers a bit more of a chance in one-day cricket. It makes the batting a bit tougher, but it definitely makes it more of an even contest. The bowlers had a chance to intimidate.

If I read some of the papers, I was lucky to play one game, let alone 240. It gave me the shits when I picked up the paper every day and saw there were people saying I shouldn't be in the team or I had one more chance. It did get me down a bit. Not so long ago I'd made a couple of hundreds in one-day cricket, and only the season before I'd been the best with the most runs.

You have to be careful in wanting to drop players so quickly. No-one has a God-given right to a spot in the team, but by the same token you've got to improve the team with the replacement. You don't just make a change for the sake of it, or because someone is thirty-six or because someone has failed twice. You have to make sure you're improving the team, then if you are, well fair enough, but I just think the media get on the bandwagon too quickly. Look at a team like Manchester United and David Beckham. The media got on Beckham's back, said he was gone, Manchester was gone. Have a look at them now.

I think the media think you're not human — you're not going to have bad days and the opposition are not going to have good days. It just doesn't happen.

It was a disappointing season, obviously, to miss the finals. Once you start losing a couple of games, it's a bit like winning — it becomes a bit of a habit. You can either get confidence or lose confidence fairly quickly, or you start trying too hard, or start looking for things that aren't there. Then you get all the talk about the rotation policy and who should be playing. It all builds up, then suddenly you're gone.

But South Africa and New Zealand played well, give them some credit. We were off the boil a bit, and the other teams took advantage. That's sport.

The South Africans headed home with rejuvenated determination after beating New Zealand 2–0 in the final. After their disappointing Test campaign, they spoke confidently about an improved showing when the Australians arrived for a further three Tests beginning in late February.

Australia's disappointing limited-overs form had immediate repercussions when on Wednesday 13 February, five days after Shaun Pollock raised the VB Trophy, ACB chief executive James Sutherland made an announcement that stunned many Australian supporters, and created headlines throughout the cricket world. With a touch of sadness in his voice, he told an overflowing media conference at the SCG that 'Stephen Waugh will not be selected in the Australian one-day team to tour South Africa and Zimbabwe in March of this year.'

Waugh, sitting side-by-side with Sutherland and chairman of selectors Trevor Hohns, vowed to fight back, but the reality was that his 325-match international career in the shortened version of the game was almost certainly over. He'd been informed of his fate by Hohns two days earlier, just hours before the prestigious Allan Border Medal night in Melbourne.

Mark didn't know of his brother's fate until the day of the official announcement. He'd heard 'whispers', but hadn't spoken to Steve about them. He recalls the sacking was a shock:

It came out of the blue. I think Stephen was expecting to go through until the World Cup (2003). Although there'd been talk in the papers, you'd think the captain was the least likely of anyone to get dropped. I was disappointed for Stephen, but he handled it well. It certainly showed no-one was guaranteed a spot.

When asked at the media conference if there was likely to be more changes, Hohns responded: 'To say only one player is a little bit unfair at this stage.'

Hohns and his panel of Border, David Boon and Andrew Hilditch weren't going to finalise the limited-overs squad until midway through Australia's Test campaign of South Africa, which preceded six one-day internationals. Mark began the tour knowing his position was 'vulnerable, but I was still hoping for the best. I was just going to enjoy the trip, and went in thinking "whatever happens, happens for a reason".'

In Australia's only lead-up match to the first Test, Mark scored 62 against South Africa 'A' in a draw at Potchefstroom. *Daily Telegraph* journalist Robert

Craddock described the innings as 'a mixture of the old Waugh and the Waugh of old'. It was obvious that every time Mark took guard, his performances were going to be closely analysed.

Three days later he played 'really well' scoring 53 on the opening day of the Test series, at Wanderers Stadium, before he gloved a ball down the leg-side to wicket-keeper Mark Boucher off fast bowler Makhaya Ntini. He shared a 111-run partnership for the third wicket with the irresistible Matthew Hayden (122), who became only the fourth Australian to make hundreds in four or more consecutive Tests. Mark's two-hour display included some handsome cuts and drives, but a fierce pull shot left the most telling impression when the ball squeezed through the helmet grid of short-leg fieldsman Gary Kirsten, who suffered a cut above an eye, and was taken to hospital for a brain scan.

However, the injury was insignificant when compared with the crushed spirits the home side suffered during a brutal display by Adam Gilchrist. In what was one of the most destructive innings ever seen, Gilchrist slammed 204 off 212 balls. It was the fastest double century in Test cricket, a record that was incredibly beaten three weeks later when New Zealand's Nathan Astle scored 222 from just 168 deliveries against England in Christchurch.

Australia reached 7 declared for 652, then South Africa capitulated for 159 and 133, handing their rivals victory by an innings and 360 runs, the second biggest margin in Test history. Admittedly the home side had been hampered by the late withdrawal of injured captain Shaun Pollock, and a hamstring strain on the first day forced Allan Donald to announce his retirement, but nothing could be taken away from the indomitable performance of the visitors. 'It showed there's a big gulf between us and them,' says Mark. 'They don't know how to beat us, they're a bit like England. They're always on the back foot, like they're too scared to be positive and take us on.'

The Australians maintained their momentum in their next outing when they beat South Africa A by an innings and 41 runs at Port Elizabeth. Mark was in blistering form, scoring 110 from just 113 deliveries, his second 50 coming off only 24 balls. The day after his performance, the final day of the match, he was having lunch when team manager Steve Bernard told him 'there's a phone call for you from Trevor Hohns'.

Mark recalls:

I immediately thought that he wasn't ringing to say hello. He told me that I
hadn't been picked in the one-day squad. He said it was a tough decision, but
the selectors felt it was time for a change. I thought I was still good enough to
perform at that level, but the selectors had their job to do. It was disappointing,
but life goes on. I'd had a very good run.

His record needs no embellishment to impress: 244 matches, 8500 runs, 18 centuries and fifty 50s at an average of 39.35. Mark Edward Waugh will undoubtedly be remembered as one of the game's most outstanding limited-overs players.

It was the end of an era. For the first time since 1986, an Australian limited-overs unit would be without a Waugh. Ricky Ponting was the new captain of a fifteen-man squad that included Queensland off-spinner Nathan Hauritz and Tasmanian all-rounder Shane Watson. Both were just twenty years old, an indication that selectors were aiming to develop a fresh mix for the 2003 World Cup in South Africa. Matthew Hayden and Queensland opening partner Jimmy Maher were also included.

Mark handled his sacking with dignity, acknowledging to the journalists covering the South African tour that he simply hadn't made enough runs during the VB series. Back home, public opinion weighed heavily against the selectors, but some prominent former players including Greg Chappell and David Hookes supported the changes.

Although he stated if the new-look team failed, he would remain hopeful of a recall, Mark realised his chances of a return were slim. In the media, the obituaries had already been written. After calling for Mark's dumping throughout the Australian summer, long-time critic Mike Coward wrote in the *Australian* (5 March):

For much too long, the selectors were so seduced by Waugh's beauty as a batsman, they effectively allowed him to do as he liked. This was a mistake and, in fairness, one of the very few serious errors of judgement Trevor Hohns and his panel have made.

Nevertheless, in the same article Coward acknowledged Mark as 'one of the greatest of all limited-over cricketers'.

Despite media speculation the timing of the one-day squad's announcement could affect preparations for the second Test, at Newlands, Cape Town, the Australians refused to be distracted, producing a performance described by Steve as being 'up there' with other memorable wins under his leadership.

Needing to score 331 in the final innings to win, the visitors overhauled the target in 79.1 overs, with four wickets in hand. Ponting held the chase together, compiling an unbeaten 100, reaching his century and hitting the winning runs with a pulled six off spinner Paul Adams. Mark had returns of 25 and 16, his second innings ended prematurely when he was given out caught behind after a delivery from Ntini deflected off his foot. 'I could have been 50 or 60 not out,' says Mark. 'I was playing well enough to do that. It just shows how fine the line between good and bad luck can be.'

His dismissal prompted media speculation that he may have played his last Test innings, but Mark bluntly asks 'Why? I'd been in good form with the fifty and the hundred, and I knew I was hitting the ball well. I was bloody annoyed with some of the media talk.'

The pressure on both Waughs was growing. Steve had made 0 and 14, taking his Test tally to 251 runs at 25.1 from his past eight matches. In the same period Mark had amassed 347 at 34.7. His figures weren't those of a player wondering where his next run would come from, but the question was being posed: Would a replacement, such as Darren Lehmann, perform better?

Only three days separated the second and third Tests, meaning there was no tour game for Lehmann to press his claims. Mark rightfully retained his spot as the Australians sought a 6–0 sweep of a shell-shocked team that just a fortnight earlier had promised to challenge their rivals' position at the top of world cricket.

Knowledgeable locals at the Kingsmead Ground in the east coast city of Durban suggested the pitch's behaviour was determined by the tidal flow. Whether the story was true or not, the South Africans belatedly discovered the crest of a wave when they beat Australia by five wickets. Leading by 148 on the first innings (Mark scored 45), the visitors crumbled for 186 in their second innings. Mark had been in free-flowing form, reaching 30 from 47 balls, before being bowled after playing across a Jacques Kallis delivery. As he left the field in typical style, leaving his helmet on, but removing his gloves, the question was asked in the press box: 'Is this his final Test?' Mark didn't think about it when he was walking off, but 'when I sat down that night I probably did. I batted well both innings, but I let myself down. It was part of my game that disappointed me that summer — getting out when I shouldn't have got out.'

The innings wasn't his last contribution for the match, as he took 2–43 in the final innings, but it wasn't enough to prevent the South Africans from successfully chasing 335.

Mark finished the series with 169 runs at 33.80, fourth behind the explosive Gilchrist, who tallied 473 at 157.66. Significantly, Steve, Justin Langer and Damien Martyn had less fruitful returns than Mark.

While Australia's squad gathered for the one-dayers, the twins returned home. Mark spent time playing golf, following the horses, and also 'quite enjoyed' watching on television Ponting's squad blitz the South Africans 5–1. It was much too early to suggest the selectors had made the right decision by removing the twins. The team had obviously performed well, but six matches weren't enough to make firm judgements.

Despite his chance to relax away from cricket, Mark was forced to endure an anxious wait until he found out if he'd be chosen for the two Tests in Zimbabwe, to be played after the Australians completed their commitments in South Africa.

His period in 'limbo' was lengthened on 27 March when the ACB withdrew from the tour citing safety and security concerns. The decision followed Zimbabwe's suspension from the Commonwealth after President Robert Mugabe's victory in the national elections earlier in the month. Outbreaks of unrest had occurred, prompting Australia's Foreign Affairs Department to issue a warning against travelling to the country. Mugabe had been condemned across the western world for his violent leadership, which included seizure of land from white farmers, and the physical intimidation of his opponents. The ACB had no choice.

Once the decision had been made, Mark contacted Trevor Hohns. He comments:

I didn't know where I stood. I just wanted to know where the selectors saw my future in the Australian team, but he [Hohns] was fairly non-committal. He said as far as he was concerned I would have been in the Zimbabwe team, so I would assume I'd be in the team for Pakistan. But then again Stephen didn't know he was going to be dropped from the one-dayers. [At the time of writing, the squad for Australia's three-Test tour of Pakistan in September 2002 is still to be chosen. The tour itself is also in doubt because of unrest in the country.]

It's tough being in limbo. It's the first time I've ever really been in that situation. I've always expected to be picked in the team throughout my career. I haven't been in a situation before where my spot has been in real jeopardy, although there have been times when other people have said I've been under pressure. I've never really thought that, but I think it now — I am under pressure. I've just got to think that if I finish now I've had a great career, so let's just get out and enjoy whatever happens.

Whatever awaits him, Mark remains confident he can still perform at the top level. Only time will tell if the selectors agree with him.

CHAPTER THIRTY

THE FINAL WORD

Throughout his life Mark Waugh has rarely relished being in the spotlight, yet he pursues a career in which it's impossible to escape the glare of publicity. While he is not a movie star, his personality traits and his rich talents have cast him in a number of headline-grabbing lead roles.

There is of course the ongoing performance of 'Mark Waugh the Everyday Bloke'. It features the boy from the 'burbs who made it onto the world stage, yet has never turned his back on where he came from. As Bankstown official Brian Freedman suggests: 'He is just as proud to wear his Bulldog cap as his baggy green.'

And what of 'Mark Waugh the Talented'? It portrays a gifted, laid-back character whose enormous ability prompts Mark Taylor to offer the simple but telling statement: 'There haven't been too many Mark Waughs in any sport.'

That is true. Cast your eye across the world's arenas and count the players who are so graceful, making their games look so easy that they set the pace while appearing to be in slow motion. Allan Border acknowledges: 'It's no coincidence that a golden period in Australian cricket coincided with Mark's arrival,' while Geoff Marsh offers:

When you think that the guy is the best slipper in the world, the best all-round
fieldsman, he opened the batting in one-day cricket, bats at four in Test cricket,
he could bowl medium quick and now he bowls off spin. There's not a better all-
round cricketer to come out of Australia since I don't know when.

'Mark Waugh the Match-Winner' is free-flowing, adventurous, entertaining, and sometimes daring. However, as Ian Healy explains, not everything is always as it seems: 'It's just Mark's natural look that makes it look easy. He is doing it as tough as any other player.'

Consider 'Mark Waugh the Worker'. It's not a description that readily springs to mind, but there's no question black-tie elegance often disguises a blue-collar approach. Recalling numerous New South Wales training sessions, Greg Matthews remembers: 'I'd see this bloke with more talent in his little finger than I had in my whole body doing extra slips catching. And I'd think: "If he [Mark] needs to do it, I'd better stay there with him."'

Then there is 'Mark Waugh the Listener'. It's a role that often shares the stage with the 'Worker'. Bob Simpson remembers Mark would always find it difficult to seek advice, but when he wasn't going well, he'd find a moment for a chat: 'The interesting thing about him is that if you did say something quietly to him, he would be at the nets trying it. He may never admit it to you, but you'd notice him there.'

Of course, there is also 'Mark Waugh the Team-Man', described by Adam Gilchrist as:

First and foremost I'd class him as a very loyal person. He's got good values,
and he stands by what he thinks, perhaps even a fraction too much on some
occasions. He's just a very happy, relaxed person to be around. He's very honest.
Loyalty and honesty to team-mates and friends are two of his key qualities and
strengths. Those, with his humour, make him a terrific person to be around, and
be in a team with.

'Mark Waugh the Opponent' is also widely regarded. Effervescent South African fieldsman Jonty Rhodes recognises his rival's ability and good sportsmanship, but he says above all else: 'Mark is always the first guy with a smile on his face, and I always appreciate that because cricket for me is a real passion, and I really love playing the game. I think Mark is similar to me in that respect. He always wants to be on the field playing for his country.'

There have of course been the more sinister roles. To some members of the public and media, 'Mark Waugh the Naive' will sadly spring to mind before other performances more worthy of recollection. However, to the people closest to him, the corruption ordeal is over. End of story. They prefer to admire the qualities that helped Mark ride out the storm. Qualities abundant in 'Mark Waugh the Man'. Close friend and manager Leo Karis comments:

'He is a very humble man, an intensely private man, and extremely honest. His honesty is precious. Mark doesn't dislike too many people, but if he does, you'll know about it. You'll never die wondering with Mark, you'll always know where you stand.'

Karis has been part of an unwavering support cast headed by Sue Porter, whose relationship with Mark has endured its own share of hardships that Sue says have all been worth it: 'It's definitely the highlight of my life to have met him. From where we started to where we've come to has been tough. It's not easy to have a marriage, a normal life, a family, and then think: "Oh God, do I give it all up?" But I made the only choice.'

The other woman in Mark's life has been there since the opening night on 2 June 1965. Bev Waugh is a resolute performer:

You are exactly the same as when they played their first game. It does not change. It never changes. Any parent, mother would know my exact feelings every time. My philosophy is: 'What will be, will be', but it doesn't change the way you feel. You feel for all [the four sons] of them equally. As for Stephen and Mark, you can pinch yourself and think: 'Look if they never do another thing, they have played for Australia for more than 10 years. Who would have ever dreamt of that happening?'

Pride is an inescapable theme for the Waughs. Rodger boasts: 'A father is always proud of his sons isn't he? All four of them are very special.'

For the brother who was by Mark's side even before birth, there is the multi-layered and typically forthright appraisal from a sibling, a cricketer, and a team-mate. Steve says:

I'm definitely proud of him. I'm just as proud of the other two brothers as well. In a way it's been harder for them than Mark and myself. Mark's going to be able to look back at the end of his career and be very happy with what he's achieved. Longevity in the game is probably the hardest thing. You can come into the team and do well, then disappear, but to come into the team and stay in it and do it over a 10-year period shows you must be doing something right, and you must have a bit of character about you to last that long.

It's a character that has been portrayed in many different ways and scenes across the world. Among others, there is 'Mark Waugh the Punter', who at the end of his career will pay Shane Warne $1000 after losing a bet that Glenn McGrath would never make a first-class 50. There is 'Mark Waugh the Immaculate', a man fastidious about his hair. There is 'Mark Waugh the Fighter', who during the last few years of his international limited-overs career walked out to bat to his chosen theme song, 'Tubthumpin' by English band Chumbawamba: 'I get knocked down, but I get up again. You're never gonna keep me down.' There is also 'Mark Waugh the Sentimental' who owns a little teddy bear that was given to him by a young boy during the corruption scandal.

All unforgettable roles.

The final word is left to the often shy, reluctant star who was once described by cricket's greatest immortal, Sir Donald Bradman, as 'the most elegant and graceful cricketer of the modern era':

Cricket has given me a great livelihood. It has allowed me to live comfortably and travel the world, which I wouldn't have done otherwise. It has enabled me to realise how good Australia is. You should never complain about living in Australia because it is a great country with a great way of life.

Cricket has taught me to live with emotional highs and lows. It has taught me to be unselfish and enjoy other people's success, and not just to think of myself. When you're playing a team game you have to think of your team-mates.

When you're playing and travelling and touring you're just so involved that you don't stop and think how lucky you are. Sometimes you actually complain and think you're unlucky. Like when you're in India or Pakistan, you're sick, it's hot, you're a long way from home and don't want to be playing, but then you see how much it means to people. Then you realise how lucky you are. Most young sportspeople would love to play any sport for their country. You're representing your country at something that's fun — it's not a job. You're in a lucky position. When old people, young people, disabled people come up to you and want to say 'hello' or get your autograph, that's when you realise how lucky you are. People travel around the world to watch you play, their commitment is so strong that it makes you aware you're in a privileged position. When you are playing you become a bit blasé about it. But when you finish, that's when you'll realise how good it was. You shouldn't take it for granted.

I've copped a fair bit of criticism from people who say I don't give my best, people who say I look lazy and don't value my wicket enough. I've had some tough times because of the corruption issue. All I can say is that I have played my guts out for my club, my state, my country, never ever thinking about, or contemplating anything but doing my best to win and perform as best as I can on that day. I get the same feeling walking out to play for Australia now as when I first started.

I'm proud of what I've achieved, and have, and always will have, enormous respect for the baggy green.

STATISTICS
(Figures accurate to 1 May, 2002)

MARK EDWARD WAUGH
(Right hand batsman, right arm medium/off-spin bowler)

BATTING AND FIELDING

First-Class Career
Debut: 1984–85 New South Wales v. Queensland, Brisbane

Season	Country	M	Inn	NO	Runs	HS	0s	50	100	Avrge	Ct
1985–86	Australia	7	11	–	167	41	2	–	–	15.18	6
1985–86	Zimbabwe	2	4	2	176	83	–	2	–	88.00	4
1986–87	Australia	1	2	–	26	26	1	–	–	13.00	–
1987–88	Zimbabwe	2	3	1	123	61	–	1	–	61.50	1
1987–88	Australia	10	16	3	833	116	1	4	4	64.08	18
1988	England	3	4	–	178	86	–	1	–	44.50	2
1988–89	Australia	11	21	3	727	103*	4	4	2	40.39	9
1989	England	24	39	4	1537	165	2	8	4	43.91	31
1989–90	Australia	12	17	4	1009	198*	1	2	5	77.62	18
1990	England	22	33	6	2072	207*	4	8	8	76.74	18
1990–91	Australia	8	13	1	840	229*	2	3	3	70.00	9
1990–91	West Indies	9	12	2	522	139*	1	2	2	52.20	13
1991–92	Australia	12	18	–	924	163	2	4	3	51.33	19
1992	England	16	24	7	1314	219*	2	6	4	77.29	27
1992–93	Sri Lanka	5	9	–	291	118	4	2	1	32.33	5
1992–93	Australia	9	16	2	883	200*	1	3	3	63.07	8
1992–93	New Zealand	3	3	–	25	13	1	–	–	8.33	2
1993	England	16	25	6	1361	178	–	9	4	71.63	18
1993–94	Australia	10	16	–	765	119	–	6	2	47.81	10
1993–94	South Africa	6	10	2	573	154	–	–	3	71.63	3
1994–95	Pakistan	4	5	–	277	71	–	4	–	55.40	3
1994–95	Australia	9	17	–	827	140	1	4	3	48.65	13
1994–95	West Indies	7	9	1	418	126	–	3	1	52.25	6
1995	England	16	29	2	1392	173	–	6	5	51.56	19
1995–96	Australia	11	19	2	805	116	1	5	2	47.35	11
1996–97	India	2	4	1	76	26	–	–	–	25.33	3
1996–97	Australia	7	13	–	564	159	2	4	1	43.38	12
1996–97	South Africa	5	7	–	395	124	–	1	2	56.43	5
1997	England	13	20	3	746	173	–	3	2	43.88	11
1997–98	Australia	11	17	2	747	115*	1	5	2	49.80	6
1997–98	India	4	7	2	332	153*	1	2	1	66.40	1
1998–99	Pakistan	5	8	–	315	117	1	1	1	39.38	2
1998–99	Australia	6	12	3	583	126	–	2	2	64.78	10
1998–99	West Indies	5	9	–	308	106	1	2	1	34.22	9
1999–00	Sri Lanka	4	6	–	72	43	2	–	–	12.00	4
1999–00	Zimbabwe	2	3	–	269	116	–	2	1	89.67	9
1999–00	Australia	7	11	1	268	100	2	1	1	26.80	15
1999–00	New Zealand	4	7	3	283	93*	–	2	–	70.75	5
2000–01	Australia	7	11	1	590	152	–	3	2	59.00	13
2000–01	India	5	7	–	375	164	2	3	1	53.57	9
2001	England	9	15	6	644	120	1	2	2	71.56	12
2001–02	Australia	8	11	–	500	168	1	3	1	45.45	6
2001–02	South Africa	5	7	–	341	110	–	2	1	48.71	8
Total		**344**	**550**	**70**	**25473**	**229***	**44**	**125**	**80**	**53.07**	**413**

Country	M	Inn	NO	Runs	HS	0s	50	100	Avrge	Ct
Australia	146	241	22	11058	229*	22	53	36	50.49	183
England	119	189	34	9244	219*	9	43	29	59.64	138
India	11	18	3	783	164	3	5	2	52.20	13
New Zealand	7	10	3	308	93*	1	2	–	44.00	7
Pakistan	9	13	–	592	117	1	5	1	45.54	5
Sri Lanka	9	15	–	363	118	6	2	1	24.20	9
South Africa	16	24	2	1309	154	–	3	6	59.50	16
West Indies	21	30	3	1248	139*	2	7	4	46.22	28
Zimbabwe	6	10	3	568	116	–	5	1	81.14	14

Team	M	Inn	NO	Runs	HS	0s	50	100	Avrge	Ct
AUSTRALIA	125	205	17	7949	153*	18	46	20	42.28	173
Australian XI	50	69	15	3720	178	3	17	14	68.89	46
Essex	80	128	19	6448	219*	8	29	21	59.16	97
New South Wales	89	148	19	7356	229*	15	33	25	57.02	97

How Dismissed:	Inns	NO	Bwd	Ct	LBW	Stp	RO
	550	70	82	310	60	8	20

Centuries
Highest Score: 229* New South Wales v. Western Australia, Perth, 1990–91

100s	Team	Opponent	Venue	Season
101*	New South Wales	Tasmania	Devonport	1987–88
114*	New South Wales	Victoria	Sydney	1987–88
100*	New South Wales	Victoria	Melbourne	1987–88
116	New South Wales	Tasmania	Sydney	1987–88
103*	New South Wales	West Indians	Sydney	1988–89
100*	New South Wales	Tasmania	Devonport	1988–89
109	Essex	Hampshire	Ilford	1989
110	Essex	Middlesex	Uxbridge	1989
100*	Essex	Australian XI	Chelmsford	1989
165	Essex	Leicestershire	Leicester	1989
172	New South Wales	South Australia	Adelaide	1989–90
100*	New South Wales	Victoria	Albury	1989–90
100*	New South Wales	Victoria	Melbourne	1989–90
137	New South Wales	South Australia	Sydney	1989–90
198*	New South Wales	Tasmania	Sydney	1989–90
166*	Essex	Worcestershire	Worcester	1990
125	Essex	Hampshire	Southampton	1990
204	Essex	Gloucestershire	Ilford	1990
103	Essex	Warwickshire	Birmingham	1990
126	Essex	Derbyshire	Colchester	1990
103*	Essex	Sussex	Chelmsford	1990
207*	Essex	Yorkshire	Middlesbrough	1990
169	Essex	Kent	Chelmsford	1990
229*	New South Wales	Western Australia	Perth	1990–91

100s	Team	Opponent	Venue	Season
112	New South Wales	South Australia	Sydney	1990–91
138	AUSTRALIA	ENGLAND	Adelaide	1990–91
108	Australian XI	Jamaica	Kingston	1990–91
139*	AUSTRALIA	WEST INDIES	St John's	1990–91
136	New South Wales	Western Australia	Perth	1991–92
158	New South Wales	South Australia	Sydney	1991–92
163	New South Wales	Western Australia	Perth	1991–92
120	Essex	Kent	Chelmsford	1992
219*	Essex	Lancashire	Ilford	1992
125*	Essex	Gloucestershire	Southend	1992
138*	Essex	Worcestershire	Kidderminster	1992
118	Australian XI	Sri Lankan Board XI	Matara	1992–93
200*	New South Wales	West Indians	Sydney	1992–93
164	New South Wales	South Australia	Adelaide	1992–93
112	AUSTRALIA	WEST INDIES	Melbourne	1992–93
178	Australian XI	Surrey	The Oval	1993
152*	Australian XI	Glamorgan	Neath	1993
137	AUSTRALIA	ENGLAND	Birmingham	1993
108	Australian XI	Essex	Chelmsford	1993
111	AUSTRALIA	NEW ZEALAND	Hobart	1993–94
119	New South Wales	Victoria	Sydney	1993–94
134	Australian XI	Northern Transvaal	Verwoerdburg	1993–94
154	Australian XI	Orange Free State	Bloemfontein	1993–94
113*	AUSTRALIA	SOUTH AFRICA	Durban	1993–94
113	New South Wales	Queensland	Sydney	1994–95
140	AUSTRALIA	ENGLAND	Brisbane	1994–95
132	New South Wales	Tasmania	Hobart	1994–95
126	AUSTRALIA	WEST INDIES	Kingston	1994–95
126	Essex	Surrey	The Oval	1995
173	Essex	Somerset	Southend	1995
136	Essex	Hampshire	Colchester	1995
121*	Essex	Derbyshire	Chelmsford	1995
121	Essex	Derbyshire	Chelmsford	1995
116	AUSTRALIA	PAKISTAN	Sydney	1995–96
111	AUSTRALIA	SRI LANKA	Perth	1995–96
159	New South Wales	Queensland	Brisbane	1996–97
124	Australian XI	Natal	Durban	1996–97
116	AUSTRALIA	SOUTH AFRICA	Port Elizabeth	1996–97
173	Australian XI	Hampshire	Southampton	1997
142*	Australian XI	Middlesex	Lord's	1997
100	AUSTRALIA	SOUTH AFRICA	Sydney	1997–98
115*	AUSTRALIA	SOUTH AFRICA	Adelaide	1997–98
153*	AUSTRALIA	INDIA	Bangalore	1997–98
117	AUSTRALIA	PAKISTAN	Karachi	1998–99
126	New South Wales	Victoria	Sydney	1998–99
121	AUSTRALIA	ENGLAND	Sydney	1998–99
106	Australian XI	West Indian Board XI	Pointe-a-Pierre	1998–99
116	Australian XI	Zimbabwe President's XI	Bulawayo	1999–00
100	AUSTRALIA	PAKISTAN	Brisbane	1999–00

100s	Team	Opponent	Venue	Season
152	New South Wales	Tasmania	Hobart	2000–01
119	AUSTRALIA	WEST INDIES	Perth	2000–01
164	Australian XI	Indian Board Pres. XI	Delhi	2000–01
108	AUSTRALIA	ENGLAND	Lord's	2001
120	AUSTRALIA	ENGLAND	Lord's	2001
168	New South Wales	Tasmania	Sydney	2001–02
110	Australian XI	South Africa A	Port Elizabeth	2001–02

Test Career
Debut: 1990–91 Australia v. England, Adelaide

Season	Opponent	Venue	M	Inn	NO	Runs	HS	0s	50	100	Avrge	Ct
1990–91	England	AUS	2	3	–	187	138	–	–	1	62.33	1
1990–91	West Indies	WI	5	8	2	367	139*	1	2	1	61.17	10
1991–92	India	AUS	4	6	–	83	34	1	–	–	13.83	10
1992–93	Sri Lanka	SL	3	6	–	61	56	4	1	–	10.17	3
1992–93	West Indies	AUS	5	9	–	340	112	1	2	1	37.78	6
1992–93	New Zealand	NZ	2	2	–	25	13	–	–	–	12.50	–
1993	England	ENG	6	10	1	550	137	–	5	1	61.11	9
1993–94	New Zealand	AUS	3	3	–	215	111	–	1	1	71.67	3
1993–94	South Africa	AUS	3	5	–	116	84	–	1	–	23.20	4
1993–94	South Africa	SAF	3	5	1	233	113*	–	–	1	58.25	2
1994–95	Pakistan	PAK	3	4	–	220	71	–	3	–	55.00	3
1994–95	England	AUS	5	10	–	435	140	–	2	1	43.50	8
1994–95	West Indies	WI	4	6	–	240	126	–	1	1	40.00	3
1995–96	Pakistan	AUS	3	5	–	300	116	–	2	1	60.00	4
1995–96	Sri Lanka	AUS	3	4	–	255	111	–	2	1	63.75	2
1996–97	India	IND	1	2	–	49	26	–	–	–	24.50	2
1996–97	West Indies	AUS	5	9	–	370	82	1	4	–	41.11	8
1996–97	South Africa	SAF	3	5	–	209	116	–	–	1	41.80	3
1997	England	ENG	6	10	–	209	68	–	2	–	20.90	6
1997–98	New Zealand	AUS	3	5	–	196	86	–	2	–	39.20	1
1997–98	South Africa	AUS	3	5	1	279	115*	1	1	2	69.75	–
1997–98	India	IND	3	6	2	280	153*	1	1	1	70.00	1
1998–99	Pakistan	PAK	3	5	–	228	117	1	–	1	45.60	1
1998–99	England	AUS	5	10	3	393	121	–	1	1	56.14	10
1998–99	West Indies	WI	4	8	–	202	67	1	2	–	25.25	7
1999–00	Sri Lanka	SL	3	4	–	29	13	1	–	–	7.25	2
1999–00	Zimbabwe	Zim	1	1	–	90	90	–	1	–	90.00	5
1999–00	Pakistan	AUS	3	4	–	105	100	2	–	1	26.25	7
1999–00	India	AUS	3	5	1	137	51*	–	1	–	34.25	8
1999–00	New Zealand	NZ	3	6	2	190	72*	–	1	–	47.50	4
2000–01	West Indies	AUS	5	8	1	339	119	–	2	1	48.43	11
2000–01	India	IND	3	5	–	149	70	2	2	–	29.80	8
2001	England	ENG	5	8	3	430	120	–	1	2	86.00	9
2001–02	New Zealand	AUS	3	4	–	140	86	1	1	–	35.00	2
2001–02	South Africa	AUS	3	4	–	129	74	–	1	–	32.25	4
2001–02	South Africa	SAF	3	5	–	169	53	–	1	–	33.80	6
Total			**125**	**205**	**17**	**7949**	**153***	**18**	**46**	**20**	**42.28**	**173**

Opponent	M	Inn	NO	Runs	HS	0s	50	100	Avrge	Ct
ENGLAND	29	51	7	2204	140	–	11	6	50.09	43
INDIA	14	24	3	698	153*	4	4	1	33.24	29
NEW ZEALAND	14	20	2	766	111	1	5	1	42.56	10
PAKISTAN	12	18	8	53	117	3	5	3	47.39	15
SRI LANKA	9	14	–	345	111	5	3	1	24.64	7
SOUTH AFRICA	18	29	2	1135	116	1	4	4	42.04	19
WEST INDIES	28	48	3	1858	139*	4	13	4	41.29	45
ZIMBABWE	1	1	–	90	90	–	1	–	90.00	5

How Dismissed:	Inns	NO	Bwd	Ct	LBW	Stp	RO
	205	17	29	123	31	1	4

Centuries
Highest Score: 153* Australia v. India, Bangalore, 1997–98

100s	Team	Opponent	Venue	Season
138*	Australia	England	Adelaide	1990–91
139*	Australia	West Indies	St John's	1990–91
112	Australia	West Indies	Melbourne	1992–93
137	Australia	England	Birmingham	1993
111	Australia	New Zealand	Hobart	1993–94
113*	Australia	South Africa	Durban	1993–94
140	Australia	England	Brisbane	1994–95
126	Australia	West Indies	Kingston	1994–95
116	Australia	Pakistan	Sydney	1995–96
111	Australia	Sri Lanka	Perth	1995–96
116	Australia	South Africa	Port Elizabeth	1996–97
100	Australia	South Africa	Sydney	1997–98
115*	Australia	South Africa	Adelaide	1997–98
153*	Australia	India	Bangalore	1997–98
117	Australia	Pakistan	Karachi	1998–99
121	Australia	England	Sydney	1998–99
100	Australia	Pakistan	Brisbane	1999–00
119	Australia	West Indies	Perth	2000–01
108	Australia	England	Lord's	2001
120	Australia	England	Lord's	2001

Sheffield Shield Career
Debut: 1985–86 New South Wales v. Tasmania, Hobart

Season	M	Inn	NO	Runs	HS	0s	50	100	Avrge	Ct
1985–86	6	9	–	150	41	1	–	–	16.67	6
1986–87	1	2	–	26	26	1	–	–	13.00	–
1987–88	10	16	3	833	116	1	4	4	64.08	18
1988–89	9	17	1	552	100*	3	3	1	34.50	7
1989–90	11	16	4	967	198*	1	2	5	80.58	18
1990–91	4	6	1	487	229*	2	1	2	97.40	6
1991–92	7	11	–	762	163	1	3	3	69.27	9
1992–93	3	6	1	343	164	–	1	1	68.60	2
1993–94	3	6	–	370	119	–	3	1	61.67	2
1994–95	3	5	–	312	132	–	1	2	62.40	2
1995–96	5	10	2	250	57	1	1	–	31.25	5
1996–97	2	4	–	194	159	1	–	1	48.50	4
1997–98	4	6	1	228	72	–	2	–	45.60	4
1998–99	1	2	–	190	126	–	1	1	95.00	–
1999–00	1	2	–	26	25	–	–	–	13.00	–
2000–01	2	3	–	251	152	–	1	1	83.67	2
2001–02	2	3	–	231	168	–	1	1	77.00	–
Total	**74**	**124**	**13**	**6172**	**229***	**12**	**24**	**23**	**55.60**	**85**

Opponents	M	Inn	NO	Runs	HS	0s	50	100	Avrge	Ct
Queensland	18	32	2	1209	159	5	9	2	40.30	20
South Australia	13	20	1	1278	172	1	5	5	67.26	9
Tasmania	14	20	4	1242	198*	3	1	7	77.63	18
Victoria	16	29	5	1345	126	2	7	6	56.04	20
Western Australia	13	23	1	1098	229*	1	2	3	49.91	18

International Limited-Overs Career
Debut: 1988–89 Australia v. Pakistan, Adelaide

Season	Tournament	Venue	M	Inn	NO	Runs	HS	0s	50	100	Avrge	Stk/Rt	Ct
1988–89	WSC	AUS	7	6	–	131	42	–	–	–	21.83	85.62	3
1989–90	WS	AUS	1	1	–	14	14	–	–	–	14.00	100.00	–
1990–91	WS	AUS	10	10	2	176	62	2	1	–	22.00	74.89	6
1990–91	WI v. Aus	WI	5	5	–	156	67	–	1	–	31.20	100.65	2
1991–92	WS	AUS	5	3	–	20	17	1	–	–	6.67	57.14	1
1991–92	WC	ANZ	5	5	1	145	66*	–	1	–	36.25	101.40	4
1992–93	SL v. Aus	SL	3	3	–	93	52	–	1	–	31.00	83.04	2
1992–93	WS	AUS	10	9	–	259	57	–	3	–	28.78	66.07	6
1992–93	NZ v. Aus	NZ	5	5	–	308	108	1	3	1	61.60	82.80	3
1993	Eng v. Aus	ENG	3	3	–	183	113	–	1	1	61.00	87.98	2
1993–94	WS	AUS	11	11	1	405	107	–	2	1	40.50	74.59	2
1993–94	SAF v. Aus	SAF	8	8	1	199	71	1	2	–	28.43	66.33	4
1993–94	AAC	UAE	2	2	1	80	64*	–	1	–	80.00	73.39	–
1994–95	SWS	SL	3	3	–	108	61	–	1	–	36.00	69.68	–
1994–95	WTS	PAK	6	6	1	243	121*	1	–	1	48.60	78.90	–
1994–95	WS	AUS	4	4	1	63	41	–	–	–	21.00	53.85	–
1994–95	NZC	NZ	4	4	–	179	74	–	1	–	44.75	89.95	1
1994–95	WI v. Aus	WI	4	4	–	125	70	1	1	–	31.25	96.15	3
1995–96	WS	AUS	10	10	–	357	130	1	3	1	35.70	73.46	4
1995–96	WC	IPS	7	7	1	484	130	1	1	3	80.67	85.51	1
1996–97	SWS	SL	4	4	–	100	50	–	1	–	25.00	80.65	2
1996–97	TC	IND	4	4	–	107	50	–	1	–	26.75	65.24	1
1996–97	CUBS	AUS	7	7	1	358	102	–	2	1	59.67	71.60	3
1996–97	SAF v. Aus	SAF	4	3	1	118	115*	1	–	1	59.00	82.52	2
1997	Eng v. Aus	ENG	3	3	–	131	95	–	1	–	43.67	81.88	–
1997–98	CUBS	AUS	9	9	–	320	104	–	–	1	35.56	73.90	2
1997–98	NZ v. Aus	NZ	4	4	–	196	85	–	2	–	49.00	76.86	1
1997–98	TC	IND	5	5	–	178	87	–	1	–	35.60	77.06	1
1997–98	CCC	UAE	5	5	1	149	81	–	1	–	37.25	82.78	3
1998–99	WI	BAN	1	1	–	74	74	–	1	–	74.00	93.67	–
1998–99	Pak v. Aus	PAK	3	3	–	43	19	–	–	–	14.33	45.74	4
1998–99	CUBS	AUS	12	12	1	542	85	–	6	–	49.27	75.28	5
1998–99	WI v. Aus	WI	7	7	–	217	74	–	1	–	31.00	68.03	2
1999	WC	ENG	10	10	1	375	104	1	2	1	41.67	76.37	6
1999–00	AC	SL	5	5	–	174	84	–	1	–	34.80	79.45	1
1999–00	Zim v. Aus	ZIM	2	2	1	160	106	–	1	1	160.00	83.33	4
1999–00	CUBS	AUS	10	10	–	305	116	–	1	1	30.50	66.30	6
1999–00	NZ v. Aus	NZ	6	6	1	206	75	1	2	–	41.20	66.24	3
1999–00	SAF v. Aus	SAF	3	3	–	11	9	1	–	–	3.67	26.83	1
2000–01	Aus v. SAF	AUS	3	3	–	66	48	–	–	–	22.00	64.71	4
2000–01	ICCT	KYA	1	1	–	7	7	–	–	–	7.00	29.17	1
2000–01	CS	AUS	9	7	2	542	173	–	2	3	108.40	83.00	4
2000–01	Ind v. Aus	IND	2	2	1	138	133*	–	–	1	138.00	95.17	3
2001	NWS	ENG	5	4	–	129	47	1	–	–	32.25	82.69	2
2001–02	VBS	AUS	7	7	1	126	55*	2	1	–	21.00	70.79	3
Total			**244**	**236**	**20**	**8500**	**173**	**16**	**50**	**18**	**39.35**	**76.54**	**108**

Opponents	M	Inn	NO	Runs	HS	0s	50	100	Avrge	Stk/Rt	Ct
Bangladesh	1	1	–	33	33	–	–	–	33.00	94.29	–
England	21	20	1	834	113	1	6	1	43.89	79.28	7
India	27	26	1	974	133*	1	4	3	38.96	80.16	15
Kenya	1	1	–	130	130	–	–	1	130.00	100.00	–
New Zealand	39	39	5	1362	110	5	9	3	40.06	76.99	16
Pakistan	29	27	2	671	121*	2	1	1	26.84	72.93	14
Sri Lanka	23	23	1	906	130	1	9	1	41.18	78.58	6
South Africa	42	41	3	1111	115*	4	5	2	29.24	69.83	16
Scotland	1	1	–	67	67	–	1	–	67.00	59.29	–
West Indies	47	45	2	1708	173	2	11	3	39.72	75.88	23
Zimbabwe	13	12	5	704	106	–	4	3	100.57	80.27	11

Innings		Inn	NO	Runs	HS	0s	50	100	Avrge	Stk/Rt	Ct
First		130	4	5181	173	6	33	11	41.12	78.12	53
Second		106	16	3319	133*	10	17	7	36.88	74.18	55

Batting	Position	Inn	NO	Runs	HS	0s	50	100	Avrge Stk/Rt	
1/2	141	11	5729	173	9	32	15	44.07	76.33	
3	34	2	1197	121*	3	8	2	37.41	74.12	
4	20	2	589	107	1	3	1	32.72	74.84	
5	37	3	934	67	3	7	–	27.47	82.07	
6	3	1	45	34*	–	–	–	22.50	88.24	
9	1	1	6	6*	–	–	–	–	66.67	

How Dismissed:	Inns	NO	Bwd	Ct	LBW	Stp	RO
	236	20	46	113	14	11	32

Centuries
Highest Score: 173 Australia v. West Indies, Melbourne, 2000–01

100s	Team	Opponent	Venue	Season
108	Australia	New Zealand	Hamilton	1992–93
113	Australia	England	Birmingham	1993
107	Australia	South Africa	Sydney	1993–94
121*	Australia	Pakistan	Rawalpindi	1994–95
130	Australia	Sri Lanka	Perth	1995–96
130	Australia	Kenya	Visakhapatnam	1995–96
126	Australia	India	Mumbai	1995–96
110	Australia	New Zealand	Chennai	1995–96
102	Australia	West Indies	Brisbane	1996–97
115*	Australia	South Africa	Port Elizabeth	1996–97
104	Australia	New Zealand	Adelaide	1997–98
104	Australia	Zimbabwe	Lord's	1999
106	Australia	Zimbabwe	Bulawayo	1999–00
116	Australia	India	Adelaide	1999–00
112*	Australia	West Indies	Brisbane	2000–01
102*	Australia	Zimbabwe	Hobart	2000–01
173	Australia	West Indies	Melbourne	2000–01
133*	Australia	India	Pune	2000–01

Domestic Limited-Overs Career
Debut: 1985–86 New South Wales v. Victoria, Sydney

Season	M	Inn	NO	Runs	HS	0s	50	100	Avrge	Stk/Rt	Ct
1985–86	1	1	–	13	13	–	–	–	13.00	48.15	–
1986–87	2	2	–	50	46	–	–	–	25.00	64.10	1
1987–88	4	4	–	129	38	–	–	–	32.25	79.14	2
1988–89	3	2	–	68	51	–	1	–	34.00	76.40	–
1989–90	3	3	–	82	50	1	1	–	27.33	62.60	3
1990–91	4	4	–	155	64	–	2	–	38.75	70.14	1
1991–92	4	4	1	159	112	–	–	1	53.00	82.81	3
1992–93	4	4	–	98	55	–	1	–	24.50	88.29	2
1993–94	2	2	–	101	68	–	1	–	50.50	150.75	1
1994–95	–	–	–	–	–	–	–	–	–	–	–
1995–96	4	4	2	93	43*	–	–	–	46.50	65.96	3
1997–98	3	3	–	153	76	–	2	–	51.00	106.99	2
1998–99	1	1	–	0	0	1	–	–	0.00	0.00	1
1999–00	1	1	–	8	8	–	–	–	8.00	34.78	1
2000–01	5	5	1	160	108*	–	–	1	40.00	68.67	3
2001–02	4	4	–	208	123	–	1	1	52.00	97.65	2
Total	**45**	**44**	**4**	**1477**	**123**	**2**	**9**	**3**	**36.93**	**80.58**	**25**

Opponents	M	Inn	NO	Runs	HS	0s	50	100	Avrge	Stk/Rt	Ct
Queensland	10	10	2	289	108*	–	–	1	36.13	82.81	7
South Australia	6	6	–	240	76	–	3	–	40.00	85.71	2
Tasmania	11	10	–	373	123	2	3	1	37.30	90.75	6
Victoria	11	11	1	461	112	–	2	1	46.10	76.71	6
Western Australia	7	7	1	114	51	–	1	–	19.00	59.38	4

Innings		Inn	NO	Runs	HS	0s	50	100	Avrge	Stk/Rt	Ct
First		28	–	885	123	2	6	2	31.61	88.24	13
Second		16	4	592	108*	–	3	1	49.33	71.33	12

Batting	Position	Inn	NO	Runs	HS	0s	50	100	Avrge	Stk/Rt
1/2	9	1	365	123	–	1	2	45.63	79.00	
3	4	–	59	32	1	–	–	14.75	64.84	
4	27	3	939	112	1	7	1	39.13	85.13	
5	1	–	51	51	–	1	–	51.00	70.83	
6	3	–	63	46	–	–	–	21.00	60.00	

Centuries
Highest Score: 123 New South Wales v. Tasmania, Bankstown, 2001–02

100s	Team	Opponent	Venue	Season
112	New South Wales	Victoria	North Sydney	1991–92
108*	New South Wales	Queensland	Bankstown	2000–01
123	New South Wales	Tasmania	Bankstown	2001–02

BOWLING

First-Class Career

Season	Country	M	Balls	Mdns	Runs	Wkts	Avrge	5	10	Best
1985–86	Australia	7	748	27	352	11	32.00	–	–	4/130
1985–86	Zimbabwe	2	258	14	110	2	55.00	–	–	1/25
1986–87	Australia	1	66	4	32	1	32.00	–	–	1/2
1987–88	Zimbabwe	2	6	–	3	–	–	–	–	–
1987–88	Australia	10	276	7	158	6	26.33	–	–	3/49
1988	England	3	72	–	75	–	–	–	–	–
1988–89	Australia	11	258	7	163	1	163.00	–	–	1/46
1989	England	24	704	19	415	14	29.64	–	–	3/23
1989–90	Australia	12	789	20	465	15	31.00	–	–	2/7
1990	England	22	1146	33	771	12	64.25	1	–	5/37
1990–91	Australia	8	186	5	138	2	69.00	–	–	2/15
1990–91	West Indies	9	560	21	271	12	22.58	–	–	4/80
1991–92	Australia	12	587	28	258	7	36.86	–	–	2/11
1992	England	16	1108	31	671	22	30.50	–	–	3/38
1992–93	Sri Lanka	5	240	6	129	2	64.50	–	–	2/77
1992–93	Australia	9	210	2	131	4	32.75	–	–	2/21
1992–93	New Zealand	3	108	6	45	1	45.00	–	–	1/12
1993	England	16	727	28	403	6	67.17	–	–	3/26
1993–94	Australia	10	807	45	261	12	21.75	–	–	2/24
1993–94	South Africa	6	234	9	119	–	–	–	–	–
1994–95	Pakistan	4	180	3	106	2	53.00	–	–	2/63
1994–95	Australia	9	618	21	308	10	30.80	1	–	5/40
1994–95	West Indies	7	216	9	146	4	36.50	–	–	2/39
1995	England	16	1535	66	789	17	46.41	–	–	4/76
1995–96	Australia	11	570	21	219	7	31.29	–	–	2/19
1996–97	India	2	209	3	130	7	18.57	1	–	6/68
1996–97	Australia	7	144	5	85	2	42.50	–	–	2/54
1996–97	South Africa	5	120	6	68	1	68.00	–	–	1/34
1997	England	13	282	10	150	4	37.50	–	–	1/16
1997–98	Australia	11	738	25	318	4	79.50	–	–	2/26
1997–98	India	4	228	1	161	2	80.50	–	–	1/44
1998–99	Pakistan	5	72	–	42	–	–	–	–	–
1998–99	Australia	6	276	7	139	4	34.75	–	–	2/55
1998–99	West Indies	5	30	–	24	–	–	–	–	–
1999–00	Sri Lanka	4	12	1	9	–	–	–	–	–
1999–00	Zimbabwe	2	24	–	19	–	–	–	–	–
1999–00	Australia	7	42	1	23	2	11.50	–	–	2/12
1999–00	New Zealand	4	–	–	–	–	–	–	–	–
2000–01	Australia	7	126	5	42	1	42.00	–	–	1/10
2000–01	India	5	276	8	133	5	26.60	–	–	3/40
2001	England	9	144	2	121	2	60.50	–	–	1/33
2001–02	Australia	8	186	4	106	2	53.00	–	–	1/19
2001–02	South Africa	5	155	5	86	2	43.00	–	–	2/43
Total		**344**	**15273**	**515**	**8194**	**208**	**39.39**	**3**	**–**	**6/68**

Best Bowling: 6/68 Australian XI v. Indian Board President's XI, Patalia, 1996–97

Test Career

Season	Opponent	Venue	M	Balls	Mdns	Runs	Wkts	Avrge	5	10	Best
1990–91	England	AUS	2	36	1	26	–	–	–	–	–
1990–91	West Indies	WI	5	390	18	183	8	22.88	–	–	4/80
1991–92	India	AUS	4	222	9	89	1	89.00	–	–	1/36
1992–93	Sri Lanka	SL	3	138	3	94	2	47.00	–	–	2/77
1992–93	West Indies	AUS	5	132	2	84	4	21.00	–	–	2/21
1992–93	New Zealand	NZ	2	90	5	27	1	27.00	–	–	1/12
1993	England	ENG	6	336	17	161	1	161.00	–	–	1/43
1993–94	New Zealand	AUS	3	288	18	94	5	18.80	–	–	1/7
1993–94	South Africa	AUS	3	108	6	30	1	30.00	–	–	1/20
1993–94	South Africa	SAF	3	180	9	86	–	–	–	–	–
1994–95	Pakistan	PAK	3	162	2	93	2	46.50	–	–	2/63
1994–95	England	AUS	5	318	10	157	8	19.63	1	–	5/40
1994–95	West Indies	WI	4	84	3	48	1	48.00	–	–	1/9
1995–96	Pakistan	AUS	3	294	12	97	2	48.50	–	–	1/6
1995–96	Sri Lanka	AUS	3	150	5	73	2	36.50	–	–	1/15
1996–97	India	IND	1	108	–	62	1	62.00	–	–	1/62
1996–97	West Indies	AUS	5	48	1	31	–	–	–	–	–
1996–97	South Africa	SAF	3	48	1	38	1	38.00	–	–	1/34
1997	England	ENG	6	42	3	16	1	16.00	–	–	1/16
1997–98	New Zealand	AUS	3	126	5	54	–	–	–	–	–
1997–98	South Africa	AUS	3	282	12	114	2	57.00	–	–	2/28
1997–98	India	IND	3	192	1	149	2	74.50	–	–	1/44
1998–99	Pakistan	PAK	3	48	–	32	–	–	–	–	–
1998–99	England	AUS	5	156	2	90	3	30.00	–	–	2/55
1998–99	West Indies	WI	4	30	–	24	–	–	–	–	–
1999–00	Sri Lanka	SL	3	12	1	9	–	–	–	–	–
1999–00	Zimbabwe	ZIM	1	–	–	–	–	–	–	–	–
1999–00	Pakistan	AUS	3	12	–	6	–	–	–	–	–
1999–00	India	AUS	3	30	1	17	2	8.50	–	–	2/12
1999–00	New Zealand	NZ	3	–	–	–	–	–	–	–	–
2000–01	West Indies	AUS	5	66	4	15	1	15.00	–	–	1/10
2000–01	India	IND	3	216	6	106	3	35.33	–	–	3/40
2001	England	ENG	5	78	1	69	1	69.00	–	–	1/40
2001–02	New Zealand	AUS	3	84	2	64	1	64.00	–	–	1/30
2001–02	South Africa	AUS	3	102	2	42	1	42.00	–	–	1/19
2001–02	South Africa	SAF	3	131	4	78	2	39.00	–	–	2/43
Total			**125**	**4739**	**166**	**2358**	**59**	**39.97**	**1**	**–**	**5/40**

Best Bowling: 5/40 Australia v. England, Adelaide, 1994–95

Sheffield Shield Career

Season	M	Balls	Mdns	Runs	Wkts	Avrge	5	10	Best
1985–86	6	748	27	352	11	32.00	–	–	4/130
1986–87	1	66	4	32	1	32.00	–	–	1/2
1987–88	10	276	7	158	6	26.33	–	–	3/49
1988–89	9	132	2	93	–	–	–	–	–
1989–90	11	726	17	429	12	35.75	–	–	2/22
1990–91	4	138	4	104	2	52.00	–	–	2/15
1991–92	7	305	16	143	6	23.83	–	–	2/11
1992–93	3	78	–	47	–	–	–	–	–
1993–94	3	316	15	115	5	23.00	–	–	2/24
1994–95	3	228	10	115	2	57.50	–	–	2/11
1995–96	5	126	4	49	3	16.33	–	–	2/19
1996–97	2	96	4	54	2	27.00	–	–	2/54
1997–98	4	204	4	109	–	–	–	–	–
1998–99	1	120	5	49	1	49.00	–	–	1/49
1999–00	1	–	–	–	–	–	–	–	–
2000–01	2	60	1	27	–	–	–	–	–
2001–02	2	–	–	–	–	–	–	–	–
Total	**74**	**3619**	**120**	**1876**	**51**	**36.78**	**–**	**–**	**4/130**

Best Bowling: 4/130 New South Wales v. Queensland, Brisbane, 1985–86

International Limited-Overs Career

Season	Tourn	Ven	M	Balls	Mdns	Runs	Wkts	Avrge	5	Best	Stk/Rt	RPO
1988–89	WSC	AUS	7	–	–	–	–	–	–	–	–	–
1989–90	WS	AUS	1	–	–	–	–	–	–	–	–	–
1990–91	WS	AUS	10	294	2	191	12	15.92	–	4/37	24.50	3.90
1990–91	WI v. Aus	WI	5	165	–	146	8	18.25	–	3/34	20.63	5.31
1991–92	WS	AUS	5	54	–	46	–	–	–	–	–	5.11
1991–92	WC	ANZ	5	30	–	40	–	–	–	–	–	8.00
1992–93	SL v. Aus	SL	3	6	–	6	–	–	–	–	–	6.00
1992–93	WS	AUS	10	213	–	159	9	17.67	1	5/24	23.67	4.48
1992–93	NZ v. Aus	NZ	5	30	–	34	1	34.00	–	1/5	30.00	6.80
1993	Eng v. Aus	ENG	3	30	–	33	–	–	–	–	–	6.60
1993–94	WS	AUS	11	246	–	184	6	30.67	–	2/26	41.00	4.49
1993–94	SAF v. Aus	SAF	8	192	1	168	4	42.00	–	1/26	48.00	5.25
1993–94	AAC	UAE	2	42	–	41	–	–	–	–	–	5.86
1994–95	SWS	SL	3	24	–	19	–	–	–	–	–	4.75
1994–95	WTS	PAK	6	143	–	131	4	32.75	–	2/43	35.75	5.50
1994–95	WS	AUS	4	66	1	46	2	23.00	–	2/43	33.00	4.18
1994–95	NZC	NZ	4	84	1	57	2	28.50	–	1/19	42.00	4.07
1994–95	WI v. Aus	WI	4	58	–	65	4	16.25	–	3/42	14.50	6.72
1995–96	WS	AUS	10	306	–	215	6	35.83	–	2/30	51.00	4.22
1995–96	WC	IPS	7	288	1	229	5	45.80	–	3/38	57.60	4.77
1996–97	SWS	SL	4	132	1	130	4	32.50	–	3/24	33.00	5.91
1996–97	TC	IND	4	120	1	86	2	43.00	–	2/38	60.00	4.30
1996–97	CUBS	AUS	7	51	1	38	1	38.00	–	1/11	51.00	4.47

Season	Tourn	Ven	M	Balls	Mdns	Runs	Wkts	Avrge	5	Best	Stk/Rt	RPO
1996–97	SAF v. Aus	SAF	4	21	–	16	–	–	–	–	–	4.57
1997	Eng v. Aus	ENG	3	48	–	44	1	44.00	–	1/28	48.00	5.50
1997–98	CUBS	AUS	9	246	–	178	7	25.43	–	2/39	35.14	4.34
1997–98	NZ v. Aus	NZ	4	30	–	30	–	–	–	–	–	6.00
1997–98	TC	IND	5	48	–	45	–	–	–	–	–	5.63
1997–98	CCC	UAE	5	66	–	46	1	46.00	–	1/26	66.00	4.18
1998–99	WIC	BAN	1	36	–	27	–	–	–	–	–	4.50
1998–99	Pak v. Aus	PAK	3	12	–	16	–	–	–	–	–	8.00
1998–99	CUBS	AUS	12	42	–	34	1	34.00	–	1/11	42.00	4.86
1998–99	WI v. Aus	W.I	7	174	1	114	1	114.00	–	1/35	174.00	3.93
1999	WC	ENG	10	54	–	44	–	–	–	–	–	4.89
1999–00	AC	SL	5	–	–	–	–	–	–	–	–	–
1999–00	Zim v. Aus	ZIM	2	18	–	14	–	–	–	–	–	4.67
1999–00	CUBS	AUS	10	54	–	43	1	43.00	–	1/28	54.00	4.78
1999–00	NZ v. Aus	NZ	6	72	–	66	1	66.00	–	1/42	72.00	5.50
1999–00	SAF v. Aus	SAF	3	24	–	20	–	–	–	–	–	5.00
2000–01	Aus v. SAF	AUS	3	–	–	–	–	–	–	–	–	–
2000–01	ICCT	KYA	1	–	–	–	–	–	–	–	–	–
2000–01	CS	AUS	9	–	–	–	–	–	–	–	–	–
2000–01	Ind v. Aus	IND	2	54	–	64	–	–	–	–	–	7.11
2001	NWS	ENG	5	48	–	27	–	–	–	–	–	3.38
2001–02	VBS	AUS	7	66	–	46	2	23.00	–	2/38	33.00	4.18
Total			**244**	**3687**	**10**	**2938**	**85**	**34.56**	**1**	**5/24**	**43.38**	**4.78**

Best Bowling: 5/24 Australia v. West Indies, Melbourne, 1992–93

Domestic Limited-Overs Career

Season	M	Balls	Mdns	Runs	Wkts	Avrge	5	Best	Stk/Rt	RPO
1985–86	1	54	1	28	1	28.00	–	1/28	54.00	3.11
1986–87	2	36	–	37	–	–	–	–	–	6.17
1987–88	4	114	3	62	5	12.40	–	3/23	22.80	3.26
1988–89	3	–	–	–	–	–	–	–	–	–
1989–90	3	113	–	86	2	43.00	–	1/26	56.50	4.57
1990–91	4	84	1	66	3	22.00	–	2/26	28.00	4.71
1991–92	4	150	1	134	3	44.67	–	2/26	50.00	5.36
1992–93	4	66	–	65	2	32.50	–	2/23	33.00	5.91
1993–94	2	–	–	–	–	–	–	–	–	–
1994–95	–	–	–	–	–	–	–	–	–	–
1995–96	4	84	1	60	–	–	–	–	–	4.29
1996–97	–	–	–	–	–	–	–	–	–	–
1997–98	3	28	–	31	2	15.50	–	2/31	14.00	6.64
1998–99	1	–	–	–	–	–	–	–	–	–
1999–00	1	–	–	–	–	–	–	–	–	–
2000–01	5	24	1	25	1	25.00	–	1/25	24.00	6.25
2001–02	4	–	–	–	–	–	–	–	–	–
Total	**45**	**753**	**8**	**594**	**19**	**31.26**	**–**	**3/23**	**39.63**	**4.73**

Best Bowling: 3/23 New South Wales v. Queensland, Brisbane, 1987–88

TEST CRICKET RECORDS

ALL TIME APPEARANCES

Player	Team	Career	M
AR Border	Australia	1978/79–1993/94	156
SR Waugh	Australia	1985/86–2001/02	148
CA Walsh	West Indies	1984/85–2000/01	132
Kapil Dev	India	1978/79–1993/94	131
SM Gavaskar	India	1970/71–1986/87	125
ME Waugh	Australia	1990/91–2001/02	125
Javed Miandad	Pakistan	1976/77–1993/94	124
IVA Richards	West Indies	1974/75–1991	121
IA Healy	Australia	1988/89–1999/00	119
GA Gooch	England	1975–1994/95	118

ALL TIME LEADING RUN SCORERS

Batsman	Team	M	Inn	NO	Runs	HS	50	100	Avrge
AR Border	Aus	156	265	44	11174	205	63	27	50.56
SM Gavaskar	Ind	125	214	16	10122	236*	45	34	51.12
SR Waugh	Aus	148	233	41	9600	200	44	27	50.00
GA Gooch	Eng	118	215	6	8900	333	46	20	42.58
Javed Miandad	Pak	124	189	21	8832	280*	43	23	52.57
IVA Richards	WI	121	182	12	8540	291	45	24	50.24
DI Gower	Eng	117	204	18	8231	215	39	18	44.25
G Boycott	Eng	109	193	23	8114	246*	42	22	47.73
GS Sobers	WI	93	160	21	8032	365*	30	26	57.78
ME Waugh	Aus	125	205	17	7949	153*	46	20	42.28

ALL TIME LEADING FIELDSMEN

Fieldsman	Team	M	Ct
ME Waugh	Australia	125	173
MA Taylor	Australia	104	157
AR Border	Australia	156	156
GS Chappell	Australia	88	122
IVA Richards	West Indies	121	122
MC Cowdrey	England	115	120
IT Botham	England	102	120
WR Hammond	England	85	110
RB Simpson	Australia	62	110
GS Sobers	West Indies	93	109

INTERNATIONAL LIMITED OVERS RECORDS

ALL TIME LEADING RUN SCORERS

Batsman	Team	M	Inn	NO	Runs	HS	50	100	Avrge	Stk/Rt
SR Tendulkar	IND	286	278	26	11069	186*	55	31	43.92	86.54
M Azharuddin	IND	334	308	54	9379	153*	58	7	36.93	73.28
DL Haynes	WI	238	237	28	8649	152*	57	17	41.38	62.87
ME Waugh	AUS	244	236	20	8500	173	50	18	39.35	76.54
Inzamam-ul-Haq	PAK	265	250	36	8494	137*	61	8	39.69	71.77
PA de Silva	SL	275	266	26	8432	145	57	11	35.13	81.41
Saeed Anwar	PAK	230	227	17	8348	194	41	19	39.75	81.60
SR Waugh	AUS	325	288	58	7569	120*	45	3	32.91	75.77
SC Ganguly	IND	191	185	14	7522	183	45	18	43.99	73.82
A Ranatunga	SL	269	255	47	7454	131*	49	4	35.84	78.00
Javed Miandad	PAK	233	218	41	7381	119*	50	8	41.70	66.93

ALL TIME MOST CATCHES

Fielder	Country	M	Ct
M Azharuddin	India	334	156
AR Border	Australia	273	127
RS Mahanama	Sri Lanka	213	109
SR Waugh	Australia	325	111
ME Waugh	Australia	244	108
IVA Richards	West Indies	187	100
CL Hooper	West Indies	205	101
JN Rhodes	South Africa	227	100

SOURCES

During the research and writing of this book, the author used the following sources.

— *Steve Waugh's Ashes Diary*, Ironbark, 1993

— *Steve Waugh's South African Tour Diary*, Ironbark, 1994

— *Steve Waugh's 1997 Ashes Diary*, HarperSports, 1997

— *No Regrets*, Steve Waugh, HarperSports, 1999

— *Steve Waugh's West Indies Tour Diary*, HarperSports, 1995

— *Steve Waugh's World Cup Diary*, HarperSports, 1996

— *Never Satisfied*, Steve Waugh, HarperSports, 2000

— *Steve Waugh's Ashes Diary 2001*, HarperSports, 2001

— *The Complete Illustrated History of Australian Cricket*, Jack Pollard, Pelham Books, 1992

— *Wisden Cricketers' Almanack*, Australia 2000–1, Hardie Grant Books

— *Wisden Cricketers' Almanack*, Australia, 1999, Hardie Grant Books

— *The World's Most Dangerous Places*, Robert Young Pelton, HarperCollins*Publishers*, 2000

— *Hands and Heals*, Ian Healy, HarperSports, 2000

— *Lord's*, Geoffrey Moorhouse, Hodder & Stoughton, 1983

— *Australian Cricket: The Game and the Players*, Jack Pollard, Hodder & Staughton–ABC, 1982

— *The 1996 Australian Cricket Almanac*, Ironbark, 1996

— *The Age 1995 Australian Cricket Almanac*, Sydney Morning Herald Books, 1995

— *ABC Australian Cricket Almanacs*, ABC Books, 1990, 1991, 1992, 1993

— *The Reasons Why*, Bob Simpson, Harper*Sports*, 1996

— *World Cup: Cricket's Clash of the Titans*, Peter Baxter, Andre Deutsch, 1999

— *Cricket Rebels*, Chris Harte, Warwick Hadfield, QB Books, 1985

— *Quick Whit*, Mike Whitney, Ironbark, 1993

— *Taylor and Beyond*, Malcolm Knox, ABC Books, 2000

— *Border and Beyond*, Mark Ray, ABC Books, 1995

— *Leading from the Front*, Mike Gatting, MacDonald Queen Anne Press, 1988

— *The People's Game*, Geoff Armstrong & Mark Gately, Ironbark, 1994

— *Caribbean Odyssey*, Mike Coward, Simon & Schuster

— *They're Racing*, Viking, 1999

— *The Entertainers*, Mark Waugh & Doug Walters, Random House, 2001

— *Waugh Declared*, Mark Gately, Ironbark, 1992

— *Bankstown Cricket Club: 50 Not Out*, Mick Stephenson, Bookworks, 2001

— *Home and Away*, Jack Pollard, ABC Books, 1995

— *Playfair Cricket Annuals* — 1989, 1990, 1991, 1993, 1995

— *Benson & Hedges Cricket Year* — 7th, 8th, 9th, 12th, 13th editions

— *Wisden Cricketers' Almanack*, 1989, 1990, 1991, 1993, 1995

— *A Year to Remember*, Mark Waugh, Random House, 1997

— *Time to Declare*, Mark Taylor, Pan Macmillan, 1999

— *Australian Cricket Board*, Annual Report, 1999–2000

— *Australian Cricket Media Guide*, 1995–96, 96–97, 97–98, 98–99, 99–00, 00–01

— *Inside Edge* Cricket Magazines (various editions)

— *Cricketer* Magazine (various editions)

— *Australian Cricket* Magazine (various editions)

— *Australian* (various editions)

— *Herald-Sun* (various editions)

— *Sydney Morning Herald* (various editions)

— *Age* (various editions)

— *Trinidad Guardian*

— *Barbados Sunday Sun*

— *The Bankstown Torch*

INDEX

A

Aamir Sohail, 133, 187, 211, 273

ABC Ashes Tour Guide, 250

ABC Australian Cricket Almanac, 96–97

Abdus Khawar, 286

Adams, Jimmy, 213, 254, 311, 318

Adams, Paul, 246, 339

Afghanistan, 2

Afridi, Shahid, 275

Agarkar, Ajit, 302

Albury (NSW), 21–22

Alderman, Terry, 93, 103, 125, 127

Ambrose, Curtly, 75, 115, 121, 122, 143, 147, 209, 233, 238, 240, 241

   asked to remove sweatband, 148–149

   best fast bowler, 123, 151

   MW bats against, 145–146

   MW's first Test wicket, 120

   Tests, 211, 240–241, 289

Anasta, Braith, 236

Anwar, Saeed, 189, 323

Anzac Cove (Gallipoli), 324

Archer (racehorse), 4

Arthurton, Keith, 70, 143, 144

Ashes, 87, 90, 91, 92, 99, 100, 101, 102, 112, 118, 152, 154, 156, 157, 159, 160, 162, 165, 166, 171, 172, 173, 185, 200, 201, 202, 249, 250, 251, 255, 256, 259, 276, 282, 285, 296, 324, 325, 326

   MW campaigns for, 67–68, 71, 79–80

   MW's views on, 169

Astle, Nathan, 331, 337

Ata-ur-Rehman, 308

Atherton, Mike, 99, 112, 167, 201, 303

Auburn Association (NSW), 15, 20, 22

Australasia Cup, 182–183

Australia A team, 202–203

Australian Cricket Board

   appoints Melick, 312

   appoints Warne, 285–86

   Australian Cricketers' Association, 257, 260–261, 277

   bans rebel players, 40

   condemned for cover-up, 277

   confirms selection, 72

   drops Steve Waugh, 336

   drops Taylor and Healey, 263

   finds no evidence against MW, 326–327

   fines Merv Hughes, 179

   fines MW and Warne, 204

   gives MW one-year contract, 331

   Gupta allegations, 309

interviews MW, 312–317, 319

Pakistan Cricket Board, 219–220

Player Conduct Enquiry Report,
140–141, 186, 204, 287

Pays for partners' holiday, 215

releases details of fines to media,
276–277

security in Sri Lanka, 226–227, 228

Simpson's comments re, 205

solicitor, 211

team manager, 256

withdraws from Zimbabwe tour, 340

Australian Cricket (magazine), 67–68

Australian Cricketers' Association, 257,
260–261, 277

Ayres, Warren, 68

Azharuddin, Mohammad, 99, 128, 290

B

Bankstown District Association, 11–12

Bankstown Junior Soccer Association, 15

Bankstown Oval, 236, 309

Bankstown Torch (paper), 16

Bankstown's Green Shield under–16s,
18, 21–22

Bankstown's Poidevin-Gray Under–21,
21, 25, 31, 35

Bannerman, Alec, 118

Bannerman, Charles, 118

Barbados (Caribbean), 207

Barnard, Mr (soccer coach), 14

Barnes, Sid, 105

Basit Ali, 244

Battersby, Dr Cam, 140–141, 269

batting, 145–146, 231–232, 318

Baum, Greg, 161, 301

Bayliss, Trevor, 62, 127

Beckham, David, 335

Bedser A.V., 160

Belvidere Cup, 234

Benaud, John, 70, 91

Benaud, Richie, 272, 275

Benjamin, Kenneth, 214, 239

Benjamin, Winston, 70, 75

Benkenstein, Dale, 243

Bennett, Murray, 33, 47, 48, 49, 58

Benson & Hedges series, 71, 74, 77, 86,
90, 92, 94, 99, 102–103, 106–107,
126, 128, 129, 134, 135, 143–144,
148–149, 175, 176, 202, 224

Bermuda, 215

Bernard, Steve, 297, 307, 337

Berry, Daren 142

Bevan, Michael, 101, 224, 233, 234, 239,
240, 246, 291, 293

Bishop, Ian, 70, 76, 143, 144, 145

Black Knight (racehorse), 197

Blewett, Greg, 214, 240, 243, 246, 247, 248

Blizzard, Phil, 45

Bolton league, 36

Boock, Steven, 44

bookmakers, 127, 183

Hong Kong Sixes, 170, 171, 309

'John' the bookmaker, 181, 184–185,
186, 198, 203, 204, 205, 220, 276,
282, 286, 327, 328

MW approached by Malik, 188–189

MW denies being warned, 140–141

MW fined $10 000, 204–205

MW makes Miracle Mile TV ad,
192–193

MW reads statement to media,
276–277

Boon, David, 42, 71, 76, 79, 90, 101, 102,
112, 114, 116, 131, 132, 140, 143,
145, 149, 151, 154, 164, 165, 169,
174, 212, 215, 254, 302, 336

Border, Allan, 57, 67, 72, 78, 79, 82, 85,
90, 95, 96, 101, 112, 114, 115, 116,
117, 120, 122, 124, 125, 137, 140,

143, 144, 149, 152, 153, 156, 160,
162, 165, 168, 174, 182, 183, 302,
303, 331, 336, 342
batting with MW, 145–147
MW at Essex, 64–65, 87–88
MW's Test debut, 111
MW's views on, 177–178
reaction when Marsh and MW
dropped, 130–131
retirement, 177–178, 180–181, 330
6524 runs, 292, 293
the two Marks, 154
v. West Indies, 145–147, 150
views on MW, 78, 139, 155, 166, 203
Border-Gavaskar Trophy, 268
Bosnich, Mark, 18
Botham, Ian, 59, 60, 94, 167
Boucher, Mark, 333, 337
Bourne, Beverly (mother) *see* Waugh,
Beverly
Bourne, Coral (aunt), 8
Bourne, Dion (uncle), 8, 17–18, 73
Bourne, Dorothy (grandmother), 5–6
Bourne, Keith (grandfather), 8
Bower, Rod, 39
Bradman, Don, 89, 105, 160, 162, 197,
275, 311, 345
Bradshaw, Keith, 50
Brandes, Eddo, 57
Brindle, Terry, 106
Brown, Courtney, 231
Buchanan, John, 304–306
Buckingham, Danny, 29
Bulldogs (rugby league), 235–236, 308
Butcher, Alan, 99
Butcher, Mark, 325, 328

C
Caddick, Andy, 162, 252, 329
Cairns, Chris, 261, 262

Cairns, Lance, 44
Campbell, Sherwin, 290–291
Canberra Raiders (rugby league), 256
Cantrell, Peter, 68
Caribbean Odyssey (Coward), 115
Carlton & United series, 242, 264, 265,
285, 286, 303, 311
cars, 28, 35–36
Chappell, Greg, 77, 79, 95, 113, 117, 118,
166, 302, 311, 338
Chappell, Ian, 77, 113, 118, 214
Chappell, Trevor, 118
Chardon, Dave, 24
Chatfield, Ewan, 40
Chip Machine (racehorse), 193
City and Country, 100
Clarke, Garth, 279
Clever Kiwi (racehorse), 193, 252
Clifford, Peter, 42
Cliftan Chief (racehorse), 193
Cockerill, Ian, 93
Commonwealth Games, 270–271
Condon, Sir Paul, 308
Conn, Malcolm, 271, 275, 276, 284, 313
Cottrill, John, 8
Courage Under Fire (racehorse), 288
Courtice, Andrew, 45
Coward, Mike, 70–71, 115, 269, 283–284,
298, 302, 332, 338–339
Cowie, Doug, 266
Cox Plate, 142, 197
Craddock, Robert, 284, 301, 333, 334,
336–337
Crawley, John, 201, 283
Crompton, Alan, 204, 256
Cronje, Hansie, 243, 244, 247, 265, 266,
306–307, 308–309
Crowe, Martin, 102–103, 155, 156,
309
Crowfoot, Gary, 32

Cuffy, Cameron, 317

Cullinan, Daryll, 238, 243, 246

Cummings, Bart, 8

Cummins, Anderson, 144

D

Daley, Laurie, 236, 278

Dandy Andy (racehorse), 60

Darling, Hugh, 278–279

Davidson, Alan, 18, 89–90

Davidson Shield (cricket), 18, 21, 22, 26

Davis, Simon 58

Davis, Steve, 266

Davis, Winston, 42

DeFreitas, Phil, 2, 199, 201

de Silva, Aravinda, 29, 137, 225, 309

Dev, Kapil, 128, 129

de Villiers, Fanie, 175

Devine, Miranda, 279

Di Venuto, Michael, 264

Dillon, Mervyn, 310–311

Dodemaide, Tony, 58, 127, 154, 170

Donald, Allan, 176, 236, 243, 245, 246, 264, 265, 295, 333, 334, 337

Dougherty, Alan and Neil, 12–13

Doull, Simon, 174

Dravid, Rahul, 322

Drivetime (racehorse), 192, 193

Dujon, Jeff, 115, 116

Dumnesy, John, 193

Duncan, Clyde, 118

Dunn, John, 23

Dyer, Greg, 47, 48, 58, 62

Dyson, John, 40, 57, 70, 71, 72

E

East Hills Boys First XI, 18–19, 26

East Hills Boys Technology High
School, 17

Egar, Col, 189

Egerton Cricket Club (UK), 36–40

Elizabeth II, Queen, 50, 256

Elliott, Matthew, 239–240, 245, 246, 252, 256

Emburey, John, 167

Emerson, Ross, 224

Emery, Phil, 89, 95

England. *see also* Essex (UK)
Carlton & United series, 286
MW bowled by Tufnell, 164–165
MW leaves Steve on 99, 201
MW's Test debut, 110–112
MW's views on, 166–167, 202, 328–329
Stewart catch, 165–166
1993, 159–161, 164
1994–95 season, 198–200
1998–99 season, 282–283
2000–2001 season, 325–326, 328–329

England, Mark, 18, 29

English Cricket Board, 84, 85

Erskine, James, 257, 260

Essex (UK), 65–67, 81–88, 97–99, 134–135, 215–218

Esso Scholarship, 37, 49, 54

Evans, Kevin, 86

Evening News, 36, 39

Expedience (racehorse), 193

F

FAI Cup, 79, 91, 96, 101, 103, 126–127, 142

Fakhruddin G. Ebrahim, Judge, 219–220, 272–273

Farhart, Pat, 51, 324

Faulkner, Peter, 71

Fernandez, Gigi, 210

first class cricket
MW plays against Australia, 85
MW selected for Australia, 73–74, 108–109

2000–2001 season, 310
    v. West Indies, 142–143
    v. Zimbabwe, 54, 56–57
Fleming, Damien, 127, 187, 207, 294–296
Fletcher, Keith, 98
Flower, Grant, 299
football cards, 14
Foster, Neil, 65, 66–67, 88, 164, 167
Frank Worrell Trophy, 122, 147, 149, 205,
    210, 214–215, 239, 241, 288, 289,
    310
Fraser, Angus, 168, 201
Freedman, Brian, 11–12, 342
Freedman, Lee, 142
Frith, David, 299
Frost, Glenn, 193, 196
Frost, Vic, 193

G
Gallipoli (Turkey), 324
gambling, 142, 159, 192–197, 252
Gatting, Mike, 114, 162, 201, 211
Germon, Lee, 231
Gibb, P.A., 134
Gibbs, Herschelle, 293–294
Giffen, George, 118
Giffen, Walter, 118
Gilbert, Dave, 37–38, 47, 48
Gilchrist, Adam, 80, 253, 265, 267, 286,
    289, 299, 300, 317, 318, 322, 328,
    340, 343
    double century, 337
    Edgbaston, 295
    MW's views on, 303
    Tests, 265, 286, 303, 328, 340
    Tooheys Cup (NSW), 80
    views on MW, 267, 299–300, 343
Gillespie, Jason, 194, 245, 248, 299, 310,
    325
golf, 161–162

Gooch, Graham, 65, 86, 88, 107, 112, 162,
    166–167, 201, 232
Gough, Darren, 199, 200, 251, 325, 326,
    329
Gower, David, 69, 232
Gravy (West Indian), 125
Greenhalgh, Iris and Peter, 36–37,
    39–40
Greenidge, Gordon, 75, 115, 117, 122
Gregory, Bernie, 15
Gregory, Dave, 118
Gregory, Ned, 118
Greig, Tony, 279
Growden, Greg, 40, 60, 103, 104
Gupta, Mukesh, 171, 309, 312, 327
Gurusinha, Asanka, 29
Guy, Dick, 40
Guyana, 116–117, 290

H
Haddin, Brad, 331
Hadfield, Peter, 19
Hadlee, Richard, 44, 139
Hagan, Bob, 236
Hair, Darrell, 132, 150, 223–224
Halbish, Graham, 204, 226
Hall, Greg, 142
Hall, Wes, 215
Harbhajan Singh, 321–322, 323
harness racing, 192–197
Harold Park Paceway (Sydney), 64, 192,
    194, 195, 196, 235, 308
Harper, Roger, 207, 224, 231
Harris, Chris, 103, 231–232
Hartshorn, Greg, 24
Harvey, Neil, 277
Hauritz, Nathan, 338
Hawke, Bob, 58–59
Hayden, Matthew, 91, 160, 170, 240, 245,
    310, 322–323, 332, 333, 334, 337, 338

Haynes, Desmond, 99, 115, 116–117, 120–121, 122, 123

Hayward, Nantie, 333

Headley, Dean, 256, 283

health. *see also* injuries
has teeth capped, 39
Osgood–Schlatter Disease, 20
resilience, 203
sickness in India, 269
viral infection, 251

Healy, Ian, 68, 75, 78, 96, 103, 112, 122, 123, 151, 170, 174, 175, 180, 187, 201, 202, 209, 231, 233, 247, 253, 263, 299, 303, 330, 343
Border's bat, 177
Haynes, 116–117, 120–121
hoists Cronje, 247
retirement, 330
Tests, 186–187, 225, 239
Thorpe catch, 252
views on MW, 78, 166, 255–256, 283
world record for dismissals, 273

helmet, 3, 21

Hemmings, Eddie, 87

Henderson, Claude, 333

Hick, Graeme, 57, 167, 199, 283

Hickey, Denis, 29, 50

Higgs, Jim, 91

Hilditch, Andrew, 336

Hill, 43

Hobbs, J.B., 160

Hogg, Brad, 237

Hohns, Trevor, 153, 310, 336, 337–338, 340–341

Holdsworth, Wayne, 18

Holland, Bob, 43, 46, 47, 48, 49

Hong Kong, 170, 171, 235, 250, 309

Hookes, David, 57, 91, 93, 94, 105, 276, 338

Hookey, Scott, 18, 62

Hooper, Carl, 76, 115, 116, 118, 122, 124, 143, 148, 209, 213, 239, 240

Hope, Jim, 67

Horan, Mike, 285

horseracing, 8, 44, 60, 62, 142, 192, 197, 288

Horsfall, R., 134

Houghton, Dave, 57

Howard, John, 277, 302

Hubbard, Ronald, 56

Hudson, Andrew, 176, 179

Hughes, Graeme, 24

Hughes, Kim, 37

Hughes, Merv, 2, 43, 58, 68, 74, 120, 124, 127, 165, 179

Hussain, Nasser, 134–135, 283, 324

Hutton, L., 160

I

Ijaz Ahmed, 273

illegal bookmaking.
see bookmakers

Illot, Mark, 134, 168

Imran Khan, 133, 211, 273, 308

India
Central Bureau of Investigation, 309, 312
descriptions of, 182, 228–229, 232, 270
Indian Cricket Board, 171
Jalandhar, 321–322
MW dropped, 129–131
MW's views on, 228–229, 270, 323
Sharjah, 182
1991–92 season, 127–129
1996 World Cup, 230–234
1997–98 season, 268–270
1999–2000 season, 302
2000–2001 season, 322–323

ING Cup, 331

injuries. *see also* health
  allergy to horse hair, 191
  bruised hand, 176
  car accident, 63
  disc in back, 220, 248
  fractured finger, 324
  hand injury, 248
  stress fractures, 50–51
Inside Edge (magazine), 172, 300, 308
International Cricket Council, 204, 211,
    220, 224, 287, 308, 312, 313, 320,
    322
Inzamam-ul-Haq, 186–187, 189, 221,
    275, 300
Irani, Ron, 216–218

J

Jackson, Archie, 111
Jackson, Paul, 49
Javed Burki, 211
Javed Miandad, 133
Jayasuriya, Sanath, 225
J-B-Dean (racehorse), 193
'John' the bookmaker, 181, 184–185, 186,
    198, 203, 204, 205, 220, 276, 282,
    286, 327, 327–328
Johnson, Graeme, 211
Johnson, Ian, 113
Johnson, Paul, 86
Jones, Alan, 278, 316
Jones, Andrew, 173, 174
Jones, Dean, 74, 76, 79, 90, 101, 103, 115,
    118, 124, 133, 140, 141, 144, 148,
    156, 176, 275, 309
Joseph, Charlie, 116, 211–212
Julian, Brendon, 209, 290

K

Kallis, Jacques, 246, 265, 339
Kaluwitharana, Romesh, 138

Karis, Leo, 192, 276, 282, 312, 314, 316,
    319, 344
Kasprowicz, Michael, 270
Kerr, Robbie, 45
Khawar, Abdus, 286
Kingsgrove Sports Centre, 32, 51–52, 53,
    54, 82, 110, 215
Kingston Town (racehorse), 197
Kinjite (racehorse), 142
Kirsten, Gary, 337
Klusener, Lance, 265–266, 294–295, 296
Knox, Malcolm, 243, 246, 260
Koiro Corrie May (racehorse), 44
Kowalski, Daniel, 271
Kumble, Anil, 237, 269

L

Labrooy, Graham, 92
Ladbrokes (UK), 165, 190
Laker, J. C., 160
Lalor, Peter, 279
Lamb, Terry, 236
Langer, Justin, 78, 284, 300, 304, 328,
    332, 333, 340
Lara, Brian, 148, 211, 214, 215, 238, 292,
    310, 317
  defends Samuels, 241
  hero of Caribbean in 1999, 289
  MW's views on, 289
  named in CBI report, 309
  Tests, 144, 147, 209, 210
  wins Honda, 318–319
Larwood, H., 160
Larsen, Gavin, 155
Law, Stuart, 232, 233, 264
Lawry, Bill, 268
Lawson, Geoff, 33–34, 57, 61, 71, 89, 92,
    93, 95, 96, 104, 105–106, 126, 127
Laxman, V.V.S., 322, 323
Lee, Brett, 311, 322, 325

Lee, Shane, 234, 308

Lehmann, Darren, 91, 92, 96, 100, 195, 295, 339

Lehmann, Tom, 161

Lever, John, 87

Lewis, Chris, 201

Light Fingers (racehorse), 8

Lillee, Dennis, 160, 179

Lilley, Alan, 67, 86

Liverpool Golf Club (Sydney), 162

Liyanage, Dulip, 138

Lloyd, Clive, 113, 117, 120

Logie, Gus, 115, 116, 125, 149

Long John Silver (racehorse), 192

Lord, David, 278

M

MCC Young Cricketers squad (UK), 49–50

McConnell, Peter, 129, 132

McCosker, Rick, 95

McDermott, Craig, 75, 94, 112, 115, 116, 120, 124, 143, 165, 177, 199, 221, 226, 230

   Australia under–19s, 29

   injured in West Indies, 114

   Tests, 57, 128, 147, 150, 207

McDonald, Ian, 204

McDonald's Cup, 49, 51, 60, 61

McEnroe, John, 179

MacGill, Stuart, 273, 283, 325

McGrath, Glenn, 173, 187, 210, 225, 234, 239, 252, 257, 296, 325, 345

McGuire, John, 37

McIntyre, Peter, 237

McKewen, Ken, 82

Mackinnon, John, 25–26

Macleay, Ken, 51, 103, 105

McMillan, Brian, 245

McMillan, Craig, 332

McNamara, Brad, 18, 32, 100, 192

McPhee, Jamie, 29

McPhee, Mark, 38, 51

Maher, Jimmy, 338

Majid Khan, 273–274, 275

Malaysia, 270–271

Malcolm, Devon, 111–112, 168, 252, 257

Malik Mohammed Qayyum, Justice, 272–273, 308

Malik, Salim. see Salim Malik

Manchester United, 335

Mandela, Nelson, 178

Marks, Neil, 100

Marks, Vic, 51

Marsh, Geoff, 74, 75, 76, 79, 90, 92, 101, 103, 116, 117, 122, 129–130, 131, 137, 149, 196, 237, 248, 296, 304, 342–343

Marshall, Malcolm, 75, 82–83, 87, 97, 114, 115, 120, 123

Martin, Rodney, 19

Martyn, Damien, 145, 147, 153, 161, 162, 170, 176, 340

match-fixing, 142, 171, 272–275, 277, 286, 307–308, 309

Matthews, Chris, 103

Matthews, Craig, 175

Matthews, Greg, 3, 24, 33, 42, 47, 48, 57, 68, 71, 81, 89, 90, 95, 104, 106, 111, 112, 118, 260, 261, 343

May, Tim, 150, 162, 174, 186, 188, 203, 211, 219, 220, 221, 257, 260, 273, 274, 277–278, 308

Mayfield (West Indian), 125

media relations

   Australian Cricket, 67–68

   Conn, 271, 275, 276

   Craddock, 301

   English team, 250

   MW ambushed by Pakistani journalists, 273–274

MW under pressure, 259, 262

MW's ACB interview, 314–315

MW's selection for Australia, 109–110

MW's views on, 284–285, 314–315, 319

Sheffield Shield, 59–60

Wisden Almanack, 86, 99, 299

Melbourne Cup, 4, 8, 44, 197

Melick, Greg, 312, 313, 317, 320, 326–327

Meman, Babu, 56

Meninga, Mal, 256–257

Mercantile Mutual Cup, 142, 157, 172, 203, 220, 234, 259, 261, 276, 309, 331

Miller, Colin, 107, 109, 283

Milliken, Geoff, 22

Mills, Bruce, 173

Miracle Mile (horse race), 192

Mohinder Armanath, 38

Monaghan, Laurie, 17

Moody, Tom, 70, 80, 90, 92, 100, 128, 137, 264, 271, 293

Moore, Andrew, 278

Moore, Peter and Marie, 236

More, Kiran, 128

Morrison, Danny, 107, 155

Moscow Olympics, 2

Moss, Peter, 39

Mugabe, Robert, 340

Muralitharan, Muttiah, 137, 138, 223–224, 226, 286, 322

Murgatroyd, Brian, 320

Murray, Junior, 144, 210

Mushtaq Ahmed, 186–187, 222

N

Naturalism (racehorse), 142

Natwest Trophy, 86

Nehru Cup, 90

Newcombe, John, 8

New Energy (racehorse), 193, 296

New Zealand

the two Marks, 154

MW dumped, 153

MW's views on, 156

1991–92 season, 152–153

1993–94 season, 173–175

1997–98 season, 261–263, 267

1999–2000 season, 303–304

2001–2002 season, 331–333

NSW Cricket Association, 89

Ntini, Makhaya, 337, 339

O

Oblico (racehorse), 193, 197

O'Donnell, Simon, 68, 76, 102, 106, 127

Odumbe, Maurice, 230

O'Keefe, Kerry, 253, 308

one-day cricket, 76–77, 182, 263–264, 295–296

O'Neill, Mark, 45, 57–58, 89

O'Neill, Normie, 232

O'Regan, Rob, 140–141, 186, 204, 287

O'Reilly, Bill, 47–48, 89

Orient Hotel (Sydney), 24

Osgood–Schlatter Disease, 20

Owens, Michael, 152

P

Pakistan

descriptions of, 272, 286

MW replaces Steve, 94

MW's international debut, 74

MW's views on, 133, 187–188, 189–190

Pakistan Cricket Board, 219–220, 275, 308. *see also* Salim Malik

1989 season, 75

1994–95 season, 187, 189

1995–96 season, 221–223

1998–99 season, 275
1999–2000 season, 299–300, 303
Panania (Sydney), 5, 6, 14–15, 41
Parore, Adam, 152
Pascoe, Lennie, 24, 201
Patel, Dipak, 132, 152
Patterson, Mark, 15, 192, 195
Patterson, Patrick, 70, 115, 143
Pearce, Kevin, 101
Perrett, Ron, 17, 19, 23, 26
Perry, Nehemiah, 289
Phillips, Ray, 48
Phillips, Wayne, 105, 137
Pisano, Raff, 312–316
pitches, 84, 85, 237
Pitty, Graeme, 24, 43
Player Conduct Enquiry Report (ACB),
    140–141, 186, 204, 287
Player Feedback Sheets, 304–305
Pollock, Shaun, 245, 264, 265–266, 294,
    333, 336, 337
Ponting, Ricky, 190, 193, 195, 215, 252,
    256, 293, 297, 302, 311, 322, 326,
    332, 338, 339, 340
Porter, Chad (son), 55
Porter, Lauren (daughter), 55
Porter, Susan
    at Edgbaston, 295
    avoids media, 314
    Border calls, 64
    cost of belief in MW, 280, 281
    encourages MW, 81–82, 316, 319–320
    engagement to MW, 235
    highlight of her life, 344
    life at home, 157–159
    MW and 'John', 186
    MW's passion for racing, 194, 196,
        197
    MW's selection for Australia, 108,
        109

MW's Test debut century, 110
    quits Kingsgrove, 215
    relationship with MW, 33, 52–56,
        62–63
    'stacks' the scooter, 215
    travels to UK, 83
Porter, Tim (son), 55
Prabhakar, Manoj, 127, 129, 171, 309
Prime Minister's XI, 58–59, 74, 93
Pringle, Chris, 155
Pringle, Derek, 65
psychology in cricket, 304–305
Pura Milk Cup, 301, 309, 310, 331

R

Rackemann, Carl, 37
Rail, Vic, 60
Ramanayake, Rami, 138
Ranatunga, Arjuna, 171, 225, 226, 233,
    286, 309
Randall, Derek, 66, 86
Randell, Steve, 222, 266
Ray, Mark, 46, 262
Reid, Bruce, 71, 101, 103, 112, 129, 143
Reiffel, Paul, 127, 130, 165, 212, 214,
    294–295
report cards, 304–305
Rhodes, Jonty, 265, 343–344
Richards, Corey, 18
Richards, Viv, 75, 93, 115, 116
    Antigua, 123–124
    in Guyana, 117
    masters of cricket, 113
    MW's admiration for, 70–71
    Tests, 76, 121, 122
Richardson, David, 246, 264
Richardson, Richie, 70, 76, 116, 117, 143,
    144, 147, 148, 208, 212, 239
Riley, Brian, 24
Ritchie, Greg, 47, 68

Rixon, Steve, 33, 57, 261, 294

Robertson, Austin, 276

Robertson, Gavin, 15, 271

Robinson, Tim, 86

Roche, Tony, 8

Roebuck, Peter, 131–132, 285, 318

rotation policy, 334–335

Ruffles, Ray, 8

rugby league, 235–236, 256, 257

Russell, Glen, 30, 192

Russia (Soviet Union), 2

Ryan, Rob, 278

S

Saeed Anwar, 189, 323

Salim Malik, 187, 218, 223, 226, 277, 286, 309

    appears at judicial enquiry, 273–274

    approaches MW, 188–189

    banned for life, 308

    cleared of bribery allegations, 219–220, 272–273

    controversy surrounding, 205

    offers bribe to Warne, 186–187

    Pakistan, 133

    sworn statements against, 211

    Tests, 168

    Warne dismisses, 221

    Wilkins' article, 204

Samuels Marlon, 318

Samuels, Robert, 241

Saqlain Mushtaq, 222

Saville, Graham, 83

Saville, Queenie (mother), 83

Sawle, Lawrie, 91, 130

scar on ankle, 9

scoring slowly, 292

Shahid Afridi, 275

Sharma, Chetan, 38

Shastri, Ravi, 128

Shatin, Michael, 314

Sheffield Shield

    MW's debut and early form, 41, 42–49, 61

    MW's views on, 157

    1987–88 season, 57–58, 61

    1988–89 season, 68–69, 71, 72, 75, 77, 79

    1989–90 season, 89, 91–93, 94, 95–96

    1990–91 season, 100–101, 102–109

    1991–92 season, 126, 127, 128, 132–133, 134, 145

    1993–94 season, 171–172, 173, 203

    1995–96 season, 220, 234

    1997–98 season, 260

    1998–99 season, 276

    changes name, 301–302

Shepherd, David, 252

Siddons, Jamie, 170

Simmons, Phil, 147

Simpson, Bob, 118, 153, 200, 226, 237, 343

    blood clot, 210

    hands out question sheet, 207

    hears of fines, 205

    impression of the twins, 34–35

    Malik's offers, 189

    Marsh and MW dropped, 130

    MW as batsman, 96, 232

    MW as bowler, 45

    MW's selection, 79, 91, 301

    MW's Test debut century, 111

    Taylor and MW late, 43

    warns about bookies, 140–141, 186

Simpson, O.S., 315

Singer World Series, 183–184, 198, 235, 237

Singh, Harbhajan, 321–322

Slater, Michael, 162–163, 174, 175, 199, 210, 212, 223, 225, 226, 273, 311

Slater, Robbie, 15
sledging, 121–122, 241
Sleep, Peter, 93
Slight Chance (racehorse), 142
Small, Steve, 40, 48, 57, 89, 126
Smith, Graeme, 62
Smith, Robin, 111, 160, 164
Smith, Steve, 24–25, 30, 40, 57
Smith Tommy, 192
Smithers, Patrick, 124, 137, 153
soccer, 14, 15, 22–23
Solomons, Harry, 31–33, 51–52, 53,
    54–55, 82, 215
Solomons, Karen (wife), 82
Soule, Richard, 29
South Africa, 37, 40
    MW's views on, 176, 247
    1993–94 season, 175–181
    1996–97 season, 242–249
    1997–98 season, 264–267
    1999 World Cup, 293–296
    2001–2002 season, 333–334, 336–337,
        339–340
South African Tour Diary, 180
Soviet Union, 2
Speed, Malcolm, 260, 273, 276, 312–313,
    314, 315–317
Srikanth, Kris, 128
Sri Lanka
    Australia under–19s, 27, 29
    descriptions of, 136, 183
    four Test ducks in a row, 138
    Liberation Tigers of Tamil Ealam, 136
    Ranatunga's runner, 225–226
    security concerns, 226–227
    1991–92 season, 137–139
    1995–96 season, 223
Srinath, Javagal, 127, 269, 324
Stephen and Mark Waugh Pavilion, 309
Stephenson, Mick, 20–21

Sterling, Peter, 192
Stevenson, Franklin, 66
Stewart, Alec, 165–166, 283, 296, 303, 309
Stone, Alan, 8
Subba Row, Raman, 290
Subzere (racehorse), 197
Such, Peter, 279
Super Impose (racehorse), 142, 197
Super League, 256, 257
Sutherland, James, 336
Sydeston (racehorse), 142
Sydney Cricket Association, 8, 26
Sydney Croatia (soccer club), 23
Symcox, Pat, 242, 248, 267
Symonds sports equipment, 32

T
Tasman Cup (soccer), 22–23
tattoo on ankle, 9
Tauffel, Simon, 253–254
Taylor and Beyond (Malcom Knox), 260
Taylor, John, 93
Taylor, Mark, 57, 61, 68, 70, 71, 79, 89,
    90, 91, 92, 95, 101, 103, 114, 122,
    124, 125, 126, 137, 143, 145, 153,
    160, 169, 174, 175, 182, 183, 199,
    202, 208, 209, 210, 212, 214, 215,
    221, 222, 225, 230, 234, 256, 263,
    264, 267, 268, 272, 286, 288, 302,
    303, 342
    captaincy, 96, 242, 249
    Edgbaston century, 251
    157 catch record, 325
    judicial inquiry in Pakistan, 273–274
    MW at team meetings, 238–239
    MW's dismissal from Tufnell, 200
    MW's ideas for, 255
    MW's playing style, 117, 144, 166,
        247–248
    MW's views on, 242

recalls young Waughs, 27
Sheffield Shield, 40
Taylor and Beyond, 260
Tests, 226, 245, 275
Time to Declare, 184
21st birthday, 43
the two Marks, 154
260-run partnership with Slater, 163
Taylor, Peter, 61, 68, 75, 89, 95, 103, 116,
133
Tazelaar, Dirk, 57, 59, 68
technology, 252–253
Tendulkar, Sachin, 128, 129, 148,
230–231, 234, 238, 268, 289, 322,
323
Texaco Trophy, 160, 251
Thompson, David, 25, 32, 54, 64, 82, 93,
171
Thomson, Jeff, 37, 48
Thorpe, Graham, 168, 252
Thorpe, Ian, 17
throwing the ball, 223–224, 286
Titan Cup, 239
Tobin, Glen, 22
Tooheys Cup (NSW), 80
Trimble, Glenn, 47, 50
Trot, Albert, 118
Trot, Harry, 118
Trumper, Victor, 89
Tufnell, Phil, 164–165, 172, 199–200, 201,
251, 255, 258
twins, 6–7

U
umpires, 253–255, 268
'Under the Southern Cross' (team song),
311

V
Vengsarkar, Dilip, 38–39, 128

Venkatapathy Raju, 322
Very Tricky (racehorse), 193
Vettori, Daniel, 261, 262–263, 304, 331
Victoria Bitter series, 334, 336, 338
Vidler, Bob, 30
V'landys, Peter, 185, 192–193, 194–195
Vo Rogue (racehorse), 60, 62

W
Wajahatullah Wasti, 296
Walkley award for journalism, 276
Walsh, Courtney, 75, 97, 114, 115, 120,
123, 125, 143, 145, 147, 150, 213,
239, 240, 241, 289, 310–311
Walters, Doug, 232
Waqar Younis, 187–188, 236, 238
Warne, Shane, 95, 142, 144, 176, 187, 188,
200, 203, 208, 211, 214, 219, 220,
223, 226, 231, 237, 241, 243, 246,
262, 273, 277, 278, 279, 282, 287,
290, 300, 306, 308, 317, 322, 326,
327, 345
ball of the century, 162
bowls Basit Ali, 244
bowls to MW, 172–173
bribe offered to Jones, 140, 141
captaincy, 285–286
catching off to left-handers, 325
character, 257–258
Cullinan, 243
eleven wickets v. Pakistan, 221
fined $8000, 204
Hudson fine, 179
Malik offers bribe, 186
MW introduces 'John', 185, 186
MW's views on, 162, 172–173
predicts Gibbs catch, 293–294
reads statement to media, 276
shares MW's racing passion, 195
shoulder injury, 272

Tests, 128–129, 147, 165, 175

three-hundredth Test wicket, 265

umpires, 254

Wasim Akram, 75, 133, 187–188, 222, 273, 196

Waterhouse, Gai, 192

Watson, Shane, 338

Watson, Willie, 154

Waugh, Beverly (mother), 325

  belief in MW, 281

  birth of twins, 4–7

  feelings about MW, 344

  overprotective, 22

  reads the comparisons, 119

  sportswoman, 8, 9

  Steve's Sheffield Shield selection, 35

  strong influence, 16–17

  Test team, 108

  twins' hundredth Test, 333

Waugh, Danny (brother), 13, 20, 22, 26, 134, 167, 234

Waugh, Dean (brother), 9, 18, 22, 26, 134, 191, 234, 277

Waugh, Edward (grandfather), 5, 7–8, 9, 292, 293, 296–297

Waugh, Ella (grandmother), 5, 8, 9

Waugh, Lynette, 109, 297

Waugh, Mark

  character

    always wears helmet, 3, 21

    as a car driver, 28, 35–36

    early fears, 9–10

    hunger for success, 32–33

    icon of Bankstown, 236

    love of gambling, 142, 159, 252

    public opinion of, 278–280

    reserved nature, 15–16

    scar and tattoo on ankles, 9

    as a twin, 6–7

    when pushed too far, 320

  childhood

    birth, 4–5

    earliest sporting memories, 8

    first sporting activities, 11–12

    backyard sporting contests, 13–14

    primary school, 10–11, 14–15

    high school, 17, 27, 31

    work experience, 23

  early career

    under–10s, 11–12

    NSW Primary Schools soccer team, 14

    Bankstown's Green Shield under–16s, 18, 21–22

    East Hills Boys First XI, 18–19, 26

    excels at sport, 19–20

    NSW under–16s, 22

    Tasman Cup (soccer), 22–23

    Bankstown grade cricket, 21, 23, 24–26, 31, 35, 51

    Combined High Schools First XI, 26, 27

    NSW under–19s, 26

    Australian under–19s, 27, 29, 31

    indoor cricket, 30–31

    NSW train-on squad, 33–35

  health. see health

  highlights

    Australia's highest individual one-day score, 318

    beats Border's 6524 run record, 292–293

    Cairns catch, 262

    centuries in successive Tests, 223

    County Player of the Year, 99

    double-century in World Cup, 230

    eighteenth limited-overs hundred, 323–324

    eleventh Test century, 246

Essex Player of the Year, 99
fifth first-class century, 70–71
fifth Test century, 174
fiftieth first-class century, 199
final innings at The Oval, 328
first hundred for Essex, 82–83
first international limited-overs century, 155
first international wicket, 39
forty-fifth first-class century, 172
four Test centuries in 1998, 275
four World Cup centuries, 293
464-runs n.o. with Steve, 104–106
1468 run record (1999), 299
fourteenth first-class century, 93–94
fourth Test century, 167–168
highest score of career (1989), 91
highest Test score, 269
hits to SCG clock-tower, 93–94
158 catch record, 325–326
hundredth Test in a row, 333
hundredth Test with Steve, 333
initial first-grade century, 31
Inzamam catch, 300
maiden test century 1991, 2–3
man of the match, 144, 178, 231, 247, 291
1996 World Cup, 231
NSW Cricketer of the Year, 62
one hundredth Test, 301, 303
opening first-class catch, 43
opening first-class century, 57–58
partners Steve in 231-run stand, 212–214
passes 1000 runs in year, 282
passes 3000 runs, 104
passes 6000 Test runs, 290
Player of the Finals, 319
Player of the Year 1990, 96
plays at Lords, 163
record in limited-overs, 338
second limited-overs century, 160–161
seventy-fifth first-class hundred, 311
sixth Test century, 180
Stewart catch, 165–166
Test debut century, 110–111
third pair of centuries with Steve in WA, 133
third Test century, 147
thirteenth Test hundred, 266
thirty-sixth birthday, 329
thirty-sixth first-class century, 138
twelfth limited-overs hundred, 293
twins' first century stand in Tests, 167–168
Vettori hit, 262–263
Wajahatullah catch, 296
injuries. *see* injuries
media relations. *see* media relations
nicknames
'Afghanistan', 2
'Audi', 139
'Blues Brothers', 127
Golden 'something', 144
'Junior', 25–26
playing style
'always trying', 77–78
at bat-pad, 174
batting, 69, 71–72, 145–146
Essex (UK), 216–218
'in a dinner suit', 143
leadership, 285–286
leg-side play, 117
with long bat, 95–96
looking ugly, 304
medium-pace bowling, 144

opening, 156
playing short balls, 331–332
ripe for Test selection, 90–91
scores on thigh pad, 98
slip fielding, 94–95, 325
upright, 88
relationships. *see* Porter, Susan
views on
ACB interview, 280
chances of getting dropped,
334–335
cricket as a livelihood, 345–346
cricket psychology, 305
crunching a cut, 104
dumping from NZ test, 153
first morning of a Test, 208–209
464-runs n.o. with Steve, 105
four Test ducks in a row, 139
hitting stumps v. South Africa,
266–267
158 catch record, 325–326
life at home, 157–159
Muralitharan's bowling, 223–224
Steve and the short ball, 148
strike rates, 149
targeting captains, 244
umpires, 253–255
waiting to play, 163
Waugh, Rodger (father), 4–7, 8, 9, 16,
167–168, 191, 234, 280, 281, 325, 344
Waugh, Steve, 101, 103, 107, 120, 127,
132, 133, 137, 143, 145, 148, 165,
169, 177, 179, 180, 181, 191, 192,
206, 209, 210, 211, 215, 221, 226,
230, 232, 234, 236, 237, 241, 243,
246, 247, 248, 260, 262, 269, 270,
271, 273, 283, 285, 289, 291, 293,
295, 296, 297, 302, 303, 304, 316,
323, 326, 328, 332, 333, 334, 339,
340, 341

best one-day innings, 293–294
birth, 4–5
captains one-day team, 263–264
captains Test team, 288
century v. West Indies, 147
childhood, 6–7
comparisons with MW, 1, 45,
118–119
dropped from one-day team, 336
FAI Cup, 126–127
fielding collision with MW, 299
first senior tour, 45
464-runs n.o. with MW, 104–106
hundredth Tests, 264, 333
Lara's out, 209
MW competitive with, 25
MW in Australian team, 2, 74,
108–109
MW leaves stranded on 99, 201
MW plays against, 85
MW proud of, 73–74
MW replaces at Egerton, 38
MW's breakthrough innings, 248
NSW under–16s, 22
partners MW in 231-run stand,
212–214
proud of MW, 344–345
Sheffield Shield, 35
Somerset (UK), 66
supports MW, 282
Test Player of the Year, 198
Tests, 118–119, 243
'the other Waugh', 90
thirty-sixth birthday, 329
twin centuries v. England, 255
twins' first century stand in Tests,
167–168
Wellham, Dirk, 42, 45, 48
Wessels, Kepler, 45, 47, 48
Westburn Grant (racehorse), 193

West Indies
    Antigua, 124–125
    descriptions of, 112–115
    Frank Worrell Trophy, 210, 214–215,
        239, 288
    Jones' dismissal, 118
    MW partners Steve in 231-run stand,
        212–214
    MW's views on, 123, 151, 311
    Sabina Park, 115
    Steve reinstated, 118–119
    1988–89 season, 75, 76
    1990–91 season, 114–115
    1991–92 season, 143–144, 145–148, 151
    1995 season, 206–207
    1996 World Cup, 233
    1996–97 season, 239–241
    1998–99 season, 289–290
    2000–2001 season, 310–312, 317–318
What A Nuisance (racehorse), 44, 197
Whitney, Mike, 33, 45, 48, 57, 89, 133, 294
    'good fella', 49
    Marsh and MW dropped, 130–131
    MW's mullet, 46–47

MW's playing style, 69, 94–95
    twins' dress sense, 80
    twins' 464-runs n.o., 105–106
Wickramasinghe, Gamini, 138
Wilkins, Phil, 3, 59, 91, 180, 203, 278, 285
Williams, David, 145, 147
Williams, Debbie Rae, 56
Windeatt, Graeme, 17
Wisden Almanack, 86, 99, 299
Woolley, Roger, 43
Woonona (NSW), 22–23
World Cup, 29, 57, 102, 126, 132–133,
        154, 202, 226–228, 230–31, 232, 237,
        263, 288, 290, 291, 293, 294, 297,
        306, 336, 338
World Cup Diary (Steve Waugh),
        229–230

Z
Zimbabwe, 54, 56–57, 340
    one-day tournament, 299
    1999 World Cup, 292–293
    2000–2001 season, 317
Zoehrer, Tim, 85